Earth's
Eleventh
Hour

Earth's Eleventh Hour

Environmental Readings from the *Washington Post* Writers' Group

Edited by

William O. Dwyer
The University of Memphis

and

Frank C. Leeming
The University of Memphis

Allyn and Bacon

Boston • London • Toronto • Sydney • Tokyo • Singapore

Vice President, Publisher: Susan Badger
Series Editor: Laura Pearson
Production Administrator: Marjorie Payne
Editorial Assistant: Sarah Dunbar
Cover Administrator: Linda Knowles
Manufacturing Buyer: Louise Richardson
Editorial-Production Service: Wordsworth Associates
Cover Designer: Suzanne Harbison

Copyright © 1995 by Allyn and Bacon
A Division of Paramount Publishing
160 Gould Street
Needham Heights, Massachusetts 02194

ISBN: 0-205-16002-6

 This book is printed on recycled, acid-free paper.

Printed in the United States of America
10 9 8 7 6 5 4 3 2 1   99 98 97 96 95 94

Contents

Preface

There is, of course, only one truth—there are, however, countless perceptions of the truth. So it is with environmental issues. There are those who maintain that Earth's ecosystem as we know it cannot last much longer than the year 2050, but there are also those who assert in all sincerity that humankind is insignificant in the big picture of Earth's environment. The truth must be somewhere between these two extreme positions. What is the truth with regard to the impact of global population growth, pollution, and resource depletion? In light of the potential gravity of such potential threats to our environment, the search for truth in these areas is certainly justified. It is difficult to imagine topics that have more compelling implications for so many people. However, the task of divining the truth about the condition of the environment is an especially difficult one.

As the Ehrlichs (1990) have pointed out, it is human nature to respond to immediate and concrete incidents rather than to trends that may extend over years or decades. We all know about the tragic Exxon Valdez incident. There is little tendency to deny such concrete events, and we can move quickly to correct or control the problems they create. Trends, on the other hand, are more difficult to recognize and evaluate but ultimately pose the greatest threat to our "spaceship Earth." It is difficult to abide by the admonition to "think globally and act locally" when what we are confronted with is a trend. Human beings generally do not forego immediate gratification in preparation for uncertain events and conditions in the distant future, a fact on which all credit card companies rely. Consider how many people reject a healthy lifestyle (e.g., proper diet, exercise) even though there is no question of the important future benefits to be gained. And even today, it is easy to find people who vehemently assert that smoking is not health threatening. This book is filled with examples of individuals and organizations refusing to alter their behaviors to provide a more healthful environment in the future. As with the smokers, they are unable to put off present pleasures for future gains.

There is much to be gained by studying the writings of accomplished newspaper journalists. Many of the *Washington Post* writers whose by-lines appear in this book have dedicated a considerable amount of time and energy to understanding, not just the events that impact our environmental quality, but also the trends—trends that may be critical to the future of "spaceship Earth." To read them is to take advantage of their efforts and their insights into a domain of modern life that has significant implications for us all. Of course, some of the events reported in these stories are now (recent) history, but their impact is current. In Washington, the Clinton administration is facing the same environmental issues that past administrations did and, like past administrations, it is acting with a degree of expediency when it comes to confronting environmental problems. There is no doubt that politics and economics often work against the pursuit of environmental quality. Through the history and the events that these writers address surface the trends: that's what makes reading them so exciting.

What are these trends that threaten Earth's environmental quality? Our population is growing at an increasing rate. It stands now at about 5.4 billion and will double in about 47 years. But even now, 40,000 children die of starvation and nutrition-related diseases each day, and the number is increasing. The amount of land suitable for farming is declining, caused by overuse, erosion, desertification, salinization, and drought. Fresh water is in increasingly short supply. The "green revolution" in farming seems to have peaked. The productivity of all those hybrid crops that are so water- and fertilizer-intensive may have leveled off. And what about acid rain, global warming, shrinking rain forests, and ozone holes? The list of trends goes on and on. How should we think about these trends? What truths should we be extracting from them and about them?

The purpose of this book of readings is to consider these questions through the eyes and pens of the men and women reporting on environmental issues for the *Washington Post*. To assemble this collection, we searched through the last five years of *Washington Post* articles that dealt with environmental issues and selected a representative sample that reflect some of the concerns central to the "environmental problem." These articles fall into three general, but interrelated categories: 1. global overpopulation, 2. land, water, and air pollution, and 3. resource depletion. Each of these areas is replete with differing opinions and variations of pessimism and optimism. We have attempted to include articles that reflect, or at least report on, this diversity. We must confess, however, that our general bias is congruent with those who believe that the environmental problems facing the planet are real and will probably have a significant impact on humanity in the not-too-distant future.

Earth's Eleventh Hour contains 15 chapters, 14 of which focus on selected topics related to environmental quality. Chapter 1 deals with overpopulation, an issue that many people feel is the root cause of most of Earth's environmental problems. Chapters 2, 3 and 4, on global warming, acid rain and air pollution, and ozone depletion, focus on environmental problems associated with Earth's atmosphere. Chapters 5, 6, and 7 deal with the environmental impact of waste and the contamination of various ecosystems. Chapters 8 and 9 address humankind's threat to Earth's water systems. Chapter 8 focuses on groundwater, lakes and rivers, and Chapter 9 treats oceans and bays.

Chapters 10, 11, and 12 deal with the problems created by the assault by human beings on the rain forests, wetlands, and endangered species. One of the major themes is the threat to biological diversity that results from environmental abuses in these arenas. Chapters 13 and 14 focus on the difficulties of protecting federal lands in the United States, lands the government has been charged to maintain and preserve in perpetuity. Of primary concern are the threats to western grazing lands by ranchers and to forests by loggers, both of which represent major threatened ecosystems. The articles in these two chapters illuminate the difficulties inherent in carrying out this responsibility and, thus, provide a good transition to the final chapter.

The articles in Chapter 15 were selected to highlight the difficulties that government faces in meeting its broad obligation to ensure environmental quality. Confronting most environmental problems places government in the classic dilemma of choosing between 1. actions that expedite short-term benefits (often of an economic nature) but risk hazardous consequences in the future and 2. actions that have short-term costs but will produce long-term benefits to environmental quality. When faced with this dilemma, governments will typically make the first choice. It is what Platt (1973) refers to as a "social trap." Just as some people cause harm to themselves by smoking, drinking to excess, or engaging in unprotected sex because of the short-term pleasures that they derive, so also are governments controlled more by the immediate rewards of their actions than by the inevitable long-term penalties. This theme runs through the articles in Chapter 15.

As a group, the *Washington Post* writers who report on environmental issues exhibit a unique sensitivity and insight into the problems facing the environment and the attempts we are making, or should be making, to address them. Not only are they excellent writers and a pleasure to read but, corporately, they write as if they have an exceedingly important story to tell. Furthermore, they tell it in a way that nurtures the desire to search for the truth about threats to environmental quality and preservation. We hope that these articles from the *Washington Post* will help provoke in the reader a heightened consciousness and a willingness to take action on behalf of this blue and white ball we all call home.

Ehrlich, P., & Ehrlich, A. (1990). *The Population Explosion*. New York: Simon & Schuster.
Platt, J. (1973). Social traps. *American Psychologist, 28,* 641–651.

Acknowledgments

We wish to extend our sincere appreciation to our students who assisted us with the preparation of this book. We are particularly indebted to Melissa Cobern, Lynette Barn, Cheryl Bowers, Diana Oliver, Paul Kelly, Bryan Porter, Joyce Day, Melissa Lofton, Kami Venema, and Matthew Bourlier for their work with the compilation and proofreading of the manuscript. We would also like to thank Bobby Lyford at the *Washington Post* for all his help with the computer searches that enabled us to locate the articles appearing in this work. Appreciation is also expressed to Kevin Stone at Allyn and Bacon for his support during this project. Finally, but by no means least, we wish to acknowledge our enormous respect for the writers at the *Washington Post* whose articles are presented in this book.

Earth's Eleventh Hour

Overpopulation: Too Much Humanity   1

W orld population growth poses an imminent threat to environmental quality and even to the survival of nature as we know it. Although some intelligent men and women might disagree with this statement, one fact that is not subject to debate is that world population is increasing at an exponential rate. If we define *human* as beginning with *Homo habilis,* it took about 2 million years for humankind to reach its first billion people. Each additional billion now takes only 10 years. That's about 184 more people every minute (after the mortality rates are accounted for). What are the implications of this onslaught? The articles in this first chapter provide some sobering perspectives.

We begin by presenting an article that clarifies the main issue of global habitability: there are simply too many people. It includes a discussion of the specter of ever-increasing immigration pressures from the more populated to the less populated countries. Articles 2 and 3 focus on this problem worldwide and in the United States in particular. Article 4 addresses the need for the United States to play a bigger role in helping much of the world control its population growth and especially focuses on our relationships with Russia and Latin America.

The next four articles present different perspectives on the issue of population growth. Article 5 presents the optimistic prediction that population growth in the United States will stabilize in about 50 years, but questions what life in this country will be like with an additional 50 million people. Articles 6 and 7 report on points of view that are hostile to population control efforts. Article 8 reflects the view that there may be considerable benefits associated with a greatly increased world population.

Articles 9–12 focus on the need for worldwide family planning and the costs that effective programs would entail. These are followed by Article 13, discussing the reentry of the United States into the world family planning effort after several years of withdrawal caused by political forces centering on anti-abortion.

Article 14 summarizes the dramatic effect on reducing fertility levels that China experienced after it introduced its controversial population control policy in 1979. Finally, as a bridge to the second topic in the book, Article 15 addresses the relationship between increasing world population and the problem of global warming.

1   Overpopulation Remains World's Defining Crisis

HOBART ROWEN
April, 1933

T he daily grist of global news can be depressing: war in the former Yugoslavia, the steady economic collapse of Russia and other states of the former Soviet empire and a deteriorating peace process in the Middle East.

Added to the negative mix are the more mundane economic troubles of the so-called "developed" nations in the Americas, Europe and Asia, which seem to enjoy trade wars when shooting wars—after a period of exhaustion—are put aside.

But all of these problems pale beside the overwhelming issue of our times, one that politicians won't face head on: excessive population that is devastating the environment and triggering an explosive, uncontrolled, illegal migration of poor people seeking food, shelter, and jobs.

The issue comes down to "global habitability," as former ambassador to Italy Richard Gardner puts it.

The good news is that President Clinton appears determined to regain the leadership abdicated by former President George Bush at the Rio Earth Summit last year. But, as Gardner wrote in an essay called "Negotiating Survival," published by the Council on Foreign Relations, Clinton will have to commit energy and money to the effort: "He must explain that prudent expenditures on sustainable development overseas are not 'foreign aid,' but investments in survival."

Yale professor Paul Kennedy explores the population time bomb in a new book, *Preparing for the Twenty-First Century*. His is a grim message, even more sobering than his earlier *Rise and Fall of the Great Powers*, and many will not want to listen.

"As Earth adds to its total population by nearly 95,000,000 people each year, the pressure upon environments and resources grows greater, the pace of illegal immigration quickens, and entire societies in the developing world collapse under the strain," Kennedy said in a *Financial Times* article.

Increasingly, the political leaders of the richer nations, panicked by the threat of invasion by hordes of poor immigrants, are being forced to pay some attention. Count Otto Lambsdorff, chairman of the Free Democratic Party of Germany, said in Washington last week: "Population growth is the number one problem of the world."

2

Another observer, critical of the rich nations of the European Community for their niggardly and increasingly protectionist attitude toward accepting imports from Eastern and Central European countries, put the issue in a simple economic framework: "Either the imports come, or the people come."

Sickening genocide and fratricide in the former Yugoslavia have produced a total of 2,053,000 displaced persons—577,000 from Croatia and 1,404,000 from Bosnia-Herzegovina, according to United Nations data as of March 24. Of these, 595,000 already have sought asylum in Europe, mostly in Germany, Switzerland, Austria, Sweden and Hungary—which naturally do not want to be overrun.

Yet, as a new report by the Trilateral Commission observes, national governments can no longer "afford to act alone as individual gatekeepers trying to build higher and higher walls." International migration, the report says, along with such issues as environmental degradation, drugs, and terrorism, "is a new fact of national and international life that requires cooperation of all kinds among all nations."

Immigration is not a problem for Europe alone, although the post-Cold War collapse of the command economies, and ethnic tension, makes it a hot political issue there at the moment.

Here in the United States, the debate over the North American Free Trade Agreement with Mexico is focused on weak enforcement of anti-pollution and work-safety laws by the Salinas government. No one wants to talk about the underlying problem: The population trap arising from fertility rates in Mexico will keep illegal migration to the United States high, no matter what NAFTA does to boost economic growth in Mexico.

The global population crisis promises to get worse instead of better. Many poor countries are unable (lack of funds) or unwilling (pressures from religious groups) to provide modern birth control information and devices to women. Most of the additional 95 million people born each year will therefore be born in the most impoverished countries in the world.

Kennedy estimates that of the extra 8.5 billion to 9 billion people to be added to the global population (now 5.4 billion) by the year 2025, 95 percent will be born in the poorest of the poor countries. Despite the expected impact of AIDS, Africa's population is expected to soar from 680 million to 1.6 billion, exceeding China's 1.5 billion, but less than India's 2 billion.

Where will all these people go? How will they survive? After a gigantic internal migration from rural areas to overwhelmed cities in the Third World, the movement will be out and away—South to North, East to West.

The solution, if there is one, requires more money for the environment, for birth control, for education programs for women, and for other meaningful Third World development (but not dams, bridges and stadiums). We have to open rich nations' markets not just to fellow-rich nations' producers, but to poor countries as well.

This is a big challenge, one the rich countries can't afford to mess up.

2   Worldwide Migration Nears Crisis

Politics, Economics Cited in U.N. Study

EUGENE ROBINSON
July, 1993

P eople are moving across international borders and from the countryside to the
city in larger numbers than ever before, and this migration "could become the
human crisis of our age," the United Nations Population Fund said today.

In its annual State of World Population report, released here, the U.N. agency
focuses on migration and paints a disturbing picture: Tens of millions of people on
the move, leaving behind desperate circumstances only to face prospects almost as
bleak. According to the report, these massive migrant flows are straining industrialized and developing countries alike.

"Migration is the visible face of social change," the report says, warning that
the trend is growing and that solutions will not be found easily. The U.N. report
estimates there are at least 100 million international migrants living outside the
countries in which they were born, or about 2 percent of the world's population. An
estimated 17 million are refugees—fleeing political strife and warfare—while 20
million are fleeing other violence or environmental destruction, including drought.

The rest are economic migrants, seeking a better life. In the past, many of those
who moved to find work eventually returned to their homes. But, according to the
report, this "circular" migration pattern is breaking down, and today "most people
move to stay."

The report says that migratory pressures are increasing, as "the growth of a
global economy has emphasized rather than reduced inequality between nations." It
notes that migration already has become a political issue, with many target nations
taking steps to stem the flow—despite the report's assessment that "where legal
channels are closed, migrants will enter by whatever means are available to them."

International migration has become an important factor in the world economy,
the U.N. agency found, with "some developing countries relying on international
migration to finance development."

According to the report, migrants sent home about $66 billion in 1989, the last
year for which an estimate was available—second only to the oil industry as a

component of international trade and greater than the $46 billion that year in foreign aid.

The report accepts the distinction between refugees and economic migrants but notes that the division is often blurred, since political turmoil and economic collapse so often go hand in hand.

Of the non-refugee international migrants, 35 million were in sub-Saharan Africa, up to 15 million in Western Europe, nearly 15 million in North America and 15 million in Asia and the Middle East. These figures were for 1991, before the Balkan conflicts displaced another 2 million people, many of whom sought refuge in European countries.

Those cross-border movements are overshadowed, however, by the relentless movement of people from the countryside to the city. Each year, according to the report, 20 million to 30 million of "the world's poorest people" move from rural to urban zones, especially the Third World's "megacities."

The report projects that by the end of the decade, seven or eight of the world's 10 largest metropolitan areas will be in the developing world. The population of some cities in Africa, the least urbanized continent, is doubling every 12 years.

"The capacity of these cities to provide economic opportunities and even modest levels of support services to newcomers is declining rather than increasing," the report says. "Migration has always been a feature of development, but today's migrants are pushing into territory already occupied by others."

Most of the poor migrants flooding the cities end up working for subsistence wages, often in the informal economic sector, and living in squalid conditions. Yet the report says that most of those who made the move are glad to have done so, preferring "poverty in the city to deprivation and desperation in the countryside."

"The decision to migrate to the city, like the decision to migrate internationally, is normally a family decision," the report says. "It should be seen as part of a family strategy to minimize overall economic risk. . . . Yet the decision in many cases is driven by necessity as much as choice."

The traditional image of a migrant, whether to a city or to another country, is of a working-age man who leaves his family at home. But the U.N. report says nearly half of all the world's migrants are women, often on their own.

According to the report, women migrants are more likely to suffer "downward mobility," ending up in the lowest-paying jobs. They are more likely to become trapped in immigrant communities and are more vulnerable to abuse. At the same time, according to the report, there is evidence to suggest that women are more likely than men to send money to those left behind.

The report recommends policies "to enable people to live in dignity in their own countries and to make migration a real choice between opportunities." Specifically, it says that industrialized nations "should consider the impact of their own economic, trade and development policies on international migration."

Overall, according to the report, the world's population grew by 93 million in 1992. The current estimated global population of 5.57 billion is expected to increase to 6.25 billion by the turn of the century, and to climb to 10 billion by 2050.

Nearly 95 percent of the increase, according to the report, is in the developing world, especially Africa and South Asia. Population growth in the industrialized countries has almost stopped.

3   U.S. Growth in 1980s Fueled by Immigrants

Newcomers Critical to Population Patterns

BARBARA VOBEJDA

December, 1990

Immigrants made up more than one-third of the nation's growth in the 1980s, driving population change more than at any time since the early part of this century.

International newcomers accelerated the extraordinary growth in the West: If California had attracted no immigrants, it would have gained two new seats in the U.S. House of Representatives instead of seven.

At the same time, newcomers from abroad replaced a rapidly departing native-born populace in a band of states stretching across the Midwest and Northeast, stemming or reversing what could have been devastating population losses.

If it were not for nearly a million immigrants settling in New York, for example, the state would have lost population; instead it registered about 3 percent growth. The same is true in Illinois, which drew more than 400,000 immigrants but grew by fewer than 40,000 residents.

And in the Washington suburbs, the arrival of Hispanic and Asian immigrants contributed to double-digit growth during the 1980s.

Federal estimates analyzed by the Urban Institute put immigration in the 1980s at 104,577 for Virginia and 93,969 for Maryland, ranking the states 11th and 12th in the nation, respectively. The District drew 25,583 immigrants, ranking 1st.

"Without immigration, you'd have a much different picture of population change," said Jeffrey Passel, a demographer at the Urban Institute.

While a detailed picture of immigration will not be available from the 1990 census for several months, existing estimates and state population totals issued last week by the Census Bureau confirm that immigration has become central in deciding the nation's gainers and losers.

Population figures are used to determine the shares of about $28 billion annually in federal funding and to determine political representation. (The Census Bureau makes no distinction between legal and undocumented immigrants in counting population for political reapportionment.)

7

California, Texas and Florida, which ranked first, third and fourth in 1980s immigration, together won 14 new congressional seats in the 1990 apportionment. New York, which ranked second in immigration, lost three House seats, a product of the departure of more than a million of its residents.

Even in states such as Indiana—more than 90 percent white and native born—immigration became increasingly important in the 1980s. The state's 36,000 immigrants provided the bulk of its population growth.

In the northwestern corner of Indiana, where steel mills and blast furnaces line the lower tip of Lake Michigan, a growing minority and immigrant community seems estranged from the rest of the state.

"They say there's Indiana, and then there's 'The Region,'" said Carlos Alvarez, president of the area's Hispanic Chamber of Commerce. "The Region," he said, refers to the northwestern industrial pocket that "was always a melting pot."

But never before has the stream of immigrants to this corner mattered so much in maintaining the state's growth.

The Census Bureau estimates that 6 million legal and 2 million undocumented immigrants came to the United States during the 1980s, when the total population grew by about 22 million. That level of immigration is second only to the 8.8 million foreigners who arrived between 1900 and 1910.

"We're in a second great wave now that's been steadily building," said Passel.

The first wave of immigration, which began in the 1840s and continued until World War I, contributed a greater percentage of growth in what was then a much smaller nation.

Still, the current proportion of increase caused by foreign migrants is greater than any since the decade between 1910 and 1920, when immigration accounted for 40 percent of the nation's population growth.

At the same time, demographers are quick to point out that the nation has attracted large numbers of foreigners for virtually all of its history and that, as a proportion of the total population, foreign-born residents still account for only about 7 percent.

"We're still a country of mass migration, but not like it was early this century," said Charles Reely, a professor of international migration at Georgetown University.

Many experts believe that the next decade will bring an equal or greater stream of immigrants, the result of liberalized laws and the continuing economic and political factors that push foreigners to American shores.

"There's every indication it will be at least as much of a factor in growth as it was in the 1980s," said Frank D. Bean, a professor of sociology at the University of Texas. "The numbers will be higher."

The uneven distribution of immigrants across the country—seven states received 75 percent of total immigration—is largely due to two factors that dominate when immigrants are choosing where to settle.

According to Bean and others, newcomers have historically selected communities with job opportunities or where friends or family have settled. In many cases, those two overlap when friends or relatives smooth the way for an immigrant to find a job.

It is this social network, for example, that explains the large numbers of Hmongs, a tribal group from the mountains of Laos, drawn to Minneapolis and St. Paul. While these cities are known more for their historical attraction to European immigrants than as a home for Asian newcomers, the stream of Hmongs began with church-sponsored refugee programs, then gained momentum as more and more family members followed.

At the same time, rapid growth in some states had less to do with immigration. Florida's 33 percent growth in the 1980s was primarily due to movement from other states. Florida attracted 2.8 million migrants, but 2.3 million of those were from within the United States.

By comparison, California drew 3.2 million migrants, 2.3 million of whom were from foreign countries.

If it were not for that level of immigration and the distribution of those immigrants, said Passel, "we'd be talking about Florida as the principal growth center, not California."

4   Clinton Must Focus on Overpopulation

HOBART ROWEN
March, 1993

I f President Clinton's meeting with Russian President Boris Yeltsin in Vancouver on April 3 actually comes off, one topic that ought to be on the agenda, but probably won't be, is the fact that modern contraceptives are almost unavailable to Russian citizens. And, as is the case in many underdeveloped countries, women's health gets a low priority in the former Soviet state.

Russian women, says Population Action International, "have little choice but to rely on abortion as their primary method of birth control," under primitive conditions, often without anesthesia.

The desperate state of family planning and reproductive health care is a highly relevant issue for the Clinton-Yeltsin summit, because the U.S. president has pledged additional assistance to prop up a nation facing a massive economic depression.

But it should be absolutely clear that no amount of economic aid to a beleaguered country—whether it be Russia, Mexico or in sub-Saharan Africa—will help if not linked with meaningful family planning.

The only factor limiting a population explosion in Russia, beyond abortions that occur in a ratio of at least 2-1 to live births, is economic hardship. According to Population Action International (formerly the Population Crisis Committee), widespread fears about using contraceptive pills and condoms can be traced to poor-quality products made in Russia or imported from Eastern Europe.

And consider the debate on the North American Free Trade Agreement with Mexico: While Mexico has taken steps to expand birth control programs, it is way behind the curve of improvement that is going on in many parts of Asia. Lindsey Grant, former deputy assistant secretary of state for environmental and population affairs, said the population of Mexico, the Caribbean and Central America, only 25 percent that of the United States in 1930, is now 60 percent, and will match the United States along about 2020.

Grant, in a bulletin for Negative Population Growth Inc., said the growth of the working-age population in Mexico and the other Latin countries has risen even faster than the overall total, putting enormous pressure on people to find jobs—or to emigrate to the United States. Reduced fertility "is the only long-term escape from the population trap they are in."

Grant is an avowed opponent of NAFTA on many other grounds with which I do not agree. But I think it is time for the Clinton administration to wake up to the fact that if population is not better controlled in Mexico, NAFTA's economic stimulus there will be overwhelmed by the sheer number of additional mouths to be fed.

U.S. Trade Representative Mickey Kantor told a congressional committee last week that Clinton is prepared to "walk away" from NAFTA unless supplemental agreements are reached with Mexico on modernized environmental and workplace regulations. It's time to add population control to the list.

The Clinton administration's instincts on family planning issues are certainly of the best. Two days after taking office, the president made good on a campaign pledge to reverse President Reagan's 1984 decision, known as the "Mexico City Policy," that barred international organizations receiving American aid money from even discussing abortion.

Reagan applied this gag rule, even when the organizations were not using U.S. funds in any abortion efforts. This ruined efforts by private international birth-control agencies to deal with the range of family planning options in various countries. Reagan (and Bush) then cut off funds to nongovernment family planning groups such as the International Planned Parenthood Federation, and withdrew support for the United Nations Population Fund. That ended 20 years of U.S. leadership in two key organizations—the ones through which Europe and Japan channel almost all of their population planning aid.

Clinton's reversal of the Reagan edict has been welcomed by the community of private organizations devoted to birth control, but they want the new administration to go much further, restoring funds to the international groups, despite budgetary restraints.

Secretary of State Warren Christopher, in congressional testimony last Wednesday, said Clinton is "absolutely" committed to participating once again in the United Nations effort.

In *Foreign Policy* magazine, Sharon L. Camp of Population Action International argues that this decade may be "the last chance to stabilize human population by the middle of the next century, through humane and voluntary measures, at something less than double the current world population of 5.4 billion."

The sad fact is that under Reagan and Bush, as Camp points out, the United States wasted 12 years in useless debates about abortion, and a commitment to the views of business professor Julian Simon that population growth "can never be a problem in a properly organized free-market economy."

Clinton needs to exert new American leadership on population control. It is, of course, true that the president has an enormous domestic agenda with which to cope. But as he said at American University less than two weeks ago, there is no way to separate domestic and international issues. The money involved for birth control is peanuts, the stakes are overwhelming.

5   With Twice as Many People, Planet Could Expect Boom or Doom

WILLIAM BOOTH
June, 1991

If the population of the Earth doubles as predicted by the middle of the next century, what kind of world will our children see?

The popular image is often nightmarish, a teeming planet covered by megalopolises, the Third World a neo-Malthusian hell where bodies are stacked like cordwood and all but the very richest are reduced to nibbling cakes of bioengineered fish meal.

This is the version of the future in the crystal ball of biologist Paul Ehrlich, the pen behind *The Population Bomb* and *The Population Explosion*, who predicts that growing human numbers spell mass starvation and environmental ruin.

Such a future, however, is anything but certain. The popular images obscure a lively debate among researchers, who are fighting over whether population growth is good or bad or irrelevant to the quality of human life.

"I venture to say no one knows," said Carl Haub, a demographer with the Population Reference Bureau here. "But it is a hell of a good fight."

Optimists vs. Pessimists

Squared off in the ring are the optimists and the pessimists, the boomers and the doomers, go-go economists and neo-Malthusian ecologists. The optimistic economists focus on labor and capital. Above all, they value human ingenuity and technological development.

The ecologists look at natural resources, at the finite supplies of land, water and air. As biologists, they speak of carrying capacity and the limits of a closed system. They point to the habitat loss, species extinction and environmental degradation.

"Ecologists are concerned with the natural world. Economists are concerned with what is valued in the marketplace. It is a very different set of approaches," said Sam Preston, a University of Pennsylvania economist with an interest in population.

"Is the world going to be more or less prosperous? That's the real question. And population growth doesn't tell you very much about that," said Duke University economist Allen Kelly, a guarded optimist. "Prosperity depends on market economics and government policies."

The optimists like to point out that, on average, standards of living have improved throughout the world. Between 1960 and 1990, as world population went from 3 billion to 5.3 billion, infant mortality dropped and life expectancy, literacy, per capita income, food production and nutrition all increased on average. Even in Bangladesh, considered a textbook case on the horrors of population pressure, literacy, infant mortality and life expectancy have all improved.

The ecologists reply that the economists fail to take into account the fact that the world is consuming its natural resources at a furious clip.

"They don't ask, 'Is there enough water? Is there enough land? Is there enough wood? What are people going to cook with? What are they going to eat?'" said Lester Brown of the Worldwatch Institute and author of the popular annual *State of the World* reports.

Debating Earth's Capacity

How many people can the world support? The upper limit of Earth's population has been debated for centuries. Abraham and Lot were concerned about carrying capacity. Chinese scholars in the time of Confucius played the game. So did the ancient Greeks, who worried about overpopulation, overgrazing and the loss of forests. (The barren, rocky landscape of today's Greece was thick with trees in ancient times.)

The United Nations is currently revising its population projections for the next century. U.N. forecasters say that instead of reaching a stable world population of 10.2 billion persons in the year 2085, today's population figure could double by the middle of next century. Almost all of the growth will occur in the cities of the developing world.

Of course, demographers have been wrong before. They missed, for example, the Baby Boom in the United States. In the 1950s, they were predicting that Japan, then a crowded, less-developed country that made rubber sandals, would be worse off than India in the future.

The United Nations now predicts world population will stabilize at 11.6 billion. The reason for stabilization is that as countries grow rich, their birthrates fall. It happened in the United States, Japan and European nations. The Greek government now frets its population growth is "too low." Germany and Hungary are shrinking.

A similar fate may await South Korea, Taiwan, Thailand and other so-called NICs, or Newly Industrialized Countries. NICs are marked by increased use of birth control, falling birthrates, growing affluence and an increased life expectancy. Some optimists see no reason why every country on Earth won't eventually be like South Korea.

But before Bangladesh can become like South Korea, some scholars fear the planet will run out of natural resources. The traditional candidates for causing limits in population growth have been energy, metals, minerals, arable land and food.

Yet even if all renewable and nuclear energies were ignored, researchers have calculated that there are enough known fossil fuel reserves to sustain population growth for 280 years.

"On the global level, existing energy resources do not appear to constitute a limiting factor for many generations to come," according to Paul Demeny, a scholar at the Population Council in New York. Moreover, minerals and metals will also probably hold out, or as the optimists contend, will be replaced by materials derived from recycling.

Food Supply in Question

Food is the subject of hottest debate. Brown and colleagues contend that the ever-increasing productivity of agriculture, supported by fertilizers and new high-yield plant varieties, is showing signs of exhaustion.

"Developing countries as a whole have suffered a serious decline in food self-sufficiency," according to the U.N. Population Fund, which estimates that about 560 million people are now living in absolute poverty.

Robert Repetto of the World Resources Institute points out that a world population twice the present size, coupled with improved dietary standards in the developing world, would mean that all the world's current cropland would have to produce 2.8 tons of grain per acre per year. This is like saying that all the world's farmers will have to be as productive as an Iowa corn farmer—the most productive in the world.

But the U.N. Food and Agriculture Organization found that in 90 developing countries, less than half the potential cropland is under cultivation. The optimists add that in addition to expanding the area under cultivation, genetic engineering and improved technologies will continue to increase yields.

"In the future, every single measurement of human life will be better than it is now," said Julian Simon of the University of Maryland and perhaps the most optimistic of the optimists. Why? Because that is the trend.

"You can't assume the future will be an extrapolation of the past," said Brown. "We're entering uncharted territory."

6   At Summit, Dueling Hemispheres

North-South Rift over Overpopulation

JOEL ACHENBACH
June, 1992

D on't say "population control" around here. "Control" bespeaks coercion, forced sterilization and supposed First World fears of a dark-skinned planet. Don't even say "population" too much—it's the word that never got credentials at the official Earth Summit.

Join the Campaign Against Population Control, says a leaflet posted inside the women's tent at the "Global Forum" alternative summit on Flamengo Beach. A poster nearby says population control is "a phrase reminiscent of 'pest control.'"

A throng jams into another tent to hear more horror stories about the dangers of population control. A Brazilian senator says such programs have resulted in the involuntary sterilization of Brazilian women. The sponsor of this panel discussion, the State Council of Women's Rights, distributes a flier arguing that the sterilizations emerge from a conspiracy by Henry Kissinger and the National Security Council to limit the birthrate in the Third World "so as to not degenerate the Anglo-Saxon race."

There are quieter voices. But the orthodoxy at the Global Forum—the huge gathering of nongovernmental organizations (NGOs) at Flamengo Beach—is that environmentalists from northern countries should spend less time worrying about population growth, and more time addressing the inequities of global wealth.

Not that population growth isn't a plausible issue here in Rio. The United Nations predicts that there will be 10 billion people on the Earth in the year 2050, nearly double today's population, and that 97 percent of that increase will be in developing nations. And since the most biologically diverse and endangered ecosystems on the planet tend to be in the tropics, the environmental impact of those additional billions of people, in terms of the potential destruction of habitat, could be enormous.

But here, the issue picks up some unsubtle shading.

Pointing Fingers

"To say that women from the South who have many babies are responsible for the environmental crisis—it's a scandal," said Rosiska Darcy de Olivera, co-chair of the Brazilian Women's Coalition.

The environmental crisis isn't caused by the billions of poor people, she said, it's caused by the relatively few rich people who drive cars and consume massive amounts of energy and other resources.

This is a spirited, emotional debate. Not totally unfairly, feminists in developing countries suspect that American environmentalists worry more about endangered monkeys than about impoverished human beings.

Into this sticky atmosphere came Karen Rindge, 28, of Washington, D.C. She works on population policy for the National Wildlife Federation's human population policy. She wanted to open a "dialogue" with the women's groups here. It turned out to be more like an argument. At one point she was vociferously accused of saying that women in the South are "uncivilized," though several listeners said she didn't say any such thing.

"It's politics," Rindge sighs. "I want to feel this great oneness with everybody, but this whole conflict really bothers me. I really feel that we have a lack of understanding between our groups. I mean, I'm a feminist!"

Another American environmentalist who came to Rio to talk about population, Jane Lyons of the National Audubon Society, says being a white American woman doesn't help in discussions like this.

"It's like being discriminated against," she said. "They don't recognize that Karen and I don't represent the government of the United States. They don't recognize that because, basically, we're white women from the North."

And worse, they're environmentalists.

Environmentalists and feminists have many overlapping beliefs, and members of one persuasion claim to be members of the other—but at the Global Forum's women's tent (newly dubbed the Female Planet), the dominant feeling is one of women's empowerment, not environmental protection.

Wanga Mumba, executive director of the Environment and Population Center in Zambia, sympathizes with Rindge. Mumba said she's tired of the bickering and recrimination.

"We are just pointing fingers at each other instead of thinking of solutions," she said. "We are wasting our time."

It has been known for many months that overpopulation wouldn't get much notice at the official Earth Summit. But it was presumed that the issue could be dealt with more informally by environmentalists and feminists attending the parallel Global Forum, the nongovernment summit in Rio. Not so, it turns out; the term *overpopulation* is too disturbing even for a casual discussion in a tent by the sea.

So, although human overpopulation may be the planet's gravest environmental threat, it is essentially not mentioned in either the official or unofficial documents coming out of Rio.

For example, the gathered nations will sign off on a declaration of principles that includes the startling non-statement that countries should adopt "appropriate demographic policies." A separate, longer document called Agenda 21, also to be approved, originally called for nations to make "modern contraception" available, but after objections from representatives of the Holy See, the language was changed to "appropriate technology dissemination."

And instead of saying that countries should try to stop the explosion of population, Agenda 21 says, "All countries will have to improve their own capacities to assess the environment and development implications of their demographic trends and factors."

At the Global Forum, the nongovernmental organizations (NGOs) plan to issue their own "treaties," including one on population. But early drafts talk mostly about misbehavior by colonialist powers. The Brazilian suggestion for the treaty wording urges adoption of "ethical principles which refuse to deem any human being as expendable or unnecessary, especially those victimized by inequitable and discriminatory international economic relations."

So it is that, at Flamengo Beach, it's not global warming that is the hottest topic, it's not biodiversity, it's not water purity. It's human ecology. Social justice.

This giant group grope in Rio is not nearly the tree-hugging event that it was supposed to be. Or maybe the press simply sold the story wrong from the very start. The press had focused primarily on the first half of the Earth Summit's official title—the U.N. Conference on Environment and Development—and didn't realize that it was the "and Development" that would dominate much of the discussion.

Don't call it the Earth Summit anymore. It's the People Summit.

7   Manila, Catholic Church Split on Family Planning

Bishop Cites '74 Data to Charge U.S. Plot

WILLIAM BRANIGIN
August, 1993

Faced with an intensified government family-planning campaign, the Philippines' Roman Catholic Church is taking the offensive, challenging the program's legality and denouncing it as part of an American plot.

According to Bishop Teodoro Bacani, a leading member of the Catholic Bishops' Conference of the Philippines, the birth control program of the government of President Fidel Ramos was the result of U.S. "demographic imperialism." He cited a formerly classified 1974 study by the U.S. National Security Council on global population growth and American interests.

The charge marks a renewed drive by the church and its allies to discredit and obstruct the population policies of Ramos and his health secretary, Juan Flavier. Ramos, the country's first Protestant president, is trying to revive a family planning program that was all but abandoned by his predecessor, Corazon Aquino, a devout Catholic who was heavily supported by the church.

In part because the program was neglected, the Philippines now has one of the lowest contraceptive-use rates in the region, health officials say. The Philippine population, currently 64 million, is growing at nearly 2.5 percent a year, compared with 1.4 percent in Thailand, 1.7 percent in Indonesia and 2.2 percent in Vietnam. Because the country's economy is not growing as quickly, increasing population is outstripping food production and the number of jobs, schools and hospital beds, officials say.

Behind the battle over birth control is a simmering feud between church and state in this predominantly Catholic country. Since the election of Ramos last year over the opposition of the Philippines' Roman Catholic hierarchy, the Catholic Church's influence on the government has been waning.

Recent surveys show that Filipinos overwhelmingly support the state's position on family planning and that there is a high demand for birth control services.

Flavier said that when he took over the family planning program, "I practically had to start from scratch." He has revived a national network of rural family planning clinics and promoted the use of condoms—despite church warnings that they are "intrinsically evil"—to combat unwanted pregnancies and AIDS. With Flavier's support, radio stations now broadcast condom commercials, unthinkable here only a year ago.

Flavier, a doctor with 30 years' experience in rural health care, has been at the center of the church-state controversy. Quick with a quip, he has reacted to church criticism by complaining, "I was 'condomed' without trial."

The war of words escalated recently when Ramos said government health workers could resign if they disagreed with his population program and a presidential spokesman called the church's stand "obsolete." The archbishop of Manila, Cardinal Jaime Sin, denounced the "foolishness" and "stupidity" of Ramos's aides, and church officials threatened to encourage resistance among the government's 7,000 health workers.

In what he described as a "bombshell" that would demolish the family planning program, Bishop Bacani said a newly obtained document showed that the United States was plotting to curb population growth in the Philippines and other developing countries for its own ends.

"We have a copy of a U.S. national security document that shows all its designs are happening in the Philippines," Bacani said. "What we are going through is a case of demographic imperialism, or the imposition of population control on other nations by a richer nation."

Asked if family planning in the Philippines could be considered a U.S. plot, the Rev. James Reuter, a spokesman for the Catholic Bishops' Conference, said, "That's exactly what [the U.S. study] implies." He added, "Certainly there is a strong belief in lay quarters that the family planning program comes to the Philippines from the U.S. [Agency for International Development] complete with targets and threats." He said the "threats" involved making new loans contingent on meeting population targets.

A U.S. Embassy spokesman said, "We plead guilty to spending millions of dollars" on poverty alleviation and development programs. "We plead guilty to promoting the idea that developing countries would develop faster if their populations did not double every 20 years."

The issue was taken up by the Council of the Laity of the Philippines, a leading Catholic lay group, which released a "summary" of the purported U.S. document at a news conference Monday. The summary, compiled by an anti-birth-control group in the United States, quotes selectively from what it says was the original 250-page document, titled "National Security Study Memorandum 200: Implications of Worldwide Population Growth for U.S. Security and Overseas Interests."

According to the summary, the U.S. study analyzed the political and economic implications of world population growth, especially as a force for instability in developing nations, and recommended assistance for family planning programs in 13 countries of strategic interest to the United States, including the Philippines. The summary describes the U.S. policy as "population intervention in the developing world."

Philippine commentators generally greeted the "bombshell" as a dud. The newspaper *Malaya* said that by invoking it, "church leaders have already lost the debate. They have, in effect, conceded that the debate is not about sin, that population growth is about political stability and development."

Disenchantment with the church position has also surfaced in other quarters here.

"The church is becoming petty and irrational," said a bank official here who formerly studied in a Catholic seminary and has two brothers in the priesthood. "The church needs to mature. It just hasn't grown."

"We need to manage our population growth rate," said Senate President Edgardo Angara. "It eats up whatever economic growth we make in this country."

The Council of the Laity, however, vowed to fight on by challenging the constitutionality of the government's family planning program in the Supreme Court and holding what one priest described as "down with the condom" prayer rallies.

8   The Numbered Days of Population Growth

JONATHAN YARDLEY
February, 1989

The good news from the Census Bureau—though precious few of those reading these words will be around to enjoy it—is that in about half a century the population of the United States not merely will stop growing but actually will begin to decline. The bad news—every silver lining, after all, does have its cloud—is that before this takes place the population will grow by about 50 million, further straining the country's natural and man-made resources.

There are of course those who see this news as rather less than good. The estimable Ben J. Wattenberg of the American Enterprise Institute, who can always be counted on to champion growth, complained last week to *The New York Times* that "This really deals with the central question of our time, 'Is America in decline?'" Wattenberg, who at times appears to relish the prospect of an America so populous that each of us is allotted an amount of space approximately equal to the dimensions of a telephone booth, fears "great turbulence" both economic and social, and counsels that we may need to bring in additional immigrants so as to keep the growth machine going full throttle.

Indeed it is true that zero population growth is a mixed blessing. An economy that for four centuries has had growth as its principal underpinning will have to undergo traumatic adjustments as the number of women of childbearing age declines. As population consolidates, the value and price of labor will rise accordingly, which means that the cost of everything else will go up as well; the potential for serious inflation is self-evident, and the possibility that the government will have to play a more restrictive, disciplinary role in the free market cannot be discounted.

A stable or declining population also means major, if at this measure largely unquantifiable, changes in the country's social life. The trend toward smaller families and single-person households obviously will not be reversed; this is most unlikely to do anything to alleviate the strain of self-preoccupation that has emerged in the American psyche in the postwar period of affluence and pop psychology. The trend toward an older population will be accelerated, with effects on the country's pension system, labor market and medical resources that clearly will be enormous; and a country dominated by older people—a "geritocracy" as one population specialist calls it—certainly is going to be different from one that traditionally has treasured youth, though the precise nature of that difference is quite impossible to suggest at this juncture.

These are problems, no doubt about it, as is the American position in the world economy and its defense posture vis-a-vis not merely the Soviet Union but also those Third World powers whose anti-Western passions have become so potent a force in global politics. Yet these problems are all within the reach of human solution, especially when one bears in mind the staggering technological resources this country has at hand; what is of far greater significance is that the benefits of stable population almost surely will far outweigh the costs, and that we—"we" of the year 2040, that is to say—will be reaping them in the nick of time.

What the growth advocates either cannot or will not acknowledge is that the price of what they regard as progress has become, in the postwar era, increasingly onerous and, in human and environmental terms, painful. Ours is to be sure a vast country, and much of it still is unsettled and unexploited, but the plain fact is that there are too many of us and that we have accustomed ourselves to demanding, as satisfaction for our needs and wants, too much in the way of natural resources. Name almost any of the problems that beset us—automobile congestion, seashore despoliation, air and water pollution, you name it—and sooner or later they all boil down to the same thing: too many people.

That over the coming half-century we will continue to add to our numbers at the rate of about a million a year can only intensify these problems. Our highways will become more crowded; our landfills will be exhausted at a breathtaking pace; our desperate inner-city neighborhoods will become more congested, in the process heightening the terrible dangers of drugs and crime; our air will become fouler and our water less drinkable. Yes, it is true that there are other explanations for these ailments than too many people; but population is at the root of all of them, and thus the long-range prospect of stable population is, in and of itself, cause for clear if moderate optimism.

Yet even that optimism must be tempered by an awareness that if we undergo as much "progress" in the next 50 years as we have in the last, there won't be much of a country left for the beneficiaries of zero population growth to enjoy. Will, for example, 50 million people mean 50 million more automobiles? Perhaps not. But quite surely they will mean 20 million more; and even if the auto industry develops a totally nonpolluting exhaust system—a most unlikely prospect—the sheer number of additional cars will place incredible demands on the highway system and the environment, not to mention the poor cities with their gridlocked intersections, parking shortages and lunatic beltways.

For anyone who believes in the notion that the most pleasant world is one in which man and his creations exist in something approximating harmony with nature and its resources, the prospect of America in 2040 is anything except inviting. We've destroyed so much in the past half-century, it's hard to imagine what will be left for our great-grandchildren by the time they reach their maturity. But at least, if the Census Bureau is right, they won't have to bulldoze more land for more houses and more shopping malls and more highways; as population stabilizes, so, presumably, will demand, and Americans of this brave new world will be able to turn their attention to other matters than merely keeping up with the needs of an ever-expanding population.

Doomsayers to the contrary notwithstanding, stable population will not mean the end of human happiness as we know it. The world will be different, of course; but heaven knows the world of 1989 is astonishingly different from the world of 1939, and somehow we have managed to survive in it. In 2040 people will still have babies and raise families and play baseball—if there's any room left for ball fields—and have picnics; there will be fewer babies and smaller picnics, perhaps, but the pleasures they afford will, if anything, be all the greater as they become less commonplace.

Stable population is nothing to dread. To the contrary, it is to be welcomed; and those of us who will not be alive to welcome it can only regret our misfortune. Stable population offers the hope, however tenuous, of a stable world; but it will be up to people to achieve that, and as history advises us, their record leaves something to be desired.

9 World Population May Hit 10 Billion by Year 2025

Birth Control Use Not Increasing as Quickly as U.N. Agency Had Predicted

SUSAN OKIE
May, 1989

The world's population, currently 5.2 billion, is likely to nearly double to 10 billion by 2025 and to reach 14 billion before the end of the next century unless birth control use increases dramatically around the world within the next few decades, according to a report released yesterday by the United Nations Population Fund (UNFPA).

The report revises an estimate that the agency made a decade ago and that has been widely quoted since. The earlier prediction was that the world's population would stabilize at about 10 billion late in the 21st century. That estimate assumed a greater increase in the worldwide use of family planning than has occurred.

"There has been a failure to address the problem on the scale that it should be addressed," said Stirling D. Scruggs, deputy director of the agency's division of external affairs.

In order to hold population growth to the older, lower estimate, the percentage of the world's women of reproductive age who use birth control would have to increase from the current level of 45 percent to 71 percent by 2025, the report said. Only a few Western European countries and China have such a high level of birth control use. In the United States the rate is about 65 percent.

The more pessimistic outlook comes despite the considerable success that international family-planning efforts have had in the last 20 years. Birth rates are declining for more than 90 percent of the world's population. Worldwide, the average number of children per woman has dropped from 6 to 3.6.

Despite these gains, the world's population is growing by 1.7 percent a year because of declining death rates and because in many developing countries, people of reproductive age make up a large proportion of the population.

"The growth rate has come down, but the number of people added to the population every year has gone up," Scruggs said.

In many countries, rapid population growth has already caused depletion of agricultural land, water, firewood and other resources. The clearing of trees to create more farm land leads to increased erosion and loss of forests needed to help counteract the atmospheric buildup of carbon dioxide, the major cause of the "greenhouse effect."

"We don't know what will happen to the natural resource base at a population of 8, 9, 10, 14 billion," said Sharon Camp, vice president of Population Crisis Committee, an advocacy group, at a news conference yesterday.

Boosting birth control use to the level required to stabilize the world's population at 10 billion would require spending at least an additional $2 billion a year for international family-planning efforts, the report said. Current worldwide expenditures are about $3 billion a year, with half of the total being spent by China and India, the most populous countries.

Scruggs said the United States spends more than any other industrialized country for international population-control programs, about $230 million this year. However, U.S. contributions have decreased from $290 million in 1985.

The United States has not contributed to the UNFPA since 1985 because the federal government yielded to antiabortion groups that objected to the agency's funding of China's population-control program, claiming China's policies were coercive. The Chinese program seeks to limit each couple to one child. Forced abortions and sterilizations have been reported.

Camp said the agency's governing council will vote next month on a new five-year program of assistance to China that emphasizes making contraceptives more available. She said the vote of the U.S. representative to the council will be viewed as a signal of the Bush administration's policy on international family-planning efforts.

10 Fertility Rates in Developing World Drop Sharply

Change Is Insufficient to Head Off Continued Rapid Population Growth, Study Finds

DON OBERDORFER
August, 1991

Fertility in the developing world has declined sharply and unexpectedly in the past two decades, but the shift is insufficient to head off continued rapid population growth, according to an international survey released yesterday.

Latest information from the Demographic and Health Surveys (DHS), a nine-year study funded by the Agency for International Development, indicates that fertility rates in the developing world have declined by about one-third since the late 1960s—from 6.1 births per woman to 4.2 births per woman.

In the 14 largest developing countries, including China and India, fertility declined by nearly two-thirds in this period, according to the study.

Demographers and other population experts attending the DHS World Conference, which convened here yesterday, said that such sharp reductions are dramatic and almost revolutionary, although they go roughly only halfway toward stopping the world's rapid population growth. In order to stabilize the world's population, the fertility rate would have to come down to about two children per woman.

Martin Vaessen, director of DHS, said the shift means that for a variety of reasons, "women don't want to have as many children." He and other experts said the change is associated with an increase in the educational level of women, the availability of contraceptives and other means of birth control as well as changes in basic attitudes about family life.

Prof. Charles Westoff, director of Princeton's Office of Population Research and senior demographic adviser to DHS, said "the media has a lot to do with this—transistor radios, television, literacy that bring an exposure to ideas [including] the idea that fertility control is legitimate and is experienced by large numbers of people in the rest of the world."

Despite the gains, said Westoff, there is an "extensive unmet need" for contraceptives and other aspects of family planning to deal with expanding world population trends.

The bad news in the new information, according to Duff G. Gillespie, director of AID's Population Bureau, is that because of the tremendously large number of young people in prime childbearing age already born, there will be twice as many people on Earth in about 30 years as there are today. "There is nothing anybody can do to hold back that tide due to the population momentum," Gillespie said.

The survey, which covered 28 countries, indicates that the fertility decline is uneven among the regions of the world and even within specific regions.

Northeast Asia, including China and Korea, is the only region of the developing world approaching zero population growth, with an overall fertility rate of 2.3 births per woman. On the other hand, fertility rates of 4-5 births per woman were recorded in Southeast Asia and Latin America, 5-6 in South Asia, West Asia and Northern Africa, and 6.4 in sub-Sahara Africa, according to DHS.

There was some change reported from sub-Sahara Africa. The studies provided "the first evidence of fertility decline" from Botswana, Kenya and Zimbabwe, according to reports to the conference.

11   Family Planning in the Family of Nations

JUDY MANN
December, 1992

T he story of the Somalian famine, the story of a people who are so terribly out of sync with their environment that they are dying out, is not just a story of economic dislocation and vanishing resources. It is a story about ineffective population control and a general failure on the part of the world to integrate reproductive health issues into international politics.

It is also a story of failed American leadership. When this nation could have served as an international model, as a developer of effective family planning techniques, as an international educator and standard-bearer for responsible family planning and infant and maternal health, it chose instead to devote its political energies to guerrilla warfare over the abortion issue.

Instead of integrating abortion into a range of population-control efforts, the Reagan-Bush administrations denied money to family planning programs that provided privately funded abortions or abortion counseling. Since 1980, the United States has gone from a world leader in contraceptive research to being a bit player.

While bipartisan efforts in Congress secured more than $330 million in international family planning funds this year, effective contraceptives such as the injectible Depo-Provera have been approved only recently for use in the United States. This has limited the drug's distribution, since many countries are reluctant to allow a pharmaceutical to be distributed to their citizens when the producing country won't let it be sold to its consumers.

About half of all married women in the world do not want any more children, according to the World Fertility Survey of 1980 and other studies, yet most do not use any form of birth control. Nancy P. Harris, director of SEATS, a program that receives $43 million from the Agency for International Development to work in Africa, Asia and the Near East, notes that contraceptive use is closely related to literacy. "The more literate the woman becomes, the higher incidence of contraceptive use. With hard times, the desired family size is going down. It is still very prevalent to define women by their childbearing, so in most Third World countries, the failure to bear a child or infertility is generally a terrible thing."

"The silent phenomenon of Africa is the rate of urbanization," she adds. "Urban areas are growing at a much faster rate than rural areas."

In similar situations in Turkey and Mexico, she said, whole villages are "migrating to sections of these humongous cities like Mexico City or Istanbul. What effect that is going to have on the poverty in some of these cities is pretty appalling." She predicts that the Food and Drug Administration's recent approval of Depo-Provera will have a "dramatic impact on contraceptive access and acceptability" among Third World women because AID will be able to purchase it and supply it through its community-based clinics.

"If we begin to adopt and implement more enlightened policies [in the United States], it will have a worldwide effect," says Kate Michaelman, head of the National Abortion Rights Action League. "It's clear when you see the pictures in Somalia that reproduction and economics is an issue we need to talk about. They are related. We are models. But we have not modeled very effectively. What we have modeled is a rigid ideology that has been destructive and harmful to our effort worldwide to integrate reproductive policy issues into all of our international policies. Reproductive issues have been separated out from all the other issues, as if one doesn't have any impact on the other, and abortion has been even more separated out."

Michaelman is counting on the new Congress and President-elect Clinton to pass the Freedom of Choice Act, which would guarantee a woman's right to abortion in the United States. "If we don't, it will continue to be an issue that everybody is distracted by. We do our world and our nation enormous good if we can sign it and move on to these more enlightened policies that understand the interconnectedness and the complexity of all these issues. The inability of people in the world to control their reproductive capacity takes an enormous toll on the world. The Somalian pictures should tell us that."

With the dawning of a new political day in this country comes the opportunity to close the book on the abortion debate and to open the book on the discussion we should have been having all along—namely, how can governments encourage sound reproductive decisions that will promote infant and maternal health and the economic welfare of everyone? That's the discussion that will take the term *human life* and infuse it with real meaning.

12   Costs of Stabilizing World Population Tallied

$10.5 Billion a Year Needed, Report Says

SUSAN OKIE
February, 1990

The world population, now 5.3 billion, could be stabilized at 9.3 billion by the end of the next century if governments and international organizations increase annual spending for family planning programs from the current $3.2 billion to $10.5 billion over the next decade, according to a report published today.

Without such a spending increase, world population is expected to grow to more than 14 billion by the year 2120, according to United Nations projections.

"What we as a society of nations do in this decade will determine population trends for the next century," said Sharon Camp, vice President of Population Crisis Committee, a nonprofit organization advocating family planning programs that prepared the report.

The added funding would be used for efforts to increase worldwide use of birth control by the year 2000 to approximately 75 percent of all couples of reproductive age. According to the report, that frequency of birth control use would result in an average family size of two children per woman and lead to population stabilization by the end of the 21st century. Recent projections of a near tripling of population by 2120 have alarmed many experts, who fear such explosive growth would strain the planet's capacity to produce food, irreparably deplete natural resources and damage the environment.

Camp said the report is the first attempt to determine, for 125 countries, what level of birth control use would be needed to modify the current pattern, and what it would cost to achieve that level. The calculations estimated it costs $16 per year per couple to provide family planning services.

By the year 2000, the U.S. government's annual contribution to family planning programs should be $1.2 billion, according to the report. Camp said the U.S. government contributed about $227 million to international family planning efforts in 1988, roughly half of it to individual nations and the rest to institutions.

The report said 29 countries have achieved an average family size of two children or less and have either stabilized their populations or are expected to do so.

They include the United States, Japan, South Korea, Australia, most West European countries and several in East Europe. More than 70 percent of couples in the majority of these countries use some form of birth control, the report said.

Another 12 countries were rated as having "good" family planning records, with between 61 percent and 75 percent of couples using contraceptives and with an average of 2.6 children per woman. Among the countries in this category were China, Thailand, Sri Lanka, Colombia, Chile and Brazil.

The Chinese government's family planning policies have been widely criticized in recent years as coercive. The United States has not contributed to the U.N. Population Fund since 1985 because part of the money goes to China, where 74 percent of couples use birth control.

Twenty-one countries were rated "fair," with rates of contraceptive use ranging from 43 percent to 60 percent of couples and with an average of 3.9 children per woman. Included in this category were Ireland, Mexico, Zimbabwe, South Africa, Indonesia and the Philippines.

Eighteen countries were rated "poor," including the Soviet Union, India, Bangladesh, Egypt, Kenya and Guatemala. Family size in these countries averaged 4.3 children per woman, and contraceptive use rates ranged from 15 percent to 42 percent of couples.

Forty-five countries were rated "very poor," with fewer than 15 percent of couples using contraceptives and with family size averaging 6.4 children per woman. Camp said it is unlikely that many of these will achieve the goal of 75 percent of couples using contraceptives by the year 2000 but said lack of progress in some countries could be offset by better-than-expected gains in others. She said countries in the "very poor" category make up only 14 percent of the world's population.

Currently, 80 percent of family planning costs in developing countries are paid by the governments and consumers in those countries, Camp said. The plan would require most developing countries to at least double their family planning budgets over the next decade. It proposes that by the year 2000 slightly under half of the projected $10.5 billion annual cost of family planning should be paid by developing countries.

13 U.S. to Resume Aiding U.N. Fund for Population Activities

JULIA PRESTON
May, 1993

The Clinton administration, extending its break with Republican policies on birth control and abortion into the international arena, announced today that it will resume funding for the U.N. population program after a seven-year suspension.

Timothy E. Wirth, the top State Department official for population issues, said here that the United States will move immediately to become "a major if not the major" contributor to the U.N. Fund for Population Activities. But he said Washington continues to regard the birth control policies of China, which limit couples to a single child, as "coercive" and will not give funds for work in China.

Wirth's speech, at a planning meeting for a 1994 U.N. population conference to be held in Cairo, drew cheers from the audience of U.N. officials and diplomats and nongovernmental birth control workers.

"It means a profound change in the attitude of the United States towards the future of the world," said fund spokesman Alex Marshall. He said the agency had been "held back in our ability to provide services," especially in Africa.

The Reagan administration stopped funding for the U.N. agency in 1986 as part of its opposition to any population control programs linked to abortion. Fund officials said the agency has never funded abortions and is barred by U.N. regulations from treating them as a form of birth control. But Reagan's officials pointed to the fact that some countries where the United Nations has population programs did allow abortions.

In 1985, the year before the cutoff, the United States gave $46 million to the fund but withheld $10 million as a signal of protest against China's approach. Renewed U.S. contributions to the fund's $230 million annual budget are expected to be at about the same level.

Wirth said that the Clinton administration would encourage debate about abortion at the Cairo conference and would remove any limits on U.S. funding for international population projects that provide abortions. "Our position is to support reproductive choice, including access to safe abortion," Wirth said.

14 China Lowers Birthrate to Levels in West

6.5 Million Sterilized in '92, Official Says

LENA H. SUN
April, 1993

C hina has dramatically slowed its birth rate, lowering the number of children Chinese women are expected to have in their lifetime to U.S. and European levels, the government announced today.

With 1.17 billion people, China is the most populous country and accounts for 21.4 percent of the world's population, so any major change in its population profile has great impact.

In a press conference, Family Planning Minister Peng Peiyun attributed the drop in the birth rate and fertility rate in 1992 to greater vigilance by the ruling Communist Party, improved birth-control measures to implement the country's one-couple, one-child family planning policy, and rising living standards that are prompting couples to have fewer children later in life.

Peng did not elaborate on what birth control measures had become more effective. But some Western specialists and reports in the Chinese press indicate a surge in 1991 in the use of intrauterine devices and sterilizations for couples who exceeded the one-child limit.

In 1992, about 6.5 million Chinese were sterilized, a family planning official said. In 1991, the figure was closer to 10 million, according to a Western specialist, nearly double the number in 1988.

Western experts say coercive measures, such as forced sterilizations, may be part of the explanation for what they describe as the surprising drop in birth and fertility rates.

"It's miraculous for a developing country to achieve this relying on just service and voluntarism," said one Western specialist in Beijing.

In China, the one-child family planning policy began in 1979. In many rural areas, couples are allowed to have two children without penalty if their first is a girl. Minorities, such as Tibetans, may be allowed to have three children or occasionally more.

China's birth rate has fluctuated in the recent past. A dip in 1983-84 coincided with widespread international charges of enforced abortions here. A low in 1979 preceded the coming to adulthood in the '80s of babies born after Mao Tse-Tung pressed for population increase in 1958.

Economic change in the countryside has strengthened the traditional preference for sons. In many cases, as peasants have become wealthy they have paid little attention to birth control because they can afford to pay the fines or bribe family planning cadres, some Chinese said.

But under pressure from central authorities to keep China's population in check, some Chinese report that local family planning cadres have tightened controls in the past two years. In parts of rural Hebei Province, for example, women who already have given birth to a son face sterilization or risk serious punishment if they again become pregnant. In China, women are the more likely to undergo sterilization, usually by tubal ligations.

"If you don't do it voluntarily, they will come and knock your house down," said a blue-collar worker, who said a relative was given such a warning last year.

Today, Peng said that the government "strongly opposes" coercive measures and added that a small number of family planning officials have been removed from their jobs for engaging in such tactics.

Stirling Scruggs, who heads the Beijing office of the United Nations Population Fund, said, "I know the minister, Peng Peiyun, has concerns about coercion because we have collaborated on projects to improve counseling skills of family planning workers and to improve the quality of contraception and the status of women, all aimed at creating programs based on freedom of choice."

The figures released today indicate that China met last year some key goals projected for 2000. Peng said that the policy would remain unchanged until the end of the century nevertheless, because "China is still in a peak period of population growth."

According to statistics from a sample survey conducted by the State Family Planning Commission last fall, China's birth rate in 1992 fell to 18.24 births per 1,000 population, compared to 21 per 1,000 in 1990. The fertility rate—the number of children a woman will have in her lifetime—dropped to 2 births per woman in 1992, down from 2.3 in 1990. The latest fertility figure is below the population replacement level. Chinese women would require a fertility rate of almost 2.2 to maintain the present population.

In Beijing and Shanghai and in northeast China, the fertility rate has plummeted to 1.5 births per woman, which is lower than that of many European countries. The U.S. rate is 2, France's 1.8 and Germany's 1.4.

At the same time that the fertility rate is dropping, the number of boy babies is growing, according to Westerners. At today's press conference, Chinese officials said the traditional preference for males to carry on the family line and work the land had produced a sex ratio higher than normal. In nearly all populations, 105 to 106 male babies are born for each 100 female babies.

According to China's 1990 census, for every 100 girls under the age of 1 there were 113.8 boys. Officials said they had not collected such data from the sample survey done last year. Unofficial specialists in the field say they believe China has new data showing the sex ratio to be even higher but was not publicizing the number because it showed growing imbalance.

While the reason for the imbalance is not known, specialists believe that three factors are probably at work: unreported births of baby girls, infanticide in poor and backward areas, and abortions of unwanted girls. Ultrasound testing to determine the sex of fetuses is common here.

15   Developing World's Role in Global Warming Grows

Population's Rise, Technology's Spread Cited

SUSAN OKIE
May, 1990

D eveloping countries, where populations are growing explosively and where personal income and use of technology are also increasing, will surpass industrialized countries in the next few decades as the major source of carbon dioxide and other gases that cause global warming, according to a U.N. report on world population released yesterday.

The report said that by 2025 the countries now comprising the Third World are likely to be spewing four times as much carbon dioxide as the developed world now produces.

The report by the U.N. Population Fund said the number of human beings, currently 5.3 billion, is increasing by a quarter of a million every day. At the current growth rate, the population should reach 11 billion by the end of the next century, but may climb to 14 billion by that time if population-control programs are not as effective as hoped.

The greatest threats posed by such massive increases in population are further global warming, deforestation and soil degradation, according to the report.

Industrialized countries currently account for most fossil fuel consumption and use of chlorofluorocarbons (CFCs), chemicals used in refrigeration and aerosols that contribute to depletion of the stratospheric ozone layer. But population growth and the spread of technology are rapidly changing that pattern.

For instance, the human population has doubled since 1950, but the car population has increased sevenfold, according to the report. Currently 400 million, it is expected to grow to 700 million in the next 20 years, with much of the increase occurring in developing countries.

Carbon dioxide, the gas thought to contribute most to global warming, is released by burning organic materials, especially automobiles and industries burning fossil fuels. Carbon dioxide emissions from industries in developing countries increased almost sixteenfold from 1950 to 1985. They are expected to soar even faster in coming decades.

Even if developed countries stabilize their carbon dioxide emissions at current levels, global emissions will triple by 2025, the report said.

CFCs, besides contributing to global warming, are believed to be the major cause of ozone depletion. Under a treaty signed in Montreal in 1987, industrialized countries agreed to reduce CFC use in an effort to cut worldwide consumption by 50 percent by the year 2000. But under the treaty's current provisions, developing countries, which now account for only a small percentage of global CFC consumption, could increase their emissions 70 percent in the next fifty years, the report said.

The findings were announced just a week after the Bush administration instructed its delegates to an international conference on CFCs held in Geneva to oppose a plan that would provide funds to developing countries to reduce their CFC use.

Population growth causes up to 80 percent of deforestation in the world and is a major reason for soil degradation caused by erosion and other factors, the report said.

More than 28 million acres of forest are cleared each year—an area larger than Virginia—and more than 17 million acres of farmland become unproductive annually because of soil erosion, according to estimates by the U.N. Food and Agriculture Organization. Erosion reduces farmers' capacity to grow food and forces them to clear more forest, establishing a vicious cycle. Deforestation is believed to contribute significantly to the levels of carbon dioxide in the atmosphere, because trees remove the gas from the air.

The report said control of world population growth must be a major part of any strategy to reduce global warming and halt damage to forests and soils. It said other steps would include improving the efficiency of energy use, shifting from fossil fuels to renewable energy sources such as wind, solar and geothermal energy, and limiting deforestation.

It said that stabilizing the world's population below 10 billion—just short of another doubling from today's level—is still possible, but would require a major increase in funding for population-control programs over the next decade.

Atmospheric Problems: The Prospect of Global Warming 2

O f all the threats to Earth's environmental quality, the specter of global warming (the "greenhouse effect") seems to have attracted the most attention by society in general. Perhaps this is because, unlike many other threats, global warming is, indeed, global in its consequences. If it occurs in accordance with some predictions, most of Earth's inhabitants will be affected. However, the issue of global warming is still subject to considerable debate and thus provides another example of how learned people disagree on almost every aspect of an environmental issue. While some scientists predict an increase of five to seven degrees in Earth's average temperature over the next 50 to 100 years, others doubt that there will be any global warming, and still others contend that what will actually occur is global *cooling* (the "parasol effect").

Similar disagreements exist over the consequences that can be expected if global warming should occur. Some predict dire consequences with radical changes in almost every aspect of life, while others predict that human beings and most other species will adapt to whatever changes occur.

Given the lack of certainty regarding the global warming issue, the only rational strategy would seem to be to "expect the worst" and take immediate steps to mitigate the potential consequences—reduce burning of fossil fuels, rain forests, and so on. On the other hand, many are quick to point out that such strategies would have an adverse economic impact. Thus, the question becomes whether to sacrifice immediate and certain benefits to guard against distant and uncertain dangers. There is much evidence showing that people in this situation will consistently choose immediate benefits even when those benefits are small and future negative consequences large. The question is whether this typical behavior pattern can be altered and, if not, will humankind's craving for immediate gratification prove deadly.

We begin this chapter with an article that provides an excellent summary of the many complex issues surrounding the global warming controversy. Articles 2–5 examine different sources of evidence and views concerning global warming, the extent of the danger, and possible causes if the phenomenon is real. Articles 6 and 7 cover proposals to reduce the risk of global warming and reactions to those proposals. The final two articles present different perspectives on the problem, with

Article 8 discussing the possibility that warming could trigger a new ice age. Article 9 reports on a group of optimistic experts who find the prospect of global warming relatively manageable through humankind's ingenuity, but also conveys the much more pessimistic forecast of many environmentalists.

1   As Earth Summit Nears, Consensus Still Lacking on Global Warming's Cause

BOYCE RENSBERGER
May, 1992

While most of the planet's heads of state converge on Rio de Janeiro for the Earth Summit to set policy on coping with global warming, most of the scientists who specialize in the subject still can't figure out whether anything unusual is actually happening to Earth's climate.

Scientists generally agree that it has been getting warmer over the last hundred years, but the average rate of change is no greater than in centuries past, and there is no consensus that human activity is the cause. And while there is no doubt that continued emissions of "greenhouse gases" tend to aid warming, it is not clear that cutting back on emissions could do much to stop a natural trend, if that is what is happening.

Seldom, in fact, has an issue risen to the top of the international political agenda while the facts of the matter remained so uncertain.

For example, in the single most comprehensive effort to synthesize the state of scientific knowledge about global warming, the United Nations Environment Program and the World Meteorological Organization called together several hundred working scientists from 25 countries—most of the top specialists with expertise in the subject—and asked them to write a comprehensive report on the situation.

That group, the Intergovernmental Panel on Climate Change (IPCC), produced a 365-page report in 1990 that was the scientific basis for a climate treaty to be adopted in Rio. It concluded that the future warming rate could speed up considerably, with Earth's mean temperature climbing about 2 degrees Fahrenheit by 2025 and 5 degrees by 2100.

That report gave impetus to one of the most ambitious international efforts ever undertaken, yet when read closely the document gives only two conclusions it calls "certain":

There is a natural greenhouse effect that keeps Earth warmer than it would otherwise be. It's been operating for billions of years, as scientists have long known.

41

Emissions of greenhouse gases from human activities are pushing up the concentration of those gases in the atmosphere. That, too, has been known for decades.

With less confidence, the IPCC scientists said there is fairly reliable evidence that the average temperature of Earth's surface has risen by about 1 degree Fahrenheit over the last hundred years and the sea level has risen by four to eight inches in the same time.

"The size of the warming is broadly consistent with predictions of climate models, but," the panel cautioned, "it is also of the same magnitude as natural climate variability."

In other words, the changes measured to date in the environment are no bigger than those the Earth has undergone in recent centuries through entirely natural processes.

"It is not possible at this time," the report said, "to attribute all, or even a large part, of the observed global-mean warming to the enhanced greenhouse effect (the extra warming attributable to those human-produced gases) on the basis of the observational data currently available."

A Matter of Perspective

If these measured words represent the consensus of climate experts, what about all the voices calling for drastic action, all those experts so widely publicized in the crescendo leading to Rio?

The fact is that most of them are part of the consensus. They differ not so much on what can be said scientifically but on what they think society should do in response. The major confrontation, as in so many scientific controversies, derives less from what the data say and more from the personalities of the scientists. The controversies reveal as much about the temperaments of researchers as the temperature of Earth.

The most visible scientists have tended to be those who express alarm and call for immediate, massive action in the name of prudence. They are most visible because many are backed by large activist organizations and because the news media traditionally give alarm calls prominence. But there are also more circumspect scientists who say the data are still much too uncertain to rush into action, especially expensive action, to curtail greenhouse emissions.

The most prominent climatologist to sound the alarm was James E. Hansen of NASA's Goddard Institute for Space Studies. He triggered much of the current concern by announcing in 1988 that "global warming has reached a level such that we can ascribe with a high degree of confidence a cause and effect relationship between the greenhouse effect and observed warming. It is already happening now."

One of the alarmists' severest critics is S. Fred Singer, the first director of the U.S. weather satellite program and a well-known skeptic of doomsday scenarios. Yet Singer calls the IPCC report "an excellent compilation . . . filled with appropriate cautions and qualifications." And he agrees that global warming is likely to continue but suspects the rate will be "modest."

What follows is a guide to the facts behind the issues to be discussed at Rio Wednesday through June 14—drawn heavily from the data published in the IPCC's original report, its update of that report and other analyses by numerous scientists, including the National Academy of Sciences' Greenhouse Warming Synthesis Panel. It may serve as a "tool kit" for nonspecialists who believe the future of the planet should be taken seriously.

The Participants

The United Nations Earth Summit, which begins Wednesday in Rio de Janeiro, will be the largest international gathering ever convened to debate the future of the global environment. Leaders of about 150 nations, along with representatives of hundreds of interest groups and nongovernmental organizations, are to take part in the event, which ends June 14. Although the meeting will stress global unity of purpose, participants fall into two groups with frequently opposed purposes:

The Industrialized Countries

They do most of the polluting, control most environmental technologies and generally want the Third World to preserve rain forests and other ecological resources.

The Developing Nations

Their rapid population growth and expanding economies are expected to put increasing strain on global ecology, but they will not defer growth without compensation in the form of grants, loans, debt relief and technology transfers.

Eliminating poverty and protecting the environment, summit planners say, go hand-in-hand, because the poorest populations often are those most driven to over-exploit their natural resources to survive. As a result, U.N. officials estimate industrialized states will need to give developing countries $125 billion annually until the year 2000—about $70 billion more than the current level of official development assistance.

Trends in History: Wild Climate Shifts

To hear the debate over global warming, you'd think Earth's climate had always been steady as a rock and is only now being forced to change on account of human activity. In fact, for at least the last 2 million years, the climate has been swinging wildly between ice ages (the most common condition) and interludes of warmth—often far more warmth than the planet is now experiencing.

Many climatologists think the chief cause of these repeated swings is a change in the intensity of sunlight as a result of shifts in the tilt of Earth's axis. Even a slight change can cause significant cooling or warming.

Some scientists note that it takes a change of only a few degrees in average temperature—6 or 8 degrees Fahrenheit—to turn a moderate climate into an ice age or vice versa. Other scientists agree but point out that such changes have been occurring all along without any human input. Extreme climate shifts are perfectly natural. Temperature swings in the past were enough to raise or lower sea level by 400 feet.

There is no way, those other scientists say, to tell whether the recent warm years (in which the temperature rise over the past century has been just 1 degree F) are part of a natural fluctuation or something new. Even if Earth warmed as fast as is predicted by many theories, the rate of change would not necessarily be faster than in the past. Recent studies of ancient climate shifts show that they can occur in just a few decades—the time scale environmental activists are warning about now. This, of course, does not mean it would be easy for people and ecosystems to adapt. Past climate shifts have caused major waves of extinctions.

Tracking natural climate change is complicated by the fact that global temperatures have not simply oscillated between warm and cold. There have been oscillations within oscillations.

Tracking the Big Chill

Take the latest ice age. It began waning about 15,000 years ago. The glaciers began melting, retreating northward. The meltwater made sea levels rise. But about 10,500 years ago, the trend suddenly reversed itself. In less than a century the ice age returned. Temperatures fell, the retreating glaciers advanced again and sea level dropped.

Nobody knows exactly what caused the change, but many experts suspect the huge volume of melting ice disrupted circulation in the oceans. The meltwater, being colder and less dense than salt water, could have suppressed, for example, the Gulf Stream, which normally heats northern latitudes with tropical water.

The cold period lasted about 500 years; then, as abruptly as the cooling began, a spell of global warming set in again.

By about 6,000 years ago the post-ice age climate reached its warmest, with a global average temperature about 2 degrees F higher than now. Then Earth cooled again, dropping about 2 1/2 degrees. So much water became locked into glaciers that the sea level during Greco-Roman times was six feet lower than it is today.

And the Little Ice Age

Then the roller coaster went up again so that between 2,000 and 500 years ago the Earth was about 1 degree F warmer than now. From about the 10th century through the 13th century, for example, Europe was so warm that Greenland was, in fact, green with plants.

Then global cooling set in again, and about the year 1550 there began an episode now known as the Little Ice Age. It didn't let up until about 1850. Iceland, which today is locked in sea ice only one to three weeks a year, was then icebound five or six months a year. In London, the Thames River froze over every winter, something it didn't do before or after.

Since 1850 Earth has generally warmed, climbing unevenly out of the Little Ice Age. Which brings up one of the contentious points of the current debate. Some experts say the warm years of the last decade are a sign of something new. Others say we may simply still be coming out of the Little Ice Age. They note that we have not yet returned to the warmth of the medieval era, when Scandinavians grew grain near the Arctic Circle.

The warming trend of the past century is by no means smooth. Much of it happened before 1940, when carbon dioxide levels were much lower than they are now. Then the warming stopped and reversed. Global cooling prevailed from 1940 to the mid-1960s, even as industrial activity soared, pouring carbon dioxide into the atmosphere. Some scientists warned then that it might signal a new ice age.

But around 1965, the warming resumed and has been increasing quite rapidly ever since. The eight warmest years of the 20th century have all come since 1979. But as the long view shows, they were by no means the warmest years ever. It was considerably hotter just a few centuries ago.

Estimating Emissions: Fossil Fuels and Deforestation

Most of the increase in carbon dioxide comes from burning coal, oil, and gas for electricity, transportation, and heating, as well as from the manufacture of cement, in which carbon-containing minerals are burned. These emissions are estimated to have grown at an average of about 4 percent per year from 1860 until the early 1970s, with slow-downs during the world wars and the Great Depression. The 1973 oil shortage halved the rate and for a while, CO_2 output did not grow at all. From

1979 to 1985 the release was steady at 5.3 billion tons of carbon per year—showing that energy conservation can have an effect. Then it started to rise again, reaching 5.7 billion tons by 1987.

About 95 percent of the emissions come from the industrialized countries of the Northern Hemisphere. Emissions there amount to about 5 tons of carbon per person per year. In developing countries, the comparable figure is about 0.2 to 0.6 tons. But the rate of increase in the Third World is about 6 percent a year, compared to 1 percent a year in Western Europe and North America.

Deforestation also releases CO_2 but estimates of the amount vary widely, from 0.6 billion tons to 2.5 billion tons. Even at the high end, this would be less than half the carbon released from burning fossil fuels for electricity, transportation and heating in the industrialized world.

Comparisons of the amount of carbon dioxide being released each year with the concentration in the atmosphere have led to a major mystery: About one-third of the CO_2 being released is—fortunately—not staying in the air. It is disappearing, going someplace where it can't intensify the greenhouse effect. The oceans may be soaking it up and incorporating it into algae or the calcium carbonate shells of marine organisms. Land vegetation may be taking it up. Perhaps soil microbes are extracting it from the air. The bottom line is: Nobody knows. More significantly, nobody knows whether a warmer Earth will reduce this beneficial carbon-scavenging effect, worsening a warming trend, or will enhance it, helping save us from warming.

Global Warming: Disparate Impact

Even if Earth warms appreciably in the next few decades, that would not mean it will get warmer everywhere. Indeed, the climate models forecast that some places will cool while the planet as a whole warms.

The bad news, according to some models, is that central North America and Eurasia are likely to get the most heating. The good news is that Antarctica may get colder or, at least, not much warmer. This is good because about 90 percent of Earth's ice is in Antarctica. Though there were early fears that the ice mass could melt and raise sea level by yards, new analyses cited by a National Academy of Sciences panel indicate it is highly unlikely to melt in the next century. In fact, it may accumulate more ice as snowfall increases, as some models predict. This could offset any sea-level rise from other causes.

Greenland's ice, on the other hand, which is about 9 percent of the world supply, is expected to melt around the edges. It is thought to have been doing that for decades, contributing to the sea-level rise of about six inches this century. Forecasts of sea-level rise vary from none to perhaps two feet over the next hundred years.

At worst, this would cause serious flooding of low regions all over the world including a third of Bangladesh and much of the most valuable real estate in Florida,

Louisiana and Texas. If the rise happened suddenly, nearly 200 million people would be flooded out.

Far more widespread are the projected effects on agriculture, though not always bad. While the latitudes suitable for specific crops would move north if growing seasons lengthened, a more significant change is likely to be in the distribution of rainfall.

In some scenarios, the United States loses enough rain to cut farm productivity by a third—until cropping patterns adapt—and Russia benefits both from more rain and the warming of parts of Siberia now unsuitable for farming. But climate forecasters emphasize that their regional prognostications are much less reliable than those for the globe overall.

Because carbon dioxide is, after all, plant food, rising CO_2 levels might well act as fertilizer, making plant growth more abundant. This would remove the gas from the air and might boost food production. In the laboratory, plants have responded this way if they had extra soil nutrients and water. But there has been no test in a natural ecosystem.

Natural ecosystems may be the hardest hit if the changes come fast. Temperature zones may move north faster than forests can keep up through natural dispersal of seeds. Margaret B. Davis of the University of Minnesota has developed computer models that show shifting climates will leave many trees standing where they cannot survive. The eastern hemlock, for example, now ranges as far south as the mountains of North Carolina. In one projection, Davis estimates that in 100 years it will retreat to the latitude of New York City; in an alternative projection she concludes that the tree will not be found south of Maine. Some experts also predict that drier weather will kill many southern temperate forests, turning them to grasslands.

The great unknown is not so much whether it will get warmer—even skeptics agree it probably will—but how fast the warming will come. If it warms slowly, humans may be able to adapt without major stress and ecosystems also may be able to change at that pace. But if it continues to heat up as it has during the past 15 years, the ecological and economic changes could be catastrophic.

The Greenhouse Effect: What It Is, How It Works

When sunlight enters a greenhouse, it passes through the glass and strikes the surfaces inside. Some light is reflected back into space and some is absorbed by the soil and plants. The light's energy is stored as heat. (Earth receives no heat directly from the sun.) The warmed objects then radiate the heat into the surrounding air.

Two things happen at this point. First, the heated air rises—a phenomenon called convection—but is trapped by the glass. This is what accounts for nearly all the temperature rise in a greenhouse but it is not a factor in Earth's atmosphere—which makes *greenhouse effect* a misleading term. Second, the heat coming off the warmed surfaces (infrared radiation) is absorbed by the glass, which gets warmer. It is this small warming effect that also happens in the atmosphere.

Most of the gas in the air plays little or no role in the greenhouse effect. Nitrogen and oxygen (which make up 99 percent of dry air) are largely transparent to light and heat. But other gas molecules act like glass. They let light in but capture heat going out. The most abundant of these are water vapor and carbon dioxide.

Environmentalists may damn the greenhouse effect, but it has been happening for billions of years and it is what keeps Earth from being as cold as Mars, which lacks natural greenhouse gases. If it were not for the natural greenhouse effect, scientists have calculated, Earth's average surface temperature would be about 5 degrees Fahrenheit. The oceans would be frozen solid. Instead the average year-round temperature is about 68 degrees.

Environmentalists don't dispute this. They point not to Mars but to Venus, where a runaway greenhouse effect is blamed for boosting the surface temperature to nearly 900 degrees.

Carbon Dioxide's Growth: A Well-Documented Worry

Contrary to popular conception, carbon dioxide is not the main contributor to the greenhouse effect. Water vapor is. But for all practical purposes, it is virtually ignored in the debates because it is not thought to be increasing significantly, there is not much that can be done about it and you wouldn't want to anyway because we need the rain.

But the concentration of infrared-absorbing gases in the atmosphere is definitely increasing—this is one of the few certainties of the current debate—and the chief contributor to the increase is carbon dioxide, or CO_2. It is growing largely because of human activity. CO_2 is produced by burning any organic matter—from fossil fuels (coal, oil, gas) in giant power plants to wood fires at backpackers' campsites.

Vast amounts of forest clearing also contribute either through burning the wood or simply by cutting it and letting it decay. Wood is a carbon-rich material and both burning and decay convert much of it back into carbon dioxide. This is the same carbon that the trees took out of the atmosphere in the process of photosynthesis as they were growing.

It is a misconception, however, that forests simply take carbon dioxide out of the air and give off oxygen. Plant metabolism consumes oxygen and gives off carbon dioxide just as animal metabolism does. The only time plants consume CO_2 is during photosynthesis, when the consumed carbon is incorporated into carbohydrate compounds and locked away in the tissue of the plant. This occurs only while the plant is growing in size. Once a forest has reached maturity, the amount of carbon dioxide it consumes is equal to the amount it loses during metabolism and from the decay of naturally dead leaves and wood. In other words, a mature forest is in a carbon equilibrium with the environment.

Along with deforestation, large parts of Earth are being reforested—especially in the Northern Hemisphere—and some estimates indicate this growth may be extracting carbon dioxide from the air in quantities comparable to those released by forest burning in the tropics.

Measurements of the concentration of CO_2 in the air over the last two centuries are extremely good. Samples of air from past centuries have been retrieved from air bubbles trapped in old ice. They show that around 1800—well before the greatest increase of population and industry—the CO_2 concentration was about 280 parts per million. Samples from younger ice show progressively higher levels. Since 1958, direct measurements have been made atop Mauna Loa in Hawaii, far from industrial sources. In what John Firor of the National Center for Atmospheric Research in Boulder, Colo., says "may turn out to be the most important geophysical measurement of the 20th century," the data show incontestably that the carbon dioxide level has grown every year since.

Today the CO_2 concentration is 356 parts per million—27 percent higher than in preindustrial times—and is growing at about 1.5 parts per million each year. These inarguable facts underlie a large part of the current worry that human-produced carbon dioxide may be enhancing the natural greenhouse effect.

Computer Models: Fine-Tuning Forecasts

If the computer simulations that predict global warming are right, Earth's climate should already have gotten hotter than it has in recent years.

In other words, the computer models that are the chief basis for forecasts of gloom and doom are flawed. The proprietors of various models have always been the first to point this out, but their caveats are usually overlooked in the popular debate.

The flaw becomes evident not when the computers are asked to simulate future climate but when they are given the climate of the past and asked what it will be like in the present if carbon dioxide levels increase from past levels to those we know exist now.

"What happens is that the computers tell you we should have gotten twice as much warming as we actually have. That tells you there's something missing in the models," said Andrew Solow, a specialist in climate models at the Woods Hole Oceanographic Institution in Massachusetts. "Everybody knows the models are crude."

Another problem is "model drift." When the models are run to predict the current climate, their results are not always the same. Sometimes, Solow said, they "predict" that we should now be in an ice age. To correct for this, computer operators tinker with the program, making "flux corrections." These change the rate at which simulated phenomena happen—such as the transfer of heat from the ocean to the air.

The tinkering continues until the model reproduces the current climate more accurately. Then the models are asked to simulate the future, without knowing if the adjusted flows of energy will stay the same.

Although there are different climate models that give different outcomes, they work much the same way: Earth is divided into a grid of several thousand boxes. The atmosphere in each box is sliced into layers; so is the ocean. The computer treats each layer in each box as a separate parcel of climate.

A set of conditions is fed into the computer for each parcel—temperature, wind, sunlight, carbon dioxide and so on, along with standard formulas for the behavior of gases, liquids and solids.

Then the computer calculates how the phenomena in each parcel would affect surrounding parcels and feeds those new numbers up, down or sideways. Once the changes propagate through all parcels, the computer recalculates everything again as if an interval of time had passed.

Modeled days pass into modeled months. To simulate a century of climate change, the world's fastest supercomputers must run continuously for about three weeks.

In recent years climate modelers have improved their methods, getting closer to how the world really works. The most dramatic result has been to roll back the early forecasts. Just three years ago some models predicted a warming of 8 to 10 degrees Fahrenheit by the middle of the next century. Today's improved models forecast considerably less warming—4 to 5 degrees—by the end of the next century.

The Other Gases: CH_4, CFCs, N_2O

Experts estimate that carbon dioxide accounts for only about 61 percent of the enhanced greenhouse effect. The other sizable contributors are methane (15 percent), CFCs (11 percent) and nitrous oxide (4 percent).

Methane is also known as marsh gas because it is produced by the decomposition of organic matter in marsh bottoms. It is also the main component of natural gas. While the amount of methane—CH_4—being put into the atmosphere is only about 1/50th the amount of carbon dioxide going up, each pound of it has 20 to 60 times the greenhouse effect of CO_2, the effect declining with time because it is taken out of the air fairly rapidly.

About 525 billion tons are released each year (compared with 26,000 billion tons of carbon dioxide), most of it from natural wetlands, rice paddies and flatus of animals. Only about 20 percent of methane comes from industrial activities that offer hope of reducing output, such as gas drilling and landfills.

The atmospheric concentration of CH_4 was fairly steady during recent centuries. Since the mid-1800s, however, it has doubled and is still climbing—twice as fast as the carbon dioxide level—mainly as the result of increasing rice cultivation.

Chlorofluorocarbons, or CFCs, are by far the most potent greenhouse gases. They are all human made, mostly for use as solvents, refrigeration coolants and aerosol propellants. They are, pound for pound, 1,500 to 7,300 times as powerful at warming Earth as carbon dioxide. One thing that keeps CFCs from roasting the planet, ironically, is that they damage the ozone layer. While the ozone hole is a different phenomenon from global warming, ozone is a greenhouse gas. So its destruction offsets much of the warming from CFCs.

Nitrous oxide, N_2O, is nearly 300 times more potent than carbon dioxide, but the amount going into the atmosphere each year is tiny by comparison. The normal sources are natural decay; but the atmospheric concentration has been growing because of increased use of nitrogen fertilizers, which soil bacteria convert to nitrous oxide.

Global Cooling: The Parasol Effect

This may be the year of the parasol effect, the year the public notices that along with phenomena that would warm the climate, there are others that would cool it. Climate change depends on which of the two forces is more powerful. This year it is almost certain to be the parasol effect from Mount Pinatubo, the largest volcanic eruption since Indonesia's Krakatau in 1883.

According to Alan Robock, a University of Maryland climatologist, Pinatubo put enough light-blocking material into the atmosphere to blot out 2 percent of incoming sunlight. The cooling effect of that event is believed to be larger than the warming effect of all the "greenhouse gases" emitted since the beginning of the Industrial Revolution.

Pinatubo's dust fell back quickly, but its sulfur dioxide is expected to stay aloft for two or three years. Each sulfur atom absorbs sunlight, shading a tiny part of Earth's surface. In addition, the sulfur causes water vapor to condense on it, creating a droplet of water. The result is increased cloudiness.

This means that the next few years are likely to be much cooler than the warm years of the 1980s. But because the sulfur will eventually come down, its cooling effect will decline and Earth will return to its previous climate trend.

Pinatubo's cooling effect, however, is a piker compared to that of Mount Tambora in Indonesia. Its eruption in 1815 caused such a cooling that 1816 became known as "the year without a summer." In New England, for example, it snowed several times that summer.

But volcanoes are not the only source of sulfur dioxide. Industries that burn sulfur-bearing coal and oil put out enough sulfur that, according to one estimate, it blocks 7.5 percent of the sunlight that would otherwise reach the ground in the northeastern United States. Unlike volcanoes, which shoot their emissions high into the upper atmosphere (where they stay for years), industrial emissions usually fall out (as acid rain) within a few hundred miles of their source. Still, climatologists suspect they may have helped keep the climate from warming as much as it might otherwise.

Because of the acid rain problem, of course, industries are being forced to cut sulfur emissions—a step that could also furl the parasol.

A cooling effect is probably also provided by natural clouds. But this remains controversial. It is widely known that daytime clouds keep the surface cool (by simple shading) and that nighttime clouds keep the surface warm (by a greenhouse effect), but it has not been clear whether one outweighed the other, or which might predominate. Climatologists have looked at clouds from both sides now and some researchers have tentatively concluded they are net coolers. Slight variations in how cloud effects are interpreted lead to changes up or down of several degrees in predicted global warming.

Some climate experts predict greenhouse warming will increase cloud cover. If so, this could offset the warming. There are indications that Earth has undergone a very slight increase in cloudiness over the last 40 years.

On the Table

Formally called the United Nations Conference on Environment and Development, the Rio meeting will address four general areas:

Two Legally Binding Treaties

One commits governments to control emissions of "greenhouse gases" and to reduce the threat of global warming; the other obliges signatories to help slow the rate of plant and animal species extinction.

The 'Rio Declaration'

A general set of principles defining individual countries' responsibilities toward the environment and their rights in pursuing economic development. It is not legally binding.

'Agenda 21'

A detailed 800-page "blueprint" of measures to be taken by states, industry and organizations to improve environmental quality between now and the beginning of the 21st century. The nonbinding program includes recommendations on air, water and land-use policies, conservation and resource management, technology transfer among nations, toxic and hazardous-waste guidelines and methods of controlling consumption and combating poverty.

'Forest Principles'

A legally nonbinding accord setting goals for management and preservation of the world's forests.

The summit—authorized by a 1989 resolution and the result of more than two years of preparation—also marks the 20th anniversary of the first U.N. Conference on the Human Environment, held in Stockholm.

2 Global Warming Continues, But Cause Is Uncertain

Buildup of Pollutants in Earth's Atmosphere Studied; Definitive Evidence Is Lacking

WILLIAM BOOTH
January, 1991

The average temperatures on Earth in 1990 were the highest since record keeping began, continuing a warming trend first detected in the 1980s.

The world's two leading authorities on global surface temperatures reported these findings jointly yesterday, but said it is not clear that the cause of the warming is the buildup of pollutants in the atmosphere.

The analyses were done by the British Meteorological Office and the National Aeronautics and Space Administration's Goddard Institute for Space Studies in New York, using a network of thermometers on land and sea.

Most climate experts say they lack definitive evidence that the observed global warming is caused by pollutants such carbon dioxide, a gas that has been steadily increasing in the atmosphere because of the burning of forests and fossil fuels, and which acts like a blanket to trap heat close to the Earth's surface.

The observed warming may instead be some completely natural, though poorly understood, phenomenon. But there is a growing feeling among many researchers that the warming trend may be fueled by human pollutants.

"I have been skeptical about saying it's an enhanced greenhouse effect," said Jim Angell, a climate expert at the National Oceanic and Atmospheric Administration's Air Resources Laboratory in Silver Spring. "But it's getting harder to defend that skepticism."

While uncertain about the cause of the warming, both the British and American researchers yesterday agreed that 1990 beat out 1988, which was previously the hottest year on record. Indeed, six of the seven warmest years in more than a century occurred in the 1980s. In descending order the seven warmest years on record are 1990, 1988, 1983, 1987, 1944, 1989 and 1981.

Angell and his colleagues, however, believe that it may take another decade to know for certain whether pollutants are causing the warming.

Based on computer simulations on how the planet operates, an international group of researchers sponsored by the United Nations predicted that the average global temperatures would increase between 2 and 6 degrees Fahrenheit by the end of the 21st century, if gases such as carbon dioxide continue to accumulate at projected rates.

The United States will host an international meeting in February to discuss possible responses to global warming. In past discussions, the Bush administration has resisted attempts to reduce carbon dioxide emission, arguing that more research is needed to prove that warming will occur.

James Hansen, head of NASA's Goddard Institute, stressed that a single record-breaking year was meaningless. Rather, he said, scientists were most interested in—and concerned about—what they view as a warming trend.

The warm weather was most evident over the United States and southern Canada, Europe, western Siberia, and the Far East.

Readings taken with weather balloons launched by Angell and colleagues at NOAA confirmed that 1990 was the warmest year not only at the Earth's surface but in the planet's atmosphere, from about 5,000 to 30,000 feet. Similarly, Angell said, the warming trend of the 1980s was also observed in the atmosphere.

Satellite data collected by Roy Spencer at NASA's Marshall Space Flight Center in Huntsville, Ala., also confirmed that the atmosphere was warm in the 1980s. However, Spencer's satellites showed that 1990 was not the hottest year, but the fourth warmest. Spencer is not sure why his temperature record is different.

Spencer said scientists don't really understand natural fluctuations in climate. Records have been kept only since the late 1800s. Indeed, there was a distinct warm peak in the 1930s and 1940s, which gave way to 20 years of relatively cool temperatures, followed by the warming of the 1970s and 1980s.

"If it was a purely scientific thing, I'd say I'm not convinced. I'm skeptical," Spencer said. "But I'm just glad I'm not a policy-maker. There is so little proof, but the possible consequences are so severe."

Last year also had by far the lowest annual snow cover ever recorded for the Northern Hemisphere, according to analyst David Robinson of Rutgers University.

Robinson said he is not sure whether the decreased snow cover was a result of higher temperatures, or the cover actually contributed to the warming. The less snow cover, the more the Earth's surface heats up. The more snow cover, the more sunlight is reflected back into space.

3 Global Warming's Effect on Sea Level Reexamined

Study Says Peril May Have Been Understated

BOYCE RENSBERGER
October, 1992

The risk of a catastrophic rise in sea level as a result of global warming could be higher than previously estimated, according to a report in today's edition of *Nature,* the British scientific journal.

The new analysis conflicts with previous studies. But if it is right, and if global warming continues to increase for several decades, the scientists say earth's climate could heat up enough to melt a large part of Antarctica's ice sheet, sending the melt water into the oceans.

If all 7 million cubic miles of ice now resting on the continent of Antarctica were to melt and flow into the ocean, it would raise the sea level by 215 feet.

The threat of even a modest meltdown has been a favorite element of the more alarmist scenarios of global warming. But it was largely laid to rest in recent years after various analyses showed that global warming might actually do the opposite: cause increased snowfall that would remove water from the oceans and build up the ice sheet. Moreover, there was evidence that the Antarctic ice sheet had been fairly stable since it formed about 14 million years ago, despite subsequent cycles of global warming and cooling.

The new analysis, which is likely to revive those earlier fears, is based on the discovery of evidence that suggests the ice sheet, far from being stable, largely melted away about 3 million years ago—just at a time when global temperatures were only a few degrees warmer than they are now.

The new evidence was obtained by Peter J. Barrett of the Victoria University of Wellington, New Zealand and colleagues. They have shown that some marine fossils found in glacial debris high in the Transantarctic Mountains belong to species known to have existed only about 3 million years ago. The fossils, remains of now-extinct microscopic creatures called diatoms, could not have been deposited there unless the ice was gone and an ocean with a higher level covered much of Antarctica.

The fossils were first found in 1984 and their age was presumed to be the same as that of an identical combination of fossils found elsewhere in deposits whose antiquity was well established. But because this implied that the ice sheet melted 3 million years ago, it conflicted with the evidence for stability and was not widely accepted.

Now, however, Barrett and his colleagues have confirmed the date by an independent method. They found a layer of volcanic ash amid the fossil deposits and determined by a well-accepted method that certain minerals in the ash were formed in an eruption about 3 million years ago.

According to David Sugden of the University of Edinburgh, who has also researched the question, Barrett's confirmation of the fossils' age raises a serious challenge to the idea that the ice sheet has been stable. In a commentary in the same issue of *Nature*, Sugden said the clash of views has produced an "impasse" that can only be solved by finding an error in the assumptions underlying one of the alternative scenarios.

Evidence against an ancient meltdown is considerable, Sugden said. For one thing, there is no sign of the land surface erosion that would have resulted from such massive melting and outflow of water. Instead, the land has geologic features indicating it was scoured by glaciers that stayed frozen as they scraped their way down slopes to the sea, where the ice broke off to form icebergs.

Also, Sugden wrote, 10° Fahrenheit of warming—the amount of increase many experts say could happen over the next century if global warming continues—would not cause major change. Antarctica would have had to warm by a year-round average of 70 to melt the ice sheet all the way to the interior of the continent. He said the far more modest warming that appears to have happened 3 million years ago should have enlarged the ice sheet through increased snowfall.

4 "Greenhouse Effect" Seems Benign So Far

Warming Most Evident at Night, in Winter

BOYCE RENSBERGER
June, 1993

G lobal warming, which has raised Earth's average air temperature by less than 1 degree Fahrenheit over the past century, is turning out to be relatively benign, scientists say. So far.

First, the effect has been to boost nighttime lows rather than daytime highs. Also, there is evidence that in the Northern Hemisphere, the warming is happening mainly in the winter and spring and somewhat in the fall. In summer, when heat stress is hardest on living things and when ice caps melt, temperatures are no warmer than they were in the 1860s and 1870s.

Moreover, according to one of several reports on global warming being released today in the June issue of the National Geographic Society's journal *Research & Exploration*, the atmospheric phenomenon thought to account for the warming at night—increased cloud cover—is probably caused by the warming itself and, thus, is likely to continue to moderate the effect as long as warming continues by keeping daytime temperatures lower.

Another article in the same journal, however, suggests the cloudiness is caused by fossil fuel pollution, which will gradually diminish.

Some scientists have warned that global warming could disrupt agriculture, damage forests and other plants, and trigger coastal flooding as melting polar ice caps raise sea levels.

"The popular vision of climate apocalypse is wrong," concluded Patrick J. Michaels, author of the most optimistic report. Michaels is Virginia's state climatologist and a professor of environmental sciences at the University of Virginia.

Michaels suggested that if the trend continues, one significant effect could be to lengthen the growing seasons in agricultural regions because the frost-free season would begin sooner in spring and end later in fall.

The evidence of warmer nights is not so much a new discovery as a new appreciation of data that have been published many times in tables of numerical data. "But nobody," Michaels said, "ever pulled it together. It was there, waiting to be synthesized from the literature."

Still, the varied views of global warming in the journal show that atmospheric scientists are still grappling with major uncertainties in their understanding of the "greenhouse effect."

This is the phenomenon named for the way the glass in a greenhouse allows sunlight in to warm the surface but blocks the resulting heat from radiating back into space. Certain gases in the air—such as carbon dioxide—have the same effect, trapping heat near the ground instead of letting it radiate into space.

The fact that this heat is held close to Earth's surface means it no longer reaches the upper levels of the atmosphere. As a result, those upper air layers become cooler than before. That, in turn, means the water vapor in the cooled air is more likely to condense into clouds.

Moreover, atmospheric scientists agree a warming climate is likely to put more water vapor into the atmosphere simply by increasing the rate of evaporation from the ground.

According to one study, cloudiness over the United States increased 3.5 percent between 1950 and 1988. A German study in 1990 reported a decline in sunshine in that country and a 1988 report by the Department of Energy concluded from numerous shipboard observations that the skies over the oceans have grown cloudier.

Clouds make the days cooler (by blocking sunlight) and the nights warmer (by absorbing the ground's heat, which would otherwise radiate into space, and radiating it back toward the ground). As a result, clouds counteract daytime warming and enhance nighttime warming.

Michaels, who long has doubted that greenhouse warming would lead to catastrophe, might be expected to emphasize data that minimize the threat.

But scientists on the other side of the controversy are in accord on this point. James Hansen of the Goddard Institute for Space Studies in New York City, the most prominent scientist to sound the global warming alarm in 1988, agrees that the warming observed so far has been mainly at night.

"We see the nighttime warming both in observational data and in our computer simulations," Hansen said. "And there is some evidence for increasing cloud cover."

Hansen, author of another report in the same journal, differs from Michaels, however, because he thinks increased cloudiness results less from warming and more from particles of air pollution in the atmosphere—mostly sulfates from the burning of fossil fuels. These have a cooling effect both by reflecting sunlight back into space before it can reach the ground and by acting as surfaces upon which water vapor condenses to form clouds.

If he is right, Hansen said, the increased cloudiness should diminish over time because the burning of fossil fuels is not increasing as fast as before and because pollution controls are limiting the sulfate output.

While this means the output of carbon dioxide will also decline, the amount already in the atmosphere will stay there for decades. Sulfates, on the other hand, fall out in days (as acid rain). As a result, the CO_2 can keep contributing to a greenhouse effect long after the sulfate levels decline, along with their cooling effects.

In the long run, Hansen said, he expects the warming factors to overtake the cooling factors and to lead to significant global temperature rise in the daytime as well as at night. Hansen's forecast, however, is not as dire as it used to be.

Just a few years ago, for example, it was estimated that CO_2 levels would double by 2030 and that the global average temperature then would be as much as 5 degrees Fahrenheit higher than now. As it happens, carbon dioxide output is not growing as fast as before and the doubling is not expected to occur until the second half of the next century, by which time it may plateau. Hansen now says the warming probably won't reach the 5-degree increase until then.

Michaels believes Hansen is wrong about both the amount of warming and the role of aerosol particles like sulfates. First, he notes that Hansen's forecast is based on computer models that overestimate greenhouse warming. Hansen acknowledges that when his computers are asked to estimate today's temperature, they say it should have risen twice as much as has been measured over the last century.

Second, Michaels believes the increased cloudiness is not a result of aerosol particles. These, he said, stay mostly in low altitude air—the haze zone visible from airplanes—whereas atmospheric cooling has been observed at cloud-prone altitudes above the aerosol layer.

Another sign that the warming is relatively benign has come from British scientists who studied global temperature variations over the last 140 years and published their findings in the latest issue of a journal called the *Holocene*. (The title refers to the most recent epoch of geological time.)

P. D. Jones and K. R. Briffa of the University of East Anglia, which maintains a major climate research center, have found that the 1 degree F. warming in the Northern Hemisphere occurred only in winter, spring and autumn. "Summers," they wrote, "are now no warmer than in the 1860s and 1870s." In the Southern Hemisphere the same amount of warming has happened throughout the year.

Jones and Briffa also found great unevenness in the temperature change from place to place. For example, the Amazon Basin has cooled on a year-round basis. In the United States, the chief variations have been a warming in winter and a cooling in spring (counter to the general Northern Hemisphere trend of a warming in spring).

Commenting on another area of uncertainty, Hansen said the poles have not warmed as fast as computers predicted they would. As a result, there is debate over the validity of previous forecasts of a dramatic rise in sea level that would flood out millions of coastal dwellers. For this to happen, the polar ice caps would have to melt faster in summer than they grow in winter.

He noted that if the poles do warm, meteorologists would expect snowfall to increase because it is now often too cold to snow there. But if air and water temperatures rise, the melting rate could increase as well. The rival trends could cancel each other out.

5   Satellite *vs.* Surface

Two Points of View on Global Warming

BOYCE RENSBERGER
July, 1993

I f there has been a planetwide warming trend over the last decade and a half—a claim repeated so often in recent years that many assume it is an established fact—it ought to have shown up by now in the 15 years of temperature readings taken by a network of Earth-orbiting satellites.

So said James Hansen, the Goddard Institute for Space Studies scientist who alarmed the world in the late 1980s with his assertion that Earth's atmosphere had been warming since the mid-1970s—caused by growing concentrations of carbon dioxide in the air, which trap heat that otherwise would radiate into space. Hansen bolstered his case with a chart showing that after 35 years of fairly steady temperatures, surface thermometer readings around the world were suddenly showing a warming trend.

Yet no sign of such warming has shown up in the satellite data.

"We've had total satellite coverage of the Earth since 1979, and we sure don't see it," said John Christy, of the University of Alabama at Huntsville.

For the last few years Christy and Roy Spencer of NASA's Marshall Space Flight Center, also in Huntsville, have been processing data collected by satellites operated by the National Oceanic and Atmospheric Administration (NOAA).

Causes for Discrepancies in Data

Each month Christy and Spencer update their analysis, issuing the planetary equivalent of a fever chart. Their latest report shows that in June, as in the 19 previous months, the average global temperature was cooler than the average for the previous decade. July, despite a local heat wave in the eastern United States, is shaping up to be cooler as well.

More significantly, instead of a global warming trend, the satellite data show no clear pattern. According to the space-based sensors, the temperature of the lower atmosphere has fluctuated irregularly—cooler than average for two or three years, then warmer for about the same time, then back, then forth.

Christy said the warmer intervals coincide with El Nino—the mysterious, periodic phenomenon in which the surface waters of the South Pacific become warmer than usual. Because heat from ocean surfaces supplies the energy that drives many weather phenomena, this warming sets off major weather shifts around the planet. El Nino appeared in 1983, recurred in 1987 through early 1988 and came back again for a prolonged stay in 1990 and 1991.

At the same time, however, Mount Pinatubo erupted in the Philippines in June 1991 and soon reversed El Nino's effect. It spewed tiny droplets of sulfuric acid into the upper atmosphere, where they eventually spread to cover much of the globe. Because the droplets reflected some sunlight back into space, they caused a global cooling. Most of the droplets have since rained out of the atmosphere.

Overall, Christy said, there has been no apparent warming trend.

Hansen's more widely reported data show similar fluctuations from year to year. But, he said, they indicate a clear warming trend that reached record high temperatures in the late 1980s before Pinatubo chilled the air.

Hansen said the readings show the lower atmosphere's average temperature rose by about a quarter of a degree Fahrenheit in that time. (Most of that warming in the Northern Hemisphere, the detailed records show, has happened at night and during the winter. Summertime high temperatures have not risen.)

Why the difference?

"Our data," Christy said, "come from satellite readings taken over the entire globe. Their data come from thermometers, mostly in industrial areas."

In other words, the temperature records were gathered in two very different ways.

The older method relies on conventional thermometers at weather stations around the world, most at airports and in cities in the industrialized world, plus scattered readings in Third World regions and aboard ships at sea. At some stations, readings have been taken regularly for more than a century. Because the readings are taken just a few feet off the ground, they are relevant to what most living things feel.

A major drawback is that many of the thermometers are in "heat islands"— places that have been artificially warmed by the growth of pavement and cities. Christy argues that this effect—as well as the fact that the limited number of stations provides uneven coverage of the globe—create the appearance of a warming trend. Hansen said the heat island effect is understood and that thermometer readings are routinely lowered a certain amount to correct for it.

The newer method uses a series of weather satellites that scan the entire surface of Earth several times a day and record the intensity of microwave radiation that comes naturally from oxygen molecules in the bottommost four miles of the atmosphere. The warmer the oxygen, the more intense the radiation. A major advantage of this method is that it monitors the whole planet evenly.

Disadvantages are that the readings go back only to 1979 and that instead of measuring the temperature near the ground, it reads an average for the bottommost four miles of atmosphere. So it's less relevant to life on the ground, though perhaps more relevant to cloud formation, which cools the surface in the daytime and warms it at night. The cooler the air at cloud altitudes, the more likely it is that water vapor will condense, forming clouds.

Moreover, Hansen points out, the satellite microwave readings can be thrown off by water droplets and other particles in the air that interfere with the microwaves' path to the satellite detectors.

Nonetheless, "if there's a greenhouse warming," Hansen said, "it should be visible in their data. The fact that it isn't tells me there's something wrong with their data. There should be similar trends."

It is also possible that the discrepancies are revealing genuine differences in the atmosphere, Hansen said. There could be a warming near the ground and little or no change a few miles up.

Greenhouse Effect Still a Concern

"The fact that we see no warming doesn't mean there's nothing to worry about," Christy said. "From simple physics we know that increasing the amount of carbon dioxide in the atmosphere raises the possibility of a greenhouse effect. A concern is certainly warranted. But, I have to add, our data show little or no warming—indicating that this problem is a lot less than what the [computer-generated] climate models would make you think."

To one climate researcher the differences are not so troubling.

"If you look at them closely, they agree remarkably well," said Jerry Mahlman, head of NOAA's Geophysical Fluid Dynamics Laboratory in Princeton, N.J., a major climate research center. "There's no data set that's perfect. They've all got problems."

For one thing, Mahlman said, the satellite data cover a fairly brief interval: "It's extraordinarily hard just to look at one decade and get any sense of a trend."

Perhaps more perplexing than the air temperature discrepancy is one involving ocean temperatures. Two of the most complete sets of global water temperatures give opposite results. NOAA's Comprehensive Ocean Atmosphere Data Set says the oceans cooled during the 1980s. The United Kingdom Meteorological Office's Global Ocean Surface Temperature Atlas says the oceans warmed during the same decade.

Because scientific efforts to monitor real-world changes yield such ambiguous results, the clamor to "do something" about global warming remains largely an emotionally guided phenomenon.

6 Carbon Dioxide Curbs May Not Halt Warming

WILLIAM BOOTH
March, 1990

E fforts to save the world from global warming by reducing greenhouse gases will not stop temperatures from rising but instead may only delay warming by a decade or two, according to energy experts and atmospheric scientists.

To slow the worldwide warming that many climate experts fear will accelerate during the next century, environmentalists, several European governments and some U.S. legislators are calling for a 20 percent reduction by the year 2000 in emissions of carbon dioxide, which collects in the atmosphere and traps heat, causing the so-called greenhouse effect. The supreme byproduct of the industrial world, carbon dioxide is produced by burning almost anything, especially fossil fuels such as coal and gasoline.

Yet a 20 percent reduction may have a barely noticeable effect on climate change in the short term, according to John Firor of the National Center for Atmospheric Research in Colorado, whose 1988 editorial in a scientific journal became the foundation for calls to reduce carbon dioxide emissions.

"What do we get for all this effort? The answer is going to be a little weak. We'll be ahead a few tenths of a degree. My instinct is that this is not going to impress a congressman very much," Firor said.

Firor's rough calculations indicate that if carbon dioxide were reduced by 20 percent, the Earth would still warm by about one-third of a degree Fahrenheit per decade. If nothing were done and carbon dioxide levels continued to climb, the world would warm by about one-half of a degree Fahrenheit each decade, according to a computer simulation.

Many climate researchers agree that the world will grow warmer, but they disagree on the amount of warming and when the change will be detectable.

"We're not talking about stopping the warming by any means, but we're talking about slowing the warming down. We're going to need all the time we can get," Firor said. "To sell the idea, you have to convince them that stabilizing the atmosphere is important and that if you can slow down the rate of change, that's very important, too."

Firor and other scientists say that slowing down the warming by a decade or two may give plants and animals, as well as agriculture, more time to adjust to new

65

conditions, which could include rising sea levels and changes in rainfall and temperature patterns.

Firor said the world might eventually have to cut its carbon dioxide production by half in order to stabilize the gas in the atmosphere but that this might not happen until the world had already warmed an average of 4 or 5 degrees Fahrenheit, an increase that still could have significant and perhaps catastrophic effects. In fact, scientists say it might even be necessary to reduce emissions by as much as 90 percent to reverse warming and to restore the climate to that of pre-industrial times before man-made carbon dioxide began accumulating in the atmosphere.

Yet because carbon dioxide emissions are so fundamental to industrial society as it is currently constituted, it is far from certain that emissions could be reduced by even 20 percent in the current decade, let alone cut in half by early in the next century. Many experts say reducing carbon dioxide would mean nothing less than a profound change in the way the world produces and uses energy.

"It's like going to war, except there's no enemy," said one researcher.

To investigate the technical feasibility of such dramatic cuts, at least a dozen studies are underway by federal agencies and private environmental and energy groups.

While they are still extremely preliminary, the studies offer a kind of first draft for a new and more efficient world, where people would drive gas-stingy cars or pay hefty "carbon dioxide taxes" to operate gas-guzzlers; where coal-fired electricity-generating stations would be shut down and replaced by a combination of solar energy collection farms, huge biomass burners and nuclear plants; where such everyday appliances as refrigerators and light bulbs would be tens to hundreds of times more efficient.

Environmentalists have argued that increasing efficiency and switching away from dirty sources of energy such as coal is economically sound and ecologically important regardless of whether global warming scenarios prove correct.

Can it be done? "Yes it can, because it is both trivial and lucrative," said Arthur Rosenfeld, an energy expert and physicist at the University of California at Berkeley.

But there is tremendous disagreement about the cost and disruption to society of such reductions. Recent calculations by a Stanford economist and colleagues put the price tag at more than $3 trillion. Other economists predict the cost to be far less. Indeed, a National Academy of Science panel is meeting next week to investigate whether it is possible to estimate costs of reducing carbon dioxide and the other greenhouse gases.

"Is change affordable? That is the big issue," said Barry McNutt of the Energy Department's Office of Policy, Planning and Analysis. "I don't think a single study has good cost estimates."

On a recent television news talk show, White House chief of staff John H. Sununu, in explaining his alteration of a speech President Bush delivered to the International Panel on Climate Change—a wording change that environmentalists criticized—said, "There's a little tendency by some of the faceless bureaucrats on the environmental side to try and create a policy in this country that cuts off our use of coal, oil and natural gas. I don't think America wants not to be able to use their automobiles."

In fact, few energy experts are talking about Americans giving up their cars. Rather, they're talking about Americans giving up big cars.

Because there is not enough time to develop exotic new fuels such as nuclear fusion or perhaps even to gain wide public and economic acceptance for atomic energy and solar cells, the centerpiece of most studies is conservation of energy through increased efficiency.

In the residential sector, analysts say there would have to be vigorous campaigns to get people to buy more efficient water heaters, lights, freezers, refrigerators, space heaters and air conditioners. But even if everyone changed their appliances and light bulbs tomorrow, Dick Rowberg of the Congressional Research Service said, this would reduce carbon dioxide emissions at best by only a few percent.

In the commercial sectors, builders would be required to use energy-saving windows, super-efficient air-conditioning systems and new types of lighting. Marc Ross of the University of Michigan believes that a substantial reduction is possible in the industrial sector if manufacturing plants were forced or encouraged to switch from coal to natural gas, and to increase overall efficiency by redesigning production systems so as to recycle more material and waste less.

Like the other researchers, Ross targets coal for severe reductions. A large part of U.S. electricity is generated by burning coal, which emits large amounts of carbon dioxide.

Curiously, however, in a speech last month spoke before the World Coal Conference in New Orleans, Deputy Energy Secretary W. Henson Moore gave an endorsement of the future of coal in the United States, even after acknowledging the threat of greenhouse warming.

Some analysts have also suggested that a massive effort to reforest the planet be undertaken. But Gregg Marland of Oak Ridge National Laboratory, who with physicist Freeman Dyson first suggested planting trees, calculated that quite a few trees would have to be planted to take up the excess carbon dioxide being pumped into the atmosphere.

For example, to soak up all the excess carbon dioxide the world produces each year, it would be necessary to plant a tree farm the size of Australia. Once the trees matured, and stopped taking up more carbon dioxide, another forest would have to be planted.

Even Bush's modest proposal to plant a billion trees, Marland calculated, would have no more effect than if each American turned off a 100-watt bulb for 90 minutes a day.

"My overall view is that it [reducing carbon dioxide] will be very difficult and very expensive," said William Fulkerson of the Energy Department's Oak Ridge

National Laboratory in Tennessee. "It's not any accident that the world depends on fossil fuel. We're still hooked on fossil fuel because it is marvelous."

And yet, even the pessimists agree that something must be done. If not, they note, carbon dioxide levels will keep growing beyond the doubling that is forecast for the middle of the next century. That doubling point has been taken as a convenient measure to factor into the predictions, but it is arbitrary and, in the absence of controls, both carbon dioxide and global warming would continue to increase as long as energy use grows.

Consumers can help reduce carbon dioxide emissions by taking these steps, according to the National Audubon Society. All the energy conservation measures recommended during the "energy crises" of the 1970s will also cut carbon dioxide.

Lower thermostat by 2° in winter. This can cut your furnace's CO_2 output by 6 percent.

Buy a high-efficiency furnace or boiler. Going from 65 percent efficiency to 85 percent will cut CO_2 by 24 percent.

Lower water heater temperature to 120°. This can save 440 to 600 pounds of CO_2 a year.

Use compact fluorescent lamps. Replacing a 100-watt incandescent bulb with a 22-watt fluorescent (which puts out the same amount of light) will save 180 pounds of CO_2 each year.

Buy an energy-efficient refrigerator (but only if the old one needs replacing, because each discard releases CFCs that damage the ozone layer). Some discards can save as much as 1,000 pounds of CO_2 a year.

Buy a high mileage car. For example, if you drive 12,000 miles a year and switch from a 20-mpg car to a 30-mpg model, you'll save 4,400 pounds of CO_2 every year.

7   Clinton Sets Plan to Cut Emissions

Programs Addressing 'Greenhouse Effect' Are Mostly Voluntary

GARY LEE
October, 1993

The Clinton administration is set to release a blueprint for reducing greenhouse gases that relies on wide voluntary participation by private industries, including many that have voiced skepticism about the dangers of the "greenhouse effect."

The plan, to be announced by the White House on Tuesday, targets major sources of emission of gases such as carbon dioxide—from automobiles to landfills—and proposes ways for gradually cutting back on their outflow so that by the turn of the century the level of greenhouse gas emissions in the United States will be at levels that prevailed in 1990.

In all, the plan outlines more than 50 projects in which industry and federal agencies can cooperate in cutting emissions, few of them mandatory. If all provisions are carried out, the plan projects an overall reduction of at least 100 million tons of greenhouse gases by the year 2000, about an 8 percent reduction.

The plan is billed as a cornerstone of environmental policy for President Clinton and Vice President Gore, who campaigned against President George Bush's environmental record in general and his policies to deal with global warming in particular. Bush had agreed to reduce greenhouse gas emissions to 1990 levels but set no date for achieving the goal and did not propose steps to get there.

Clinton, to underscore the importance of his plan, will present it in a White House Rose Garden ceremony, officials said.

After a briefing on the plan late last week, however, many officials of environmental groups sharply questioned its effectiveness, largely because of the voluntary nature of many of the proposals.

According to a copy of the plan made available by an administration official, one key provision calls for employers to offer cash vouchers rather than subsidize parking—a move that should encourage employees to use public transportation rather than drive. The blueprint says that this provision would reduce carbon emissions 8.2 million tons in 2000, a significant cut in transportation-produced emissions, which account for a third of all greenhouse gases in the United States.

The Climate Change Action Plan, as the new policy is called, is designed to hold down the rise of global temperatures, which some specialists predict could increase 8 degrees Fahrenheit by the end of the next century unless measures are taken to check it. Although many experts agree that a gradual warming is taking place across the globe, there is wide disagreement over the pace and causes, with some arguing the process is occurring too slowly to pose any real environmental danger and that such changes have occurred in the past.

In an Earth Day speech last April, Clinton set the goal of returning to 1990 levels by the year 2000 and pledged to make the fight against global warming a domestic policy priority.

The United Nations Framework Convention on Climate Change, signed at the Earth Summit in Rio de Janeiro in June 1992, binds signatories to cut greenhouse gas emissions to 1990 levels. After initial objection by Bush administration officials, the United States signed the agreement and ratified it a year ago. The document, ratified so far by 36 countries, will become effective after 14 more countries endorse it.

Michael Oppenheimer, a greenhouse specialist at the Environmental Defense Fund, said some of Clinton's measures are sound. "But I have doubts as to whether even taken all together they can achieve reductions to 1990 levels. The problem is that almost all of the measures are voluntary and there is very little to encourage industry to participate and punish those who don't."

"It's a repackaging of some old ideas and a few scattered new ones. There is no guarantee that any of this will get us anywhere. The only thing worse than this policy would have been no policy," said Steve Kretzman of Greenpeace.

Greenhouse gases are largely produced by the burning of industrial and transportation fuels, making any policy for reducing them politically sensitive. Six million tons of greenhouse gases will be added to the atmosphere over the United States between 1990 and 2000 if no policy is adopted, the plan says.

When an interagency task force began devising the plan last spring, environmentalists encouraged members to take several bold measures, including increasing federally mandated fuel efficiency standards for vehicles and imposing new taxes on gasoline to discourage driving. Those proposals, opposed by the big auto makers, were not included.

But officials said the types of approaches advocated by environmentalists would have been expensive and entailed major legislative battles that an administration already facing tough fights over trade and health care legislation wanted to avoid.

So the centerpiece of the package is cooperation and it suggests ways for federal agencies and private sector firms to work together to reduce emissions. It involves little legislation and virtually no new spending.

Under one program in the plan, federal agencies would remove regulatory barriers to and encourage private investment in hydroelectric power. In another, the Department of Energy would set up housing technology centers to advise home builders on reducing carbon emissions in home energy systems. The two projects, according to the plan, would cut greenhouse emissions by 2 million and 4.3 million tons, respectively, by the turn of the century. Another DOE project encourages private utilities to reduce their greenhouse emissions.

In all, the plan seeks $68 billion in private investment to develop more alternative, fuel efficient and environmentally sound technologies. The $1.6 billion the plan would cost the government could come from other programs, an official said.

The plan also calls for strengthening greenhouse gas sinks, or natural environmental systems such as forests that absorb greenhouse gases.

It proposes increased efforts to preserve forests that it says would result in a net reduction of 8.5 million tons of carbons by the year 2000.

The blueprint establishes a White House task force to monitor the progress of the programs every two years. But it does not mention sanctions or other means by which nonparticipants will be forced to take part.

The new plan also establishes a pilot "joint implementation" program through which federal agencies would assist other countries in developing technologies to combat greenhouse emissions. Private U.S. companies are also encouraged to invest in anti-greenhouse gas efforts abroad, particularly in developing countries.

8 Climatology

Warming Could Trigger Cold Spells

KATHY SAWYER
July, 1993

I magine the polar front in the North Atlantic suddenly dipping down to Spain with sheets of sea ice expanding in behind it, plunging Northern Europe into a deep freeze. Or picture major lakes formed by retreating glaciers, draining catastrophically into the North Atlantic, disrupting the patterns of ocean heat transfer that drive the world's climate.

These images are conjured by unexpected evidence from ice samples recently dug out of ancient glaciers. It suggests that global warming could, ironically, cause sudden, potentially devastating cold spells.

In addition to the gradual increase in global temperature that many have predicted as a result of human air pollution, the findings indicate, warming could trigger sudden wild temperature swings—downward as well as upward—with consequences that make this summer's Midwest floods look like fun.

The reason scientists believe this might happen in the future is that it happened in the past.

What the new ice-core evidence suggests is that modern civilization may have enjoyed, for the last 10,000 years, a rare period of climate stability on a planet where, at least for most of the last 250,000 years, conditions have veered swiftly from warmer to colder and back again.

In the continuing struggle to understand the immensely complex subject of global climate change, links between cause and effect are often murky.

But scientists had long assumed a certain rhythmic steadiness in the climate. There were the ice ages (cold, but changeable because of the disturbing presence of massive glaciers or sea ice) and then there were the periods between the ice ages (warm and stable, like now).

This reassuring view has been severely shaken by international teams of scientists working on GRIP (the Greenland Ice-core Project). They report in the July 15 *Nature* that "recent climate stability may be the exception rather than the rule." Drilling almost to bedrock some 10,000 feet into the Greenland ice sheet last summer, they retrieved the first detailed samples from the Eemian era—the last relatively warm interglacial period like this one, which is called the Holocene.

The samples surprised them because analysis showed the Eemian—between 115,000 and 135,000 years ago—was punctuated by episodes of extreme cold. These temperature swings developed with startling speed and lasted from 70 to 5,000 years.

The researchers analyzed the ratio between various forms of oxygen (which varies in a predictable way with temperature), as well as greenhouse gas concentrations trapped in air bubbles and other properties of the ice samples to determine the air temperatures of the period.

The Eemian period is believed to have been, on average, a few degrees warmer than today. If that additional warmth triggered the instability, this raises "disturbing questions about the likelihood that current global warming might prompt the present climatic regime to adopt this unstable state," according to *Nature*.

The scientists found that, in the Eemian period, when temperatures rose an average of 3.8 degrees Fahrenheit above today's levels, they also began to fluctuate by as much as a stunning 18 degrees within decades.

"Previously we just assumed the last warm period was very similar to the present period and just stable like it is now," Eric Wolff of the British Antarctic Survey told Reuter. "Finding that it wasn't raises fears about what could happen if it gets warmer."

In a separate paper, Andrew Weaver of Canada's University of Victoria cites findings that the continued release of "greenhouse gases" such as carbon dioxide into the atmosphere could increase temperatures by as much as 13 degrees Fahrenheit over the next five centuries, causing a rise in sea level of as much as six feet.

In a companion article to the GRIP reports, J. W. C. White of the University of Colorado's Institute of Arctic and Alpine Research described the previously unthinkable prospect of a sudden ice age engulfing Northern Europe and the derangement of the oceanic heat-transfer system.

"We don't know which is the norm for interglacial periods: the stable, one-state Holocene or the multiple-state, rapidly changing Eemian," White wrote. "We do know that answering this question will be a priority for global change research in the coming years."

9   So What If It's Getting Hot?

Don't Worry about Local Warming; These Experts Say We'll Adapt

WILLIAM BOOTH
September, 1991

Last week, as eco-technocrats from a hundred countries bumped heads in Nairobi over how best to confront global warming, and as Washington wilted in a freak September heat wave, the National Academy of Sciences quietly issued a report with a remarkable conclusion: When it comes to the greenhouse effect, there's nothing to worry about.

If global warming is indeed a reality, if the temperature and the seas rise in the course of the next century, humans will adapt quite nicely, the report concludes. Stripped of its caveats, that is the gut-level impression of the dozen agronomists, economists, engineers and environmental scientists assembled to consider the matter by the Academy, the august body that advises the federal government.

The National Academy of Sciences has been wrestling with the greenhouse issue for years. In the spring, it issued another of its cautious reports, concluding the United States should adopt "effective but inexpensive" actions to slow down projected warming. That means reducing carbon dioxide and other gases produced by automobiles and industry, but doing so gradually, at least to begin with.

But this latest Academy panel takes another approach. It assumes Earth is going to warm, and then dares to ask the politically incorrect question: So what?

A temperature rise of two or three or four degrees spread out over 50 or 60 years? No big deal, say these adaptationists. We'll crank up the AC and increase electric power generation by 12 to 22 percent. So what if it costs $400 billion? It all depends on how you discount the investment over time.

What about climatic refugees? It's happened before, say the adaptationists, and it'll happen again. The Irish fled the warm, moist summers of the 1840s that led to the potato blight. Midwesterners fled the Dust Bowl. This time around, Texans might move north to Minnesota. It costs, on average, $1,500 to transport the contents of a 450-square-foot apartment 400 miles to a six-degree-cooler climate. That's not going to break the bank.

A rise in sea level of one or two or three feet? The adaptationists envision dikes, levees, pumps and berms to hold it back. The Dutch had to build them, and they're doing okay. What's a seawall cost these days? In South Carolina, about $2,000 a foot, or about 6 percent of the value of the property the seawall is protecting.

Agriculture? If the greenhouse world is drier rather than wetter, which is entirely possible, we'll extend irrigation. We'll create genetically altered super-wheat. We've done it before. A new strain of cultivated plant, used these days for only about six years before it is replaced by another strain, costs about $1 million to develop. Farmers are among the most adaptable and ingenious of people in the pursuit of commerce.

The report has already attracted criticism for its complacent, almost breezy, even hopeful tone. Part of the reason is that the adaptationists rely for their analysis on economics and engineering, and not on ecology, a science that is still struggling valiantly to connect enough dots to present Earth's big picture.

It is precisely this difference in approach that will color every report and discussion of global warming and related environmental issues for years to come. Economists have not yet found a way to put a price tag on an acre of wetland or a species of warbler, and until they do, they will not enter the equation; there is not much salable meat on a warbler.

The report is also being criticized for its optimism. For the most part, the adaptationists see a very different future than do many environmental activists, who tend to be a more pessimistic bunch.

Look, for example, into the crystal ball of Michael Oppenheimer, a senior scientist with the Environmental Defense Fund, and his colleague Robert Boyle, the authors of the briskly selling book *Dead Heat*.

Here is an example of their vision of the mid-21st century: "In the Chesapeake Bay, Long Island Sound, Narragansett Bay and other coastal waters that once gave purpose and delight to sailors, swimmers, fishermen, and children building sand castles, the water is rankest in the summer. . . . Stimulated by warm, still weather, algae blooms deoxygenate the water below. Suddenly half a million menhaden, maybe a million, go belly up. After a week, the oily fish stink too much even for the gulls, but eels still burrow into the bloated fish to gorge on internal organs. Above the rotting carcasses washed up on shore, next to the shattered houses half tumbled into the water, the air is filled with the ceaseless buzzing of greenhead flies and the scurrying of rats' feet over broken glass."

No place to spend the weekend with the kids. To Oppenheimer and many others, including not a few scientists, the greenhouse world is no vacation land. It is downright terrifying.

The adaptationist panel's report was even too much for one of its own members. Jane Lubchenco, an ecologist from Oregon State University, issued a strong dissent, stating "I disagree with the report's implicit message, that we can adapt with little or no problem."

Yet according to the majority of the panel, Lubchenco is overreacting, or rather reacting in the absence of good data. The results of a warming "will be no more severe, and adapting to them will be no more difficult, than for the range of climates already on Earth and no more difficult than for other changes humanity faces."

What about food riots and dust bowls, massive forest death and global economic chaos? What about melting polar ice caps and water lapping at the foot of the Washington Monument?

The panel is not so hysterical. It pleads for perspective. "Human adaptability is shown by people working in both Riyadh and Barrow and seeking out both Minneapolis and Galveston. Recent American migration has on average been toward warmth."

In fact, the adaptationists suggest we should be glad it's getting warmer and not colder, as some of the scientists who now predict warming once suggested would happen. If the world got nine degrees cooler, instead of nine degrees hotter, the upper midwestern United States would be crushed under a sheet of glacial ice. "None of the projected effects of the warming would make large areas uninhabitable."

The panel assumes the world will warm moderately and not all at once, as most computer simulations suggest. It notes that something weird and awful could happen, such as a reversal of the balmy Atlantic Ocean current that keeps Britain from freezing. But such an event is unlikely, it says. Better to monitor the situation than to react prematurely to nightmare scenarios.

As far as megaproblems go, the adaptationists rank global warming relatively low, concluding that "epidemics from causes already known, failure to control population growth, and chemical pollution are more serious threats to human health than climate change."

The farmers will probably do all right, they say. Increased levels of carbon dioxide in the atmosphere makes plants happy, at least in the laboratory. Things grow well in warm weather.

However, higher temperatures will also mean shorter growing seasons in some states, and therefore reduced yields. There may not be more pests, but there could be different kinds of pests. But farmers adapt. In fact, they exploit their neighbor's misfortunes. They plant earlier. They rotate crops. "Ask a farmer who is 70 or 80 years old what is different now compared to when he was a child," the panel suggests. Horses to tractors. Dirt roads to paved highways. Hybrid corn. The introduction of soybeans, pesticides, canola and Belgian endive.

"We did not foresee that people would dumbly suffer and so we did not use a 'dumb-people scenario.' We assumed people would adapt. We assumed people don't have feet of clay," said panel chairman Paul Waggoner, an agronomist and meteorologist at the Connecticut Agricultural Experiment Station in New Haven.

The adaptationists, heavily influenced by such economists on the panel as William Nordhaus of Yale University, stress that the human activities that generate most of the national income will be little affected by gradual climate change.

Some 97 percent of U.S. income, Nordhaus notes, is generated by the industrial and energy sectors only 3 percent by agriculture and forest products. The adaptationists believe that national economies will not be disrupted by the kind of climate change that is generally predicted. Bogs, reefs and deserts aren't big income generators in the United States.

Of course, the natural world could be the big greenhouse sweepstakes loser. And it is the disconnect between the natural world and the world of commerce that so disturbs Lubchenco and other ecologists. "Divorcing humans," Lubchenco writes, "from their ecosystems ignores the intimate, if often complex and subtle, dependencies of humans on the natural landscape."

The panel concedes there is not much that humans can do to help the natural world adapt to warming. "At present, the potential for human intervention to ease adaptation in marine ecosystems seems quite limited." So, too, for inshore waters and terrestrial systems.

The group suggests the establishment of seed banks, gene libraries, zoos and gardens, though Waggoner concedes such schemes sound lame. The problem is that natural communities of plants and animals do not migrate very quickly. A Texas hack berry tree, and its associated lifeforms, cannot rent a U-Haul and move to Minnesota.

Based on pollen records, scientists believe a temperate forest can move at a rate of about 100 kilometers per century. Not fast enough, the panel says, to match the speed at which warming is expected to come. But to give the natural world a chance, the scientists suggest that natural "corridors" be preserved to allow for movement of seeds and animals.

"For the sort of climate change we are assuming," the panelists write, "the timely adaptation of every species and conservation of the countless cooperators in the natural landscape are highly unlikely."

What that means is major extinctions and major transformations of ecosystems are likely. The woods will not be the burned-out wastelands envisioned by hysterics, but they might turn into savannah. We'd still have photosynthetic plants, but we wouldn't have elms, at least where elms are now. Plants that thrive in Florida, though, may do quite well in Tennessee. In any event, things are not likely to look the same.

A sea-level rise of three feet would cause a loss of 30 to 70 percent of U.S. coastal wetlands. Is that a big problem or a little one? The panel doesn't say, mostly because the value of a wetland—what its loss means to Americans and to the economy—is hard to evaluate.

Many activists and some economists are hoping for the day when such "environmental costs" can be tabulated. While there is not yet a pricetag for a wetland, researchers say that building a man-made system that would duplicate a hectare of natural wetland's waste water treatment and fish spawning capabilities would cost $205,000.

What's to be done? The adaptationists recommend improving our ability to monitor climate and predict changes and impacts. Don't hobble the market, they advise; doing so will only hamper our ability to adapt and improvise to change. And, they say, let's improve our ability to roll with the environment. If we dealt better with the kinds of climatic change we already experience—hurricanes, drought, floods—we would be better prepared to deal with any catastrophic changes that lie ahead.

Depending on how you view the world, the academy's report can be a little comforting, or extremely disturbing. It concludes, in essence, that the systems dominated by humans will, at worst, muddle along. There will be costs. There will be winners and losers. But the crops will grow. Industry will continue. Humans will adjust and adapt.

As for the warblers, elms and menhaden, the adaptationists say they'll have to fend for themselves.

Atmospheric Problems: Ozone Depletion   3

The ozone layer, 10 to 30 miles above the Earth, acts as a filter in the upper atmosphere to screen out ultraviolet (UV) radiation from the sun. More than 99 percent of the sun's UV radiation is absorbed by atmospheric ozone, and humanity could not survive on Earth without this filtering system. It is widely believed that exposure to even modestly increased levels of UV radiation would have serious detrimental effects on plant and animal life. Laboratory studies have related UV radiation to a variety of human problems such as cataracts, skin cancer, and depressed immune system functioning. UV radiation also affects plant growth and photosynthesis, and phytoplanketon have been found particularly sensitive to UV levels.

Ozone molecules, comprised of three oxygen atoms, can be broken down by reactive substances such as chlorine and nitrogen oxides. In the mid 1970s, a National Academy of Sciences panel reported that the ozone layer was being damaged by a group of industrial compounds called chlorofluorocarbons (CFCs). CFCs include a number of chlorine-based compounds used as aerosol propellants, refrigerants, solvents, and for an array of other purposes. When released, CFCs are broken down primarily in the stratosphere by UV radiation to form chlorine atoms. Each chlorine atom, in turn, is able to destroy hundreds of thousands of ozone molecules.

The report of declining concentrations of ozone was cause for considerable alarm, both in the United States and worldwide. In the mid 1980s, it was reported that dramatic changes in ozone concentrations occurred each spring over Antarctica, leading to the term *ozone hole*. Subsequent satellite measurements indicated reductions in ozone concentrations of 2 percent to 10 percent over various parts of the Northern Hemisphere and another hole over the Arctic. In 1987, delegates from 24 countries signed the Montreal Protocol, an agreement to curtail CFC production worldwide. In 1990, 93 nations signed the London Ozone Agreement, agreeing to phase out all use of CFCs by the year 2000, and to limit use of several other potentially harmful substances as well.

The articles in this chapter treat several aspects of the ozone problem. Articles 1, 2 and 3 describe evidence of declining ozone concentrations worldwide, but particularly over the United States. Articles 4 and 5 speculate on possible health consequences of increased UV radiation as a result of a thinning ozone layer. Articles 6, 7, and 8 are concerned with replacements for CFCs in industry, the problems associated with such a massive technological alteration, and the finding that substitute compounds are likely to be more harmful than first believed. Finally, Articles 9 and 10 present a far more optimistic picture, suggesting that ozone concentrations will begin increasing earlier than expected and that relatively trivial increases in UV radiation will occur in the meantime.

1 First Summer Thinning Found in U.S. Ozone Layer

Skin Cancer Risk Increases, Experts Say

MICHAEL WEISSKOPF
October, 1991

S cientists reported yesterday the first summertime thinning of the protective ozone layer over the United States, raising the risk of skin cancer as heavier doses of ultraviolet radiation leak to the ground during the time of year when people are most exposed.

E.I. du Pont de Nemours, the world's largest producer of chlorofluorocarbons (CFCs), the most damaging of the man-made chemicals to ozone, responded to the new data by pledging to halt production of the chemicals by 1997—three years ahead of schedule—and to speed the phaseout of substitutes that are less destructive than CFCs but still capable of fraying the ozone layer.

The data included in this recent assessment underscore the urgency for a more rapid and aggressive response, du Pont vice president Joseph Glas said in a statement to the media.

Along with a report in April that wintertime ozone has thinned twice as fast as previously projected, yesterday's data is expected also to fuel diplomatic efforts to accelerate the timetable of an international treaty calling for the phaseout CFCs at least by the turn of the century.

"The problem is more serious than we believed," said Environmental Protection Agency Administrator William K. Reilly. "The world community needs to reconsider the course that it's on, as to whether it's fast enough and whether substitutes can be brought on more quickly."

A vaporous veil lying 15 miles above the surface, ozone shields life on Earth from the damaging effects of ultraviolet rays. Yesterday's findings of significant depletion between May and September when people wear less clothing and spend more time outdoors deepens concerns about skin cancer, experts said.

EPA officials said they factored in possible summertime erosion of ozone in last April's projection of a near-doubling of skin cancer cases and deaths over the next 40 years. According to the American Cancer Society, there are now more than 600,000 cases of skin cancer a year in the United States and nearly 9,000 deaths.

According to Edward De Fabo, a photobiologist at George Washington University Medical Center, the increased doses of solar rays during the growing season could endanger certain crops and jeopardize planktonic organisms at the base of the oceanic food chain.

Yesterday's report was based on what is considered the most comprehensive data gathered since monitoring of the ozone layer began in 1985.

Readings were taken by National Aeronautics and Space Administration satellites and ground-based spectrometers, and the data were analyzed by a panel of international scientists that was convened by the United Nations Environment Program and the World Meterological Organization.

The data confirmed earlier findings of winter ozone depletion as high as 5.6 percent in the Northern Hemisphere, including the United States and Western Europe.

But for the first time, the instruments recorded summertime depletion of 2.9 percent to 3.3 percent at latitudes reaching roughly from Florida in the south to central Canada in the north.

According to Jack Kaye, manager of NASA's atmospheric chemistry modeling and analysis program, scientists are uncertain whether the summertime findings result from refinement in analytical tools or from increased atmospheric levels of chlorine, which comes from the breakdown of CFCs and destroys ozone molecules.

He said some scientists believe the destructive chemical reactions may be catalyzed not only by polar ice clouds interacting with the chemicals in the winter but also by sulfate particles all year long. Sulfates, put into the air by volcanoes and burning of fossil fuels, may remove some of the nitrogen compounds that suppress the activity of chlorine, he said.

In another important finding, scientists discovered that ozone loss in the lower stratosphere has a cooling effect on global temperatures, apparently countering the warming effect created by CFCs.

2 Ozone-Hole Conditions Spreading

High Concentrations of Key Pollutants Discovered over U.S.

KATHY SAWYER
February, 1992

T he danger that a new ozone "hole" could open over densely settled areas of the Northern hemisphere, exposing the population to increased amounts of harmful radiation, is greater than previously suspected, scientists reported yesterday.

New indications of ozone depletion by NASA satellite and multi-agency airborne instruments are so alarming, the scientists said, that they decided to release them before completion of the data analysis in late March.

Two weeks ago, detectors aboard a converted spy plane flying over New England and eastern Canada recorded the highest level of the ozone-destroying chemical chlorine monoxide ever measured anywhere around the globe. The level— 1.5 parts per billion—was approximately 50 percent greater than any previously seen over Antarctica, the site of the infamous ozone hole first discovered in the early 1980s.

Chlorine monoxide, which results from the presence of man-made chlorofluorocarbons (CFCs), is a potent ozone-destroyer by itself. And when combined with small amounts of its chemical cousin, bromine monoxide—which the NASA researchers also found at elevated levels—the effect is enough to destroy ozone at a rate of about 1 or 2 percent per day for brief periods in late winter, said Michael Kurylo, NASA's program manager for the airborne studies.

Ozone in the stratosphere protects the Earth's surface by absorbing much of the ultraviolet radiation that causes skin cancer, cataracts and immune-system damage in humans and devastates many microscopic marine organisms.

Weather conditions permitting, ozone over parts of the Northern hemisphere could be depleted by 30 to 40 percent, the scientists said. By comparison, about 50 percent of the ozone has been depleted from the ozone hole over Antarctica.

To emphasize how ozone-destroying chemicals have become widespread over populated areas, Kurylo described the experience of the science investigators' flights out of Maine. "There were some flights directly out of Bangor where the aircraft encountered these parcels [of chlorine gas] before it ever got to operating altitudes."

In addition, researchers found evidence of reduced concentrations of nitrogen oxides in the lower stratosphere. Nitrogen oxides help preserve ozone by reacting with chlorine and bromine compounds before they can damage the ozone layer.

"Our conclusion is that the 'immune system' of the atmosphere—its nitrogen-mediated ability to fight ozone-destroying chemicals—is weaker than we had suspected before," said James G. Anderson of Harvard University, lead scientist for the airborne observations program. "None of the news is good."

Ozone-depleting compounds in the stratosphere from the Arctic as far south as the central Caribbean were found to be much more abundant than computer analyses had predicted. Part of this is a result of the eruption of Mount Pinatubo in the Philippines last June, the scientists said.

The new observations, including some from NASA's new Upper Atmosphere Research Satellite (UARS), suggest that the chemical processes that apparently work to deplete ozone throughout the atmosphere are not confined to the polar areas, where conditions are more conducive to ozone destruction.

The Antarctic hole was discovered in 1985. Concern has grown since then that Earth's ozone shield is being destroyed by human industry, primarily by the release into the atmosphere of CFCs used as refrigerants, thermal insulators and in cleaning solvents. These break down into chlorine atoms or compounds, which interact with and destroy ozone.

Ozone is a form of oxygen whose molecules contain three oxygen atoms instead of the usual two—a configuration that gives ozone its peculiar ability to filter ultraviolet rays from sunlight. But highly reactive chlorine or bromine compounds, atmospheric scientists believe, snatch one of the oxygen atoms away. The remaining two-atom molecules of ordinary oxygen cannot block ultraviolet radiation.

How severely the ozone is depleted depends on weather conditions, especially the size and duration of the so-called polar vortex—a supercold mass of air penned in by high winds swirling around it. When the air is cold enough inside the vortex, ice particles form. These, along with liquid droplets, provide platforms for the ozone-destroying chemical reactions, which are triggered by sunlight.

The vortex over the Arctic is more broken, because of turbulence caused by surrounding mountains, than is the one over Antarctica, scientists noted. The greatest danger of high ozone loss—a "hole"—over the Arctic will occur when the vortex there remains intact until late February, according to Kurylo.

Based on an estimated 10 percent ozone loss in mid-latitudes during the 1990s, a panel of the United Nations Environment Program reported in November that increased ultraviolet radiation leaking through the ozone layer by the turn of the century could cause 1.6 million additional cases of cataracts and 300,000 additional skin cancers a year worldwide.

Most nations have agreed to phase out CFCs by the year 2000, but some potential replacements also involve ozone destroyers.

The new findings yesterday moved Sen. Albert Gore Jr. (D-Tenn.) to introduce new legislation that would speed the phase-out of ozone-depleting chemicals.

A NASA official compared the decades of buildup of ozone-destroying chemicals to the way a head of foam forms on a glass of beer. The chemicals rise through the lower atmosphere and bubble into the stratosphere.

Scientists noted that, once in the atmosphere, the ozone destroyers are very persistent. Even if CFCs were phased out at once, said Kurylo, to restore the ozone layer to its former health "would take until 2060 or 2070. . . . This legacy will be with us for a long time."

3   Ozone Layer Thins Further, Possibly Because of Volcano

But Scientists Still Expect Turnaround by 2000

BOYCE RENSBERGER
April, 1993

T he ozone layer, long under assault from industrial chemicals, has taken an added hit—probably as a delayed effect of the eruption of Mount Pinatubo in 1991—and may still be reeling, atmospheric scientists reported yesterday.

As a result, during late 1992 and early 1993 the average amount of ozone over the planet as a whole was 2 to 3 percent lower than at any time since 1979 when scientists started taking such measurements. Over all some parts of the temperate zone, including the western United States and Eurasia, the loss this past winter was as severe as 14 percent.

The researchers said that if the additional depletion is a Pinatubo effect, it should dissipate over the next year or two, allowing the natural process of ozone creation to replenish the lost amount. They also said that the new findings are not likely to alter the forecast that the protective layer, which absorbs much of the sun's potentially harmful ultraviolet rays, will continue to thin until around the year 2000 and then start getting thicker.

That turnaround is predicted to result from the phase-out of ozone-destroying chlorofluorocarbons (CFCs) and other chemicals mandated by an international treaty called the Montreal Protocol.

The 14 scientists who announced their findings at a news conference are mostly from the National Aeronautics and Space Administration's Goddard Space Flight Center in Greenbelt and the National Oceanic and Atmospheric Administration. They emphasized that the findings do not mean that the Northern Hemisphere is experiencing an "ozone hole" like the one that forms annually over the South Pole, and that the ozone loss does not pose a significant health hazard.

"This is not an ozone hole," said Goddard's Richard S. Stolarski, one of the group's leaders. Moreover, he added, the greater depletion seen last winter came when ozone levels were naturally at a high point in their annual cycle. Though the amount was reduced, it did not drop as low as it normally does in mid- and late summer.

"The ozone highs are being reduced," Stolarski said, "but there are still significant amounts overhead."

The new findings are based on observations by several Earth-orbiting satellites operated by NASA and NOAA, including preliminary data from the latest space shuttle flight, and confirmed by ground-based ozone monitoring instruments.

James F. Gleason, an atmospheric scientist with the University Space Research Association who works at Goddard and another leader of the research group, said that if Pinatubo was to blame for the ozone loss, it was a delayed effect. He said the reason is that the Philippine volcano is in the tropics and its output reached into the stratosphere and began circling the globe in equatorial latitudes.

Then, Gleason said, it took several months for the particles to spread slowly to the north and south. They now cover the entire Earth and are diminishing in tropical latitudes. After a brief episode of unusually large ozone destruction in late 1991, Pinatubo appeared to have no further effect on the ozone, although its particles, which shade the ground, did contribute to a global cooling trend that has temporarily reversed global warming.

Then in April 1992 the global average ozone level began dropping, reaching its current low in January of this year. Gleason said ozone levels appear to be staying low but should rise as particles wash out of the atmosphere.

The scientists speculated that Pinatubo could have affected the ozone layer in three ways. One is by injecting large quantities of particles into the stratosphere. The volcanic particles would act as platforms on which ozone-destroying chemical reactions take place, playing much the same role that microscopic ice particles play in the Antarctic ozone hole.

The second hypothesis is that Pinatubo altered the pattern of winds in the stratosphere. This can happen as the particles absorb sunlight, become warmer and heat the surrounding air, causing it to rise. This rising air could block the normal winds that carry ozone-rich air from equatorial latitudes (where most ozone creation takes place) toward the poles.

A third possibility is that the warmed stratosphere would also alter the rates at which new ozone is formed or old ozone is destroyed. The ozone data for 1992 are being published in today's issue of *Science.*

4   Ozone Depletion Tied to Infectious Diseases

U.N. Report Could Prompt Bid to Speed Phaseout of Chlorofluorocarbons

MICHAEL WEISSKOPF
February, 1992

Increased exposure to ultraviolet radiation expected to leak through the Earth's thinning ozone layer may worsen the danger of certain infectious diseases, including AIDS, a new report by the United Nations says.

The report, an update on environmental hazards threatened by damage to the ozone shield—which absorbs much ultraviolet radiation before it strikes the Earth's surface—confirmed earlier estimates: researchers projected 1.6 million new cases of cataracts and 300,000 new cases of skin cancer per year by the turn of the century.

In the wake of this week's disclosure by NASA that erosion of the ozone layer over the Northern Hemisphere may be worse than anticipated, the U.N. findings are expected to fuel diplomatic efforts to accelerate the timetable of an international treaty for phasing out the most depleting chemicals—chlorofluorocarbons (CFCs).

Alarmed by the NASA findings, the administration is likely to propose at an April meeting of treaty signatories that they move up the phaseout date from the year 2000 to 1996 or 1997, officials said Wednesday.

On Thursday, the Senate, in a 96 to 0 vote, called on the administration to speed up the timetable, but did not specify a date for phaseout of the chemicals, which are widely used as solvents, coolants and agents to shape foam products.

Sen. Albert Gore Jr. (D-Tenn.), who sponsored the provision, has called for a halt in production of the chemicals no later than Jan. 1, 1995—a target date echoed by most environmental groups.

In the House, Rep. Henry A. Waxman (D-Calif.) accused the administration of failing to implement four provisions of the Clean Air Act aimed at the chemicals, including requirements to recycle CFCs in auto air conditioners and refrigerators and to ban nonessential uses of CFCs. Regulations were due out months ago.

"Putting these rules in place is far more important than the administration's empty talk of finally taking a responsible position at the next international meeting," said Waxman.

The U.N. report, compiled by a panel of international scientists, confirmed earlier research indicating that ultraviolet radiation has a "profound influence" on weakening the human immune system that might lead to an increase of infectious diseases, including AIDS.

In addition to skin cancer, the scientists noted new findings that cancer of the lip and salivary gland could result from excess exposure to ultraviolet radiation.

5   Ozone Hole's Effects Are Measured

UV Exposure Jumped in Argentine Town

BOYCE RENSBERGER
June, 1993

For the first time in the long debate over ozone depletion, scientists have detected and measured the result that environmentalists had warned about: a large increase in the amount of ultraviolet rays striking a populated area.

For several days in December of 1990, residents in and around Ushuaia, Argentina, a small town at the southern tip of South America, were exposed to a 50 percent increase in the amount of ultraviolet radiation (UV) that is normally filtered out by the Earth's ozone layer.

According to a report in the May issue of the *Journal of Geophysical Research,* the UV increase occurred when a section of the seasonal Antarctic ozone hole broke away from its main polar location and drifted north. Afterward, the breakaway hole is assumed to have dissipated.

Scientists calculated that the added UV dose brought the level up to the intensity that normally occurs 20 degrees closer to the equator, or at the latitude of Buenos Aires. In the Northern Hemisphere, the equivalent UV dose occurs normally at the latitude of Cape Hatteras.

Although the debate over depletion in the UV-absorbing ozone layer often has proceeded as if such increases were commonplace, scientists had never before been able to confirm an instance. The problem is that amounts of UV radiation always fluctuate wildly for entirely natural reasons. In some urban areas, levels have dropped over the years as a result of air pollution, which absorbs UV. These factors have made it difficult to blame any given increase on ozone loss from human causes.

"These are the first measurements to show a large increase in UV radiation over a populated area of the world," said John Frederick, a University of Chicago atmospheric physicist who led the research and was the lead author on the scientific paper.

Frederick said the UV dose measured in Ushuaia was especially potent because the incident occurred in December, which is summer in the Southern hemisphere, and the sun was relatively high in the sky.

When ozone depletions occur, it is often during seasons when the sun is low and its rays slant through a greater thickness of ozone than when the sunlight comes straight down. For example, when the sun is 30 degrees high in the sky—one-third of the way from the horizon to the zenith—the rays pass through twice as much ozone as when the sun is directly overhead.

Because very little is known about the effects of increased UV on plants and animals, it is not clear what impact the brief incident might have had. Although wildlife in tropical latitudes is often adapted to higher UV levels, biologists fear that species native to more temperate zones lack such adaptations and may be harmed. When domesticated plants in this country are exposed to artificial UV, many species are harmed, some grow better and some never seem to notice the difference.

"Our quantitative understanding of the biological effects of UV radiation is far, far behind our understanding of ozone depletion," Frederick said. "Maybe this report has biological relevance and maybe not."

The incident in Ushuaia is known to have resulted from human-caused ozone depletion because the annual ozone hole is caused by synthetic chlorofluorocarbon compounds (CFCs). Unlike chlorine that enters the lower atmosphere from seawater and volcanoes but quickly rains out, CFCs travel nine or more miles high into the stratosphere where the ozone layer is.

There the molecules are broken down by UV, releasing their chlorine atoms, which go on to break apart ozone molecules (made up of three oxygen atoms), converting them into ordinary two-atom oxygen, which does not absorb UV.

Because of special conditions that exist only over Antarctica during its spring-time (fall in the Northern Hemisphere), half or more of the ozone is destroyed—but only inside a huge ring of winds that roughly encircle the continent. This is the ozone hole.

As the springtime sun rises higher in the sky, it warms the air and breaks up the winds. Large masses of ozone-depleted air are freed and drift away from the South Pole. It was one of these, Frederick said, that moved over Ushuaia, where he and his colleagues happened to have installed a UV-monitoring station.

As always happens after the ozone hole breaks up, natural processes created enough new ozone to replace nearly all the lost molecules.

6 The Costly Race to Replace CFCs

Ozone-Depleating Chemicals Force Historic Industrial Retooling

MARTHA M. HAMILTON
September, 1991

It was the perfect substance—cheap, nontoxic, nonflammable and easy to dispose of. Used in air conditioning, refrigeration, foam packaging, insulation and solvents for electronics manufacturing, chlorofluorocarbons (CFCs) helped usher in the age of microelectronics, air conditioning, frozen food and fast food.

Now, an international agreement to phase out production of CFCs and other ozone-depleting chemicals by the year 2000 is ushering out this ubiquitous substance and forcing one of the most sweeping retoolings in the history of U.S. industry.

This giant step sideways—equivalent to redesigning several of the major technological achievements of the past decades—may be unprecedented. The chemical was "on the leading edge of many of the developments that have defined the American lifestyle in the last 30 or 40 years," said Kevin Fay of the Alliance for Responsible CFC Policy, an industry group.

"There could be as many as 3,500 specific applications where CFCs are involved to some degree, either in manufacturing or operations. It goes across every industry," said Tony Vogelsberg, the environmental manager for Du Pont Co.'s fluorochemicals group.

Consumers probably won't notice most of the physical changes made as a consequence of getting rid of CFCs. Most of the products that depend on them will probably look and function pretty much as before. But the price of replacing CFCs with more expensive substitutes may ultimately mean higher prices for autos, appliances and other products that use CFCs.

Eliminating CFCs and other ozone-depleting chemicals by switching to alternatives could cost as much as $36 billion between now and 2075, according to the Environmental Protection Agency. As a result, companies worldwide—including major chemical companies—are jostling to grab a piece of the huge new markets up for grabs.

In the mid-1970s, scientists discovered that the chlorine atoms in CFCs were thinning the earth's ozone layer. In the 1980s, scientific evidence for a hole in the ozone led to the international agreement to phase out CFCs.

Efforts to find replacements for some uses of CFCs began as early as the 1970s, when they were banned as propellants in aerosol cans. In addition, the chemical is no longer used to make polystyrene cups and the "clam shell" boxes in which fast food is sold.

As expensive and as daunting as the substitution process will be, it may produce some unanticipated bonuses. Forced to reexamine products and processes to make them work without CFCs, some industries are finding improvements.

Still, some of the proposed substitutes may have their own unanticipated complications. Several could require more energy to produce, thereby contributing to increased carbon emissions—and global warming. At least one has produced disappointing results in tests of its toxicity in animals.

One class of potential substitutes—hydrochlorofluorocarbons (HCFCs)—have come under tougher scrutiny by environmentalists. Although they still contain ozone-damaging chlorine, HCFCs produce less damage to the ozone than CFCs and have been viewed as a transitional substitute while industry continues to search for better alternatives.

But the rapidly increasing damage to the ozone may rule out using HCFCs as widely as once thought possible, according to environmentalists. "The timetable keeps changing because we keep learning that CFCs are causing greater damage than we thought two years ago," said David D. Doniger, senior attorney for the Natural Resources Defense Council, an environmental organization.

The huge quantities of CFCs sold worldwide—2.2 billion pounds in 1986—have principally been used in the categories of air conditioning and refrigeration; foam packaging and insulation; and cleaning solvents. Air conditioning and refrigeration usage account for about 40 percent of all CFCs. Just to name those three broad categories, though, doesn't convey how ever-present CFCs are.

They "really [were] like water," said David R. Chittick, environment and safety engineering vice president for AT&T, where CFCs have been used as a solvent for cleaning. "How do you go around and manage the household without water?"

The National Aeronautics and Space Administration uses 20,000 gallons of CFCs a year to decontaminate the inside of its space shuttles and the orbiters and to scrub down the hardware on the launch pads. The chemicals also are used in medical services, to sterilize and preserve whole blood, and to sterilize artificial joints, heart pacemakers and other implants.

The market for the chemical substitutes for CFCs is likely to be only half of what the market was for the earlier ozone-depleting chemicals, according to Fay. "Better conservation and use practices and more environmentally aware considerations of how [such chemicals are] to be used" have helped reduce demand, he said.

For example, CFCs used in air conditioning are now being recovered and recycled rather than released into the atmosphere, and NASA distills and recovers 10,000 gallons a year of the 20,000 gallons that it uses.

"People have come to recognize that there are a richer set of alternatives than they had thought and that there are opportunities for substitutes that people might not have considered that may have superior attributes—not just to other substitutes to the chemical they are replacing," said John S. Hoffman, director of EPA's Division of Global Change.

CFC comes in different formulations for different purposes. For example, CFC-12 has been used for automobile air conditioning and in home refrigerators, while CFC-113 is used as a solvent in the electronics industry.

The automobile industry has reached a consensus on substituting HFC-134a for CFC-12 in car air conditioning beginning next year. HFCs are hydrofluorocarbons.

In other areas—household refrigerators, for example—the choice of coolants is less clear. Du Pont is betting that HFC-134a will become the substitute of choice for appliance manufacturers, although EPA officials are investigating whether another chemical, HFC-152a, can do the same job while consuming less power. Du Pont produces the competing chemical as well as HFC-134a but has raised questions about its flammability. In an effort to dramatize that shortcoming, the chemical company produced a video that shows a drum of HFC-152a exploding when it is ignited and distributed a German-made video that shows a refrigerator exploding in a ball of flames.

Du Pont, which invented and has been the world's largest producer of CFCs, plans to invest $300 million this year to develop CFC alternatives, including plants that will have the ability to produce up to 34,000 million tons a year of HFC-134a.

Ultimately, according to Du Pont's Vogelsberg, the appliance manufacturers will decide on a substitute.

Bob Johnson, director of product evaluation for refrigeration products at Whirlpool Corp., said that his company has two primary candidates to replace CFC-12. Both would require some redesign of the refrigerator to maintain performance, as would the substitution of two products to replace the CFC-11 foam used as insulation in refrigerators.

The biggest problem with the two products to replace the CFC used in refrigerator insulation is "they are more chemically reactant" than the chemical they would replace, said Johnson.

"The industry uses plastic liners in refrigerators, and the new blowing agents tend to attack those plastic liners," he said. "A large part of the challenge there is coming up with modifications to the foam or to the plastic itself to inhibit this chemical attack, or it's possible that we will use a barrier film to isolate the plastic from the foam."

In addition to finding new equipment that operates with CFC substitutes, industry also must deal with retrofitting old equipment.

"There's about $135 billion worth of equipment dependent on CFCs here and probably in the range of $200 billion worldwide," said Du Pont's Vogelsberg. "This equipment has a lifetime of anywhere between 15 years for the typical refrigerator to 30 years or more for large industrial chillers."

One area where CFCs have been replaced with less difficulty than anticipated is in the electronics industry, according to EPA and industry officials.

"In the solvent field, we were not locked in to the extent that refrigeration is," said AT&T's Chittick. "We don't have massive equipment that is dependent on CFCs, like a compressor, but we do have the requirement to clean."

At AT&T, the need to eliminate CFCs caused the company to look at its processing to determine why cleaning was needed, he said. In some areas, AT&T replaced the resin flux that had been used as a soldering agent for circuit boards with another process that eliminates the need for cleaning. Where cleaning couldn't be eliminated, AT&T has substituted turpines, a material made from citrus, for CFCs.

Substitutes have drawbacks compared to the industrial perfection of CFCs, however, he said. Turpines are flammable. In addition, its toxicity in high concentrations has yet to be determined, so "we use it with caution," he said. "It all comes under the grand scientific principle of no free lunch."

Expensive as replacing CFCs may be, the cost of doing nothing could include major damage to human health and the environment—including higher numbers of skin cancers and cataracts, suppression of the immune system in both humans and animals and increased smog. As one recent report prepared for the EPA put it: "Under all reasonable assumptions about ozone depletion and the uses of [the chemicals], the benefits of regulating ozone depleting chemicals far exceed the costs."

Still, said AT&T's Johnson, toting up the balance sheet is hard. Although the company found opportunities and improvements as they sought to eliminate CFCs, "We spent a lot of money getting there, and we had to replace a lot of capital equipment.

"What's the true cost-benefit to the world to eliminate the ozone depleting chemicals? I don't know how to put that on my books."

7 U.S. to End CFC Production Four Years Earlier Than Planned

Schedule for Other Ozone-Protecting Action Reexamined

MICHAEL WEISSKOPF
February, 1992

President Bush yesterday announced that United States will stop making certain industrial chemicals four years earlier than planned because of new estimates of their damage to the protective ozone layer over the Northern Hemisphere.

The president's pledge to halt production of chlorofluorocarbons (CFCs) by Dec. 31, 1995, commits the United States to a faster phaseout schedule than most of the industrialized nations that signed the Montreal Protocol—an international treaty that sets a deadline of 2000 for elimination of the chemicals, which are widely used in consumer products.

The White House was quick to characterize the decision as the latest example of U.S. leadership in defense of the ozone layer. But the new timetable will pose little or no hardship to American producers, most of which have long been planning to get out of the declining market for CFCs.

Nor does the decision speed the phaseout of many substitute chemicals already in use that are less damaging than CFCs but still erode the veil of ozone molecules. The ozone layer in the stratosphere screens out much harmful ultraviolet radiation, which can cause skin cancer, cataracts and damage to the immune system.

The president called for a reexamination of plans to stop production of the substitutes by 2030. E.I. du Pont de Nemours & Co., the largest CFC producer, plans to phase out the substitutes 10 years earlier.

Under the terms of the Clean Air Act Amendments of 1990, Bush is authorized to accelerate the phaseout schedule without new laws or congressional action.

"The president has taken at best a half step," said Sen. Albert Gore Jr. (D-Tenn.), who has called for a faster phaseout of CFCs and its substitutes. "His deadline is welcome, but still inadequate."

The destructive power of CFCs was first reported in the 1970s, prompting a U.S. ban on them in aerosol products in 1978. But industry found increasing uses for the inexpensive gases as refrigerants, computer chip solvents and foam-blowing agents. By 1986, the world was producing 720 million pounds of the chemicals per year.

Unlike many pollutants, CFCs do not break down in the lower atmosphere. Gradually, they waft high into the stratosphere where they come apart under the intense bombardment of solar rays. Chlorine released in the process snares oxygen atoms from three-atom ozone molecules, changing them into conventional two-atom oxygen molecules which do not absorb ultraviolet light.

The CFC explosion of the past 20 years has put so much of the chemicals into the atmosphere that there is no way of stopping continued depletion of the ozone shield. Even with the faster phaseout, the protective layer is not expected by scientists to be restored to its 1970s condition until the middle of the next century.

Last week, NASA scientists reported that a converted spy plane flying over New England and eastern Canada recorded the highest level of ozone-threatening chlorine compounds ever measured anywhere in the world. The level was 50 percent higher than previously seen over Antarctica, where an ozone hole was first discovered in 1985.

Scientists predict an additional 1.6 million cases of cataracts a year and 300,000 new cases of skin cancer as result of ozone depletion by the year 2000.

The Montreal Protocol of 1987, signed by 71 nations, provides for regular reevaluations of whether a faster phaseout is warranted. A working group is scheduled in April to set an agenda for a full meeting of signatories in November.

Germany has pledged to eliminate CFCs by Jan. 1, 1995, and one of the most popular substitutes by 2000. The European Community is committed to a deadline of July 1997.

To keep pace with the phaseout schedule announced yesterday, U.S. industry will have to cut its production to half of the 1986 baseline in the protocol. But industry already has cut output by 42 percent, spokesmen said.

Bush provided for "limited exceptions" to the ban, allowing continued CFC production to service the $135 billion in existing equipment that uses the chemical. According to industry estimates, 15 percent of 1986 levels will be needed for such servicing.

8 Study Finds Alternatives More Damaging Than Believed

Faster Phaseout to Protect Ozone Layer Supported

MICHAEL WEISSKOPF
February, 1992

Only a few years ago, they were hailed as "environmentally enlightened" chemicals, capable of performing the many tasks of chlorofluorocarbons (CFCs) without poking as large a hole in the protective ozone layer.

But now the replacements—known as HCFCs because of hydrogen added to the original compound—are themselves under attack. An environmental think tank released a report last week showing that while the alternative chemicals are much less damaging to ozone, they are three to five times more destructive than previously thought.

The report by the Washington-based Institute for Energy and Environmental Research supports pleas in Congress for a faster phaseout of CFC alternatives than the 2030 deadline set by statute. After NASA earlier this month warned of a potential hole in the ozone layer over North America, President Bush announced plans to halt U.S. production of CFCs four years earlier than scheduled, but left intact the timetable for eliminating HCFCs.

"It's a mistake to replace one ozone-destroying chemical with another," said Sen. Albert Gore Jr. (D-Tenn.), who wants HCFCs gone by 1999. "Any added increments at this point represent true insanity."

For industrial users, however, HCFCs are an invaluable "bridge," allowing production lines to keep going until nondepleting substitutes for the ubiquitous chemicals are perfected. HCFCs also are needed to service an estimated $200 billion worth of existing air conditioners and heat pumps that use the chemicals.

"There's nothing else to turn to right now," said Kevin Fay, who heads a trade association of CFC users and producers.

Work on alternatives began in the late 1970s after the first warnings of CFC damage to the veil of ozone molecules 15 miles above ground. The layer screens out much of the ultraviolet radiation that can cause skin cancer, cataracts and other ailments.

Chemical companies stopped HCFC research in the early 1980s when ozone risk estimates softened, then resumed efforts after the ozone hole over Antarctica was discovered in 1985 and industrialized nations signed the Montreal Protocol in 1987. The treaty was the first step to weaning their societies off the cheap, easily produced chemical used as coolants in air conditioners and refrigerators, solvents for electronic parts and "blowing agents" for plastic products such as Styrofoam.

Unlike most pollutants, CFCs do not break down in the lower atmosphere. Eventually they rise into the stratosphere, where intense solar rays splinter them, releasing chlorine that destroys ozone molecules.

By adding hydrogen to the chemical formulation, chemists make CFCs less stable in the lower atmosphere, assuring that the compounds will break down before reaching the ozone layer. Thus, although they still release some chlorine, HCFCs are about 95 percent less powerful as ozone depleters than the original compounds, industry experts say.

Chemical companies promote HCFCs, which have replaced 10 to 25 percent of CFCs at up to five times the price. Du Pont, the largest producer, advertises the chemicals as "environmentally acceptable."

But Arjun Makhijani, the environmental researcher who is coauthor of last week's report, criticized such characterizations as "deceptive."

HCFCs are 95 percent less ozone-depleting than the original compounds only if the analysis assumes that the alternatives release chlorine at the same, slow rate as CFCs. In fact, Makhijani's research indicated, they free chlorine much faster; and because the coming years are critical for arresting the chlorine buildup, the contributions of HCFCs will be "far higher" than indicated by the earlier analyses of their destructive power.

For example, HCFC-22, North America's most commonly used refrigerant, is 75 percent less depleting than CFCs, not 95 percent as originally estimated, Makhijani said.

Increasingly used as a substitute for aerosol propellants in Europe and foam-blowing agents worldwide, HCFC-22 production has increased 9 percent a year since the mid-1980s and is expected to continue to rise at that rate until 2000, he said.

Getting HCFC-22 off the market in 2005, or 25 years earlier than planned, would significantly cut chlorine levels in the atmosphere, the think tank report concluded.

Tony Vogelsberg, environmental manager of Du Pont Fluorochemicals, acknowledged that HCFCs are less benign than previously described, but insisted that they are vital as transition chemicals. HCFC-22, for instance, may be used to replace more depleting CFC gases used in supermarket refrigerator cases.

Meanwhile, development of non-chlorine-based chemical compounds is proceeding rapidly. It is expected that within three years, new auto air conditioners will run on nondepleting chemicals.

9   After 2000, Outlook for the Ozone Layer Looks Good

BOYCE RENSBERGER
April, 1993

A fter nearly a decade of headlines and hand-wringing about erosion of the Earth's protective ozone layer, the problem appears to be well on the way to solution.

As a result of the Montreal Protocol, an international treaty obliging signatory countries to phase out ozone-destroying chemicals, scientists expect the threat of ozone destruction to peak in just seven years. In 2000, according to the latest scientific estimates, the ozone layer should start slowly getting thicker and better able to block the sun's harmful ultraviolet (UV) rays.

In fact, researchers say, the problem appears to be heading toward solution before they can find any solid evidence that serious harm was or is being done.

This hopeful trend—at variance with the dark scenarios of environmental doom that were pronounced after discovery of the Antarctic ozone hole in the 1980s—is supported not only by growing scientific evidence but even by scientists in the environmental movement.

"The current and projected levels of ozone depletion do not appear to represent a catastrophe," said Michael Oppenheimer, an atmospheric scientist with the Environmental Defense Fund. "But I'm flabbergasted that we let it go this far before taking action. It was a potentially very serious problem."

Richard Stolarski, an atmospheric scientist at NASA's Goddard Space Flight Center, agreed: "I happen not to be of the disaster school. It's a serious concern but we can't show that anything really catastrophic has happened yet, or that anything catastrophic will happen in the future."

Attempts to detect the most feared effect of ozone depletion—increased bombardment of the Earth's surface by UV rays—have failed to turn up any evidence of increased ultraviolet influx outside the Antarctic region during the few weeks each year that the ozone hole is open.

If there has been any increase in UV, researchers say, it is too small to measure against a background of normal ultraviolet levels that rise and fall by large amounts for entirely natural reasons on time scales from hours to decades.

Given the expected improvements in the ozone layer, even the ozone hole eventually could stop opening. Already scientists see signs that the hole is not likely to grow much bigger than it has.

Even when the problem reaches its worst in 2000, scientists expect summertime ozone losses over temperate zones to be about 6 percent, double what they are now. Because each percentage point of ozone loss theoretically leads to an increase in UV intensity of 1.3 percentage points, the potential increase in ultraviolet would be about 8 percent.

Scientists calculate that the increased UV exposure a Washingtonian would get in midsummer then will be the equivalent of moving south about 3200 miles now. In other words, if you want to know what this area's ultraviolet level will be like in July 2000, go to, say, Raleigh, N.C., this July.

Worst Depletion Occurs in Late Winter

Latitude is crucial because, like time of day and season, it affects the amount of atmosphere that UV must pass through to reach the ground. When the sun is directly overhead, for example, its light penetrates one thickness of atmosphere, but when it is on the horizon, its rays take a slanting path roughly equivalent to 40 thicknesses, and 40 times as much ozone.

This is key to understanding why, even though ozone depletion is worst in late winter (ozone is reduced by 8 to 10 percent), less ultraviolet gets through than in summer, when the ozone loss is milder. Sun angle is so low in winter that the UV passes through more ozone then than during summer when there is less depletion. (Over the tropics, where sun angle is high all year long, there has been no observed ozone depletion.)

"One reason we haven't seen any increase in UV is that we didn't start taking good data long ago," said Stolarski, who nearly 20 years ago was among the first researchers to assert that the ozone layer could be damaged if certain chemicals—especially chlorine—traveled high enough in the atmosphere.

Ultraviolet Rays Fluctuate Naturally

Because of natural fluctuations in ultraviolet, it is impossible to detect a trend in a short period of data collection.

While there is evidence that the ozone damage is happening, it has proven impossible so far to detect any resulting increase in UV reaching the ground because ultraviolet fluctuates so much naturally.

"The amount of increase that the theory says we could be getting from ozone depletion is smaller than the error of our best measuring instruments," said John E. Frederick an atmospheric physicist at the University of Chicago.

"People get all excited about a few-percent change in UV, but it's nothing to get a 20 percent increase naturally," Frederick said. "If an increase of 20 percent were going to be so damaging, there should be no life in Florida," where ultraviolet always exceeded the allegedly dangerous levels once forecast for more northerly latitudes.

Los Angeles Pollution Cuts Levels of UV

Stolarski, Frederick and other atmospheric scientists say that even if there were good UV measurements going back many years, they still might not show an increase because other factors such as increased cloudiness (one of the predicted effects of global warming) and air pollution (including pollution by ozone in the lower atmosphere) might be shielding the ground, compensating for the lost upper-atmosphere ozone.

That, in fact, was a conclusion of one of the most exhaustive studies of the ozone problem ever undertaken, an effort in which nearly 150 scientists from 28 countries collaborated under the auspices of five American, British and United Nations agencies.

"The decreases in UV-B [the damaging form of UV] caused by increases in [air pollution] since the industrial revolution probably exceed the increases due to ozone depletion," according to the group's latest report, "Scientific Assessment of Ozone Depletion: 1991."

In Los Angeles, Frederick said, there is so much extra ozone in the lower atmosphere in the form of air pollution from cars that it cuts the ultraviolet level on an average day by 6 to 9 percent. On smoggy days, the UV level drops by 20 percent.

Without Shield, Almost Uninhabitable Earth

If any of this comes as a surprise, it may be because most of the mass media coverage of this complex issue has focused on cries of alarm by environmentalists who feared a worst-case scenario in which the planet's protective ozone layer would be thinned enough to let in massive amounts of solar radiation.

If the ozone shield did not exist, the surface of the Earth would be virtually uninhabitable. The amount of ultraviolet that reaches the top of Earth's atmosphere would be lethal to most forms of life if it penetrated to the ground.

The world responded to the environmentalist case. The main threats to the ozone, synthetic chemicals called chlorofluorocarbons (CFCs) used chiefly as refrigerants, solvents, foam-blowing gas, and once as spray-can propellants, are being phased out. In fact, production and sales of CFCs are declining faster than originally projected by negotiators of the Montreal Protocol.

So well are the corrective measures proceeding that scientists who have been looking for effects of ozone depletion say it may not be possible to document any before the massive injection of CFCs into the atmosphere fades away, ending humanity's inadvertent experiment in perturbing Earth's atmosphere.

10   Decline of Ozone-Harming Chemicals Suggests Atmosphere May Heal Itself

BOYCE RENSBERGER
August, 1993

The amount of ozone-destroying CFCs in the atmosphere, which had been rising rapidly for decades, suddenly slowed its rate of increase in 1989 and has nearly leveled off since then, scientists at the National Oceanic and Atmospheric Administration have found.

The NOAA researchers credit a surprisingly rapid decline in the production and use of the chemicals—called chlorofluorocarbons and sold mainly as refrigerants and plastic foam-blowing agents—and forecast that their concentration will peak around the year 2000.

If current trends continue, they say, CFC levels will slowly decline, allowing the ozone layer to heal itself naturally and provide steadily increasing amounts of protection against the sun's ultraviolet rays.

"This is extremely good news for the environment," said James W. Elkins of NOAA's Climate Monitoring and Diagnostics Laboratory in Boulder, Colorado. Elkins led the research effort, with colleagues at NOAA and the University of Colorado, that has been tracking CFC concentrations since 1977. Elkins said that when his group first saw the drop in the CFC growth rate, it was so dramatic, "our first reaction was [that] we've got something wrong with our instruments."

The data—which have been circulating privately among scientists for more than a year, and on which *The Washington Post* based an earlier report that the ozone problem would peak in 2000—are published in today's issue of the scientific journal *Nature*. The findings were submitted to *Nature* in June 1992; but because the journal prohibits scientists from presenting their work publicly while it is undergoing peer-review, Elkins and the other authors could not talk about their findings until now.

"I'm very pleased that this is out," said Richard Stolarski, an ozone-layer researcher at NASA's Goddard Space Flight Center in Greenbelt. "It's very welcome experimental confirmation of what many of us had projected on the basis of [CFC] production figures. It's actually amazing how fast some of these growth curves drop off."

CFCs, which were invented in the 1920s but did not come into widespread use until the 1950s and '60s, are blamed for about three-quarters of the depletion of ozone. In recent years, the loss over temperate zones has been about 3 percent to 4 percent. In the last two years, however, occasional losses have surged to as much as 10 percent to 15 percent for brief periods. These are generally attributed to effects from the 1992 eruption of Mount Pinatubo, which are expected to fade in coming years.

The new CFC report was based on measurements of air samples collected at seven stations around the world in polar, temperate and tropical regions. Starting in 1977, samples of air were taken weekly from each station and shipped to Elkins's laboratory for analysis.

The new report concerns the two most common and fastest growing types of the chemicals: CFC-11 and CFC-12. From 1977 through 1984, the concentration was rising at an annual average of 9 parts per trillion (ppt) for CFC-11 and 17 ppt for CFC-12.

In 1984 production and use of the chemicals increased; and from 1985 to 1988, the CFC-11 concentration grew at a rate of 11 ppt each year while CFC-12 grew 19.5 ppt each year.

Then, Elkins said, something "surprising" happened. After 1988 the rate of increase plummeted, reaching levels this year of 2.7 ppt for CFC-11 and 10.5 ppt for CFC-12.

After establishing that the instruments were not malfunctioning, Elkins recalled, he became puzzled as to why CFC release would be slowing its growth even though the Montreal Protocol—a global treaty signed in 1987 to phase out use and end the production of ozone-destroying chemicals—was not due to take full effect until 1996. He called E. I. du Pont de Nemours & Co., which makes the chemicals, and learned that their estimates of the amount produced around the world showed a parallel decline.

Elkins and colleagues estimated that if CFC output trends continue to fall and production ceases in 1996, as planned, the concentration of CFC-11 in the lower atmosphere will peak in 1998 and CFC-12 a year later. Because it takes two to four years for molecules in the lower atmosphere to reach the stratosphere, where the ozone layer is, the amounts there would not be likely to peak until shortly after 2000.

At that time, the group estimated, the concentration of chlorine (the atom that breaks off CFC and attacks ozone) in the stratosphere would be about 4 parts per billion, up from the current 3.4 ppb.

After the peak, however, the chlorine would slowly fall out of the atmosphere. Small amounts are removed all the time as the chlorine combines with hydrogen to form hydrochloric acid in water droplets that eventually fall in rain.

The scientists estimate that it could take 50 to 100 years before the concentration of stratospheric chlorine returns to levels thought to have existed before the widespread use of CFCs—about 0.5 ppb. Elkins said that if the world can make it to 2000 without suffering any major harm from ozone depletion, he would not expect any catastrophes to arise during the long recovery period.

He credited the CFC decline to public pressure. "This is all driven by U.S. public opinion," he said. Adverse publicity about CFCs has meant "consumers won't buy products made with CFCs."

At the same time, the chemical industry apparently has embraced the goals of the Montreal Protocol, at least in part because firms saw profitable new markets in costlier CFC substitutes.

"This is a beautiful case study," Elkins said, "where science, the law, industry and the public worked together."

One caveat remains. Third World signatories, which include such large and growing refrigeration markets as China, India and Indonesia, are allowed to delay their phaseout of CFCs for 10 years. To help them meet the higher costs of substitute chemicals and refrigeration hardware built to use the substitute, the protocol allows them to draw on a fund to which the rich countries would contribute.

Although these countries are not large users of CFCs now, there is a fear that in their drive to develop economically and to improve public health through wider use of food refrigeration, they may increase use of the cheap ozone-destroying chemical rather than more costly substitutes.

In the industrialized world, the phaseout is likely to be smoother. According to the Air Conditioning and Refrigeration Institute, all home air conditioners, including central and window units, already use one of the substitutes—HCFC-22, or hydrochlorofluorocarbon-22. Pound for pound, HCFC-22 can do only about 5 percent as much harm to the ozone layer as CFCs. Home refrigerators use CFC-12 but rarely need recharging before the unit wears out mechanically. Refrigerators that use ozone-safer coolants are starting to come on the market.

Most automobile air conditioners, until the 1994 model year, were built to use CFC-12. Nearly all '94 models will use a hydrofluorocarbon coolant, HFC-134a, that contains no chlorine and thus cannot harm ozone. Because car air conditioners are notorious for leaking (mainly because of vibrating hose connections), most existing units will eventually need recharging with CFC-12 or replacement with a new unit that works on HFC-134a.

Even after the ban on making new CFCs, however, experts say it should still be possible for a few years to recharge older units with recycled CFC-12. The cost of retrofitting a car with an HFC-134a air conditioner has been estimated at $200 to $800.

Atmospheric Problems: Air Pollution and Acid Rain   4

O n any given day, the U.S. Environmental Protection Agency asserts that millions of people in the United States breathe air with smog levels judged to be harmful to their health. The city of Los Angeles is notorious for its smog, but other cities such as Mexico City are even worse. The problem of air pollution is compounded when the oxides of nitrogen and sulfur spewed into the air, largely by automobiles and coal-burning electric generation plants, combine with water to produce nitric and sulfuric acids that fall downwind as acid rain or acid snow.

Like the greenhouse effect, the issue of acid rain has attracted a considerable amount of public attention. Many scientists believe that this precipitation is responsible for significant damage to forests and lakes. In North America, the problem is particularly severe along the east coast of both the United States and Canada. Trees are dying from North Carolina all the way into Canada, and some lakes are so acidic that they are no longer able to sustain the diversity of flora and fauna they once were. The lakes in Canada have been particularly affected by this insidious form of pollution. The acid rain problem is also present in other parts of the world; the Black Forest region of Germany has received particular public attention.

As with other environmental issues, it is difficult to achieve consensus among the experts as to the extent or seriousness of the problem. Significant reductions in pollution levels of nitrous and sulfur oxides would certainly be costly to industry and possibly would curtail economic growth. Naturally, any expansion-oriented economy will be reluctant to make these reductions.

The articles in this chapter review the issue of air pollution and acid rain and provide an overview of the difficulty of dealing with a threat to the environment that is not yet fully understood in terms of its causes, scope, or significance. Article 1 provides some insight into the severity of the problem of air pollution with a vivid description of conditions in Mexico City. Article 2 illustrates how the intent of Congress in passing environmental legislation can be subverted by the regulatory agencies charged with its enforcement. In this case, the issue concerns use of tall smoke stacks by industry to circumvent antipollution regulations. Article 3 continues this theme with a description of changes in implementation of the Clean Air Act that allows industry to increase emissions without following specified procedures.

On a different topic, Article 4 discusses a finding that the pollutants causing acid rain may actually mitigate the greenhouse effect, and finally, Article 5 discusses an under-reported finding that acid rain may not be as devastating as many fear.

1   Mexico City Choked by Pollution Emergency

Worst Air Quality on Record Disrupts Daily Life

EDWARD CODY
March, 1992

S ince playing basketball with his teenage son over the weekend in the poisonous Mexico City air, Erick Alcantara has been swallowing asprin tablets nonstop to combat a throbbing migraine.

His six-month-old daughter, Irene, has suffered bronchial problems almost since birth in what the Alcantara family says is a reaction to the increasingly polluted atmosphere. School authorities this winter have forbidden the Alcantara's first-grader, Andres, and their 11-year-old daughter, Mary Carmen, from running during school recess for fear that they and their boisterous playmates will breathe the befouled air too deeply.

"We can sit down in the playground, but we can't run," Andres, six, complained. "Whoever runs is taken to the principal's office."

These have become the realities of everyday life for the Alcantaras and millions of other Mexico City families who reside in what is arguably the world's most polluted city, which in recent days has been going through what environmentalists and local authorities have classified as its worst air-quality emergency on record. Mexico City's problem is in part simple geography: it is ringed by mountains that trap pollution.

As ozone readings soared to record levels last week, President Carlos Salinas de Gortari's government imposed the most draconian antipollution measures so far on the city's 20 million inhabitants. Although some grumbled at the inconveniences and industrialists warned of slowing the economy, acceptance seemed widespread. After years of resignation, many here have begun to demonstrate increasing impatience with the government's apparent inability to clean up the air they breathe.

A day-without-a-car program, in place for two years, was temporarily expanded to two days a week and weekends for some cars. That meant 40 percent of the city's nearly 3 million vehicles are kept off the road each day until conditions improve. Automobiles produce about 75 percent of the region's ozone.

Reacting to his inability to use the family car on Wednesday, Thursday and Saturday under the intensified restrictions, Alcantara said, "I am ready to use a bicycle, or even roller skates, if it will improve the pollution situation."

Subway use jumped by about a million passengers to 5.5 million a day, stuffing an already crowded system. Executives in suits and ties were forced to leave their cars at home and ride alongside workers in the minibuses that swerve up and down the capital's main arteries.

In addition, the most polluting of the some 30,000 factories around Mexico City were forced to cut production 30 percent, and Salinas announced a crackdown under which they will be forced to reduce contamination by 1994 or move out of the Valley of Mexico.

The government's emergency moves helped bring pollution down a bit. Also buoyed by favorable winds and atmospheric pressure, city antipollution officials said they were considering scaling back their restrictions, that is, until the next explosion of high readings.

But Mayor Manuel Camacho Solis and his environmental aides have acknowledged that, given political and economic realities, permanently reducing ozone levels will take at least a decade. Steps already in place have reduced other pollutants, such as lead and carbon monoxide, but increasing gasoline consumption, combined with Mexico City's 7,300-foot altitude, means only long-term hopes are realistic for getting ozone under control.

As a result, Carmina and Erick Alcantara and their four children have begun to talk of moving to a provincial city. So far, however, it has only been talk, since outside Mexico City employment opportunities are less numerous and schooling, particularly college preparatory classes for 16-year-old Erick Jr., is less prestigious.

In the meantime, they and their neighbors have been forced to play out their lives engulfed by pollution. Although the long-term effects on health have not been scientifically assessed, the Health Ministry has said contamination has become a major source of respiratory irritation, minor illnesses and debilitation. "People here just live tired," Carmina said. "My kids are always coming home with headaches and stomach aches. And the baby is always having bronchial troubles."

Carmina, who does not own a clothes dryer, has taken to drying the laundry for a family of six by draping it around bathroom fixtures. She used to hang it out on the roof, she said, but "it came out smelling like smoke" when she brought it in.

Erick Alcantara, 47, a mid-level manager in a downtown bank, winced at the thought of paying taxi fares because of the restrictions on driving the family car. Usually, he explained, he drives Carmina to her job as a lab technician for the government health system, dropping the children off at their schools and day-care center on the way. Now that will have to be done morning and evening in a taxi on another no-driving day.

Alcantara said his daily routine is to return the car to the apartment-house parking lot and take the subway to his bank, with a five-minute walk to the station nearest his home and another 10-minute walk from the station nearest his bank. But because of the rise in pollution, he added, he has begun resorting to minibuses or taxis for the final leg of the trip to avoid the headaches he gets from walking in the polluted streets.

Pollution has made life in Mexico City a series of such compromises. The Health Ministry has recommended against outside exercise, and Alcantara knew he should not be playing basketball on the outdoor court last weekend, for example, but Erick Jr. wanted to practice for his school team.

"I promised him I was going to play with him no matter how high the smog reading," the father said.

Another compromise is necessary every time the Alcantara family takes its car into the Mexico City streets.

"We drive along with the windows closed to have more security [from the foul air], but then the sun comes along and beats down on the car roof," Alcantara said. "So we open the windows anyway. Then a truck comes along shooting out smoke—and ugh."

Andres and Mary Carmen have struggled with their own compromises at school, where teachers say children strain under the prohibition against outdoor exercise at recess. According to Andres, many of the boys at his school disobey the injunction and run until they are caught by teachers. Marycarmen said her girl-friends are more disciplined and spend their recess playing table games.

The Public Education Ministry's ban on outdoor exercise was handed down last December and is scheduled to last until the summer rainy season reduces pollution. Despite the restriction, a dozen pupils at the Simitrio Ramirez primary school in the southern neighborhood of San Bernabe fainted from the effects of pollution last Friday—one of the worst smog days—and two were hospitalized.

2 "Tall Stacks" and Acid Rain

Northeast Suffers from Faraway Emissions

MICHAEL WEISSKOPF
June, 1989

A mid the floral sprays of a late spring on Camels Hump, a 4,000-foot Green Mountain peak, are patches of death. Once too dense to penetrate, the forest opens broadly to stands of defoliated red spruce, teetering like charred victims of fire. At their feet lay 200-year-old firs, violently snapped from their bases. The gloomy scene contrasts sharply with the explosion of new growth 600 miles away in the Ohio River Valley, but to many scientists there is a crucial connection.

Rising incongruously from the rolling, midwestern farmland are utility smokestacks almost as high as the Empire State Building. Known simply as "tall stacks," the tapered, concrete towers enable utility companies to emit large quantities of sulfur dioxide and technically still comply with the Clean Air Act because no pollution occurs in the valley below. Instead the gases that the stacks shoot thousands of feet into the air move downwind to Canada and the Northeast, turn acidic and eventually fall in rain and snow.

Scientists say that much of the acid fallout in Vermont comes from the valley, and Vermont officials and environmentalists blame tall stacks for the forest damage.

Congress and federal courts have repeatedly prohibited reliance on tall stacks to achieve local air quality standards. But 108 have been erected nationwide since the Clean Air Act was passed in 1970 and still stand today, monuments to the power of special interests.

By building the stacks—typically 400 to 600 feet high—utilities have been able to continue burning cheap, high-sulfur coal, avoid the expense of sulfur-removal devices and still meet limits on sulfur dioxide near the plant.

The power companies were able to do this because they pushed the Environmental Protection Agency until they got what they wanted, blanketing the government with lobbyists, exploiting ambiguities in the law, ignoring court rulings and manipulating public opinion. The EPA, guardian of the nation's air resources, handed out one concession after another. The EPA's handling of tall stacks illustrates a larger truth about the federal attempt to clean up the environment.

A groundbreaking piece of legislation when it was enacted 19 years ago, the Clean Air Act in many respects seems almost futile today. While no one disputes that things would be worse without it, the legislation has not prevented unhealthy levels of pollution for more than half the population, depletion of the ozone level by industrial gases, contamination of drinking-water sources by airborne toxins and acid damage to lakes and forests.

Critics turn the blame not on the act but on those charged with implementing it. The EPA, they say, failed to force industry to make the changes necessary to save the nation's air.

Few laws have required more dramatic action from the industrial sector—utilities, automakers, oil and chemical companies and steel manufacturers. According to government statistics, corporations have spent $400 billion on technology to cut auto pollutants 90 percent, take lead out of gasoline, filter out industrial soot and remove sulfur from coal combustion gas.

But the steps were not taken voluntarily. Industry fought the changes every step of the way, and the history of tall stacks illustrates the pattern of accommodation that has been followed by EPA.

The concessions that industry has won have come at a heavy price. Scientists and environmentalists cite these costly results: Ozone levels may not have reached the critical stage they are at now had the EPA in the early 1980s not extended deadlines and relaxed standards for auto emissions. The stratospheric ozone layer—the "good" ozone—may not have become so depleted if the EPA had observed the scientific consensus as far back as the 1970s and banned chlorofluorocarbons (CFCs). Northwest Indiana may not have been covered in so much soot if the EPA had not allowed steel companies in the Gary area to avoid requirements for particulate emission controls in the early 1980s and operate without a state control plan since 1977.

Industry resistance was anticipated by sponsors of the act, but they were ready to prescribe strong medicine to deal with what was commonly seen then as a national crisis.

"It is a tough bill because only a tough law will guarantee America clean air," then-Sen. Edmund S. Muskie (D-Maine), the act's chief sponsor, told the Senate in September 1970. "Industry has been presented with challenges in the past that seemed impossible to meet, but has made them possible."

Such rhetoric was not surprising given the political climate then. The previous April, on Earth Day, millions of people demonstrated around the country for environmental protection. President Richard M. Nixon, then in his first term and fearing Muskie's presidential ambitions, was unwilling to cede him the environment as an issue.

Industry lobbyists were far fewer and did not take the bill seriously at first, recalled Leon Billings, who served as Muskie's top environmental aide. The chief lobbyist for General Motors never visited Muskie and no top auto company executive testified at subcommittee hearings. "They honestly believed we'd go away," Billings said.

The toughest provisions of the bill, such as the 90 percent cuts in auto emissions, were drafted in closed meetings. When the subcommittee emerged with a tough bill, industry "had never seen anything like it," Billings said.

But special interests learned from the defeat. Since then they have missed few opportunities to influence the act and its enforcement at the legislative, regulatory, and judicial levels.

The number of lobbyists representing air polluters has mushroomed, and they include many former staff members of the key Senate and House committees who have ready access to their old colleagues.

Special interests give generously to congressional and presidential campaigns. Since 1981, political action committees of firms and organizations with a direct interest in clean air legislation have contributed $21.8 million, according to records compiled by *The Washington Post* and the Public Interest Research Group.

Utilities, with plants in nearly every legislative district, are among the most effective pressure groups. The industry has dozens of full-time Capitol Hill lobbyists and retains a special team of lawyers to fight regulatory and legal battles.

Campaign contributions are funneled through an industry-wide donor—Power Pac—and sent by individual companies. They have totaled $6.4 million since 1981. An industry group, Citizens for Sensible Control of Acid Rain, has used mail and phone calls to warn consumers of the costs of acid rain legislation, citing utility estimates widely regarded as inflated.

"They fight at every stage of the process, from the moment legislation is being formulated, continuing at the stage legislation is actually being considered, through markups and into conference committees," said Curtis Moore, until recently the Republican counsel to the Senate Environment and Public Works Committee. "If you succeed in enacting something, they will be immediately at the agency. When regulations are proposed, they are fighting them. When they're final, they challenge them in court. Then they start the process all over again and find the loopholes." The rise of tall stacks reflects that general pattern.

Since the early 1980s, scientists have been able to trace the origin of acid rain by analyzing emission patterns, air pathways and the chemical composition of pollutants. Certain airborne particles have regional signatures, such as arsenic and selenium. They originate in the Midwest, where power plants burn coal rich in those elements.

Scientists generally agree that half of the acidic particles in Vermont come from the Midwest, primarily the Ohio River Valley. On days of the highest acid levels, the pollution is very likely to have originated in the valley.

The bucolic setting by the banks of the Ohio seems an unlikely source of industrial pollution. But the tall stacks that sprout from the rich farmland release enormous volumes of sulfur dioxide. Seventeen tall stacks tower over the weathered barns and farmhouses along a 150-mile stretch of the Ohio.

The General James M. Gavin plant near Gallipolis emits more sulfur dioxide through its 1,105-foot stack than any source in the nation, more than the total emissions of some states—350,000 tons a year. A mile away, the Kyger Creek plant, through its 1,000-foot stack, releases 220,000 tons a year of the pollutant.

Utility officials defend tall stacks as a legitimate way of meeting local sulfur dioxide limits at the least expense to ratepayers. Moreover, they say, tall stacks shore up local economies by permitting use of high-sulfur coal mined in the Midwest.

Do tall stacks simply shift the damage elsewhere in the form of acid rain? "The answers aren't in yet," said John M. McManus, an environmental engineer at American Electric Power, owner of Gavin and other Ohio Valley plants. He said industry studies indicate that most sulfur dioxide and its byproducts fall from the air after traveling far shorter distances than from Ohio to Vermont. "On balance, tall stacks have resulted in environmental benefits," he said.

That view does not have many adherents among Vermont officials. "Utilities reflect their own self-interest—to avoid the costs of cleaning up pollution," said Jonathan Lash, Vermont's secretary of natural resources. "I find that understandable. The EPA reflects the unwillingness of industry to confront the problem. Perhaps that was understandable in 1970. In 1989, it's unforgivable."

Scientists say there is a clear pattern to the emissions. The gases move quickly from the valley, change into acidic particles called sulfates and travel hundreds of miles to the Northeast. The particles pass in and out of clouds, liquefy and eventually fall as precipitation, which in Vermont is said to be 10 to 100 times more acidic than normal rain.

Camels Hump is a good laboratory to assess the effects of acid rain and fog. Since 1965 it has been the subject of an ecological study counting and measuring trees.

A 1986 survey marked dramatic changes. Nearly every species had declined in number, most prominently the red spruce. Once a dominant tree on Camels Hump, pushing its bushy, evergreen crown 100 feet high, the red spruce had declined by 65 percent; sugar maples had dropped by 37 percent.

"The proportions of dieback are staggering," said Hubert Vogelmann, chairman of the University of Vermont's botany department and head of the survey team. "In 1965, the trail was just a tunnel through a dense forest. You could barely see the sky."

No one knows the cause of forest damage on Camels Hump and other high-elevation forests along the Appalachian spine. Normal stresses—insects, fungus and drought—may play a role. But Vogelmann said he believes air pollution is a contributing factor, if not the decisive one—the final blow to trees already weakened by natural enemies.

One piece of the evidence that he said tends to implicate acid rain is that the most damaged side of Camels Hump faces west—toward the land of tall stacks. The fact that tall stacks simply transfer pollution rather than eliminate it was known to Congress at the time it drafted the 1970 law. While the final legislation did not explicitly rule out tall stacks, it called for plans that include "emission limitations" to achieve air quality standards.

Utilities were undeterred, erecting tall stacks at new plants such as Gavin and raising stacks at old plants while lobbying EPA and state officials responsible for implementing air quality standards. They argued that technology to scrub sulfur from coal was too expensive and unproven, that low-sulfur coal was in short supply and that tall-stack dispersion was the only practical alternative.

The EPA was persuaded. In January 1972, it gave the first official blessing to tall stacks. Specifically, it approved a plan in Georgia that relied on the raising of utility smokestacks to meet the new ground-level sulfur dioxide standard.

Two years later, the EPA and tall stacks received their first judicial rebuke. The U.S. Court of Appeals in New Orleans, ruling in 1974 on a suit by the Natural Resources Defense Council (NRDC), found that states could approve tall stacks, but only after utilities tried to reduce emissions by other means.

Utilities, however, paid little attention to the ruling and took their case to Congress, using the Arab oil embargo to drive home the need for tall stacks. The Federal Power Commission, using statistics from the utilities, issued a report predicting power shortages if plants were forced to meet sulfur dioxide standards by the 1975 deadline.

Although the EPA had judged scrubbers feasible by then, the utilities were unwilling to invest in the costly devices. American Electric Power ridiculed scrubbers in national newspaper ads. And a company executive warned Congress that mandating "this primitive, monstrously expensive technology" would create a "national energy tragedy."

The stack for the Gavin plant cost less than $10 million to build in the mid-1970s, according to the company. Outfitting it with scrubbers today would cost $756 million.

Congress met the utilities halfway, passing legislation in June 1974 that permitted temporary reliance on tall stacks on a case-by-case basis. But efforts to legitimize tall stacks as a permanent control strategy were soundly defeated.

In 1976 the EPA issued new guidelines that grandfathered all stacks raised before 1972 and set a height limit of 2.5 times that of the boiler house for newer stacks.

By 1977, Congress began to link tall stacks with acid rain damage then being reported in lakes and forests in Canada and the Northeast. Seeking to close loopholes in the 1976 guideline, lawmakers amended the act. Utilities were not to rely on stack height to meet sulfur dioxide standards, unless "necessary" to avoid "excessive concentrations" of pollution caused by air turbulence. If necessary, they could raise the stack to 2.5 times the height of the pollution source.

David Hawkins, then head of the EPA's air office, said that in hindsight, Congress apparently intended to permit tall stacks to avoid excessive pollution—but only after the use of scrubbers or clean fuels to reduce emissions. He said that is consistent with the 1974 court ruling.

Under that reading, Hawkins said, power plants like Gavin would have had to use scrubbers or low-sulfur coal to meet sulfur dioxide limits, relying on their tall stacks only if excessive concentrations persisted because of turbulence.

But power company lawyers had a different interpretation, which Hawkins, as the EPA's air chief, initially accepted. Because air turbulence always causes excessive levels of pollution from low stacks, utilities claimed the automatic right to raise stacks to 2.5 times the height of the pollution source, and proceeded to do so. "It was one of those times when the adversary system didn't function properly," said Hawkins, now a senior attorney at NRDC.

By early 1980, Hawkins said, "we started to wake up." That June, the EPA, citing acid rain concerns, turned down the request of a Cleveland utility to raise its stacks and was formulating a program to reduce sulfur emissions nationwide.

But it never had a chance. Ronald Reagan entered the White House in 1981, and one of the first decisions of Anne Gorsuch, the new EPA administrator, was to rescind the Cleveland decision. In 1982, she issued a new regulation affirming the industry's view of the 1977 amendment and allowing unlimited stack heights case by case.

The NRDC sued again, and in 1983, the U.S. Court of Appeals for the District of Columbia Circuit ruled that utilities were not entitled to an automatic 2.5-fold increase for stacks that were heightened after the 1970 act.

In 1985, Lee M. Thomas, then EPA chief, proposed eliminating the automatic 2.5-fold credit but grandfathering in the scores of utilities that had already received approval.

In January 1988, the D.C. Circuit declared the grandfathering provision excessive and sent it back to the EPA, where the issue remains today.

"The moral of the story is that Congress has to be pretty damn clear when it adopts these requirements to give directions to the agency that can't get confused," Hawkins said. "Confusion encourages the agency to take the path of least resistance, which is almost always to accommodate the industry dogging it."

William D. Ruckelshaus, who as EPA administrator opened the door to tall stacks 17 years ago, said that "the decision to approve it is hard to justify today. We didn't give enough attention to the long-range transport of those pollutants. You'd have to say that while you were solving one problem, you were creating another," he said.

3   EPA Eases Final Rules on Industrial Pollution

Plant Emissions Could Rise without Approval

TOM KENWORTHY and DANA PRIEST

June, 1992

After losing a prolonged internal administration debate with White House conservatives the Environmental Protection Agency yesterday issued final rules governing industrial air pollution that will allow some polluters to increase emissions without prior government approval.

The rules implementing provisions of the Clean Air Act amendments approved by Congress in 1990 were immediately attacked by critics on Capitol Hill and in the environmental community as a betrayal of the law's intent. The regulations represent a defeat for EPA Administrator William K. Reilly and a victory for the White House Council on Competitiveness. The council, headed by Vice President Quayle, had argued that the clean air rules should be written to guarantee maximum flexibility for industry.

But just hours before the EPA announcement, in an ironic quirk of timing, the House Appropriations Committee voted to terminate the council's funding for next fiscal year. The 30 to 18 party line vote reflected growing Democratic dismay over the activities of the council, which many Democrats say has secretly operated to advance the business community's agenda by controlling the writing of rules implementing legislation.

"What the competitiveness council is all about is ideological purity." Rep. Vic Fazio (D-Calif.) said. The council is where business interests go, he said, to get "intervention at the highest level if you're not satisfied with the normal course of procedures."

Assistant EPA Administrator William G. Rosenberg yesterday characterized the new clean air rules as striking a balance between ensuring compliance with the new act and giving about 34,000 industrial polluters the opportunity to make minor changes in their operations in order to compete more effectively.

"We want to protect clean air, we also want to protect [business'] ability to make changes," said Rosenberg.

But critics said the rules violate the letter and spirit of the 1990 legislation. "The permit regulations blatantly violate the Clean Air Act," said David Doniger, senior attorney with the Natural Resources Defense Council. "They transform a program to protect people from polluters into one that protects polluters from people."

Rep. Henry A. Waxman (D-Calif.), a chief architect of the law and one of Congress' most outspoken critics of the Council on Competitiveness, accused the administration of "carving the heart out of the new Clean Air Act that the president used to point to as the high point of his domestic program."

The rules announced yesterday will allow factories to make "minor" modifications in their emissions without prior government approval or the need to get new permits. What constitutes a "minor" change varies widely by type of pollutant and geographical area, but critics say the rules could allow plants to increase their emissions by thousands of tons per year.

Although the EPA would have 45 days and state government would have 90 days to reject such minor changes, in the interim the facility could continue to emit more pollutants than allowed under its permit. An earlier draft of the rules required industries to give states seven days' notice of changes—a requirement that was dropped from the final version.

An administration spokesman said yesterday that President Bush would likely veto the Treasury, Postal Service and General Government appropriations bill if it includes the competitiveness council funding cut.

The amendment, sponsored by Rep. David E. Skaggs (D-Colo.), strips from the appropriations bill the $86,000 requested by the president to pay the two part-time staff members who run the council. It also would prohibit any other money from being used to support the council or any similar organization.

The subcommittee appropriations bill would not prohibit the White House from temporarily detailing employees from other federal agencies to work as council staff.

4   Primary Ingredient of Acid Rain May Counteract Greenhouse Effect

WILLIAM BOOTH

September, 1990

S cientists have gathered preliminary evidence that sulfur dioxide, an air pollutant produced by burning some fossil fuels and a major contributor to acid rain, also may be cooling the planet and counteracting global warming.

The perverse possibility that one pollutant may tend to cool the Earth while others tend to warm the planet is likely to present policy-makers with a profound dilemma over what to do about the apparently linked problems of global warming and acid rain.

Among researchers, there is growing awareness that man-made aerosols such as sulfur dioxide may play a significant and perhaps crucial role in climatic change. The findings have emerged in a spate of recent papers and technical presentations. Scientists who study climatic change have begun to suspect that while "greenhouse" gases trap heat and warm the planet, other pollutants may be counterbalancing the greenhouse effect. Sulfur dioxide appears to be having this effect by modifying clouds so they become more effective in shading the planet from the sun's rays and bouncing sunlight back into space.

Because of this effect, scientists fear that reducing acid rain may accelerate potential global warming. But failing to control acid rain will cause further harm to lakes, streams, and forests and will perhaps only delay an inevitable worldwide warming that, instead of coming slowly over the next century, could arrive quickly in what one scientist called "a tremendous heat pulse."

The magnitude of the "sulfur effect" remains unknown, but some climate experts believe the cooling produced by sulfur pollution may offset half the warming that most scientists predict will be caused by all greenhouse gases or by carbon dioxide alone.

"It's the wild card in climate change," said Robert Cess of the State University of New York in Stony Brook.

"It's the million-dollar question," said George Kukla of Columbia University's Lamont Doherty Laboratory.

Until recently, researchers focused on the potential warming effects of carbon dioxide, whose concentration in the atmosphere is steadily increasing because of the

120

burning of fossil fuels and destruction of forests. Carbon dioxide and certain other gases act like the glass in a greenhouse, letting sunlight reach Earth's surface but then holding in the heat that results. Experts fear that the accumulations of such greenhouse gases, which is expected to double in the next century, will trap more and more heat and raise temperatures several degrees, setting off a chain of events that could include rising sea levels and mass extinction of plants and animals.

But now many scientists are beginning to turn their attention to a group of man-made aerosols, microscopic particles that drift in the air—especially sulfur dioxide, which is produced by the burning of fossil fuels, in particular coal.

When sulfur dioxide enters the atmosphere, the particles act as reflectors that bounce some of the sun's rays back into space. Robert Charlson of the University of Washington and colleagues have suggested that the cooling effect of the particles alone might mask half the warming caused by greenhouse gases.

However, sulfur dioxide particles also serve as the nuclei on which water vapor condenses to form tiny droplets. The result is a droplet of dilute sulfurous acid. Because the droplets are smaller than normal, the clouds look brighter. The brighter the clouds, the more they reflect the sun's energy back into space.

Cess of the State University of New York compares the effect to sugar. A bowl of powdered sugar, with its tiny particles, is a brighter white than a bowl of ordinary granular sugar. "It is the same with clouds," Cess said.

There is also evidence of increased cloud cover. James Angell of the National Oceanic and Atmospheric Administration, for example, reported recently that cloud cover over the United States appears to have increased between 2 and 3 percent since 1950.

"There's some pretty convincing observations from satellites that the aerosols are producing thicker clouds and they are reflecting more solar radiation back into space," said Kukla of Columbia. "We are finding that the cooling impact of man-made aerosols could be quite large."

Scientists have long suspected that sulfur affects climate. Benjamin Franklin, for instance, noted that sulfur aerosols produced by volcanoes reflect sunlight back to space. Franklin went on to suggest that the eruption of Laki Volcano in Iceland produced unusually cold weather in 1783–84. The much larger Tambora eruption in Indonesia in 1815 resulted in the "year without a summer," although much of that was due to the clouds of pulverized rock and other material ejected into the atmosphere.

Paul Mayewski of the University of New Hampshire and colleagues have examined ancient ice from Greenland and reported last month that the quantity of man-made sulfur in the atmosphere now rivals the amount of sulfates produced by the large eruptions of Laki and Tambora and trapped in the ice.

"One way to look at it is that acid rain is good. But I'd never want to say that," Mayewski said. "But I would say that we're underestimating the effect of warming due to carbon dioxide because we're dumping so much sulfur dioxide into the system." Back in the 1970s, researchers referred to the sulfur loading in the atmosphere as a "human volcano." In recent years climate experts thought the carbon dioxide would overwhelm the sulfur pollution. Now researchers are not so sure.

Based on observed sulfur loading in the atmosphere and computer climate simulations, Tom Wigley of the University of East Anglia in England has reported that sulfur clouds already may have "significantly offset the temperature changes that have resulted from the greenhouse effect."

If the sulfur effect is real, it would explain a central enigma in the climate record. Despite the fact that the world on average appears to have warmed about 1 degree Fahrenheit in the last century, the warming has not been uniform all over the world. From 1940 through the 1980s there has been little or no net warming in the Northern Hemisphere, where most of the Earth's people, industry and sulfur pollution are. There has, however, been warming in the Southern Hemisphere.

"Some of us have been wondering where all the warming was," said Patrick Michaels of the University of Virginia. "The sulfur explanation ties up a lot of disparate facts. It shows why the Northern Hemisphere hasn't warmed and why the Southern Hemisphere has shown more of a magnified greenhouse effect." Unlike the buildup of greenhouse gases such as carbon dioxide, which stays in the atmosphere for tens of years and spreads evenly over the globe, the effects of sulfur are short-lived and regional. The sulfur particles stay aloft for only days or weeks before they fall to the ground in rain or snow.

If the role of sulfur cooling proves to be large, and this is still far from certain, some researchers say it could be necessary to continue burning fossil fuels in order to produce sulfur dioxide to fight the carbon dioxide-driven warming.

"I would not be surprised if somebody suggested concentrating fossil fuel power plants on the eastern margins of continents, which would put a lot of sulfates into the atmosphere, which would rain out over the oceans, which have a tremendous capacity to absorb acidity," Michaels said. This plan would make sense, Michaels said, because the prevailing winds blow from west to east.

Such a scheme, however, flies in the face of arguments by many researchers and environmentalists who have been calling for a commitment by the United States and other governments to reduce their fossil-fuel burning.

James Hansen and Andrew Lacis of the National Aeronautics and Space Administration recently reported that continuing to produce sulfur pollution to slow warming would commit earthlings to "a Faustian bargain." Sooner or later, the two said, "fossil fuels would run out, whereupon a huge carbon-dioxide-induced warming would begin." This is because the carbon dioxide gas would linger for decades after the sulfur dioxide particles precipitated out.

Moreover, Hansen and Lacis said that while sulfur pollution may play a significant role in climate change, its effect probably will not be large enough or last long enough to prevent warming entirely. But the magnitude is not yet known. Given the uncertainties, the two scientists recommend limiting the ultimate magnitude of the "experiment" by taking steps—such as increasing energy efficiency and slowing deforestation—that make sense on other grounds regardless of whether global warming takes place.

5　Is Acid Rain a Tempest in News Media Teapot?

Study Questioning Harm Gets Little Attention

HOWARD KURTZ
January, 1991

According to "60 Minutes," a $500 million federal study released last fall "takes the conventional wisdom about acid rain and shoots it full of holes."

According to the *Wall Street Journal,* the report's findings "expose the irresponsible hysteria fomented by environmental groups and encouraged in hyperventilating media reports."

According to Reed Irvine, head of Accuracy in Media, a conservative media watchdog group, the report discredits "the fearmongers in the environmental movement, the government and the media who have been portraying acid rain as one of those critical problems that must be solved if we are to save the country, civilization and the planet."

The focus of this rhetorical assault is a 10-year study by the National Acid Precipitation Assessment Program (NAPAP) an inter-agency body created by Congress in 1980 to settle once and for all the debate over the effects of acid rain caused by industrial pollutants.

In three volumes weighing more than five pounds, the study concluded that acid rain, while still a problem, has caused far less damage to the nation's forests and lakes than previously estimated. Yet the report was virtually ignored by *The Washington Post* and given scant attention by most other major news organizations last year, even while Congress debated and approved new acid rain controls that will cost as much as $4 billion a year.

Some reporters say privately that it is difficult to write stories that debunk the conventional wisdom of environmental activists, whom the press treats more deferentially than industry spokesmen and other lobbyists. Striking the right balance is particularly difficult on complex science stories, where reporters must rely on "experts," many of whom have ideological axes to grind.

In that regard, critics say the recent acid rain report on CBS's "60 Minutes" was one-sided because correspondent Steve Kroft included none of the prominent scientists who believe the NAPAP report understated the dangers of acid rain.

Why Was Report Ignored?

Still, the question remains: Why has the most expensive acid rain study ever conducted received so little media coverage? Several factors are involved:

The findings were released in dribs and drabs, in "draft" reports and at scientific conferences, from 1987 through last year, so journalists were never presented with a dramatic "new" report.

The report's credibility was hurt by charges from some scientists and environmentalists in 1987 that NAPAP softened its findings under political pressure from the Reagan administration.

By the time the massive "external review draft" was released in September, Congress, the Bush administration, the utility industry, and environmental lobbyists had cut most of their deals on revising the Clean Air Act, and the news coverage was largely being driven by politics. "The legislative debate was essentially over before the report came out," one reporter said.

The study contained such voluminous data that many groups found something to support their view. While industry officials hailed the report, William G. Rosenberg, assistant administrator of the Environmental Protection Agency, said it "did show a lot of damage" from acid rain and that skeptics are "interpreting the data the way they want to. There are people in the tobacco industry who still argue that tobacco is not so bad."

The NAPAP report said there was "no evidence of a general or unusual decline of forests in the United States and Canada due to acid rain," except for red spruce trees at high elevations.

While acid rain is helping to damage aquatic life in about 10 percent of eastern lakes and streams, the study said, the number of lakes damaged has remained unchanged since 1980. The report also said that acid rain is contributing to the erosion of buildings and statues and is reducing visibility in the eastern United States.

Michael Weisskopf, *The Washington Post's* environmental reporter, said he was on vacation when the report was released. But he said many people involved in the acid rain debate told him it had little news value.

"Just because the government threw a load of money at this thing doesn't mean it's a precious document," Weisskopf said. "There are enough reports on this subject to line your bookshelves. . . . This is such a dynamic city, with so many pressure groups pushing their point of view, you don't have to do investigative reporting to find these reports. If they are truly important, they are promoted and put forward."

New York Times reporter Philip Shabecoff noted in a story last March that the NAPAP report "has come under criticism from some distinguished scientists that are reviewing it," some of whom charged that the program "ignored a number of studies suggesting serious air pollution problems." But he reported that other experts found the conclusions "essentially right."

Shabecoff said last week that the report gave "fairly short shrift" to a body of evidence compiled by highly regarded scientists that acid rain is one of a number of air pollutants that at high altitudes . . . have led to substantial death and deterioration of trees." Nevertheless, he said, "It should have been given more serious treatment by the media. There's a lot of good science in it."

The controversy was rekindled two weeks ago when James R. Mahoney, NAPAP's director, said on "60 Minutes" that news accounts had presented an "extreme" view of acid rain. Mahoney, in an interview, criticized *The Washington Post* for its acid rain coverage, saying the paper "has never, ever carried any article about this program, even though *The Post* holds itself out to be the paper of record about government business. . . . If you read only *The Washington Post,* you wouldn't know this program existed." Weisskopf did mention the NAPAP study in a November story, and *The Post* published two articles about it in 1987.

Mahoney also said his report never claimed "that acid rain is no problem. We find damage to lakes, damage to materials, risk to public health. . . . The only question is how much reduction is appropriate and how much benefit are we going to get from the cost."

Documenting the Obvious

David Hawkins, senior attorney with the Natural Resources Defense Council, called the study "a very extensive exercise in documenting the obvious." For example, he said, NAPAP focused on lakes that are constantly acidified, while three times as many lakes are subject to occasional acidification.

Hawkins, who appeared on the "60 Minutes" broadcast, said the program "essentially took industry's characterization of NAPAP's findings. . . . Many scientists were shocked by the one-sidedness of the scientific presentation."

All the "60 Minutes" guests except Hawkins supported the NAPAP findings, including Sen. John Glenn (D-Ohio), conservative columnist Warren Brookes, an Ohio coal company president, Mahoney and Edward Krug, chief watershed scientist at the University of Illinois, who worked on the study.

Even some of the NAPAP participants disagree on its findings. Twelve scientists who worked on the study have charged in a letter that "60 Minutes" misrepresented the report's data on water damage. And the EPA said in a statement that Krug has "limited scientific credibility" and "is well outside the mainstream of scientific consensus on the acid rain issue."

Krug called the EPA's criticism "peculiar" because the agency was part of the NAPAP study. He said that despite "outrageous claims" by some scientists, the effects of acid rain are less than 1 percent of what people were claiming 10 years ago."

Jeff Fager, a "60 Minutes" producer, said the segment was meant to focus on "a very expensive government study which wasn't paid much attention."

Solid Waste: Where Should We Put It All?   5

A s most municipalities are painfully aware, the question of what to do with solid waste—garbage—is becoming increasingly costly and problematic. In recent years the federal government has begun regulating the design and use of landfills, largely in an attempt to protect underground water supplies. It is no longer a matter of merely finding a valley nobody wants, backing the garbage trucks up to it and filling it with the discarded "tailings" of modern society. To reduce this burden, the recycling alternative has come of age—not without problems of its own. We are collecting far more recyclables than we are able to process, and the ultimate solution may lie, not in "recycling," but rather in throwing away less. In the meantime, the garbage trains, garbage barges, and interstate garbage "deals" will continue.

Articles 1 and 2 in this chapter address the heated issue of interstate dumping of solid waste. Article 3 reports on community resistance to the prospect of new landfills, even though they would mean economic development and a greater tax base. Article 4 addresses the growing concern municipalities have over the dumping of residential yard waste into their landfills.

Article 5 reports on McDonald's efforts to reduce the amount of solid waste generated by its fast-food outlets. Finally, in an attempt to demonstrate the diversity in the solid waste problem, Article 6 describes the difficulties being created by climbers trashing Mount Everest.

1   Garbage on the Rails

Out of Sight, Out of Mind; Containers Mask Cargo as Trains Roll Past D.C.

DON PHILLIPS
December, 1991

E very day, nearly all the trash created by the 840,000 people of Bergen County, N.J., is carried down the East Coast to a giant landfill south of Richmond in Charles City County, Va.

Although the trash rolls within sight of the Capitol and the Transportation Department, past Crystal City and through Alexandria, it is barely noticeable because the trains are neither unsightly nor smelly. The refuse essentially is "stealth" garbage: out of sight and out of mind, stuffed in a new generation railroad container that masks its cargo.

The shiny aluminum containers, designed to travel on flat cars or on a truck chassis, have cryptic markings, with the only real clues to their contents being the name of the company in small letters and the letters "BULKBOX."

"We have people calling sometimes saying, what have you got in those cars? Those are really neat-looking cars," said Steve L. Watson, assistant vice president for industrial and solid waste of CSX Transportation, which owns the rail line over which the Bergen County trash travels for the last part of its journey.

Few environmental issues have become as emotional as the interstate hauling of garbage. A rising tide of trash is spilling over state lines as East Coast urban areas run out of landfill space and out of environmentally acceptable options for disposing of their waste locally or transporting it long distances to a decreasing number of approved landfills. The Environmental Protection Agency estimates that 14,000 of the nation's 20,000 landfills closed between 1978 and 1988, and half the rest will close by 1995, some under fire from state and federal officials.

For years, trucks and barges were the only means of transporting municipal, solid waste and sewage sludge. But with ocean dumping of sludge banned, and communities becoming angrier at truck congestion on highways and around landfills, waste companies are turning to railroads.

Long-distance trains now run from New York and New Jersey to Texas, Illinois and Virginia and from Seattle to rural Oregon. Plans are under way to transport most of the Los Angeles basin's trash to the Mojave Desert or to abandoned mines.

More than trash is moving. Dried New Jersey sludge is hauled in sealed containers to the Midwest, and a considerable amount of New York sludge probably will move long distance by rail when New York ends its ocean sludge dumping by July 1. New York is considering several rail routes, including shipping sludge to midwestern plants that would convert it to fertilizer.

Railroads and the major waste companies have learned a lesson from the days of the "poo-poo choo-choo," a dripping, smelly trainload of 5,000 tons of Baltimore sludge that was rejected by Louisiana, Mississippi and Arkansas and became a national joke before returning to Baltimore in late 1989.

Railroads once paid little attention to the special needs of garbage, leaving that detail to the shipper, but soon realized "if you end up with homeless solid waste, whose name gets in the paper?" said E. L. Wefel Jr., manager of Conrail's solid waste business group.

Waste companies and railroads have discovered that the same equipment that protects high-tech freight—the sealed rail container—can be used to conceal garbage from the public eye—and ire—and at the same time provide a cost-effective alternative for moving garbage long distances.

"It's kind of amusing since you're carrying something that's useless," said CSX's Watson. "Just in the last year, we've seen a realization that you can't treat garbage like garbage."

The Bergen County-Charles City County train is run by Chambers Development Co., of Pittsburgh, using equipment developed by Intermodal Technologies Inc., one of several companies that have entered the garbage-by-rail equipment business. Every evening, eight flat cars, each carrying four containers, leave the sprawling Bergen County Baler Transfer Station at North Arlington, N.J.

Each of the 32 containers, about half the size of an average truck trailer, carries as much trash as the average individual creates in 27 years.

Economics drives most decisions to ship garbage by rail; when the distance is more than 400 to 500 miles, trucks are more expensive. But the desire to avoid truck traffic is a major element in nearly all decisions to ship garbage by rail. The Bergen County train, for example, removes 80 truck trips a day from Interstate 95, and that will grow to up to 200 a day when containers of incinerator ash are added in January.

But even when garbage is being shipped a short distance railroads can be attractive when there are reasons to shield communities from garbage trucks. The city of Roanoke and surrounding communities have contracted with Norfolk Southern to haul all the area's trash to a landfill only 32 miles away in Smith Gap because trucks would have to traverse mountainous back roads through peaceful back country communities.

Montgomery County plans an 18-mile container train run from a Shady Grove loading station to a proposed incinerator at Dickerson, a plan tied up in court battles. "The roads out to the site are very rural roads, and we don't want to increase truck traffic," said Robin Depot, project manager for the Northeast Maryland Disposal Authority.

The largest single movement driven largely by public relations is the Seattle trash train. Seattle's garbage rolls down the scenic Columbia River Gorge to a landfill in north-central Oregon partly because local groups objected to truck traffic in the gorge. The white containers are washed after almost every trip.

"That's the way you tell our train, they're the cleanest containers out there," said Devera Uhl, Union Pacific Railroad's product manager-consumer products.

Although environmentalists would prefer that the garbage not move at all until every possible scrap is recycled, they tend to view rails as a lesser evil than trucks.

"The more trucks you have on the road, the more congestion and the more air pollution you have," said Daniel J. Weiss, Washington director of the Sierra Club's Environmental Quality Program. "In the long run, it may cost less to society to ship by rail than by truck."

According to the EPA, Americans produced 179.6 million tons of solid waste in 1989, a total estimated to reach 216 million tons by 2000.

About 13 percent of solid waste was recycled in 1989, the EPA said; most of the rest ended up in landfills. Recycling will grow, but not by enough to end the need for more landfills.

The rapid shutdown of landfills will be accelerated by a new EPA regulation that puts restrictions on landfills beginning in September. They must have double layers of liners inside clay barriers and pipes under the liners to capture water that leaches through the trash. They must be continuously monitored, and the area around them will have to be managed for 30 years after the last trash is dumped. The rules affect not only new landfills but also any landfills that continue in business.

Most experts say that the great expense involved in building landfills will mean that the country must build regional megalandfills in rural areas to take trash from several surrounding states.

"We see the [rail] business growing greatly because of the new rules," said George Stern, president of the Chicago & Illinois Midland Railroad, which serves a major landfill in Illinois.

But the states that have been the major recipients of other states' trash are trying to punch holes in that scenario. Indiana, West Virginia and Pennsylvania have all but declared war on New York and New Jersey, which account for 53 percent of the trash that crosses state lines.

These states have attempted to take action to slow or halt the flow of interstate garbage, but courts repeatedly have ruled that the Constitution's Commerce Clause forbids one state from banning another state's garbage or charging higher fees for out-of-state garbage. The Constitution reserves that power strictly to Congress.

Led by Sen. Dan Coats (R-Ind.), who made out-of-state trash a major plank in his last campaign, the states are turning to Congress to give them the power to halt the westward and southward flow of garbage. Trash promises to be the major environmental issue of 1992 as Congress faces a rewrite of the Resource Conservation and Recovery Act.

In an effort to block or tone down the "not in my back yard" sentiment in Congress, waste management companies and railroads formed the Environmental Transportation Association, which wants to persuade Congress that regional landfills can be located in politically acceptable areas.

The Bergen County train and the Chambers landfill in Charles City County are designed to prove that trash disposal can be environmentally and politically sound. Despite initial protests, the mostly rural Virginia area has come to appreciate at least one aspect of the dump. "Tipping fees" from Chambers have allowed the county to build a new school system while cutting taxes.

County Administrator Fred A. Darden said that some people near the landfill were "madder than heck and I don't blame them. Nobody likes to have a landfill there, even our own." But he pointed out that the county supervisors who ran for reelection in November won, and the landfill, somewhat to his surprise, was not a major campaign issue.

2   Proposal to Curtail Interstate 'Pass-the-Trash' Contracts Foments Senate Oratory

HELEN DEWAR
July, 1992

The Senate would like to be regarded as the "world's greatest deliberative body," capable of lofty discourse on war, peace and other profound matters. But the truth is that nothing moves senators to impassioned oratory more than garbage.

For the better part of the past two days, the Senate debated—at times fiercely—a bill that has euphemistically been entitled the "Interstate Transport of Municipal Solid Waste Act of 1992."

In ordinary language, that means not-in-my-backyard, or, more specifically, as senators from largely rural states kept telling the New Jersey senators, take your garbage and stuff it in your own landfill.

"The game of pass-the-trash must end," said Sen. David L. Boren (D-Okla.), whose state is among the reluctant trash importers.

New Jersey is exporting its garbage only because "our landfills filled up with the garbage that came from our neighboring states" and because New Jersey is trying to clean up its own environment, complained Sen. Bill Bradley (D-N.J.).

At issue was the latest effort by Sen. Dan Coats (R-Ind.) and his allies to allow states to reject other people's garbage. Two years ago, the Senate approved a proposal to allow states to ban unwanted garbage from outside their borders, only to lose the provision in a House-Senate conference. This year, several senators banded together in an attempt to reach a compromise that would allow states to restrict new garbage-dumping contracts while leaving existing contracts in force.

But Coats contended that many existing contracts were open-ended or indefinitely renewable, meaning that states like Indiana would continue to be treated as the nation's trash dump.

So he proposed an amendment to allow states to cancel existing private contracts, prompting hours of oratory before a new compromise was negotiated to permit contract abrogations after seven years.

The saga of what senators called the "P.U. choo-choo," the garbage-loaded New York train that rumbled around the Midwest earlier this month before it was forced to return its pungent load to New York, was a favorite of the ban-the-trashers.

"While some of my colleagues had the opportunity of enjoying New York City, the Big Apple, over the recess, the state of Missouri was threatened with the apple cores," said Sen. Christopher S. Bond (R-Mo.) as he traced the itinerary of the "40 cars of rotting, maggot-filled trash" around Illinois, Kansas and Missouri.

"For two weeks, it simmered and boiled in the hot sun with plenty of rain to moisten it and keep it nice and juicy," he said, hardly missing a single sickening detail. "Fortunately, the trash train kept on moving," he said. "Ultimately, it went back to New York City, where it should have been dumped in the first place."

A little sensitive about the image of New Jersey, New York and other garbage dumpers, Sen. Frank R. Lautenberg (D-N.J.) sought to "set the record straight about New Jersey," becoming as lyrical in his own way as Bond had been in his way.

Not only does New Jersey rank "among the top states in developing patents," but it has "more horses per square mile than any state in the country," Lautenberg claimed. Anticipating the amazement of colleagues who had not noticed many horses or pastures along the New Jersey Turnpike or Amtrak rail line to New York, Lautenberg tried to explain. "We may not have a lot of horses. But we do not have a lot of square miles either."

Bradley saw the issue from a different perspective: trash-bashing as a political issue.

"You stand there . . . in front of the television cameras and say, 'I stopped the garbage, elect me,'" Bradley said. "That is, until next year, of course, or the year after that, or the year after that, when you want to export the garbage because your state is filled up and now you need to export. But that will be down the road. 'I will not have to worry about that. I will be reelected.'"

3   Even Cash for Trash Fails to Slow Landfill Backlash

Public Resistance Widens U.S. Garbage Gap

MICHAEL WEISSKOPF
February, 1992

S hunned for years, Yorkshire had a rare suitor last summer. A company wanted so badly to move into this sleepy village that it came bearing lavish promises: jobs, property tax breaks and an economic development package worth more than $1 million a year.

It seemed like a last chance to arrest the rigor mortis of Yorkshire, to modernize a town of 3,805 people that has no sewage system, no occupants for empty plaza shops, no entertainment outside a drive-in movie and no future for its educated youth. Wells are running dry, and one of the fire trucks is 29 years old.

But given the choice, residents overwhelmingly rejected Browning-Ferris Industries (BFI) and its plan to build a regional landfill for nontoxic waste in the rolling pastureland southeast of Buffalo. Despite the powerful incentives, they were unable to trash their town.

The day after the decision, BFI officials closed their storefront on Main Street and left town with another pink slip in hand. Since July 1990, they have traversed the burgs and backroads of New York in search of a community "partner" willing to host a landfill for a share of the profits. So far, they are batting zero.

New York is no exception. The rejection of BFI's trash-for-cash deal by an obscure hamlet like Yorkshire illustrates the depth of Americans' aversion to landfills. Once, every town had a garbage dump somewhere on its outskirts to bury the banana peels and tin cans of daily domestic life. Overflowing and under-protective by today's standards, they are shutting down at an alarming rate: Fewer than 4,000 of the 14,000 landfills nationwide in 1977 are still open, and the number is expected to drop to 1,800 by the turn of the century.

Larger, modern facilities are coming on line, but such ribbon-cuttings are rare events in Northeast, Mid-Atlantic, California and Great Lakes cities. For every U.S. garbage bier that has opened since 1986—usually after years of protest and litigation—six have closed, according to recent industry statistics.

The trash backlash has all the fury of previous campaigns against nuclear plants and hazardous-waste dumps. In fact, landfills are far less menacing depots for "solid waste," the universe of mostly innocuous household and commercial garbage. But in an era of environmental horror stories from Love Canal in New York to the Exxon-Valdez oil spill in Alaska, the NIMBY (not-in-my-back-yard) syndrome breaks out even when communities confront the specter of low-level pollution.

It could not have come at a worse time in the history of U.S. trash, which is fast proliferating even as its burial grounds diminish. The average American dumps 4 pounds of garbage every day, up from 2.6 pounds per day in 1960, and roughly twice the per capita rate of Japan, according to U.S. government studies.

In an effort to close the garbage gap, BFI and other large landfill operators are opening their wallets to demonstrate the profit of a little pollution. Some companies pledge college scholarships, others offer to build community centers and new sewer systems or pay huge "host fees" for every ton of trash hauled.

The payoff can be big. "If you're the only landfill in the area, you've got a monopoly," said Jay Busbee, who edits a newsletter published by a solid waste consultant in Alexandria. "It's a very aggressive fight between all the major disposal companies."

As BFI is discovering, however, it is a buyer's market. Even Yorkshire, where opportunity rarely knocks, reacted with "the ultimate slammed door," said Philip S. Angell, assistant to the chairman of BFI. "We were told to get out of town, politely, but it was still out of town."

BFI never expected a red carpet. The waste management company had tried four times since the mid-1980s to site a landfill in New York, taking the conventional route. It quietly optioned land, announced its plans and braced for the public uproar. The firm was sued to keep it from moving into one town. A company official needed police protection at a public meeting in another town. And after investing millions of dollars and years of effort, the company emerged empty-handed every time.

The "community partnership" program was born out of that frustration and a new realization: The main reason people fight landfills is a sense of powerlessness in the decision of whether and where to put one.

Under "principles" of the program announced 20 months ago, BFI chairman William D. Ruckelshaus, who twice headed the Environmental Protection Agency, pledged not to even look for a site until a town formally voted to host a landfill and its officials negotiated a package of profit-sharing benefits.

New York seemed like a ready proving ground. Only 130 landfills were receiving trash last year, down from 294 in 1986, according to the Legislative Commission on Solid Waste Management. To compensate, the state has become a major trash exporter, sending 20 percent, of its 20 million tons to other states in 1991. And with half of today's dumps scheduled to close by the mid-l990s, the problem is expected to worsen. Just three new facilities have been permitted since 1986.

Paradoxically, more and more trash exports have come from upstate, where sparsely populated communities have plenty of land for landfills. Much of Yorkshire Township is wide open space in western New York dotted every few miles by a frame farmhouse.

As other states follow New York's pattern, trash exporting is expected to have a limited market. The District of Columbia and 16 states exported more than 100,000 tons each during 1989 and 1990, mostly to the South and rural parts of the Midwest, according to the National Solid Waste Management Association.

Yorkshire was one of hundreds of towns to receive letters and videotapes from Ruckelshaus, inaugurating the partnership program. His pitch was straightforward: New York was heading for a serious garbage crisis; BFI wanted to build modern, environmentally safe landfills; and communities willing to host one would benefit as full shareholders.

"It's your choice," Ruckelshaus emphasized in a letter to town officials.

More than a dozen towns were interested enough to be briefed by BFI officials. But only Yorkshire's town board has gone so far as to invite in the landfill salesmen to campaign for the community's support.

They rented space in the plaza, held open houses at the Knights of Columbus hall and coffees at the firehouse. On display were models of the large landfill that BFI hoped to build on up to 500 acres and a list of the economic goodies in store for this shopworn, working-class town.

There were promises of up to 100 jobs in a town wracked by three major plant closings in recent years; $1.6 million in yearly fees, enough to cut local taxes of the average family by three-quarters; $100 million in construction expenditures, most of which would go to local workers and businesses; and $1.15 million in annual grants to foster the long-term economic development of Yorkshire, whose budget is $810,000.

"Most companies are coming in here looking for tax breaks or what we could give them to start up," said town supervisor Frank Smith. "BFI came in and said, 'This is what we can do for you.' That's why I took the hook."

But few of his constituents wanted to build their future on top of a garbage dump, even one as safe and modern as BFI promised. Two neighboring towns had waste disposal sites forced upon them unhappily. And opponents quickly organized here under the banner, "Keep Yorkshire a Hometown, not a Dumptown." Their campaign was based on fear of everything from noisy truck traffic to the shipments of detritus from less wholesome places such as New York City.

"It was not going to be disposable diapers," said Cindy Bradfield, a leader of the opposition. "What price do you put on your health and the health of your children? There are other ways to bring money into an area."

Solid waste is not supposed to be toxic, although it can include processed medical debris and ash of hazardous waste incinerators. Household batteries rust and leak lead. Plastic products break down and release a variety of hazardous substances.

But if landfills are built to New York standards, the nation's toughest, the release of wastes to the environment should be prevented.

Two liners made of plastic and clay are supposed to undergird the site, protecting ground water. A double system of pipes is to pump out any liquid seepage. And a layer of dirt covers the site nightly to keep out vermin.

BFI was willing to go even further to ease fears here by negotiating the source of the waste and excluding any undesirable contents, said Angell.

Still, the opposition mounted almost as soon as BFI opened its office in early July. By July 29, Bradfield enlisted 200 townspeople to pack a hearing, armed with information on the toxic contents of landfills and a map of the region. On it, she marked off the two nearby landfills and scrawled the words, "A Toxic Triangle?"

A week later, Bradfield presented the town board with the signatures of 70 percent of Yorkshire's 1,640 registered voters on a petition opposed to the BFI plan. She received a standing ovation from hundreds of people at the meeting.

The board voted 5 to 0 to ban landfills in Yorkshire, including BFI's.

Supervisor Smith said recently that by rebuffing BFI, voters killed the goose that may have laid a golden egg for Yorkshire. And, in the process, they passed up an opportunity to "do our share in solving the landfill problem. Not that we had the answer for the entire country, but maybe we could've done our part."

Sitting in her living room several months later, Bradfield acknowledged that by helping to block a landfill here, she transferred her fears—as well as her garbage—somewhere else.

"Maybe it's very selfish of me to say not in my backyard, but I don't want it here," she concluded. "Maybe there's a place where the economy is so bad, or people don't care about the quality of their land, and want it."

4   Much Ado about Yard Wastes

Area Governments Moving to Keep Clippings Out of Landfills

D'VERA COHN
June, 1993

T he tons of grass clippings and shrub trimmings that Washington area homeowners will bag this weekend and put out at the curb are increasingly unwelcome in local landfills.

Governments in the region are beginning to ban dumping of yard wastes as landfills reach capacity. Some communities are imposing added fees for picking up such waste. Others are offering incentives to encourage homeowners to recycle it—preferably in their own back yards.

For the foreseeable future, homeowners still will be able to put yard waste out with the garbage. But most will have to bag it separately from other trash, as they already do with newspapers, bottles and cans.

Branches, leaves and grass account for an estimated one-fifth of all garbage tonnage, and one-third of what homeowners throw out. In Fairfax County alone, more than 150,000 tons of yard waste are thrown out each year.

"It's a very important part of the waste stream, and it's important that we concentrate on reducing it," said Joan Rohlfs, a recycling specialist with the Metropolitan Washington Council of Governments.

Instead of being dumped in landfills, grass and leaves are being trucked to a growing number of government and private composting sites locally, where they rot into a rich organic soil additive that can be sold to recoup costs.

Yard waste will be banned next year at two of the area's biggest landfills, the Lorton regional facility and Montgomery County's landfill. Montgomery plans to impose a pickup charge for leaves and grass. Fairfax County, which runs Lorton, will require all garden waste in the county to be recycled and is looking for a composting site.

Charging fees for picking up yard waste can be controversial, as Falls Church learned when it imposed the area's first fee for yard waste pickup April 1.

Residents must buy special trash bags for garden waste at local stores and purchase stickers from local government that must be attached to the bags before pickup. The total cost is about $1 per bag. The bags, which each hold 30 pounds, go to a private composting facility in Loudoun County.

"Some people have not been particularly happy about the bag and sticker fee," said Annette Mills, the city's recycling coordinator. "Others are happy because they've . . . seen neighbors put perfectly good clippings at the curb for the landfill, at taxpayer expense."

Homeowner Jean Mess, of Falls Church, said she does not like the 30-pound bags, which she says are big and heavy when they are filled, "but I don't see any other way to do it."

As for the charge, "at first I didn't like the sticker thing, but I've gotten used to it," Mess said. "They're trying to balance the budget, and they're doing it in the most fair way possible."

S. N. MacPherson, who lives in the Falls Hill neighborhood of Fairfax County, said changes in yard waste pickup wouldn't be a hardship for her because she already has a compost pile and leaves her grass clippings on the lawn to add nutrients to the soil.

But, she said, "A lot of people live in town houses, and they have limited space. There's a point at which the county will have to pick up."

Loudoun County is trying another twist: Starting April 1, it began requiring yard waste to be sorted from other trash brought to its landfill and charging $50 a ton for disposing of it. The charge rises to $80 a ton in July.

"That's going to discourage people from bringing in yard waste, which is why we did it," said county recycling coordinator Steve Carfora. Local garbage haulers now take most yard waste to local composting sites, where fees are lower, he said.

Prince George's County and Prince William County also are trying incentives. Both counties permit yard waste to be left at composting sites at no charge, but fees to dispose of it at the landfill are $62 a ton in Prince George's and $49 a ton in Prince William. Many private haulers in both counties also require customers to bag yard waste separately.

The District has required residents to separate yard waste from other trash for several years. Leaves are taken to a mulching facility on Children's Island, but the city hopes to open a composting facility that will produce a more sophisticated soil additive that can be sold.

Maryland is discouraging yard waste dumping in landfills by banning loads that contain only yard waste beginning Oct. 1, 1994. The Virginia General Assembly passed a law this year to encourage compost sites by imposing less-strict permit rules than for other waste facilities.

As an alternative, localities are touting back yard composting, saying it's not as complicated, smelly or time-consuming as many people believe. They also promote "grasscycling"—that is, leaving the clippings on the lawn to act as a fertilizer.

"The best thing to do with yard waste is to keep it in your own back yard," said Jeff Dunckel, Montgomery County's yard waste program manager. "That's one of our key messages: Not only is it the environmentally right thing to do, but it saves you time."

Fairfax has given away 1,200 free bins to participants in composting workshops. It is encouraging gardeners who recycle their own debris to put up signs telling their neighbors that they are volunteers in the YIMBY (Yes, In My Back Yard) program. Arlington is studying how to promote more use of mulching lawnmowers. Montgomery plans to offer discount bins next year and has trained more than 100 "compost commandos" to offer workshops.

One is Cynthia Bennett, of Rockville, who signed up because her own efforts produced stinking, clumpy, slow-to-rot compost piles.

Now, she said, "I get just beautiful stuff. . . . It's almost spiritual. The compost pile is never dead. There's so much life that comes out of it. It's a wonderful thing."

The next wave of composting could be in Loudoun, where a 12-acre, $10 million indoor mechanized facility to process food scraps has been proposed west of Dulles International Airport. Natural Recycle Systems, an affiliate of Eastern Oil recyclers, wants to compost more than 150 tons a day, plus lesser amounts of yard waste and possibly sewage sludge.

For the avant garde in home composting, there's always vermiculture, the four-syllable equivalent of a worm box. In the recycling office on the fifth floor of the Montgomery County office building, Paul Kaldjian keeps bloodworms in a blue plastic recycling bin to turn leftover fruit and vegetable scraps from lunch into good dirt.

The worm box, Kaldjian said, does not smell. And the worms stay put, he said, sifting his hands through the stew of dirt, orange rinds, banana peels and apple cores in the blue bin. Two-inch red worms slithered from view.

"They like to stay where their food is," he said. "They're not going anywhere."

5 Big Mac Attacks Trash Problem

McDonald's Aims for 80 Percent Reduction of Its Solid Waste

MARTHA M. HAMILTON
April, 1991

McDonald's Corp. and the Environmental Defense Fund yesterday announced a series of steps designed to reduce by up to 80 percent the amount of trash that the fast-food giant sends to the nation's landfills. Many of the changes will be where the customer won't notice them—behind the counter, where 80 percent of the hamburger purveyor's trash is generated in the form of throwaway supply packaging.

But McDonald's said it is implementing or testing other measures that the customer will see, including replacing bleached paper bags with brown ones; reducing the size of napkins; offering reusable coffee mugs; and providing condiments such as catsup in bulk dispensers instead of throwaway pouches.

None of the moves is as dramatic as its decision last November to phase out the durable polystyrene clamshells it had used to package meals.

But McDonald's and Environmental Defense Fund officials said that the steps represent something more meaningful—weaving waste management into the corporate fabric. "We had to quit looking for the grand slam. We had to start looking comprehensively," said Keith Magnuson, McDonald's director of operations development. "We've taken solid-waste management and made it a day-to-day part of our business."

The company also will begin to recycle corrugated cardboard containers; require suppliers to include more recycled content in paper products; test composting food waste; and replace the disposable supply containers with reusable containers.

McDonald's said the moves would reduce the trash generated at its 8,500 outlets by up to 1.6 million pounds a day.

"This is not a marketing ploy," Magnuson said. "It was never intended to be. If that was our intention, we could have stopped on Nov. 2," when the company announced it would stop using plastic foam containers.

Taking steps to reduce the solid waste that it generates probably will neither cost nor save the fast-food giant money in the long run, according to Magnuson and EDF senior scientist Richard A. Denison.

Although eliminating throwaway products used by McDonald's customers would eliminate only about 5 percent of the waste produced by the company—recycling accounts for the rest of the saving—Denison said that reducing waste at the consumer level is important to get consumers to focus on the solid-waste dilemma.

Other steps that McDonald's is considering at the consumer level include using reusable lids on salads. Some of the lids would walk out with carry-out customers, but lids on salads served to customers eating in the store could be removed before the salads crossed the counter to make it easier to collect them for wash and reuse.

In addition to testing large pump-style dispensers for condiments, McDonald's is also looking at using larger throwaway pouches so that drive-in and carry-out customers won't need to take more than one.

Requiring more recycled content in products used by McDonald's also has an important ripple effect, Denison said.

"We try to make what they want to buy," said Ira Stone, senior vice president for communications for Stone Container Corp., which produces brown paper bags and white bags made of 65 percent recycled paper for McDonald's and other customers. "McDonald's is certainly one of the ones that drove us toward developing the product."

The task force formed by McDonald's and EDF last August to study the solid-waste issue went further than either side envisioned in producing solutions, both organizations said yesterday. Representatives of other environmental groups said the results look promising.

6   Everest: A Mountain of Trash

Even Corpses Clutter Peak's Worn Trails

JOHN WARD ANDERSON
June, 1993

As Santosh Yadav inched her way toward the top of Mount Everest, the world's highest peak, each toe-kick into the ice and lunging hand grasp was a fight against howling wind, blinding sun, thin air and bitter cold.

Yadav had left camp 11 hours earlier—at 1 A.M.—and now, after a grueling 2,000-foot ascent, she fought back physical and mental fatigue, pushing on, ignoring frostbitten hands, trying to become the first woman to scale Everest twice.

Suddenly, 120 feet short of the summit, she was forced to stop. "There was a traffic jam, like Delhi," she said in an interview, describing the queue of climbers she encountered at the top of the world on May 10. That day, a record 40 people, including Yadav, 26, a member of the Indo-Tibetan Border Police, conquered Everest. Climbers reported hearing shouts to hurry up, that others were waiting.

Even more disconcerting than the crowd, Yadav said, was the garbage left behind by years of climbers who do not lug their trash down the mountain. Environmentalists estimate 50 tons of rubbish are scattered across Everest as well as a more macabre form of litter—the corpses of dozens of climbers, some of which have lain there for years.

A vast snowfield called South Col, a camp at 26,500 feet that is the most popular staging area for the final assault on the top, is littered with ripped tents, butane stoves, old sleeping bags, empty food containers, ropes, broken tent poles, more than 2,000 oxygen bottles and about 20 corpses.

For every five people who have climbed Everest, at least one person has died in the attempt, including 34 in the past five years. Some bodies are carried down but others are left behind, usually because of risks involved in retrieving them. T. C. Pokharel, former head of the Nepal Mountaineering Association, estimates that more than 100 corpses are on Everest.

"The rubbish and bodies make you stop and think: 'This is one hell of a dangerous place to be,'" said Col. Michael Kefford, the British defense attache in Katmandu, who led his country's unsuccessful 1992 attempt up the difficult west ridge. "Perhaps it focuses the mind so you don't become part of the pile."

"The problem of too much rubbish and too many people is quite substantial," said Sir Edmund Hillary. He and Tenzing Norgay became the first climbers to reach the summit of Everest, on May 29, 1953. Hillary, who has called for a five-year moratorium on climbing the mountain, added, "At a minimum, everything should be put in a single pile, rather than spread around carelessly, and the bodies could be buried underneath it."

Once considered the pinnacle of human achievement, climbing Mount Everest now is almost commonplace—for those with sufficient personal wealth and physical endurance. Aided by better equipment, commercial guides and discovery of the easiest route to the top, more than half of the 600 people who have climbed Everest since 1953 have done so in the last five years.

Across the Himalayan range, which stretches from northwest Pakistan through northern India, Tibet, Nepal and Bhutan, some of the poorest governments in the world are debating how to exploit their chief asset—the mountains—without polluting both the landscape and the indigenous cultures.

Nepal's relatively unregulated, open-door policy is cited as a prime example of how not to do it.

"With so many aspiring to go to Everest, and with the money Nepal gets, they did not heed advice for rationing the expeditions," said M. S. Kolhi, president of the Indian Mountaineering Foundation and chairman of the Himalayan Environment Trust. "They became so enamored of the money that was coming in, they were tempted to put no stop to it."

"When Mount Everest opened for the first time, we were not paying much attention, and it was done very helter-skelter," admitted Nepal's tourism minister, Ram Hari Joshi, who said Nepal earns about $70 million a year from tourism—24 percent of all its foreign exchange. "We realized very late we'd have to do something to stop it."

Now, the country has limited the number and size of expeditions. Previously, as many as 20 teams, some with dozens of climbers and up to 1,000 porters, jammed the slopes at the same time. Beginning this fall, only four expeditions with a maximum of seven climbers each will be allowed in a season, and the teams must use different routes.

Nepal also is gradually opening other mountains to tourists, hoping to relieve the pressure on Everest and the popular trekking area around Mount Annapurna.

While mountaineers and environmentalists largely praise the initiatives, a huge increase in permit fees to climb Everest—from $10,000 per expedition to $10,000 per person—has drawn intense criticism.

"Raising fees that substantially is making climbing Everest a rich man's sport, even more so than it is already," complained Hillary, a New Zealander, who said he hopes Nepal will keep its promise to pour 40 percent of the revenue into cleaning and preserving the area.

Ang Rita Sherpa, whose deceptively frail frame belies the fact that he has climbed Everest a record eight times, said raising fees and limiting the size and number of expeditions could greatly reduce the standard of living and increase unemployment in local communities of Sherpas that serve climbers.

Noting that commercial outfits charge a minimum of $35,000 to lead people up Everest, Kefford said it already is a rich man's sport. "The trouble is, the mountaineering fraternity does not have the ability to regulate itself," he said. "It's all about ambition and ego and commercialism."

Before the fee increase, there were 50 teams on a 10-year waiting list to climb Everest. Officials said they doubt the price increase will reduce the mountain's popularity. Bachendri Pal, leader of an all-woman team from Nepal and India that put 18 climbers on top this spring, said 90 tents from more than a dozen expeditions were pitched at 22,000 feet.

Environmentalists and climbers said a cleanup funded by the World Wildlife Fund has cleared the most unsightly garbage from the 17,552-foot base camp. But they said the problem is as bad as ever above the camp, where retrieving the trash is physically demanding, time consuming, costly and dangerous.

According to mountaineers, cleanup is complicated by moving glaciers, opening and closing crevasses, winds and snowfalls. Garbage visible one day is hidden the next. Bodies that vanish into a crevasse may surface down the mountain years later. Stories abound of climbers rounding a corner or scaling a ledge to find a corpse blocking the path.

Katmandu's *Himal Magazine* said the body of one climber could be seen for six years above South Col, her face gone but her hair blowing in the wind. Then in the mid-1980s it disappeared, only to emerge a few years later, thousands of feet below.

The corpses left on Everest belong to mountaineers and high altitude porters who may have succumbed to any of a variety of mishaps—avalanches, falls, altitude sickness, hypothermia, exposure or exhaustion. Many people simply disappear, such as George Leigh Mallory, the mountaineer who said in 1923 that he wanted to scale Everest "because it's there"—and who vanished at around 28,000 feet in 1924. His body has never been found.

Like the garbage abandoned on Everest, the corpses are preserved by the extreme cold and can take years to decompose. Often, they are left by teams forced to abandon everything and retreat to lower altitudes in the face of fierce blizzards that can rip tents to shreds and bury a camp under three feet of snow in a matter of hours.

Under such circumstances, according to climbers, no one risks their own life carrying a body down the mountain, and once a body is abandoned, it might not be found again for years. Even in good weather, climbers are near exhaustion after the weeks of toil it takes to climb Everest, and they do not have the energy to haul a body down steep cliffs and across narrow ice bridges.

Much of the trash comes from an era when people were not environmentally sensitive, and when expeditions mounted militaristic siege-style assaults, using hundreds of people and tons of equipment. Today, a lightweight alpine style is more in vogue.

The garbage is not solely climbing equipment. In 1987, a 16-member American team left almost a ton of trash strewn about the base camp, including baseball bats, Frisbees, dozens of empty beer cans and liquor and champagne bottles.

"While it seemed that no cost had been spared to outfit it, every cost had been avoided in cleaning up after it," wrote adventure writer Robert A. Hutchison, who catalogued the debris in his 1989 book, "In the Tracks of the Yeti."

The Nepalese government now demands a list of an expedition's equipment and a $4,000 refundable deposit to ensure that none of it is left on the mountain.

Toxic Waste   6

The articles in this chapter deal with the problem of managing the tons of toxic waste that are released each day into our air, water, and land. As with the other areas of environmental concern, there is considerable controversy over the magnitude of the problem, as well as the strategies to attenuate it. Since the famous 1978 Love Canal episode, in which homeowners in Niagara Falls discovered that their houses were built over an old toxic dump site, and some of the more than 300 escaping chemicals were making their families sick, there has been an increasing public consciousness in the United States about what we are doing with our discarded poisons.

It is common knowledge that the Environmental Protection Agency and the Superfund for cleaning up hazardous chemical dump sites are woefully behind schedule; there is not much movement in the list of the 100 most dangerous sites. The Department of Energy has reported thousands of pounds of missing plutonium buried somewhere in Idaho. And the global dumping of toxic waste has reached scandalous proportions. The list of such problems goes on and on.

The first article in this chapter describes the difficulty residents in the Chicago area are experiencing with their attempts to remove toxic waste from their neighborhood. Articles 2 and 3 discuss attempts by government to deal with selected toxic waste issues. These are followed by Articles 4 and 5 focusing on financial and political realities that weaken government's resolve to deal with the toxins generated by U.S. commerce. Article 6 addresses the special risks women face from exposure to environmental toxins.

Another aspect of the toxic waste problem is the significant threat nuclear waste poses to countries that "joined the nuclear family." The former Soviet Union already carries a dreadful burden in this area, and Article 7 describes the crisis it faces in this regard.

1   Chicago's 'Toxic Wasteland' Breeds Blue-Collar Environmentalism

MICHAEL ABRAMOWITZ
November, 1992

To the casual driver, the shattered steel mills and landfills rising around the "Skyway" connecting Chicago and northwest Indiana are the remnants of a long-past industrial age. To people living in the shadows of the elevated highway, they are visible signs of a continuing environmental nightmare.

"We feel like we're living in an island of garbage," said Virginia Cap, 70, a 35-year resident of Hegewisch, a tightly knit, working class neighborhood on the far southeast side of Chicago.

Cap exaggerates only a little. Hegewisch borders what is arguably one of the nation's most polluted areas, a six-square-mile region known as Lake Calumet, named for the shallow lake and marshes that have been Chicago's official dumping ground since the mid-19th century.

By the city's count, the Lake Calumet area has 51 landfills and dump sites, more per square mile than any other region of the country, according to environmentalists. In addition, thousands of tons of chemicals, sludge and other pollutants have been dumped illegally, creating what Mayor Richard M. Daley has termed a "toxic wasteland."

Such contamination has helped to create a thriving grass-roots environmental movement amid what seems an unlikely, blue-collar setting. Far from the stereotype of environmentalists as yuppies in Birkenstock sandals and L. L. Bean shirts, this assortment of schoolteachers, factory workers, public-housing residents and young activists has struggled for more than a decade to fight polluters and the waste industry.

Their rallying cry is simple and pointed: "No Dumps, No Deals."

In recent years, the activists have enjoyed notable successes. They persuaded the late Mayor Harold Washington to ban new dumps and incinerators on the southeast side, and they focused attention on environmental problems at a Chemical Waste Management Inc. incinerator, shut down since an explosion damaged its furnace last year.

This summer, residents won what they considered their greatest victory when Daley declined to build the region's proposed third airport near Lake Calumet. His airport plan ignited anger on the southeast side largely because thousands of resi-

148

dences would have been demolished. Environmental activists said it would have destroyed valuable wetlands.

The Lake Calumet area was almost entirely marsh or swamp until the late l9th and early 20th centuries, when industrialists began filling in the area to build factories while discharging untreated liquid and garbage into its rivers and lakes.

The area became one of the country's most vibrant manufacturing centers, with giant steel and chemical plants taking root near easy access to Lake Michigan and a national railroad network junction in southeast Chicago. The region's fortune soured in the early 1980s with the decline of the steel industry and the loss of thousands of manufacturing jobs, which left behind empty plants and many environmental problems.

Today, one of the most curious aspects of Lake Calumet is that alongside heaping mounds of trash and abandoned buildings are stretches of prairies, marshes and open space that constitute the last place one can legally hunt in the city of Chicago.

On the banks of Indian Ridge Marsh, a visitor can watch the flight of the great egret, a giant white bird with a nearly four-foot wingspan. Seven endangered birds, including the egret and the black crown night heron, live in the vicinity of Lake Calumet.

Bud Polk, an amateur birder and a civic activist, said many workers grew up in this "urban wilderness" and are instinctively receptive to environmental concerns. "People may not be able to name a bird or a plant," he said, "but there is a deep appreciation."

Many residents have more basic concerns. Cap, a homemaker, said she began organizing after becoming fed up with the smell of steadily advancing incinerators near Hegewisch. "We couldn't open our windows," she said. "It stunk. Seven days a week, we were like prisoners in our own home."

Marian Byrnes, a retired public schoolteacher, tells of finding in her mailbox one day in 1979 a notice that the Chicago Transit Authority was planning a bus garage on 150 acres of beautiful open space in the back of her house. She helped to organize protests that blocked the garage and has been among principal organizers of protests against toxic-waste dumps, to the point of getting arrested during a rally blocking entrance to Chemical Waste Management's incinerator in 1990.

"We've been receiving the city's garbage for the last 100 years," said Byrnes, 66. "It's enough already, and it's definitely unfair for any more of it to come to the southeast side."

For state Rep. Clem Balanoff (D), who represents the region in the Illinois House, the issue struck home when he met several children with cancer during his first campaign for public office a few years ago. No one has documented a link between Lake Calumet's toxic waste and elevated cancer rates, but Balanoff and others have expressed strong suspicions.

They point, for instance, to state Department of Public Health studies that found higher-than-expected rates of lung and bladder cancer among area residents. "Cancer is something that touches the lives of just about everyone on the southeast side, whether it's your family, neighbor or child," Balanoff said.

Citizens in similar working-class areas nationwide have become increasingly vocal about environmental issues. Not only have such neighborhoods frequently been the target of industries that treat and dispose of waste, but national environmental groups also have often ignored local concerns while focusing on such national legislation as the clean air and water acts, according to Kevin Greene, research director for the Chicago office of Citizens for a Better Environment.

"You have a number of grass-roots groups emerging to deal with local problems in the absence of the [national] groups," he said. "The people were very frustrated. They decided to take matters into their own hands."

Not everyone is happy with the results. Mary T. Ryan, a vice president of Waste Management of North America Inc., which operates a landfill in the area, said activists focus considerable ire on the waste-disposal industry, which cleans up after the fact, rather than on large manufacturers that initially caused the pollution.

"I find that kind of amusing," she said. "Is it because these industries provide more jobs and are viewed more differently than we are?"

For all of their success in halting new landfills, activists have little to show in actual cleanup of spilled waste. Some experts said the price of a cleanup could reach $2 billion.

City officials said neighbors squandered a major opportunity to obtain a large portion of that money by opposing the new airport, because Daley had promised to set aside hundreds of millions of dollars for environmental cleanup. Now activists are promoting a long-standing idea to turn the area into a 2,400-acre ecological park.

Another obvious source of money, the federal Superfund program, has been unavailable to southeast Chicago because of a Catch 22: Superfund dollars are rare, so priority is given to cleanup sites where toxic contamination directly threatens drinking water.

No such link has been established here, although there are indications that groundwater beneath Lake Calumet, contaminated from years of environmental degradation, has been leaking into Lake Michigan, the source of drinking water for 5 million Chicago-area residents.

Rep. George E. Sangmeister (D-Ill.) recently obtained federal funds to study the possible link.

While an industrial revival occasionally appears to be underway around Lake Calumet, activists said business will never embrace the region until its environmental problems are solved.

"Businesses are reluctant to relocate here because of the potential liability," Balanoff said. "People understand that if we take care of the environmental problems, this is one of the only ways we're going to attract development."

2 Incinerators May Face Tougher EPA Standards

Hazardous Waste Burning Is Targeted

TOM KENWORTHY
May, 1993

The Clinton administration, facing a mounting political outcry over hazardous waste incineration, yesterday announced that it would temporarily halt the industry's growth while it seeks to impose tougher health and safety standards on existing facilities.

Promising to "immediately strengthen our program for the regulation of incinerators and industrial furnaces that burn hazardous waste," Environmental Protection Agency administrator Carol M. Browner announced a de facto moratorium on the licensing of new plants for 18 months.

During that time, she said, EPA would undertake an effort to reduce generation of hazardous wastes and to involve the public more in decision-making about incinerators. Another goal, she said, is to tighten the agency's regulation of 171 boilers and industrial furnaces now operating but awaiting final federal permits.

More stringent regulation, she said, could cut down on emissions of harmful byproducts of incineration such as mercury, lead and dioxins.

"The Clinton administration will use every tool under existing law to assure real change for the safest possible hazardous waste disposal," said Browner.

Browner's announcement came as opponents of a controversial new commercial Waste Technologies Industries (WTI) incinerator in East Liverpool, Ohio, have increased political pressure on the Clinton administration to shut down the facility, located close to the Ohio River and an elementary school.

During the presidential campaign and immediately after the election, Vice President Gore sided with the plant's opponents. But the new administration has done nothing to reverse a decision by the EPA late in the Bush administration allowing the plant to begin test burning and proceed toward full commercial operation.

Opponents of the WTI incinerator brought their protest to the White House on Monday, escalating a campaign to embarrass the Clinton administration for failing to live up to its pledge to keep the facility from operating. More than 50 people were arrested during the protest.

Browner and other EPA officials said the new policies and rules announced yesterday would have no immediate impact on the WTI plant, at least until its permit is due for renewal. The facility is in limited commercial operation after failing two components of its test burn.

"That's sort of like exempting Love Canal from Superfund," said Rick Hind, an official with Greenpeace, the environmental group that has helped lead the campaign against the WTI incinerator.

The most immediate effect of the new EPA rules would be felt at 171 industrial furnaces. Most of those are on-site disposal facilities run by waste-generating industrial plants and do not operate as commercial incinerators. But the group also includes 34 cement kilns that operate as commercial incinerators.

In a recent memo from Hugh Kaufman, an EPA hazardous waste official, Browner was advised that many of the boilers and kilns in this group are operated unsafely and violate air pollution regulations.

Browner said yesterday that the 171 facilities awaiting final federal permits would be required to conduct full-scale risk assessments of their operations, adhere to a new EPA emission standard for dioxin (a carcinogenic byproduct of incineration of some chemicals), and comply with tougher controls on the emissions of particulates of metals such as mercury.

The risk assessments would have to include possible indirect health effects through contamination of food and water supplies.

Other hazardous waste facilities, including 15 commercial incinerators that have full federal permits, would be subject to the new strictures when their permits come up for renewal. In addition to the 171 burners and industrial furnaces, the U.S. has 184 facilities classified as incinerators, most of which are operating under final federal permits.

Browner also said that the EPA, in cooperation with state governments, will undertake a reevaluation of the role of incineration in controlling hazardous waste, with the goal of reducing the amount incinerated from the current level of about five million tons per year.

Kaufman, a frequent internal critic of EPA, praised Browner yesterday for highlighting the issue of the safety of hazardous waste incinerators but said the announcement "was a nothingburger in terms of substance."

The EPA, said Kaufman. already has full authority to impose tougher regulations on existing incineration facilities at virtually any time, and does not have to wait for permit renewals. "There's nothing new here," he said.

3   Environmental Law Presses Compliance on U.S. Facilities

THOMAS W. LIPPMAN

December, 1992

S ome subjects can be found on everyone's list of early challenges President-elect Bill Clinton can expect to face: Somalia; the budget deficit; job creation. But as with any incoming administration, unknown monsters lurk in the bureaucratic deep.

Take the Federal Facilities Compliance Act.

This new law, signed by President Bush on Oct. 6, allows the states and the Environmental Protection Agency to impose the same environmental rules on federal government facilities that they do on private business and to sock them with stiff fines if they fail to comply.

The main target is the Energy Department's network of nuclear weapons factories, which have dumped toxic and radioactive materials into the soil and water for more than 40 years. But the law also applies to military bases and any other federal installation that discharges hazardous solid waste.

Penalties for failure to reach agreement with the states on long-term cleanup and compliance plans can be as high as $25,000 a day.

The enforcement clock, which sets dates when federal departments must submit information and compliance plans to the states, began running when the bill was signed. The Energy Department's deadline for delivering a compliance schedule comes up less than three months after secretary-designate Hazel R. O'Leary is to take office.

"We would administer the sanctions in the law against the federal government the same as we do against the private sector," said Thomas "Tad" McCall Jr., director of the EPA's Federal Facilities Enforcement Division. "The Bureau of Prisons, Department of Interior, Agriculture, they're all subject to it."

Dubbed the Eckart bill for its chief sponsor, Rep. Dennis E. Eckart (D-Ohio), the compliance act waives the doctrine of sovereign immunity to expose federal facilities to state environmental regulation. It envisions that states, working with EPA, will use the threat of fines and penalties to negotiate compliance agreements and timetables with federal agencies.

"Punitive enforcement actions" should be taken only if a federal agency fails to make a good-faith effort to meet negotiated timetables or fails to request enough money in its budget to carry out the agreement, an EPA-sponsored "Dialogue Committee" of federal and state officials and environmental activists recommended Nov. 25.

Agreements to comply are not the same thing as bringing facilities into compliance, which may take many years, experts said, but they are acceptable to state regulators and environmentalists because they are legally enforceable.

"Compliance agreements are not environmentalists' heaven, they are realistic steps," said Shira Flax, who has been studying the issue for the Sierra Club.

McCall said EPA is "talking with the states and our regional offices about how to go about doing this. EPA has to promulgate regulations on some of it, such as how munitions will be regulated." The Pentagon, he said, "is very concerned that we would start regulating ammunition storage" at potential hazardous waste cleanup sites.

The states are eager to force the Defense Department to clean up waste oil, toxic chemicals, explosives and other contaminants, he and other officials said, because they want to be able to use military bases as they are closed in defense spending cutbacks.

But the principal target of the law is the Energy Department's 12-state network of factories that produced the uranium, plutonium and nuclear warheads that underpinned the nation's strategic defense for decades. The department has estimated that it will take 30 years, and cost more than $100 billion, to clean up the mess.

At most of these sites, the department has stocks of "mixed waste," part radioactive material—regulated under the Atomic Energy Act—and part hazardous waste—regulated under other laws—for which no disposal technology has been developed, partly because of the legal confusion.

Under the new law, the Energy Department has a three-year grace period to develop mixed-waste storage and treatment plans acceptable to the states, which were not encouraged by its first proposal, published in the Dec. 3 Federal Register.

That notice read: "The Energy Department believes that a two-step process— development of a national plan followed by development of site-specific plans—is the most prudent and . . . viable approach to managing its mixed waste program." Most Energy Department sites are developing treatment and disposal plans on an "individual, site specific basis," the notice said, describing that procedure as a "high-cost, inefficient method . . . that may result in unnecessary duplication of efforts among sites."

This proposal, to develop a nationwide management plan first and site-specific treatment and disposal plans later, ran into immediate opposition when the department presented it to EPA and state officials earlier this month.

"We said forget it," McCall said. "It's going to be state-led, not DOE-led."

"The states gave DOE a clear message," according to Flax. "They rejected the national compliance plan. They said, start with site-specific plans and use those to develop a national plan."

"We think the Dec. 3 proposal is upside down," said Tom Curtis, director of the natural resources group at the National Governors Association. He said that the cleanup plan for each site must be tailored to the specific types of waste, the terrain, and the political climate of the state.

The Energy Department said in its Dec. 3 notice that it has 530,000 cubic meters of mixed waste at 37 sites, and is generating an additional 52,000 cubic meters yearly. Construction of a treatment facility can take five to 15 years, the department said.

Curtis explained that probably means treatment facilities will not be constructed at every site, so some states will have to accept waste from others—a process that could result in high-stakes interstate negotiations.

"This is going to be an extremely interesting exercise to watch unfold," Curtis said. He offered a hypothetical example: Idaho might agree to accept some waste now stored at the Hanford plutonium site in Washington state, but only if Washington agreed to take down some dams so salmon could return to Idaho's rivers.

4   Environmental Programs Getting Short Shrift in '93 Budgets

D'VERA COHN

March, 1992

One hundred thirty-seven tons of litter may not be picked up along Fairfax County roads next year. Montgomery County plans to hire no employees to enforce its tough new tree-protection ordinance.

Arlington County wants to cut in half the number of trees and flowers it plants.

All those environmental programs and more—from expanding recycling efforts to policing illegal dumps—are slated to be cut or postponed under 1993 budgets proposed by the area's county executives.

Many local governments are trying to save programs with user fees, such as Alexandria's proposal to charge a trash collection fee to single-family houses and Montgomery County's proposed tax to raise $10 million for storm-water-drainage improvements. But government officials say they do not dare cut environmental programs too deeply because the programs have strong public support.

"Environmental programs have a standing of their own, and we didn't have that 10 years ago," said Victoria Greenfield, a top official in the Prince George's County Environmental Resources Department. "Traditionally, environmental programs are the first things to bite the dust."

The area's most drastic environmental cuts are proposed in Fairfax County. Acting Executive Richard A. King's "doomsday" budget is an extreme blueprint that would be enacted if supervisors do not approve tax increases. It would close the county arborist's office, which enforces tree-planting requirements, turn over illegal dumping enforcement to the commonwealth's attorney and stop maintaining county property except to correct building code violations.

"This [arborist's] office has been on the hit list of the developers," said Ed Mainland, a tree activist from McLean. "If the arborist's office is out of the way, there isn't going to be anybody around to . . . enforce that law."

But even if Fairfax increases taxes, King still proposes to end county spending for roadside litter pickup, which supplements state efforts and picks up 137 tons of trash a year. He would stop payment for 38 community cleanup programs, and suspend county efforts to recycle more yard waste, a program already facing trouble because a composting site cannot be found.

Montgomery County Executive Neal Potter's spending blueprint would drop financing for the Energy Services Center, which gives advice to homeowners on how to conserve energy. Some funds came from utilities to compensate for past overcharges, a source that's now running out.

Potter's budget also proposes no new hiring to implement the county's tough new tree ordinance. Until officials agree on how to pay for garbage-disposal programs amid declining revenue, Potter proposes to suspend plans to recycle more yard waste through composting and to delay a program that would encourage tenants in commercial and apartment buildings to recycle more.

"The composting program is a key target the county needs to focus on," said Neal Fitzpatrick, of the Audubon Naturalist Society. "I'm concerned."

Prince George's County Executive Parris N. Glendening will announce his budget later this month. Greenfield said the county may drop one of its three household hazardous-waste collection days, when homeowners can drop off used batteries and leftover pesticides. For the second year in a row, the county will not pay for spraying against gypsy moths, which damage trees.

District Mayor Sharon Pratt Kelly wants to tighten spending for the city's tree-planting program, while at the same time planting more trees than in past years, something environmental groups believe is unlikely.

"We're proposing to do as much or more with less," said Richard Hebert, a spokesman for the Department of Public Works.

In Arlington, proposed trims would eliminate the residential street-sweeping program to save $99,000, and reduce by half the numbers of trees and flower beds planted annually. Valerie Lemmie, the county's top environmental official, said Arlington hopes to get a state or federal grant to make up the loss in street-sweeping money.

After Loudoun County supervisors turned down their budget request, park officials are relying on donated supplies and volunteer labor to plant up to 65 acres of trees in a new park in Purcellville, according to park director Cindy Welsh. So far, however, county supervisors have turned down requests to pay for an access road to the new Franklin Park, so the public may not be able to get in.

Alexandria officials say they plan no such cuts. Budgets have not yet been released in Anne Arundel and Howard counties.

5 Some Toxic Substance Rules Being Dropped

Administration Did Not Appeal Court Decision

FRANK SWOBODA
March, 1993

R egulations governing hundreds of toxic substances at workplaces from dry cleaners to large factories will be watered down or eliminated today as a result of a Clinton administration decision not to appeal a federal court ruling.

The administration decision leaves nearly 400 hazardous substances, ranging from carbon monoxide to wood dust, either unregulated or governed by weaker standards that were voluntarily set in 1968 by the industries being regulated.

It also puts a cloud over the Labor Department's ability to regulate health and safety hazards in the workplace, and may give new impetus to legislation now before Congress that would overhaul federal job safety laws.

The administration had until yesterday to appeal a July ruling by the U.S. Court of Appeals for the 11th Circuit, which struck down permissible-exposure limits set by the Labor Department's Occupational Safety and Health Administration in the waning days of the Reagan administration. The appeals court said OSHA could not issue broad standards for hundreds of chemical substances, but had to justify scientifically each change in a standard.

OSHA has issued only 24 substance-specific health standards for the workplace since the agency was created in 1970.

The court stayed its ruling until yesterday to allow an appeal. According to the Labor Department, regulation of 212 chemicals will revert to the 1968 standards as a result of the ruling, 164 will be left unregulated and 52 will be unaffected.

An OSHA official said that under the old carbon monoxide standard, which will again govern the workplace, "You can die from carbon monoxide poisoning and still be within OSHA's limit."

The appeals court acknowledged the potential blow it was striking to OSHA's regulatory efforts. If OSHA is forced to continue using the case-by-case approach to standards setting, the court said, "It would take decades to review currently used chemicals and OSHA would never be able to keep up with the many chemicals which will be newly introduced in the future."

But the court said that if OSHA wanted to change the way it set standards, it had to go to Congress and get the law changed.

Labor Secretary Robert B. Reich issued a statement yesterday saying he understood that the Justice Department would not appeal the case to the Supreme Court. Labor Department sources said Reich was notified of this decision in a March 19 letter from Acting Solicitor General Lawrence Wallace. They said Reich had recommended the case be appealed.

A Labor Department source said few of the Clinton administration's top appointments at either the Labor or Justice departments were in place as the decision was being made.

"It may just have fallen between the cracks," he said.

Reich said he was "heartened by and supports the use of the innovative approaches such as those used by OSHA in developing the [tougher] standards."

The statement appears to give a boost to OSHA reform in Congress being pushed by organized labor. Under legislation introduced by Rep. William D. Ford (D-Mich.), chairman of the House Education and Labor Committee, OSHA would be able to use the broad standards-setting approach that the appeals court said it had no authority to use. The proposal would also require an automatic review of each standard every three years.

Organized labor has made changing OSHA one of its top legislative priorities in this Congress.

Peg Seminario, health and safety director of the AFL-CIO, said yesterday that labor did not push the Clinton administration to appeal the case because "we thought an appeal to the Supreme Court was unlikely to result in a different decision. We didn't want to have more bad law."

6 Many Toxins Target Women Specifically

SANDY ROVNER
June, 1993

W omen are uniquely susceptible to toxins in the environment, including pesticides and lead, leading to seemingly unrelated medical problems from cancer
to chronic fatigue syndrome, according to testimony at a recent seminar on women's
health and the environment.

"Although there are many principles of health research that are the same for
males and females, there are special susceptibilities experienced by women [and
children]," said Kenneth Olden, director of the National Institute of Environmental
Health Sciences (NIEHS) of the National Institutes of Health. The seminar was
sponsored by the Washington-based Society for the Advancement of Women's
Health Research.

Differences are due to female hormones such as estrogen and the physiological
changes brought on by menstruation and menopause. Interaction of these factors
with environmental toxins can lead to a range of disorders.

For example, chemicals like polychlorinated biphenyls (PCBs), organo-
chlorines (DDT), dioxin and other industrial byproducts all have estrogen-like
activity, said Olden and NIEHS scientific director John McLachlan.

Many of these toxins replace natural estrogen in cells, sometimes stimulating
the production of various hormones or blocking such hormones. The toxins often
lodge in fatty tissue—such as the breast—where they can influence cellular function
over decades.

A recent study of stored blood from 14,000 participants in the New York
University Women's Health Study found significantly higher levels of DDT in
women who developed breast cancer.

Target sites for estrogen, McLachlan said, include bones, brain, cardiovascular
system, liver, skin, uterus and vagina. Diseases related to estrogen include breast
and uterine disease, including cancer, as well as endometriosis, fibroid tumors,
premenstrual syndrome, reproductive dysfunctions such as infertility or lactation
suppression.

Exposure to lead usually occurs in the first few years of life. With treatment,
some of the immediate effects on the brain, other parts of the central nervous

system, kidneys and heart are reversible, said Ellen Silbergeld, University of Maryland epidemiologist and toxicologist for the Environmental Defense Fund. Still, some 90 percent of lead settles in the bones and is handled much as calcium is. This means that during pregnancy, lactation, and menopause, lead—with the calcium—is released from the bone back into the blood.

Lead levels in the blood of pregnant women, Silbergeld wrote in a 1991 paper, "change over pregnancy, and lead is rapidly transferred across the placenta to the fetus." She noted that women whose diets are low in calcium and Vitamin D will have "substantial bone demineralization" during pregnancy and lactation during which lead as well as calcium subsequently migrate into the hearts, brains and kidneys of both mother and fetus or infant.

During menopause, Silbergeld said, remobilization of lead reoccurs. "In postmenopausal women, compared to premenopausal women, there is about a 22 percent increase in blood lead levels." This again puts them at risk of lead's neurotoxic effects, she said.

7 In the Former Soviet Union, Paying the Nuclear Price

Radioactive Accidents and Dumps Sicken Generations

MICHAEL DOBBS
September, 1993

I t was the happiest day of Sergei Davydov's life: Aug. 29, 1949. The retired engineer still remembers the blinding flash and his "feverish joy" at the sight of a huge, mushroom-shaped cloud erupting over the desert of northern Kazakhstan. The Soviet Union, the world's first communist state, had become a nuclear super-power—and he had pressed the button.

In a squalid wooden hut 600 miles away in southern Russia, by the bank of the Techa River, Mavzhida Valeyeva remembers 1949 for a different reason. It was the year her health began to deteriorate dramatically. Along with practically all her neighbors, she now suffers from violent headaches and constant nosebleeds. Her blood is anemic. Her four children and five surviving grandchildren are all invalids.

It took Valeyeva more than four decades to make a connection between her family's devastating health problems and the Soviet Union's nuclear bomb project. In 1990, the Soviet government finally acknowledged that millions of tons of highly toxic radioactive waste had been secretly dumped in the Techa by a plutonium plant 49 miles upstream from Valeyeva's village, Muslyumovo. The river the villagers saw as a source of life was in fact a source of death.

"It would be better if they had never discovered this nuclear energy," said Valeyeva, who visited the river daily to collect drinking water and wash her family's clothes. "It would be better to be poorer, but at least to be healthy and give our children and grandchildren a chance of living a normal life."

The communist politicians who launched the Soviet Union on a program of breakneck industrialization and transformed the country into a military and political rival of the United States, believed that the natural resources under their control were inexhaustible. Yet future generations of Russians and Tatars, Balts and Ukrainians, Czechs and Poles will pay a heavy price for the hubris of their leaders. There came a point when nature simply rebelled.

Based on a two-month journey from the center of Europe to the Russian Far East, this is the third in a series of articles about the legacy of Marx, Engels, Lenin and Stalin. Today's article looks at the destructive impact that communism had on the environment in Russia—one of the scars left by the combination of totalitarian rule and socialist economics that will almost certainly take generations to heal.

The environmental catastrophe left behind by 70 years of communist rule is visible in poisoned rivers, devastated forests, dried-up lakes and smog-polluted cities. Some of these disasters, such as the evaporation of the Aral Sea following the diversion of rivers for an irrigation project, have permanently changed the contours of the vast Eurasian landmass. But, according to Russian scientists and ecologists, the most lasting physical damage will probably have been caused by the unleashing of nuclear power.

"Radioactive contamination is the number one environmental problem in this country. Air and water pollution come next," said Alexei Yablokov, a biologist who serves as President Boris Yeltsin's chief adviser on environmental matters. "The way we have dealt with the whole issue of nuclear power, and particularly the problem of nuclear waste, was irresponsible and immoral."

The scale of nuclear contamination in the former Soviet Union has only become clear over the last few years, with the advent of free speech and the lifting of censorship restrictions. In the wake of the 1986 Chernobyl catastrophe, Russians learned about other disasters, including a series of accidents at a plutonium-producing plant near the southern Urals city of Chelyabinsk between 1948 and 1967. They also learned about dozens of ad hoc nuclear dumps, some of which could begin seeping radioactivity at any moment.

The seas around Russia—from the Baltic to the Pacific—are littered with decaying hulks of nuclear submarines and rusting metal containers with tens of millions of tons of nuclear waste. Russia itself is dotted with dozens of once secret cities with names like Chelyabinsk-70, Tomsk-7 and Krasnoyarsk-26, where nuclear materials have been stockpiled. Unmarked on any map, they hit the headlines only when there is an accident. Vast areas of the country have been treated as a nuclear dump, the result of four decades of testing.

"We were turned into human guinea pigs for these experiments," said Bakhit Tumyenova, a senior health official in the Semipalatinsk region, the main Soviet nuclear test site until 1989. "They kept on telling us that it was for the good of the people, the Communist Party, the future. The individual never counted for anything in this system."

'A Pernicious Philosophy'

The testing of the Soviet Union's first atomic bomb in 1949 represented a huge achievement for a backward, semi-Asiatic country. It had mobilized vast economic and human resources, from the team of elite scientists who designed the bomb to the army of slave laborers who mined the uranium and disposed of the nuclear waste.

The two sides of the Soviet nuclear project—the epic achievements and the disregard for human life—are symbolized by the man initially in charge of it. Lavrenti Beria, the chief of Stalin's secret police, was a great organizer. But he was also a great destroyer, willing to obliterate any obstacle to achieve his goal.

"It was a heroic epoch," recalled Igor Golovin, a leading scientist and biographer of Igor Kurchatov, the head of the nuclear project. "We worked days and nights and really believed in what we were doing. The propaganda instilled the idea that the United States had the bomb and wanted to enslave us, so it was vital that we acquired our own nuclear weapons as soon as possible, whatever the cost."

Few of the scientists and engineers working on the project gave much thought to the dangers of radioactive fallout. After pushing the button that triggered the first nuclear device, Davydov rushed to the site of the explosion without any protective clothing or gas mask. He was later sick with leukemia for some 20 years.

"They gave me special injections, and it somehow stabilized. Now I feel all right," said the 76-year-old pensioner, proudly displaying a chestful of medals. "Personally, I think that all those people who demand privileges from the government because their health suffered as a result of these tests are just crooks and swindlers."

The idea that any sacrifice was justified in the effort to turn the Soviet Union into a superpower was a fundamental part of the communist ethos. ("You can't make an omelette without cracking eggs," Lenin liked to remark.) It permeated the nuclear project right from the start, and still exists to some extent among older people. The system elevated the state above ordinary individuals—and this was its basic flaw.

"The postwar generation was brought up with the idea that they should be ready to sacrifice themselves for the state. This was the philosophy of the time. It was a pernicious philosophy because it prevented any thought being given to ecological problems," said Natalya Mironova, an environmental activist in Chelyabinsk. "For many years we were unable even to discuss such matters."

Little attention was paid to such issues as nuclear safety and the training of responsible personnel. The manager of the Chernobyl plant at the time of the 1986 disaster had previously been in charge of a heating plant. According to officials, roughly 50 percent of the accidents in nuclear power stations and 75 percent of accidents on nuclear submarines are due to "human error."

This year alone, there have been at least three accidents at nuclear facilities in Russia involving the release of radioactivity. The government has been inundated with dozens of letters from scientists at both military and civilian nuclear facilities warning of "further Chernobyls" because of rapidly deteriorating working conditions and the departure of many highly qualified workers.

Into the Food Chain

For the 1,000 inhabitants of Muslyumovo in the southern Urals, the Soviet Union's experiments with the atom are a curse that will blight the lives of many generations. According to the local doctor, Gulfarida Galimova, four of every five villagers are "chronically sick." She says the effects of radiation have altered the genetic code of the local Tatar population, with the result that babies are often sick from birth.

"We do not have a future," said Galimova. "We have been so genetically harmed that our descendants will not be able to escape this curse. Patients come to me, and I know I can never cure them. Radiation has entered the food chain. Our cows eat radiated grass. The potatoes we grow in our back yards are poisoned. The only solution is to close this entire region off—and not let anyone come here for 3,000 years. But they won't do that, because there isn't enough money."

The 2.75 million curies of radioactive waste flushed into the shallow Techa was equivalent to half the fallout from the bomb that fell on Hiroshima, but nobody bothered to inform local inhabitants. In the late 1950s, signs were posted along the Techa warning people not to bathe in the river. The nature of the danger was never explained, so most villagers paid little attention.

In the early 1980s, Galimova first started noticing that something was terribly amiss with the health of Muslyumovo residents. Nearly 10 percent of births in the village were premature. Many of her patients were anemic. There was a high incidence of cancer. When she reported her findings to her superiors in Chelyabinsk, the problems were blamed on bad food and a lack of hemoglobin. She was accused of being a bad doctor.

What local people refer to as "the river illness" is now affecting the third and even fourth generation of Muslyumovo residents. Valeyeva's eldest son, Ural, 33, is mentally retarded. His three children—aged 6, 4 and 18 months—can barely summon up the energy to get out of bed. Another daughter, Sazhida, 29, has a chronic craving for chalk that has destroyed all her teeth. Her oldest son, Vadim, 11, has been sick from birth. Timur, 6, has chronic bronchitis and anemia.

It was not until April 1986 that Galimova finally guessed what was the matter. Chernobyl played a crucial role in convincing Mikhail Gorbachev and other Soviet leaders that the country's problems could not be solved without glasnost, openness. Discussion of ecological problems was no longer taboo.

When they finally came clean about the contamination of the Techa, the authorities also admitted two disasters involving the Mayak plutonium-producing plant at Kyshtym, some 60 miles northwest of Chelyabinsk. In 1957, a waste storage tank exploded at the plant, releasing 20 million curies of radiation. A decade later, a drought dried up nearby Lake Karachai, which had been used as a storage tank for 120 million curies of waste products from Mayak. High winds scattered radioactive dust over a wide area.

According to an official Russian government report released earlier this year, the three disasters at Mayak affected 450,000 people living in a contaminated region roughly the size of Maryland. The amount of radioactivity still stored at Mayak—much of it in insecure conditions—is equivalent to the fallout from 20 Chernobyl disasters.

Nearly 20,000 residents of the Chelyabinsk region were evacuated from their homes. By a tragic twist of fate, some of these people were moved from one high-risk region to another.

Valentina Lazareva, for example, was evacuated from a village near Mayak in 1957 as a 9-year-old orphan. There were rumors of an "explosion" at the plant, but nobody knew anything for sure. She spent the rest of her childhood in an orphanage in Brodokalmak, a village a few miles downriver from Muslyumovo. The children crossed the Techa every day on their way to school and drank water from a nearby well. In the summer, they would swim in the village.

"Now we are all sick," said Lazareva, who is 46 but looks much older. There were 32 people in my class. We have already buried five of my classmates. Another 10 are dying. But all are invalids, in one way or another."

Glasnost without Rubles

Today, there is no shortage of glasnost about the man-made environmental disaster confronting the former Soviet Union. But there is a desperate shortage of resources to do much about it. The amount of money the government has earmarked to clean up the Chelyabinsk region—roughly $20 million—is minuscule compared to the $40 billion to $60 billion cost the United States has projected for the cleanup of its main plutonium-producing facility, the Hanford nuclear reservation in Washington state.

In Razakhstan, which declared itself an independent state in December 1991 following the breakup of the Soviet Union, health officials say they are unable to provide even basic medical care to villages exposed to four decades of nuclear tests. The lack of basic health services has encouraged many people to turn to charlatans and faith healers for help. In Semipalatinsk—the site of 470 nuclear explosions, including 116 in the atmosphere, between 1949 and 1989—a Muslim preacher named Sary-Aulie has been attracting crowds of 10,000 with his promise to cure aches and pains through "vibrations."

"We can't do much for these people, so it's not surprising that they put their trust in charlatans," said Tumyenova, the regional health administrator. "The Semi-palatinsk test site served the entire Soviet Union. Now the other republics have gone their own way—and we have been left alone, sitting on top of a gigantic nuclear rubbish heap."

Pesticides   7

Rachel Carson's *Silent Spring,* published in 1962, dealt primarily with the indiscriminate use of pesticides in the environment and the harm to the ecosystem they were causing. More than thirty years later the issue is still with us; in fact, today's farmers are using far greater amounts of pesticides, fertilizers, weed killers, and so on, than were used in Rachel Carson's time. Although food production has increased greatly despite shrinking numbers of farmers and acres of farm land, we appear to be paying a heavy price for this increased productivity. It is well known that only a small percentage of the chemicals used in agriculture ever reach their intended targets; the leftovers linger to pollute land, water, and air. Further, chemical residues on or in the food we eat have often been linked to a variety of health problems. Identification of hazardous pesticides and legislation concerning pesticide use are complex issues involving the often conflicting interests of government agencies such as the Environmental Protection Agency, the Federal Drug Administration, and the Department of Agriculture on the one hand, and various farmer and food-marketing organizations on the other hand. To further complicate the issue, some chemicals such as DDT are known to be hazardous and their use is banned in this and other industrialized countries, but they often can be manufactured and exported, usually to developing countries. The people of those developing countries are, of course, then exposed to dangerous pesticides, but also people of other nations are exposed through imported products.

The articles in this chapter treat some of these problems associated with the use of pesticides and other chemicals in agriculture. The first article presents data on the extent of groundwater pollution caused by pesticides and suggests that pesticide use could be greatly reduced without lowering production. Article 2 discusses public concerns over food safety, and Article 3 describes the debate over use of pesticides for the sole purpose of marketing "pretty produce." Articles 4–7 focus on existing and proposed new laws concerning use of pesticides and health standards, including topics such as testing procedures and differential risks for children and women.

1   Drastic Cut in Pesticide Use Is Possible

Group Says Alternatives Such as Crop Rotation, Predator Insects Found Effective in Preventing Crop Loss

JAY MATHEWS
May, 1991

J im Durst stopped spraying insecticides on his tomatoes three years ago, yet they burst forth as round and red as ever.

Chemical pesticides have been banished from his 600 acres of tomatoes, melons and sunflowers near Esparto, Calif., one small sign of a turnabout in U.S. agriculture that a national environmental group said this week could cut pesticide use as much as 80 percent with no crop or income loss.

The report by the Natural Resources Defense Council (NRDC), the group that created a panic about tainted apples in 1989, was released Tuesday with favorable reaction from farmers and backhanded compliments from the chemical industry.

"I couldn't agree more with the report," said Durst, who controls harmful insects by growing plants that attract their natural insect enemies. "The problem with pesticides is that they are not very selective. If you spray, you kill everything," good bugs and bad.

Lawrie Mott, an NRDC biochemist and co-author of the report, said the two-year study marked the most ambitious effort "to attach hard numbers" to alternatives to heavy pesticide use, such as crop rotation, genetic improvements and predator insects.

The alternative technologies are available, the report said, but are being introduced slowly because interested federal agencies and environmental groups have not had resources to compete with chemical companies in distributing information to farmers.

Pesticides that helped to make American farmers the most productive in the world have become increasingly controversial as studies revealed pesticide contamination of groundwater, the source of drinking water for more than half of the U.S. population.

The NRDC cited a federal report showing 46 different pesticides in the groundwater of 26 states, although critics of such studies have noted only slight contamination rarely shown to affect human health.

Bob L. Vice, president of the California Farm Bureau Federation, said some of the NRDC report, entitled "Harvest of Hope," was based on "flawed information" and drew conclusions "not supported by research."

He endorsed its support of integrated pest management (IPM), a system of carefully monitored pesticide use combined with biological controls and other alternative methods, while noting that a study examining only a few farms may miss the impact of different soil and weather conditions.

Jay J. Vroom, president of the National Agricultural Chemicals Association, said his industry has supported IPM since 1972 and is sponsoring several efforts to keep hazardous chemicals out of drinking water.

Frank Zalom, director of the statewide IPM project at the University of California at Davis, said industry and government must make available more information on alternative methods.

Jennifer Curtis, principal author of the NRDC report, said her examination of university research, ongoing private studies and work on individual farms in California and Iowa revealed a potential for reductions in pesticides from 25 percent to 80 percent with no loss of crops or income.

She said tons of pesticides were sprayed on Iowa corn to eliminate just one pest, the corn root worm, which could be more safely controlled through crop rotation that disturbs the pest's life cycle.

Curtis cited several barriers to pesticide reduction. Chemical companies, she said, are very aggressive in getting pro-pesticide information to farmers, and growers of major crops such as corn and wheat risk losing significant federal subsidies if they substitute another crop in one growing cycle to reduce pesticide use.

The Environmental Protection Agency, she said, also has been slow to approve new pest-control substances made from plants and other safe, biological materials.

Although Curtis and Mott emphasized that they were not calling for conversion to organic farms like Durst's that forsake chemical pesticides, they endorsed a plea by organic growers that consumers judge fruits and vegetables on taste and nutrition, not appearance.

The Alliance for Food and Fiber, representing California growers who defeated last year's "Big Green" environmental initiative supported by the NRDC, congratulated the environmental group for what it called "a summary of the positive direction the industry has been headed for the past several years." Mott and Curtis estimated that more than half of U.S. farmers are attempting to reduce pesticide use.

2 Paradox over Produce Safety

Consumers Opt for More Fruits and Vegetables, Despite Worry over Pesticides

CAROLE SUGARMAN
May, 1992

D o Americans trust the safety of the food supply? Not as much as they used to, say two surveys released last week. Since last year, there has been a significant decline in the level of confidence, according to the Food Marketing Institute's annual Trends Survey.

Only 12 percent of consumers are completely confident that food is safe, and 60 percent are mostly confident. This is a 10 percent drop in the combined categories from last year, and the first time in three years that there has been any decline.

Nevertheless, Tim Hammonds, senior vice president of FMI, a trade association representing the nation's supermarkets, said he thought the finding was a "blip this year." The survey was conducted at the same time there was a lot of negative publicity on the issue of fish safety, Hammonds said.

When asked, "What, if anything, do you feel are the greatest threats to the safety of the food you eat?" The most common response was spoilage. Hammonds said that during a recession, it is not surprising to see a high level of concern over maintaining quality and freshness.

"When money is tight, people are much more concerned about what they have to throw away," he said.

From a list of potential health hazards, respondents chose pesticide and herbicide residues as the most serious, a category that has been No. 1 since 1986. "There continues to be a fair amount of publicity," about the subject, noted Hammonds. Consumers are "telling us it's a very real and continuing issue for them."

Antibiotics and hormones in poultry and livestock were viewed as the next most serious hazard, followed by nitrites in food and irradiated foods. Additives, preservatives and artificial coloring were next, showing a steady decrease from previous years.

Concern over food safety issues in general and pesticide residues in particular are consistent with another survey released last week, this one conducted for the Center for Produce Quality, an arm of the fruit and vegetable industry.

That survey found that 61 percent of consumers are concerned about pesticide residues, a 6 percent increase over 1989 and the peak of the Alar crisis. In March 1989, an environmental group released a report indicating that Alar, a pesticide then used on apples, was a potent carcinogen. Apple sales plunged, and some schools even stopped serving them.

Nevertheless, the produce industry survey showed consumers saying they eat more produce than they did last year. What's more, 86 percent said they were confident in the safety of fresh fruits and vegetables.

How can consumers be more confident and more concerned at the same time? And if they are concerned, why are they eating more produce?

Peter Sandman, director of the environmental communication research program at Rutgers University, said these findings indicate "a genuinely rational consumer" who believes the benefits of eating produce outweigh the risks.

"You have people whose attitude is, 'Produce is good for me and I eat a lot of it, and because I eat a lot of it, I want to be very sure it's safe.' Pesticide residues are a "big enough" concern for people to want it corrected, "but not big enough to change behavior," he said.

Among the other significant findings in the survey:

More than 75 percent of consumers polled agreed that current regulations do not sufficiently take into account the risk that pesticides may pose to children. Of those with children in their household, 85 percent said they were concerned that their "own children's health may be at risk because of pesticide residues on fresh fruits and vegetables;" 15 percent said they might reduce the amount of fresh produce they serve their children.

These findings are significant in anticipation of a National Academy of Sciences report on pesticide residues and children's health, which is due out this fall.

People were most confident in the safety of fresh fruits, vegetables and milk, followed by meat, eggs, poultry and fresh fish.

The gender gap has narrowed. While men are still more likely than women to believe that the benefits of eating produce outweigh the risks from pesticide residues, the difference is smaller. Women's confidence in the produce supply also increased and is now about the same as men's.

3 Growing Debate on Appearance's Sake

USDA, Consumer Advocates Divided over 'Pretty Produce' Pesticides

SHARI RUDAVSKY
September, 1992

D are you eat a peach?

As tempting as the fresh fruits and vegetables of summer might seem, they have become the focus of a heated debate between the Agricultural Marketing Service and consumer advocates.

The argument, which has raged this summer, centers on whether some pesticides are used only to improve the cosmetic appearance of produce or whether healthier produce would result if the industry eliminated the use of pesticides that contribute only to appearance.

Consumer advocates contend that some of the pesticides the agriculture industry sprays on plants serve only to enhance the physical appearance of fruits and vegetables—resulting in what they term the "pretty produce" syndrome.

USDA and industry officials respond that there is no "convincing evidence" that farmers use any type of pesticide exclusively to improve the appearance of their crops. Furthermore, agency and industry officials say, consumer—not agency—preferences drive the cosmetic standards, and what consumers say in market surveys may differ vastly from what they do in a supermarket.

The debate has proved largely fruitless, for neither side can point to conclusive research to support its contentions. Indeed, one of the few points on which all sides agree is that such research has yet to be conducted.

The 1990 Farm Bill mandated that such research should be carried out but included no funding to do so. USDA officials say the agency has not considered such research a priority.

Signed into law last month, the agriculture appropriations bill included $250,000 for research on cosmetic standards for fruits and vegetables.

And both sides continue to debate the question of whether the research needs to be conducted.

Public Voice, a consumer advocacy group, has no doubt as to its answer. Either further research should be conducted or pesticide sprayings that research has already identified as being done solely for cosmetic reasons should cease, the organization says.

"Do we know exactly what the impact is on consumers of eating a peach a day that has been treated by fungicide? No," said Allen Rosenfield, director of government affairs for Public Voice. "Do we have reason to believe there may be a health risk we can't assess successfully? Yes."

But Daniel Haley, an administrator for the USDA's Agricultural Marketing Service, said that in a time of limited resources, allocating money for research that might not yield conclusive results is not a priority. What makes this a particularly thorny research problem, Haley said, is the difficulty of separating pesticides' effect on produce appearance from simply killing pests.

In order for the USDA to alter its grade standards, research would have to prove such a pesticide-appearance link, Haley said. "We certainly can conclude that the linkage has not been established. We don't need to spend another 10 research projects to come up with the same allegations," Haley said. "We are not opposed to research in this area, we are merely opposed to prioritizing this issue in light of many other pesticide-related issues before us."

John McClung, vice president for government relations of the United Fresh Fruit and Vegetable Association, agreed that additional research would be extraneous. McClung called the debate on cosmetic standards "a tangent" of the larger, more important debate of how to reduce pesticide use.

"The real issues are whether or not pesticides are necessary, to what extent they are necessary, and whether they represent any risk to the consumer," McClung said. He finds the debate problematic, he said, because it implies that pesticide use poses a health hazard to consumers, which he said research has discounted.

Public Voice's Rosenfeld said that fear of finding links among cosmetic standards, pesticide use and health risks is what has prevented the USDA from pursuing such research. "I don't buy the argument that scarce resources are what's kept the USDA from doing this research," he said. "We've asked what they're afraid of; they are afraid of what they would find. That's why they're stonewalling."

4 EPA Issues List of 35 Suspect Pesticides

Action Might Spur Hill Efforts to Overhaul Food Safety Laws

TOM KENWORTHY
February, 1993

The Environmental Protection Agency yesterday released a list of 35 agricultural chemicals whose use could be prohibited under a recent appeals court ruling that struck down the agency's interpretation of a 35-year-old law that bans even trace levels of carcinogenic pesticides in processed foods.

Although EPA emphasized the list is not definitive, many of the chemicals named, as well as many more yet to be reviewed, eventually could be restricted or banned unless the ruling is reversed by the Supreme Court, Congress enacts new legislation or new scientific information is produced demonstrating they do not cause cancer.

The agency's disclosure of the list—which includes pesticides commonly used on fruits, vegetables, grains and other food products—is expected to spur efforts on Capitol Hill to undertake a comprehensive overhaul of food safety laws that many regard as outdated.

"NEPA does not believe that the [listed] pesticides . . . pose an unreasonable risk to public health based on available data," stressed EPA Administrator Carol M. Browne, who pledged to work with Congress, consumer and industry groups to develop a response to the decision by a federal appeals court in San Francisco last year.

At issue in that case was the EPA's most recent attempt to reconcile the conflicting demands of federal law, that apply different standards to raw and processed foods. One provision of law allows the government to balance a chemical's economic benefits against its health risks when applied to raw foods. But another provision of a 1958 law, known as the "Delaney Clause," prohibits the use on crops of cancer-causing chemicals whose concentration increases during the cooking or other processing of foods.

Four years ago, following the development of new technologies that allow detection of chemicals in unprecedentedly minute amounts, the EPA proposed a new standard of "negligible risk" for processed foods. It would have allowed use of cancer-causing pesticides if the risk did not exceed one additional case of cancer per million people resulting from daily exposure to the chemical over a lifetime.

But in a suit brought by consumer advocates and environmental groups concerned about pesticide use, the appeals court overruled the "negligible risk" standard last July, saying the EPA "has no discretion" under the old statute and must comply with the Delaney Clause's complete ban.

The Supreme Court is to decide next month whether to review that appeals court ruling.

Yesterday's publication of the list was the first official response to the decision by EPA as it seeks public comment on dealing with the ruling.

Representatives of the food industry and the environmental community expressed optimism yesterday that the listing would help to break a logjam in Congress over reassessing food safety and pesticide laws.

"This is an exercise in demonstrating just how outdated the Delaney Clause is," said Juanita Duggan, a senior vice president of the National Food Processors Association. "Congress acts when they have to, and maybe the court decision is that forcing event."

Al Meyerhoff, a senior attorney with the Natural Resources Defense Council, said the court's decision and the EPA's response was a graphic demonstration of the need for a "uniform approach" to food safety and pesticide regulation whose "principal goal should be reducing pesticide use."

5 Three U.S. Agencies Announce Joint Commitment to Cut Pesticide Use

TOM KENWORTHY and JOHN SCHWARTZ
June, 1993

The Clinton administration, anticipating the release next week of a major scientific study on the health effects of pesticides, yesterday pledged to reduce the amount of the chemicals used in U.S. food production.

In an unusual joint announcement by three agencies that in the past have sparred over agriculture and food safety policy, Secretary of Agriculture Mike Espy, Environmental Protection Agency Administrator Carol M. Browner and Food and Drug Administration Commissioner David A. Kessler said the administration is "committed to reducing the risks to people and the environment that are associated with pesticides."

"This is a very significant commitment," said Browner. "There has been a lot of inaction at the federal level."

At the same time they pledged to reduce pesticide use, the three officials sought to reassure the public of the overall safety of U.S. food supplies in what seems to be a concerted federal effort to dampen anxieties that may come with next Tuesday's release of a National Academy of Sciences report on pesticide risks to children.

Many experts believe that the report will conclude that federal standards, because they are based on adult dosages, may underestimate the health risks to children.

"We are not saying that food is unsafe," said Kessler. "What we're saying is that we can do better. There is no reason for a scare, and there is no reason for alarm. . . . There's no doubt that the benefits of fruits, vegetables and grains far outweigh the risks of residues of pesticides on these products."

In their joint announcement, which Kessler termed a "major landmark in the history of food safety," the three officials said they would carefully use the academy study, as well as another study by an environmental group scheduled for release on Monday, as the basis for legislative and regulatory initiatives to reduce pesticide use. About 900 million pounds of pesticides are used annually on U.S. food crops.

In addition to the overall goal of reducing pesticide use, the three officials said the administration would seek to promote alternative pest control methods (such as exploiting various natural biological processes), and change government regulations to make it easier for industry to develop and register safer pesticides. The regulatory and legislative changes to implement those goals are expected to come later this year.

The National Academy of Sciences report to be released next week is one of a number of developments that are expected to spur a thorough review this year of federal policies on pesticides.

EPA is grappling with a court decision last year invalidating its policy of permitting the use of chemicals that pose only a negligible risk of causing cancer. And Congress is considering legislation to establish a single risk standard for pesticides rather than the two different standards that now exist for the chemicals' use in processed and fresh foods.

Rep. Henry A. Waxman (D-Calif.), a sponsor of that legislation, yesterday hailed the administration announcement making reduced pesticide use a priority. "Implicit in this statement is the acknowledgment that pesticides pose a serious risk to the public health," said Waxman.

6   Pesticide Risk May Be Higher in Children

Citing 'Potential for Concern,' Panel Calls for More Stringent Federal Exposure Standards

CAROLE SUGARMAN
June, 1993

A long-awaited report released yesterday has found serious scientific and regulatory deficiencies in the way the federal government assesses the health effects of pesticides on infants and children.

The study, conducted by a committee of the National Academy of Sciences (NAS), concludes that far too little is known about how such chemicals affect the young, and that there is "potential for concern" that some children may be ingesting unsafe amounts of pesticides.

It recommends that when adequate data on a given chemical are lacking, "there should be a presumption of greater toxicity to infants and children." In such cases, the NAS panel called for exposure standards 10 times more stringent than would normally be applied.

But the study emphasizes that parents should not reduce their childrens' consumption of fruits or vegetables.

"The single most important point is that the current system for regulating pesticide residues for foods in the United States needs to be fundamentally restructured so that health concerns become the priority, especially when it comes to children," said pediatrician Philip J. Landrigan, chairman of the NAS committee that prepared the report.

Currently, the Environmental Protection Agency regulates pesticide levels by balancing agricultural benefits with health risks, based on an extrapolation from figures on average adult consumption. That system does not take into account the dietary patterns of children, who eat fewer foods and consume much more of certain foods per unit of body weight than adults, the panel concluded.

"The study notes that children may be more sensitive or less sensitive than adults, depending on the pesticide to which they are exposed." Landrigan said that in general, children may be more susceptible to pesticides than adults "for the simple reason" that children's organs and immune systems are still growing.

"To improve regulation of pesticides and increase understanding of how they affect children, the NAS panel urges federal regulators to:

> Use immature animals in addition to adult animals (usually rodents) to test for the toxicity of pesticides, to provide better information about how young organisms react to the chemicals.

> Conduct food consumption surveys at one-year intervals up to age 5, as well as surveys of children age 5 to 10 and 11 to 18. Surveys now use only broad groupings that do not reflect dramatic changes in dietary patterns at different ages.

> Increase sampling of pesticide residues from foods consumed by infants and children.

> Consider all sources of dietary and non-dietary exposure to pesticides, including drinking water and water added to foods, as well as air, soil, lawns, pets and indoor surfaces.

> Apply new statistical methods in estimating risk for children.

Numerous experts emphasized yesterday that the report's recommendations should not be construed as a call to throw away produce in the refrigerator.

"There's no reason for alarm, no reason for panic," Food and Drug Administration Commissioner David A. Kessler said yesterday. "Just because the food supply is safe doesn't mean we can't work to make it even safer."

The report, originally scheduled for release Tuesday, was made public on Sunday after excerpts appeared in the *New York Times*. Anticipation of the $1.1 million report—commissioned by Congress in 1988 and three years overdue—was generating so much anxiety that Clinton administration officials and the food and chemical industries had been planning months in advance ways to head off public panic. For weeks, organic food companies, environmental groups and food industry associations have been distributing press kits.

"This is a huge chunk of the economy that's very sensitive to panic-driven scares," said Jeff Nesbit, a consultant to the Grocery Manufacturers of America, a trade group representing the food industry. Annual revenue of the food industry totals more than $360 billion; agricultural chemical sales reach nearly $7 billion a year.

On Friday, the Clinton administration issued a statement announcing its commitment "to reducing the risks to people and the environment that are associated with pesticides." The joint announcement, made by the Environmental Protection

Agency, the Department of Agriculture and the Food and Drug Administration, included a pledge to promote alternative pest control methods and to make it easier for industry to develop and register safer pesticides.

That announcement, originally scheduled for Tuesday, was pushed ahead after an environmental group held a press conference Friday releasing the results of its own study. The Environmental Working Group, a nonprofit research organization, concluded that children can receive up to 35 percent of their entire lifetime dose of some carcinogenic pesticides by age 5, and that infants and children are routinely exposed to combinations of two or three (or in some rare cases, eight) pesticides per food. The group said that the health effects of these exposures are not known.

In a letter to the Environmental Working Group, John Peter Wargo, an associate professor of environmental policy at Yale University and a consultant to the NAS committee, urged the environmental group to refrain from preempting the NAS report with its own study. Wargo called the environmental group's study "primarily a piece of advocacy, not yet a work of science." Richard Wiles, the author of the environmental group's study, was formerly the project director for the NAS report.

Industry and environmental groups reached for comment yesterday supported the academy's recommendations, as well as the administration's commitment to reducing pesticide use.

"The academy's recommendations are very good news for consumers and the industry, said Jeff Nedelman, a spokesman for the Grocery Manufacturers of America. "It will help us achieve our goal of eliminating detectable residues in food." The National Agricultural Chemical Association said in a statement: "We will work with everyone to further strengthen the food safety system."

Wendy Gordon, program director for Mothers and Others for a Livable Planet, an environmental group, said that the agencies' joint announcement "signals a real change in direction."

NAS panel chairman Landrigan, of the Mount Sinai School of Medicine in New York City, said he was "very pleased" that the administration appeared to support the panel's findings. But he expressed concern that "the remedies proposed by the agencies are vague promises for actions for the future" and said he "didn't see anything that spoke to the here and now."

7 Relaxed Food Safety Rules on Pesticides to Be Sought

JOHN SCHWARTZ
August, 1993

The Clinton administration is preparing to ask Congress to relax a long-standing ban on cancer-causing pesticides in food. The move is part of a plan to revise food safety standards, administration officials said.

The most controversial part of the package is the new uniform standard for pesticide use in all foods, known as the "negligible risk" standard. It would prohibit use of pesticides that present a strong cancer risk and allow those that present a lesser risk. The cutoff point is still being debated but could amount to one cancer death per million.

That proposal would replace the Delaney Clause of the Federal Food, Drug and Cosmetic Act, which strictly prohibits carcinogens in processed foods.

The Delaney Clause is flawed, officials said, because it applies only to processed foods and left the EPA regulating different kinds of foods by different standards, some of which were considerably weaker than the new standard. A 1987 report by the National Academy of Sciences suggested moving to a broad-based risk standard. Legislation to that effect has been proposed by several lawmakers, including Sen. Edward M. Kennedy (D-Mass.) and Rep. Henry A. Waxman (D-Calif.).

The new legislation is being developed by the Environmental Protection Agency, Agriculture Department and Food and Drug Administration. Administration officials have spent much of this week briefing farming interests, chemical manufacturers and environmental groups and circulating a one-page "white paper" outlining the plan. The White House is seeking comment from different groups before proposing legislation, which could come as early as mid-September.

The package also calls for a complete review of pesticides against the new standard, new regulatory tools for the EPA to phase out chemicals that violate the standard and promotion of safer pesticides. The plan would ban export of pesticides that have been prohibited here. Such a move could break the so-called "circle of poisons," in which U.S. firms export dangerous substances to other countries, which then export their pesticide-grown produce back to the United States.

Environmental groups are opposed to any weakening of the Delaney Clause. "It's very difficult to conceive of a food safety plan that is worth its name if it doesn't contain a strong support for Delaney and an expansion of that concept, rather than a weakening of it," said Jay Feldman, executive director of the National Coalition Against the Misuse of Pesticides. "The so-called negligible risk standard is certainly not horrible, but it's not quite as good as a ban on cancer-causing pesticides," said Michael F. Jacobson, executive director of the Center for Science in the Public Interest.

EPA officials said that while the negligible risk standard might appear to weaken food safety, it was only part of a larger package that would make food safer overall. "The intention is to strengthen the nation's food safety laws," said EPA spokeswoman Loretta Ucelli. "Our goal is to move toward a health-based standard on residues, while at the same time find a way to move safer pesticides to market more quickly and remove unsafe pesticides from the market more quickly."

Representatives of the food industry, who have long worked to see pesticide restrictions loosened, voiced cautious support for the package. Jeff Nedelman, president of the Grocery Manufacturers of America, said, "The administration deserves some considerable credit and strong public support." Nedelman expressed hopes that the government would make the package preempt state laws, however, to avoid a patchwork of conflicting standards across the country.

On June 25, the administration announced a commitment to reduce use of pesticides and to promote pesticide-free, or "sustainable," agriculture, although officials said current levels of pesticide use did not present a public health threat.

Threats to the Water Resource: Groundwater, Rivers, and Lakes 8

M ost environmentalists claim that the threats to Earth's supplies of unpolluted waters present a far greater problem than some of the better known issues, such as the dwindling supplies of fossil fuels. Much of the world does not have safe water to drink, and with the rapidly increasing population this problem can only get worse. Aquifers, those underground bodies of water on which millions depend for drinking water and agricultural irrigation, are being depleted and polluted. The increasing problem of polluted oceans and bays and their decreasing ability to sustain commercial fishing is, of course, common knowledge and is covered in this chapter.

Two chapters are devoted to *Washington Post* articles in this arena. This chapter focuses on the problem of polluted groundwaters, rivers, and lakes. The first article discusses plans EPA made in 1988 to help protect U.S. groundwaters. The second article, written three years later, discusses how EPA may not be achieving its goal of groundwater protection. The next two articles provide examples of specific instances of reported problems with polluted drinking water. As an example of the cyclical nature of the government's efforts to deal with environmental problems, the fifth article reports on another EPA proposal to guarantee safe drinking water.

The sixth and seventh articles focus on one of the common threats to fresh water: the extensive use of lawn chemicals. Articles 7 and 8 treat the international problem of water pollution at the United States–Mexican border. Article 9 addresses the problem that Poland is experiencing with water pollution.

The final article reports on a plan to improve the environmental quality of the Great Lakes. This is the largest collection of fresh water bodies in the world and has for many years suffered from major threats to its ecosystems.

1   EPA Unveils Proposal to Protect Groundwater

A 'Yellow Light-Green Light' Pesticide Plan

MICHAEL WEISSKOPF
February, 1988

The Environmental Protection Agency announced plans yesterday to protect the nation's underground drinking water supply from pesticides by setting limits on their levels in groundwater, restricting their use in areas "vulnerable" to contamination and banning them once they exceed the prescribed limits.

In a proposal open to public review, the EPA unveiled its long-awaited strategy for controlling pesticide pollution of the underground streams that irrigate crops and serve as the source of drinking water for half the American population.

With up to 60 pesticides—many of them carcinogens—found in the groundwater of 30 states, the agency has come under increasing pressure to draft a plan. Although there are laws regulating the quality of drinking and surface water and use of pesticides on crops, none comprehensively addresses pesticides in groundwater.

"The actual and potential contamination of our nation's groundwater resources by pesticides poses one of the most critical and difficult environmental concerns of this agency," Assistant EPA Administrator Jack Moore told reporters.

As Moore unveiled the EPA plan, Sen. David F. Durenberger (R-Minn.) introduced legislation calling for more stringent controls in what is expected to be a contentious congressional debate, with environmentalists, farmer interests and the pesticide industry fighting for their causes.

The 150-page EPA proposal is designed to protect current and potential drinking water sources, essentially writing off brackish or nonpotable groundwater.

Brushing aside the goal of "pristine" groundwater as unobtainable, the plan would limit each pesticide to levels as protective of public health as possible given economic and technological constraints. Until a standard is set, carcinogenic pesticides would be restricted to levels of "negligible risk," which means they could not expose people to a risk of cancer higher than one in a million.

As preventive measures, the EPA would establish certain national policies for chemicals known for their penetrating power, limiting their application to certified operators or restricting their use in irrigation waters. Moore said such preventive schemes could be applied to states or regions depending on their soil.

Stricter measures would be applied to such areas as Florida, the Central Valley of California, the southeastern coastal plain, and parts of Wisconsin where loose, sandy soils invite pesticide leaching, Moore said.

The EPA blueprint calls for active participation of states to tailor their prevention to local conditions, sizing up soil characteristics and groundwater quality.

Moore called the agency's prevention plan a "yellow light–red light" warning system in which the discovery of pesticides would trigger restrictions. As the levels increase toward unacceptable limits, the regulation would intensify to the point of banning the chemical.

Once levels reached the point of "imminent and substantial endangerment to public health," according to the plan, EPA could order the polluter to provide bottled water.

Different portions of the plan are expected to raise controversy. The pesticide industry worries that state-by-state regulation could lead to 50 different standards.

Environmentalists want protection expanded beyond current and potential sources of drinking water to all groundwater. They want pesticides limited to levels at which they cause adverse health effects instead of economically and technologically feasible levels and stricter enforcement measures.

Durenberger's bill comes closer to the environmentalist demands by setting a goal of "nondegradation" of all groundwater and standards based on health considerations only. His bill would require states to control the sources of groundwater pollution, restricting pesticide application before pollution occurs.

2 EPA Falls Far Short in Enforcing Drinking Water Laws

MICHAEL WEISSKOPF

May, 1991

With unusually high levels of radioactive elements found in its drinking water in 1984, the city of Batavia, Ill., seemed a prime target for environmental regulators.

But seven years later, city officials say Batavia's drinking water is just as polluted with the cancer-causing elements. Its 17,000 residents still face an estimated lifetime risk of cancer from the tap hundreds of times higher than the Environmental Protection Agency considers acceptable.

The EPA, charged with enforcing the nation's drinking water laws, never issued a warning—not when Batavia hooked up more residents to its water system and not when the city reneged on its agreement with the state to clean up the pollution.

"They just looked the other way," Jacob Dumelle, a member of the Illinois Pollution Control Board, said of the EPA.

Like thousands of other drinking water systems nationwide, Batavia's slipped through the EPA's loose enforcement net. Despite a strong congressional mandate to protect drinking water, the agency and the state officials deputized to enforce its regulations have taken action against less than 9 percent of the 20,000 persistent violations of the law that occurred in each of the past three years, according to statistics from the EPA.

The lax enforcement record highlights what congressional critics describe as a larger breakdown of the nation's system for protecting the public from the health hazards of unsafe drinking water.

According to interviews, federal documents and congressional reports examined by *The Washington Post:* Dozens of toxic chemicals, including such carcinogens as dioxin, remain unregulated years after standards were mandated by Congress. Those standards that have been set for carcinogens are not as protective as required by law, and the recent attempt to regulate lead has been stretched out for more than 20 years despite its well-known dangers to children and pregnant women. The requirement to test water quality at least quarterly has been widely violated. One utility in Washington state went seven years without checking its water. Exemptions from the restrictions on small utilities that claim economic hardship are

186

expected to be broadly liberalized, exposing their customers to unusually high risks from certain contaminants. Public notice requirements for violations of standards are largely ignored.

Failures to implement the law fully are not necessarily an indictment of the nation's water quality. Nor is there direct evidence of excess cancer cases caused by tainted water. Such links are difficult to prove because of cancer's long latency period.

Nevertheless, the EPA considers drinking water pollution one of the four greatest environmental risks facing Americans, causing as many as 1,000 cancer cases a year and stunting the mental development of as many as 240,000 children.

Acknowledging that his drinking water program "cannot be considered perfect," EPA Administrator William K. Reilly said at a recent congressional hearing that many of the agency's lapses stem from unrealistic statutory deadlines, inadequate staff and scientific uncertainties.

Reilly emphasized, nevertheless, that the nation's drinking water supply is widely recognized as "among the best-protected in the world."

Standards have been set since the 1970s for 58 of the most pervasive contaminants, including the major disease-causing microorganisms. The biggest cities, including Washington, are generally in compliance with the standards.

Speaking for most of the nation's utilities, Jack Sullivan, of the American Water Works Association, said that while small systems still have "serious problems," the U.S. water supply deserves "high levels of confidence. Versus other places I've been in the world, you just don't see the number of outbreaks [of disease] here."

But Rep. Henry A. Waxman (D-Calif.), a principal author of 1986 amendments to the law, said no one has a basis for judging the safety of drinking water because of the spotty testing done by utilities.

He said the best evidence of EPA's failure is found in its own studies, showing, for example, that more than four-fifths of the excess environmental risk of cancer in Philadelphia comes from drinking water contaminated chiefly by chloroform.

"We don't see people suffering immediately from drinking water, so the EPA can decide it's not a problem they have to deal with right away," he said. "The program is a shambles."

The Safe Drinking Water Act of 1974 required the EPA to set target standards for contaminants that, if met, would eliminate health dangers. Enforceable standards were to be fixed as close to these targets as feasible, given the best pollution control technology.

Unhappy with the regulatory pace, Congress directed the EPA in 1986 to set standards for 83 unregulated contaminants within three years, step up water testing and public notification procedures and take action to enforce the law within 30 days if the state government deputies fail to act.

Although enforcement has picked up significantly in recent years, the EPA's efforts still fall far short of the congressional mandate, according to the agency's records. In each of the three years from 1988 through 1990, about 33,000 mostly small utilities failed to test and report their water quality, as mandated, on a total of about 86,000 occasions. In the same period the utilities exceeded the limits for contaminants 15,000 times a year. Officials said 80 percent of those roughly 100,000 infractions a year were corrected within four months.

This means that there were about 20,000 violations a year that were persistent. In those 60,000 cases, about 8.3 percent resulted in some form of enforcement action. But in the last three years, state government with primary enforcement responsibility ordered remedies in just 2,172 of the cases, sometimes years after serious violations were discovered, officials said. The states also referred another 505 cases for civil or criminal prosecution.

The EPA provided little enforcement backup. In those same three years it imposed just 41 fines, recommended civil litigation in 36 cases and issued 507 administrative orders to stop violations. It also issued 1,714 other enforcement notices or proposals.

"The message to water systems is that there's no risk in violating the law," said Erik D. Olson, a lawyer for the National Wildlife Federation. "It renders meaningless all the effort that the EPA puts in setting standards if they're not enforced."

The Washington state utility that repeatedly violated testing requirements, for example, was finally sanctioned seven years later, according to a study by the General Accounting Office.

James Elder, director of the EPA's office of drinking water, blamed a lack of staff for the spotty enforcement. But he acknowledged that governing "fellow public entities" has bred a "non-enforcement culture" at the agency.

In the Batavia case, the city signed an agreement with the state in 1985 to reduce radium that occurs naturally in deep groundwater and exceeded the standard by nearly three times. The plan called for new wells to tap less contaminated aquifers and a treatment plant to be completed in five years.

None of the plan's milestones was achieved on time, and the project is still three years from completion, but the state never penalized the city, instead it allowed the city to hook up more homes and businesses to its water line. State officials said reports of progress from Batavia stayed their hand. The water office has one attorney to prosecute dozens of violators of the radium standard alone.

In Chicago, the EPA's regional office was kept well informed of Batavia pollution. But Daniel Wilson, chief of the drinking water section, said he saw no need to force a costly cleanup of radium after the EPA announced plans to review and possibly relax the standard.

The announcement was four years ago, and the review is still pending.

Radium is one of the contaminants for which Congress required standards by June 1989. Thirty-two other pollutants, including 10 carcinogens, remain unregulated two years later and are not expected to be regulated for another 18 months.

Elder said the three-year deadline was too short for regulation of so many chemicals. The process, he said, was slowed by debates between agencies and among scientists assessing the contaminants.

Included on Congress's list was a class of the most toxic substances, such as solvents and pesticides, for which especially stringent standards were required. The law required limits based on technology at least as protective as granular activated carbon (GAC). In a filtration system, the pulverized charcoal takes up chemicals from drinking water and, at least in theory, can reduce the public's cancer risk.

But the EPA balked at the potential costs of GAC, and instead of using it as the basis for establishing a regulation, the agency set standards according to a different principle—a contaminant need be reduced only to the lowest level that can be reliably measured by most laboratories. Rather than requiring the best pollution reduction that technology offers, the EPA chose to be guided by the limitations of labs to analyze data.

"The divergence from the statutory directive is plain," the Congressional Research Service concluded recently.

In practical terms, the standards for some pollutants ended up more lenient than Congress intended. For most dietary risks, the EPA sets a threshold of 1 in 1 million odds of getting cancer over a lifetime of exposure. But for such water-borne carcinogens as polychlorinated biphenyls (PCBs), the agency set a standard that poses a cancer risk of 1 in 10,000. For the pesticide heptachlor, the allowed risk is even higher.

Reilly said he plans to review the decision to regulate pollutants on the basis of measurability.

Another problem is a loophole in the law that allows small, economically strapped utilities to avoid compliance with standard as long as the contaminant does not pose an "unreasonable risk" to health. Until now, their pollution levels had to be more than twice as high as the standard to be considered unreasonable.

But in the draft of a new guideline for such exemptions circulated internally last October, the EPA would allow levels of certain pollutants to reach 20 times the standard.

EPA officials said these higher concentrations would be permitted because the temporary nature of the exemptions meant periods of exposure would be limited. They run up to three years, but can be extended indefinitely.

The guideline, expected to be completed later this year, would open a "Pandora's box," said Olson, allowing small utilities to supply tainted water for years.

3 Two Maryland Wells Tainted by Leaks

Montgomery Landfill Is Chemical Source

RETHA HILL

August, 1992

C hemical compounds leaking from a government landfill in Montgomery County have contaminated the wells of two nearby houses, prompting specialists to test the drinking supplies of other houses in the area for possible pollution, local officials said yesterday.

The leaks at the Oaks landfill near Laytonsville in northeastern Montgomery were first detected during testing last year. Recent tests showed that solvent compounds and freon compounds had tainted the wells at the two houses, one of which is abandoned, officials said.

A county water-quality specialist said the solvent compounds were similar to those used in paint thinners and dry-cleaning chemicals, and the freon compound is commonly used in refrigerator systems.

Small quantities of the compounds were first detected last year in monitoring wells bordering the 220-acre landfill.

Yesterday, county officials completed sampling of well water at 10 other houses northwest of the landfill and said they will know in about two weeks whether runoff from the dump has contaminated any of those.

The county has supplied bottled water to the family that lives in the occupied house with a contaminated water supply. County officials said they would provide bottled water to other families if tests show their drinking water contains chemical runoff from the landfill.

"What we have are indicators that cause us to take prudent actions," said Alan Bergsten, chief of the Solid Waste Management Division of the local Department of Environmental Protection.

The early findings, he added, do "not indicate we have an environmental disaster here."

James Caldwell, a water quality specialist for the county, said the level of contaminants was below that which the federal government considers hazardous. Caldwell said that although there was no immediate danger in drinking water from the contaminated wells, residents should avoid it.

"If people were to consume the water now there would be no health effects, but we don't want them to consume it," Caldwell said. "That is why we are supplying them bottled water."

However, residents who live in the area where the wells have been tested for contamination said they were concerned.

"It was going to happen sooner or later," said Ann Handler, who lives directly across the road from the northwest boundary of the landfill with her husband and three young children.

Handler said she and her family were drinking well water until Sunday, when they learned of the two contaminated wells. She then switched to bottled water for drinking and cooking, while continuing to use well water for bathing, which officials said was a safe practice.

William J. Jaffurs, chairman of the Oaks Landfill Advisory Commission, who notified residents who live near the problem area, said he was "greatly dismayed and distressed" by the landfill leaks.

"We are trying to keep everybody as calm as possible," he said.

Jaffurs said if contamination is found in other wells and if the county cannot keep it from spreading, a 1982 agreement between the county and area residents could require the county to pipe in water to the residents, an expensive job. The closest water lines are about four miles away.

"It wouldn't be cheap," said Ted Graham, director of the Department of Environmental Protection.

The Oaks landfill opened in 1982 after a bitter seven-year fight over where Montgomery would put a trash dump, after the closing of its landfill at Gude Drive in Rockville.

Using what was then the state-of-the-art technique for containing trash, the landfill was lined with clay soil. Solid waste planners envisioned the landfill would be used for all types of trash until a waste-to-energy plant could be built on Shady Grove Road by the mid-1980s.

Then, for the next 18 years the Oaks site would be used for trash that could not be converted into energy, Bergsten said.

The Shady Grove facility was never built, and expansion at the Oaks landfill began two years ago. Bergsten said the expanded landfill will have impermeable double-lined plastic to protect groundwater from further runoff.

County officials said that after they determine the extent of the contamination, they will perform engineering studies to devise a way to contain the runoff.

The runoff is created when rainwater soaks through mountains of garbage and trash, including household waste and appliances, and then leaks through the clay liner.

Tests showed that the runoff contains dichlorodifluoromethane, a freon compound, and traces of the solvents tetrachloroethylene, methylene chloride, dichloroethylene and other substances.

All but one, the tetrachloroethylene found in the well water of the unoccupied house, were under maximum containment levels set by the U.S. Environmental Protection Agency, county officials said.

County officials and residents said the discovery of leakage at the Oaks site is likely to intensify debate over building an incinerator in far western Montgomery.

In September, solid waste and environmental planners are supposed to suggest a plan to the County Council for handling the county's trash over the next 10 years.

4   D.C. Ordered to Urge Boiling of Tap Water

EPA Threatened Fine of $5,000 a Day

D'VERA COHN
October, 1993

U nder threat of a $5,000-a-day fine, District officials agreed yesterday to tell residents of a Northeast neighborhood to boil drinking water because harmful bacteria was found in water from a former school building faucet. They emphasized that the city's water supply is safe.

Meanwhile, federal inspectors toured one of the city's two treatment plants to try to determine why unusual levels of general bacteria contamination turned up there as well.

City and federal officials announced Wednesday that a water sample drawn last week from the now closed Woodson Junior High, at Minnesota Avenue and Grant Street, tested positive for fecal coliform, a bacteria found in human and animal waste.

Routine water testing in September also turned up unusual levels of general bacteria contamination, a less serious problem, at about a dozen other sites and in disinfected water leaving the city's two treatment plants. No problems have been reported at nearby suburban water systems.

The Environmental Protection Agency urged the city Monday to issue a boil-water notice in the Woodson area. When city officials did not, EPA ordered them to do so Wednesday and said the city could be fined $5,000 each day it failed to comply.

District officials said yesterday that city workers would go door-to-door in a six-block area near the school distributing notices that say residents "may wish to boil tap water before drinking or using it for food preparation or use bottled water for these purposes." The advisory will be lifted Saturday if four days of follow-up tests are negative, the notice said. Tests were negative Wednesday and yesterday.

"We do not believe there is any significant risk to our water supply," said Richard Hebert, a spokesman for the Department of Public Works. "The water supply is essentially safe."

"You don't want to play around with something like that," said City Councilman Kevin Chavous (D), who represents the 7th Ward neighborhood near Woodson, in endorsing the public notice.

In that neighborhood, the discovery of the fecal coliform was greeted with anger and concern.

"Some of my neighbors have been boiling the water for a long time because they find things in the water," said Viola Simmons, 78, of the 4000 block of Minnesota Avenue. "I'm going to start boiling it myself."

"I am very angry that no one has informed me," said Gloria Dandridge, 48, who lives nearby. She said she has sickle-cell anemia and must drink a lot of water. "I don't need additional things making me ill."

"We are tax-paying citizens of the nation's capital who deserve clean, fresh water, and we also deserve to be told when it is not," said resident Preston Gibson, 74, who did not learn until last night of the water problem.

Presence of fecal coliform could be a sign of disease-causing organisms that cause symptoms similar to stomach flu: cramps, nausea and headaches. Hospitals are not reporting increases in such symptoms, Hebert said.

The news of the city's water problems came on the heels of a report this week by the Natural Resources Defense Council, a national environmental group, criticizing federal enforcement of drinking-water laws. In a move that indicates high-level involvement, officials from EPA headquarters in Washington yesterday toured the Dalecarlia water treatment plant, operated by the Army Corps of Engineers, which sells water to the city. Normally, EPA's Philadelphia regional office inspects the local water system.

EPA officials said they do not believe the District water supply poses a serious public health problem but that follow-up tests and inspections are needed.

Erik Olson, author of the defense council report released this week, criticized the city for not notifying people sooner, even though the city obeyed the law's deadlines.

"What's troubling is that the District people have known about this for so long and haven't told anyone about it," Olson said. "It basically took EPA stepping in for them to notify the public."

EPA also ordered the city to institute a systemwide program of water-main flushing and to inspect for possible sewer and water cross-connections in the Woodson area.

EPA officials said the District has not regularly cleaned its 1,300 miles of underground pipe in several years. Hebert said the city never had a regular program but flushes pipes when bacteria levels rise from contamination buildup.

The city began flushing hydrants last week. The region's other large water systems periodically flush their pipes to clean them.

Staff writers Santiago O'Donnell and Serge F. Kovaleski contributed to this report.

5 Drinking Water Proposals Combine Aid, Flexibility

TOM KENWORTHY

September, 1993

The Clinton administration yesterday proposed legislation to give states and local water systems more financial assistance and regulatory flexibility in meeting federal drinking water requirements.

"The way we guarantee safe water for the American people is broken and it needs to be fixed," said Environmental Protection Agency Administrator Carol M. Browner in unveiling the proposal during a speech to the National Association of Towns and Townships. At the same time, the administration sent detailed recommendations for rewriting the 1974 Safe Drinking Water Act to Congress.

The legislative proposals are designed to achieve a balance between assuring the public that water supplies are free from contamination and meeting the concerns of local officials about the costs and technical burdens of complying with federal mandates.

"We need to be absolutely uncompromising about the goals of environmental protection, but at the same time we need to incorporate more flexibility, more local and regional decision-making in how we reach those goals," Browner said.

The last reauthorization of the drinking water act in 1986 required EPA to set standards for 83 specific contaminants. Since then, Congress and the executive branch have been besieged by complaints about the costs of meeting the standards, particularly from thousands of small systems facing the highest relative costs. Rather than pay those costs, many water systems have simply refused to comply with federal standards.

In its report to Congress yesterday, the EPA estimated the annual cost of meeting existing drinking water standards at $1.4 billion. Those costs are minimal for users of the largest municipal water systems. But for the roughly 16,000 systems serving fewer than 100 people, the average household expense is $145 per year.

To ease that financial burden, the administration is proposing a $599 million revolving fund that would help states and communities meet the capital costs of assuring safe drinking water. In addition, the legislation would allow states to charge customers fees to help cover the costs of administering the federal requirements.

At the same time, the legislation would permit smaller systems that are strapped for funds to use less expensive technology than is required for larger systems. Browner also is proposing that Congress overhaul the current requirement that it set standards for 25 new contaminants every three years, replacing it with a risk-based system. In some cases, the deadline for complying with new standards would be extended from 18 months to five years.

And to shift the act's emphasis to prevention rather than treatment of water pollution, the proposals offer incentives to states and communities to rely more on protecting their sources of water and less on monitoring and treatment of contaminants.

Although Browner said the administration is determined to reduce regulatory burdens on local communities, she also underscored its commitment to providing the highest level of safety. "All Americans, whether they live in big cities or in small trailer parks, must be safe from harmful bacteria and toxic chemicals in drinking water," she said.

Environmental groups generally praised the administration's new approach. "A lot of what they are proposing is a good first step toward strengthening and improving the law," said Erik Olson, an attorney with the Natural Resources Defense Council. But Olson said the NRDC remains wary that the "fine print" giving flexibility to local water systems might allow them to "evade national standards completely."

John H. Montgomery, a Washington representative for the National Rural Water Association, said small systems would likely remain skeptical about the proposal's promised relief until they see the actual legislation. "The devil's in the details," he said.

6　The Chemical Quest for the Perfect Lawn

Pesticide, Fertilizer Runoff Ending Up in Area's Water Supply

D'VERA COHN
April, 1991

A h, springtime in Washington: azaleas in bloom, a rolling green lawn, a perfect rosebush, the smell of pesticides in the air.

To environmentalists, spring brings the stink of too much fertilizer—spread by homeowners just before a rainstorm so that it runs off into streams—the spraying of insect-killers that also wipe out helpful bugs, the pouring on of weed killers on weeds that are already dead.

Homeowners make few choices with as many ecological consequences as when they care for their lawns and gardens, or hire someone else to do it. Yet despite the growing public concern about the environment, most homeowners still use large amounts of chemicals in the quest for a perfect lawn—although more and more do it with a guilty conscience.

"I am the worst. . . . When all else fails, I'll pour the chemicals on it," said Margaret Kincheloe, of McLean, president of the Garden Club of Fairfax. "It's very hard to be a good person in gardening. I admire those who do it."

Kincheloe said the lawn-care company she uses urged her to have her soil tested to see what nutrients it needed. But she told them to just put on fertilizer anyway without a test.

Like many other gardeners, she applies pesticides before insects show up, a practice that one local extension service agent likened to taking an aspirin because you're afraid of getting a headache. She also uses a quick-release fertilizer for "instant results," a product that is more likely to run off than a slower-release treatment that takes longer to turn grass bright green.

Bill Stewart, an extension service agent in Prince George's County, said most spring fertilizing is unneeded, and estimates most people could use 70 percent less fertilizer and 90 percent less weed killer if they used them properly.

A survey of Fairfax County homeowners included in a Virginia Tech report for the state legislature found that most of them had no idea how much nitrogen they put on their lawns when they fertilize, they do not read pesticide directions, and they apply chemicals in a way that could endanger local water supplies.

Natural-gardening advocates refuse to use any chemicals. Extension service gardening experts say chemicals can be used in moderation without harming the environment, but that most people use too many of them. Cutting back on chemicals, experts say, can be better for the lawn, because organic materials condition the soil and strengthen the plants' ability to fend off weeds and pests.

But there are tradeoffs: Few non-chemical weed killers exist, so lawn owners either learn to live with weeds or dig them up. Being cautious about bug-killers risks waiting until it is too late. Organic fertilizer is costlier and must be used in larger quantities than its chemical cousin. Chemical-light gardening may take two years to green up a lawn; a commercial service can do it in three months.

"It's nice to have a nice lawn but . . . I think people should relax their standards somewhat," said Claire Hardy, a horticultural technician with the Fairfax County Extension Service.

The consequences of chemical overuse have shown up in Fairfax County streams, where phosphorus levels have doubled since 1986. Officials blame the problem on homeowners dumping so much fertilizer on their lawns that it cannot be absorbed by plants and runs off into creeks and rivers. Phosphorus produces algae blooms that steal oxygen, which fish and water plants need to live.

Tests regularly turn up traces of pesticides and herbicides in streams leading to the county's Occoquan drinking water reservoir—levels that peak during the spring lawn care season.

Thomas Grizzard, director of Virginia Tech's Occoquan monitoring laboratory, said the amounts are not high enough to harm humans, but "the fact that we see them at all is an indication it's something we should keep an eye on."

Michael Heller, of the Chesapeake Bay Foundation, said even low levels are worrisome because the harm from chemical contamination often shows up decades after use. "We can't assume that even if we stop today, we won't have a problem," he said.

The U.S. Environmental Protection Agency found potentially harmful levels of nitrate—much of it comes from chemical fertilizer—in more than half the drinking water wells it tested nationwide. High nitrate levels can cause "blue baby" syndrome, a potentially fatal oxygen-depriving disorder in infants.

Officials blame fertilizer, mainly from agriculture, for high nitrogen levels in the Chesapeake Bay.

The General Accounting Office, the investigative arm of Congress, reported last year that the lawn pesticides industry "continues to make prohibited claims that its products are safe or nontoxic," and the government does little to stop their false promises. The GAO said no product that kills living organisms can be described as safe.

The EPA is reviewing the risks of 32 commonly used and potentially hazardous lawn pesticides, but the GAO expressed concern that none of those reviews has been completed.

The GAO report especially criticized the EPA's failure to finish reviewing two of the most popular home pesticides: Diazinon, an insect-killer that is the most widely used lawn pesticide and is linked to bird kills, and 2,4-D, a common weed killer with possible links to cancer. The EPA has banned use of Diazinon on golf courses and sod farms.

"Given what we know about potential risk and all the unknowns, the most responsible decision is to try to use nonchemical pest practices," said Jay Feldman, of the National Coalition Against Misuse of Pesticides. Feldman said his own chemical-free lawn in the District "has a lot of clover," but is "very lush."

The lawn care industry argues that its products are not dangerous if properly used, and that fewer chemicals are being used on each lawn, although the total amount is growing because the nation's acreage of lawns is increasing.

"Lawn care has not been a major problem throughout the country," said Thomas Delaney, government affairs director for the Professional Lawn Care Industry Association in Atlanta. "In cases where there is misuse, most of it is attributable to homeowner misuse."

The lawn care group's guidelines now include "integrated pest management," which means using a blend of techniques to fend off insects rather than relying only on chemicals. Most lawn care companies, the trade group says, offer "natural" alternatives, and a small number of all-organic companies have sprung up.

In some states, including Maryland, lawn care companies are required to post signs warning neighbors that the area has been sprayed, and legislation has been introduced in Congress to require the same in all states.

Woodbridge homeowner Dick Crane has made the switch. His Featherstone Terrace lawn was the test plot for Prince William County extension agent Marc Aveni to show a neighborhood group how to reduce chemical use.

Crane said he had abused his lawn for 19 years, drowning it in fertilizer, letting weeds choke out the grass and ignoring the bare patches. On Aveni's advice, he had a soil test that told him to use lime, which he has applied several times since then.

He applied only one bag of fertilizer last fall, a quarter of what he had used in the spring in past years. He is not scalping his grass when he mows, but letting it grow longer.

When his neighbors showed up at his "dustbowl" last August, he said, "everyone was laughing at my lawn. This year, the last laugh is going to be mine. . . . I'm definitely a converted environmentalist."

7   Growing Lawns a Cut Above

Program Teaches Homeowners How to Cultivate Environmentally Safe Grass

CARLOS SANCHEZ
May, 1993

M arc Aveni knows well the Washington area's recipe for spring: generous portions of lime, fertilizer and herbicides, plenty of grass seed, add water and wait for the lawn to turn green.

Unfortunately, that rite of spring is damaging the environment, Aveni said. So, his office—the Prince William Extension Service—has begun a unique countywide project designed to change destructive lawn and gardening habits.

"The basic theory is: You have to work one on one with people to educate them," Aveni said of the program.

Called the Water Quality Program, the pilot project is based on the premise that millions of good-intentioned homeowners unknowingly are suffocating area waterways and the Chesapeake Bay with their lawn maintenance practices, as well as the other chemical runoff from modern living.

"For the Chesapeake Bay, probably the biggest challenge is fighting against nutrient pollution," said Elliott Finkelstein, with the Chesapeake Bay Program in Annapolis. "We see a lot of nitrogen and phosphorous, which are probably the major components for the degradation of the bay."

Nitrogen and phosphorous are two major components for most lawn fertilizers that mingle with groundwater that runs into streams and eventually flows into the bay. More than 304 million pounds of nitrogen gets into the bay annually, Finkelstein said. In addition, about 23.8 million pounds of phosphorous run off into the bay.

Those two chemicals promote algae growth, which results in cloudier waters and, ultimately, robs the water and marine life of oxygen.

"A typical farmer probably applies less material per acre than a homeowner," Aveni said.

While there certainly are other sources of the pollution, Aveni said, educating gardeners and others about environmentally safe lawn practices is a good first step in cleaning up local waterways.

200

And the U.S. Department of Agriculture apparently agrees. That's why the department has given Aveni's program part of a $100,000 grant to develop a model program that other areas in the region and nationwide can emulate.

What began three years ago as field days that allowed specialists to discuss lawn practices with visitors to Prince William parks has evolved into the Volunteer Lawn Program, offered through the Water Quality Program.

The 100 volunteers in the program signed an agreement with the extension service to learn and apply the new lawn practices by attending seven field days throughout the year and by meeting with trained master gardeners.

After one year, volunteers are asked whether they would like to have demonstration lawns. If they agree (five people have), the extension service places a sign on the homeowners' lawns saying they have been trained by the agency. The hope is that neighbors will see firsthand the results of this training and ask the demonstration homeowners what they did.

"We get a lot of referrals," Aveni said. "People have a need to know how to care for their lawns. And when it comes to lawns, we find a lot of homeowners are prone to buying into things."

While that works wonders for the $16 billion-a-year lawn and garden industry, it often leaves homeowners out of a lot of money and with a breadth of knowledge—borne from the marketing of lawn and garden products—that frequently is wrong, Aveni said.

And the most fundamental error that people make, he said, is working so hard every spring. "In this area, fall is really the time to be working. It's the time to fertilize, put seed down, aerate, plant trees and shrubs," he said.

By taking those steps, program participants say they have achieved miraculous results.

"They told me that I wouldn't believe my lawn next spring," Lake Ridge resident Bob McNamara said of his first shot at the program last fall. "I didn't expect what I saw. I don't work nearly as hard as my neighbors do now and [my lawn] is better than most."

Joel Contrucci, another Lake Ridge resident, said he has done a 180-degree turnaround with his lawn practices since joining the program.

"You always get the hard sell that your lawn can't survive without four feedings a year," he said. "And that's not the case."

The training those two homeowners received is offered four times in the spring and three times in the fall, Aveni said. The workshops are free and currently are offered at Anne Moncure Wall Park in Montclair and Lake Ridge Park.

Topics include mowing and pruning, back yard composting, pest management and native plants. The next workshops are scheduled for June 5 at Lake Ridge and June 12 in Montclair. Horticulturist Ed Milhous will discuss planting native species and how to avoid problems.

8   Pollution under Scrutiny at U.S.-Mexican Border

WILLIAM BRANIGIN
October, 1989

On a given day, up to 12 million gallons of raw sewage from this booming city in the northwestern corner of Mexico flows untreated into the Tijuana River. Illegal aliens wade through it to cross into the United States, people use it to wash their cars, and farmers siphon off some of its flow to irrigate crops.

All this might not make much difference to Americans, except that the Tijuana River does not recognize the U.S. border. Its "black waters," as the Mexicans describe the river's contents, flow northwest into California, meander through a federally protected salt-water estuary and empty into the Pacific Ocean just south of Imperial Beach.

As a result, 2 1/2 miles of U.S. beaches north of the Mexican border have been closed for most of the last 10 years. The 2,500-acre estuary—one of only three of its kind in the United States—is gradually being poisoned. Endangered species of birds that live there are disappearing. And nearby communities have been plagued by mosquitoes and a variety of diseases.

Among the illnesses associated with the reeking, greenish-black river, according to U.S. health officials, have been amoebic dysentery, vibrio cholera, staphyloccal disease, hepatitis, encephalitis and two outbreaks of malaria in the last three years. Coliform counts, indicators of fecal matter in water that provide the basis for closing beaches, have also turned up polio agents in the Tijuana River. Consisting almost entirely of raw sewage, the river ranks as the most polluted in the United States officials in San Diego say.

Long a sore point in relations between Tijuana and San Diego, the Tijuana River has come to symbolize a problem of increasing concern along the 2,000-mile U.S.-Mexican border: worsening air and water pollution. Smog that drifts into the United States from Mexican border cities, flows of untreated sewage and the dumping of industrial wastes have raised fears that, as one U.S. environmentalist recently put it, the border could turn into "a 2,000-mile Love Canal," the highly polluted area near Niagara Falls.

Now, however, authorities of both countries appear to be turning their attention to the problem. Among several accords reached during a visit to Washington by

President Carlos Salinas de Gortari earlier this month was an agreement in principle to build a unique joint sewage treatment plant on U.S. soil just north of this city. The agreement is viewed as another example of increased Mexican cooperation with the United States under the Salinas as administration.

The $144 million project—including a 25 million-gallon-a-day treatment plant and a pipeline to carry treated waste water to the Pacific Ocean—is aimed at cleaning up the Tijuana River and saving the estuary. Details are now under negotiation by U.S. and Mexican representatives at the International Boundary and Water Commission.

"We are moving rapidly to resolve sanitation and pollution problems on the border," said Narendra Gunaji, the U.S. head of the l00-year-old commission. He said he expects the new joint sewage treatment plant to start operating by 1993.

Pollution problems on the border long have been overshadowed by those of illegal aliens and drug trafficking. In recent years, however, the problems have worsened as populations on both sides of the line have grown. Many of the new inhabitants are poor Mexicans who live in unauthorized settlements lacking sanitation services.

One of the most serious problems, U.S. officials say, is the pollution of the Rio Grande which forms the border between Mexico and Texas. According to the International Boundary and Water Commission, up to 25 million gallons a day of raw sewage flow into the river from Nuevo Laredo, the Mexican city across the border from Laredo, Tex.

At El Paso, where the commission is based, water pollution problems have been supplemented by winter smog that drifts over from the sister city of Ciudad Juarez. As in the rest of Mexico, cars in Ciudad Juarez are not required to have antipollution devices, and controls on industrial emissions are not as strict as on the U.S. side.

Near Mexicali, opposite the California town of Calexico, sewage and industrial wastes have severely contaminated the New River, which flows north to California's Salton Sea, a national wildlife refuge.

In the case of the Colorado River, Mexico suffers the consequences of high salinity acquired in the water's usage for irrigation as the river passes through seven U.S. states before entering Mexico's Gulf of California. The United States is obligated under a 1974 agreement to reduce the salinity.

Here in Tijuana and neighboring San Diego County, pollution from the Tijuana River has been compounded by breakdowns and overflows of Tijuana's sewage treatment system. After rejecting previous American proposals for construction of a joint treatment plant as too costly, the government of Salinas' predecessor, Miguel de la Madrid, opted to build its own plant, which de la Madrid proudly inaugurated in 1987.

However, the plant, the first of its kind in the country, ran into problems from the start. With capacity to treat 17 million gallons of sewage a day, it was inadequate to handle the 22 million gallons a day actually pumped into it, much less the overall 32 million gallons a day produced by Tijuana's 1.3 million residents. The plant promptly broke down in October 1987, remaining out of service for seven months. During that time, raw sewage was discharged directly into the Pacific Ocean surf, a source of concern for San Diego because of currents that occasionally flow north.

Even now, San Diego city officials worry about the surf discharge of sewage that they say is inadequately treated at best. "The Mexicans are very proud of what they've done," said one official, "but it's not up to the standards we have here. It's a touchy issue."

While U.S. authorities have declared beaches just north of the border unsafe, said California state parks official Ed Navarro, "directly across in Mexican waters, activity goes on as if there's no problem."

Although the agreement for a new joint treatment plant is generally welcomed, some U.S. officials remain bitter about the whole issue. "I don't think anyone is thrilled about having to pay to treat someone else's sewage," said San Diego County supervisor Brian Bilbray, noting that the U.S. government is expected to foot $100 million of the new plant's cost.

9 Expanding Waste Line along Mexico's Border

EDWARD CODY
February, 1992

For the last 15 years, Armando Beltran has been pulling up in his green-and-white tanker truck and connecting to a six-inch pipe that gushes with free—and chemically polluted—drinking water.

Along with dozens of other piperos here, Beltran has made a business of trucking the municipal water around a city struggling with an exploding population and an outstripped water system. The contaminated output from Nogales's Tomatera well, he said, goes to water-starved local factories, where it runs through faucets, sinks and toilets, and into the city's sprawl of plywood-and-cinderblock shacks, where thousands of poor families without plumbing store it in metal barrels to drink and wash with.

Although Beltran professes not to know it, his daily trips to the Tomatera pipe have come to symbolize a legacy of filth and toxicity along Mexico's border with the United States. The water that comes out there was found more than a year ago to contain potentially dangerous industrial solvents. But hard-pressed city authorities have yet to cut off the flow.

All along the 2,000-mile frontier with the United States, Mexico's municipal, state and federal governments have been similarly slow to react to the accumulation of environmental horror stories that have become an important part of life in a string of dingy factory towns, industrial parks and slums from Matamoros on the Gulf of Mexico to Tijuana on the Pacific Ocean.

A week-long trip along that string made evident a tragic despoiling as industry—much of it American-owned—sprang up without effective enforcement of environmental controls. The new factories also have attracted hundreds of thousands of new workers, submerging the border strip's infrastructure and turning the Rio Grande from a river where children used to swim into a gently flowing cesspool.

As a result, the south side of the U.S.-Mexican border has become a picture of neglect, of factories leaking foul-smelling effluents into brackish green and yellow canals, of muddy lanes connecting rows of slapdash huts where workers' children drink polluted water from drums that used to hold toxic chemicals, of culverts spewing human feces into rivers and ditches while garbage and chemical leftovers putrefy nearby in open dumps.

As Mexico and the United States negotiate along with Canada for a North American Free Trade Agreement, environmental activists have voiced alarm that similar deterioration could occur in the Mexican interior over the coming decade unless environmental controls are enforced. Although comparatively low Mexican wages are the main attraction for American and other investors here, they have warned, some companies have moved plants to Mexico—and may again in the future—partly to take advantage of traditionally lax antipollution enforcement.

"Once these problems take place in the interior, no one will be able to do anything about them," said Richard Kamp, a longtime environmental militant who monitors border pollution as head of the Border Ecology Project in Naco, Ariz.

President Carlos Salinas de Gortari, who has made the free-trade accord his top foreign priority, repeatedly has pledged to get a grip on Mexico's environmental mess, in the smog-infested capital as well as along the border. He enacted tough new antipollution laws soon after coming to office and has set aside $460 million for his Ecology and Urban Development Secretariat (known by its Spanish acronym SE-DUE) to strengthen enforcement over the next three years.

Mexico's enforcement practices to date are likely to provide ammunition for U.S. congressional opponents of a free-trade accord.

In part to meet environmental fears in Congress and bolster a free-trade accord, Mexico's ecology secretariat and the U.S. Environmental Protection Agency also have negotiated an Integrated Border Environment Plan due for publication late this month. Officials of the two environmental agencies have described the document as the first comprehensive survey of border pollution and recipe for cleaning it up.

Local activists on both sides of the border have dismissed the plan as a public relations ploy, however, asserting the governments are putting on a display to assuage congressional concerns and assure passage of the trade agreement once negotiations are completed, probably later this year. The critics have made their assessments on the basis of nearly complete drafts of the plan made available last week by SEDUE officials in Mexican border towns.

"I don't think there's any meat to this, how do you say, this circus between Mexico and the United States, between SEDUE and the EPA," said Fernando Medina, who heads the civic Committee for Ecological Disclosure in Mexicali.

Campaigning for Change

On both sides of the border, vocal environmental groups have expressed skepticism on promises from environmental officials because of what they say has been a historical refusal by Mexican authorities to move from declarations of good intent to actual enforcement.

"We don't trust the authorities to monitor this enough to know that we will be safe," said Laura S. de Durazo, part of a group opposing a seaside toxic-waste incinerator due to begin operation soon on the outskirts of Tijuana.

On the other side of Tijuana, in a ravine filled with ramshackle houses along muddy streets without drainage, Maurilio Sanchez Pachuca also has concluded that getting authorities to deal with pollution can be difficult. Since 1983, he has been leading a petition-writing campaign, visiting offices and inviting officials to visit— all without response.

The 25,000 families of his Chilancingo neighborhood have been frightened by what happens when rain falls heavily on the Otay Mesa industrial park, a flat hilltop just above their homes where a number of American-owned factories have gone into operation over the last decade. A 48-inch drain pipe serves the mesa, Sanchez said, but it overflows during heavy downpours, sending factory wastes into three gullies that lead directly into Chilancingo's rutted streets, past a kindergarten and on to the Canon del Padre River.

Sanchez said he started his campaign to eliminate the pollution by writing Tijuana health authorities. For three years he wrote and waited for answers, fruitlessly. Then he started writing to health authorities in the Mexican state of Baja California, also fruitlessly, and to the state governor.

"We didn't get an answer from him either, nothing," Sanchez said, flipping through a file of his letters.

Finally, after four more years of letter-writing, Sanchez was told President Salinas planned to come and see for himself. Local residents prepared for his visit. But it never happened, and they still do not know why.

"He could at least fly over in a helicopter, because I am sure he doesn't know about our case," Sanchez said. "We have confidence in the president. If he knew, we could get something done."

In his correspondence file, Sanchez also has a copy of some pages from a sampling he said was done by the Autonomous University of Baja California showing that the wastes flowing into Chilancingo contain lead, copper, zinc, cadmium and chrome, all presumably from the factories up on the mesa and all presumably dangerous to the neighborhood's health.

Partly because of a tradition of confidentiality in the Mexican government and partly because Salinas's antipollution orders are only now beginning to take effect, shortage of official data has plagued cleanup efforts along the entire length of the border.

Kamp said, for example, that the 1990 binational study of Nogales drinking water remains the only comprehensive look at what has happened to city water since the rise of factories alongside a highway south of the city.

City authorities closed down two water wells after the study, he said, but have refused to accept the unofficial data as conclusive. The Tomatera facility was closed for several days, but reopened to whoever wants to draw water there even though it lies near the polluted Nogales River waters that run through town. After the river crosses into the United States, however, the garbage-lined wash has been posted by U.S. health authorities with a sign saying: "Danger, Keep Out, Polluted Water."

Rise in Birth Defects

Carmen Rocco, a physician and medical director at the Brownsville, Tex., Community Health Center, has encountered similar frustration in her efforts to determine why an unusually high number of babies are being born without brains in the city's Valley Regional Medical Center and Brownsville Medical Center hospitals, just across the Rio Grande from a zone of factories in Matamoros, Mexico.

She said her research has shown that 42 births troubled by neural tube defects, including 28 anacephalics, took place between November 1989 and January 1991. This is about six times the U.S. average, but nobody knows why, Rocco said.

She and some colleagues have an idea, however. They have begun pursuing the chemical wastes that she said regularly turn Matamoros canals into "orange and brown rivers" that empty into the Rio Grande and nearby lagoons that flow into the Gulf of Mexico.

Along the broad avenues of Matamoros's Finsa industrial park, where brightly painted factories are flanked by lawns and soccer fields for employees, the extent of filth has long been difficult to discern with scientific certainty.

Shampoo-like bubbles foamed one recent day, for instance, where wastes flowed directly into a canal from a concrete trough leading from an electrical-components factory. Juan Nicolas de Leon, an architect who until last week ran the local SEDUE office, said the factory has its own pretreatment plant for water-borne wastes that should make them "crystalline" when they pour into the canal.

Another, nearby plant that finishes automobile bumpers recently received certification from SEDUE that its operations are environmentally harmless, de Leon said. But a sampling taken just downstream from its discharge for a report last May by the U.S. National Toxic Campaign Fund showed 23.2 million parts per billion of the chemical xylene—which the researchers said is 52,700 times the U.S. standard for drinking water.

Xylene was identified as a solvent that has been connected to respiratory irritation and damage to the lungs, liver and kidneys. The discharge sampled for the report is released into a series of canals that eventually flow to the Rio Grande and the Gulf of Mexico.

The Baja California state SEDUE representative, Cesar Ruben Castro, said the problem with treatment equipment in many factories is that it is only partly effective, removing all waste in some cases but only half the waste in others.

Sights for Sore Eyes

Monitoring wastes has been easy at some spots along the border. The Mexican city of Nuevo Laredo, for example, with a population of more than 600,000, discharges about 27 million gallons of raw sewage a day directly into the Rio Grande at more than 25 points. Fecal matter can be seen floating in the current as the river curves southward—toward towns downriver that pump their drinking water from the same stream.

A new sewage-treatment plant has been scheduled for construction. But Nuevo Laredo's population has been growing so fast the plant's capacity will be inadequate even before it is completed, said Adolph Kahn, a retired veterinarian and environmental activist from Laredo, Tex., just across the river.

As Kahn looked on, pigs rooted contentedly in an open Nuevo Laredo dump only a few hundred yards from the river. Oily black residue covered some patches of the dump. Chalky yellow residue covered others.

Guillermo Giron, president of the environment committee of a national assembly-plant association, estimated recently that some 260,000 tons of toxic wastes produced by American-owned firms are dumped illegally in Mexico every year. U.S.-Mexican accords since 1986 have obliged assembly plants to return to the United States any toxic material brought into Mexico. In fact, authorities on both sides acknowledge no one has kept track of how much comes in or how much goes out, and the officials suspect much of it is dumped after use.

The U.S. General Accounting Office estimated that of the 1,449 assembly plants along the border, about 800 create hazardous wastes. Of these, only 446 have registered with authorities to allow tracking of incoming and outcoming materials as required by the U.S.-Mexican accords, the GAO reported.

Salinas, as part of his environmental push, has pledged to quadruple the number of inspectors along the border to 200 as part of the three-year binational plan.

In Matamoros, for example, SEDUE recently hired three university-trained inspectors to visit plants. When Castro took over SEDUE's Baja California operations two years ago, the state had 23 inspectors; it now has 43 and is recruiting 40 more.

Also as part of the new get-tough rules, the Matamoros SEDUE office ordered closure of Productos de Preservacion, an American-owned pesticide factory, and the Mexicali office closed Quimica Organica last month. Both factories had been cited for dangerous leaks of chemical gases.

These were among some 700 such closures, most of them temporary, ordered by SEDUE in the last year under the campaign by Salinas to crack down on offenders.

10   Poland Faces Communist Legacy of Pollution

Water That Burns Skin Is Reminder That Freedom Is No Quick Cure for Fouled Environment

BLAINE HARDEN
December, 1991

It spurts yellowish-brown from the tap, laced with heavy metals, coal-mine salts and organic carcinogens. It stains the sink, tastes soapy and smells like a wet sock that has been fished out of a heavily chlorinated swimming pool.

Given a few weeks, it will eat a hole in a steel pan. Better to wear rubber gloves while washing the dishes. Better to boil it before cooking. Best not to drink it.

Tap water drips daily into the collective consciousness of Warsaw as part of the pernicious legacy of four decades of communism. The water is a long goodbye from a totalitarian system that scorned environmental common sense and poisoned people in the name of the masses.

More than two years after Polish voters dumped communism, each morning's grungy dribble from the tap is a dispiriting reminder that political freedom and free-market economics offer no quick cure for a catastrophically fouled environment. Wretched tap water sends the same dismal message in Prague and Budapest.

Residents of these capitals need go no farther than their kitchen sinks to see—indeed, to taste and smell—that the old Eastern Bloc remains a poor, polluted and unhealthy appendage of the new Europe.

"When I washed my face with tap water, it caused little red blotches. My skin felt stretched and itchy. I felt like it might crack or split open if I spoke or laughed too much," said Barbara Matusevicz, 36, a secretary at Warsaw University's department of law.

Like many Warsaw residents whose skin hurts after washing with tap water, Matusevicz has experimented for years with boiled water, bottled water, skin lotions and home remedies. She finally settled on a cheap, if unorthodox, cure.

"I started making a facial mask out of porridge, the same stuff I serve my son for breakfast. It moisturizes and makes my skin feel smooth," Matusevicz said.

Jan Dojlido, head of the department of water chemistry and biology at the Polish Institute of Meteorology and Water Management, does not smear porridge on his face—but neither does he drink Warsaw water directly from the tap.

Strictly speaking, Dojlido said, the tap water is not "toxic." The water's tendency to irritate human skin, he said, is caused by its high concentration of chlorine, and heavy chlorination is required to de-fang the noxious cocktail of industrial and human waste that is present in river water as it is sucked into the Warsaw's water-treatment plants.

For his own family's supply of drinking and cooking water, Dojlido runs tap water through an activated carbon filter and then boils it. He advises mothers to bathe their babies only in tap water that has been boiled for a full 15 minutes; this rids the water of cancer-causing organic compounds that he regularly measures in tap water at concentrations he said are more than twice as high as minimums set by the World Health Organization.

As a scientist who has been studying water quality for much of his adult life, Dojlido has a difficult time talking about Warsaw tap water without occasionally resorting to an unscientific adjective like "horrible."

"I came to Warsaw in 1948 and the water here is steadily getting worse. Warsaw is very unlucky when it comes to water," said Dojlido.

The causes of the pollution are many but the problem begins with Warsaw's principal source of drinking water, the Vistula River.

That river, Poland's longest, flows clean and drinkable out of the Carpathian mountains in the south of the country. But about 150 miles before it reaches Warsaw, the Vistula soaks up the runoff from Silesia, Poland's industrial heartland. Few areas of the world are more polluted.

Using the river as a lifeline and a toilet, Communist central planners concentrated the nation's steel, chemical fertilizer and pulp-and-paper plants in Silesia. People who live there have significantly higher rates of cancer, along with circulatory and respiratory diseases, than other Poles, according to recent studies. Rates of mental retardation in Silesia have been described as "appalling" by the Polish Chemical Society.

Over the years, the Communists' central plan did not insist that Silesia's toxic waste be kept out of the river. The Ministry of Environmental Protection reported last month that about a quarter of Poland's big industrial plants either have no waste-water treatment or use devices of insufficient capacity. The ministry said half of the country's small industrial plants use no waste-water treatment.

Silesian factories seed the Vistula with pollutants including ammonia, phosphates and heavy metals such as lead and mercury. For example, the average concentration of mercury in the Vistula in 1990 was nine times higher than the Polish norm for safe drinking water. Existing water treatment technology in Warsaw can do little to remove heavy metals from river water, according to Robert Latawiec, central waterworks manager.

Coal mines in Silesia are the biggest polluters of the Vistula. They dump about 6,600 tons a day of chlorides and sulfates into the river, according to the Ministry of Environmental Protection. These corrosive salts are the reason why Warsaw tap water can eat a hole in a baking pan and why rusted-out water pipes have to be dug up and replaced every 10 years. The ministry says corroded water pipes leak about one-third of the water they are supposed to carry.

The river is going to get even saltier. According to the Ministry of Environmental Protection, the amount of such salts in the river will increase by about 70 percent over the next decade as coal mines continue to be exploited. Lacking oil, natural gas or nuclear-power plants, Poland needs the coal to produce electricity.

Salts are the major reason why 57 percent of the Vistula is classified as unfit for any purpose.

Polish cities and towns also contribute. About 40 percent of the country's sewage is untreated. A large proportion of it goes straight into the Vistula, both upstream and downstream from Warsaw. This city treats only about one-third of the waste it pumps into the river.

"The Vistula is a sewer for half the country," said Dariusz Jan Stanislawski, a scientist at the Polish Department of Water economy and an adviser to the minister of environmental protection.

Cleaning up a national sewer that also happens to be Poland's main source of drinking water is a complex and costly project that environmental officials say will take at least 20 years.

The World Bank, along with Sweden and the Polish government, is paying for studies of a comprehensive cleanup of the Vistula. Sweden is keenly interested because the river is the largest single source of pollution in the Baltic Sea.

Poland has put together an ambitious cleanup program. Nearly 3,000 new waste-water treatment plants are to be built. Desalination plants are also proposed. Some of the worst-polluting industrial plants have been closed, and others are being forced to pay heavy fines. Excepting salts, pollution is no longer getting worse.

But the Warsaw government, already running a deficit and struggling with a free-market economic transformation that most Poles no longer support, cannot pay for cleaning up the entire river using modern technology. Nor are foreign donors rushing in to pick up a tab estimated at tens of billions of dollars.

Environmental officials here said that the fastest and cheapest way to improve the quality of tap water is for Poles to stop wasting it.

The average resident of Warsaw, for example, uses about twice as much tap water as the average resident of Western Europe—about 98 gallons a day per person in Warsaw compared to 53 a day in the West. The average Pole produces four times as much waste water as West Europeans.

"In Poland, like all of Eastern Europe, there was no economic incentive to save water. Nobody thought of charging for water. houses don't have water meters," said Bronislaw Kaminski, president of Poland's National Fund for Environmental Protection and Water Management.

Kaminski said technocrats from his water fund have been rushing around Poland in the past year preaching conservation and ordering a halt to the construction of 50 water-treatment plants "that are too big, too expensive and which use old technology."

Kaminski is the father of a nationwide crusade to cut back on water usage by making consumers pay a market price for the water they consume and the sewage they create.

"In a market economy, the money for good water has to come from taxpayers. If we reduce consumption and make consumers pay for water, we will have resources to build smaller, more efficient plants that use the best technology," said Kaminski.

Warsaw residents will probably have to wait several years before conservation, higher water bills and new treatment technology can purify water drawn from the Vistula.

Even then, the Vistula may prove a poor source of good-tasting drinking water. As Robert Latawiec, manager of Warsaw's waterworks, explained, "From this quality, you can't make miracles."

In the meantime, there is a less polluting alternative, a man-made reservoir north of the capital. Warsaw already draws more than a third of its drinking water from the reservoir, which is called Zegrzynskie Lake.

Still, as water chemist Dojlido likes to point out, Warsaw is very unlucky about water.

"The rivers that flow into Zegrzynskie Lake drain wetlands where there is something called humic acid. It makes for a bad color. When this water is treated with normal amounts of chlorine, it can produce very toxic haloforms," said Dojlido.

The most common haloform in Warsaw tap water, Dojlido said, is chloroform, a known cancer-causing agent when its concentration in drinking water exceeds 30 parts per billion.

"It often happens that the concentration of chloroform is over the permissible limits. In fact, it happens that the level is more than double the limits set by the World Health Organization. The water is not safe then for drinking," said Dojlido.

Warsaw does have one other option—underground water. The city lies on an artesian basin, with clean drinking water lying at a depth of about 650 feet.

During the Communist era, the city drilled a small number of public wells and made water available to residents willing to line up outdoors with plastic jugs. Over the years, as the quality of tap water has deteriorated, the lines for well water have grown longer. Huge plastic jugs, along with portable rollers, sell briskly in local markets. The usual wait for good water is about half an hour.

As part of the government's low-tech cure for the capital's clean-water crisis, scores of new wells are to be dug throughout the city in the next few months. The wait for underground water should soon disappear. Unfortunately, according to water experts, so will the good water.

11 Great Lakes Governors Endorse Pollution Plan

EDWARD WALSH
April, 1991

The Environmental Protection Agency and the governors of the Great Lakes states announced a voluntary "pollution prevention" program today that EPA Administrator William K. Reilly predicted would meet the agency's goal of a 50 percent cut in the discharge of certain toxic chemicals into the lakes by the end of 1995.

"Pollution prevention" is the buzzphrase for changes in manufacturing that generate less pollution. The approach stands in contrast to older methods that try to remove pollutants from a factory's output.

Environmental groups generally praised the program as an important "first step," but some warned that a purely voluntary approach would never end pollution of the Great Lakes, the largest collection of fresh water bodies in the world.

"Voluntary reduction of a few pollutants is only a starting place," Carolyn Raffensperger, staff director of the Illinois chapter of the Sierra Club, said in a statement. "That alone will not clean the Great Lakes without other strong, well-funded programs. We need the big stick to match this carrot."

The sharpest criticism came from Jack Weinberg, coordinator of the Green-peace Great Lakes project, who called today's announcement a "feel-good program targeted at public approval ratings, not at cleaning up the poisons in the Great Lakes." He said the program was inadequate in part because it covers only 17 toxic chemicals among thousands that flow into the lakes and did not include "a single enforceable pollution prevention" measure.

Reilly replied that EPA and the states will continue to enforce all existing pollution laws while encouraging voluntary steps toward additional cuts in toxic discharges and that there would be no "vacation" from the terms of those laws for industries that join the voluntary effort.

Reilly was joined at a news conference here by the five Republican governors of Great Lakes states—Arne H. Carlson of Minnesota, Jim Edgar of Illinois, John Engler of Michigan, Tommy G. Thompson of Wisconsin and George Voinovich of Ohio. Christine Perovich, spokeswoman for the Council of Great Lakes Governors, said it was "pure coincidence" that the three Democratic members of the council were not here because of scheduling and other conflicts. She said the Democrats— Govs. Evan Bayh of Indiana, Robert P. Casey of Pennsylvania and Mario M. Cuomo of New York—fully supported the voluntary program.

Under the plan announced today, the EPA and state governments will encourage industries and others to adopt pollution prevention programs targeted at specific toxic chemicals and certain geographic areas of the Great Lakes region. The geographic targets include the heavily industrialized area of northwest Indiana, the Niagara River and Milwaukee. The 17 toxic chemicals covered by the plan are among those targeted by a nationwide EPA effort to reduce the discharge of those substances by 33 percent by the end of 1992 and 50 percent by the end of 1995.

Incentives to industry include promises of public recognition of voluntary pollution prevention measures that could be used in advertising and marketing campaigns. Among the specific projects included in the plan is a cooperative effort between the states and the Big Three U.S. auto makers to identify and reduce toxic substances that are part of the automobile manufacturing process.

Threats to the Water Resource: Oceans and Bays 9

This chapter contains articles focusing on environmental problems associated with oceans and bays. The first two articles address ocean pollution; Article 1, written in 1991, provides some cause for optimism, reporting that quality of the coastal waters around the United States may be improving. However, there continue to be numerous problems, and Article 2 is but one example of many that report on ocean pollution incidents, this time in California and caused by untreated sewage spills.

The remaining ten articles address the pollution problems in the Chesapeake Bay and the efforts to restore this body of water. The Chesapeake provides an excellent prototype of the fight to protect the environment from threats posed by the industrial development and urban expansion associated with a growing population. The story of the Chesapeake is similar to numerous others that are being played out in our nation, as well as in the rest of the world. Hopefully, the lessons we are learning from the Chesapeake will improve our strategies for environmental preservation in the myriad of other ecosystems whose very survival is threatened.

Article 3, the first discussion of the Chesapeake Bay, indicates one source of the problem, describing the efforts of a major petroleum company to obtain a permit to drill for oil and natural gas in the immediate area. The next five articles provide a clear picture of the difficulties encountered in the attempts to restore the Chesapeake Bay in the face of conflicting agendas of numerous interest groups. Articles 4, 5, and 6 all suggest a need for more stringent controls, but make very clear the difficulties associated with such an approach. In one area, officials who promoted stringent restrictions were voted out of office and replaced by others favoring fewer controls and more reliance on voluntary changes. Environmentalists object that voluntary programs are hopelessly inadequate. Article 7 suggests that the most important focus now should be on individuals rather than on industry and should target contamination from urban development, automobiles, and yard chemicals. However, Article 8 makes it clear that there still is a long way to go in reducing industrial pollution and describes a plan to reduce the increasing level of nitrogen contamination.

The final four articles concern the state of marine life in the Chesapeake Bay. Articles 9, 10 and 11 concern the drastic reduction in the oyster harvest over the past ten years, and one article suggests that there may be similar danger to the crab population. Finally, Article 12 provides a ray of hope, reporting that conservation efforts appear to have restored the once devastated rockfish population.

1   Is Coastal Pollution Ebbing?

Some U.S. Waters Reported Cleaner in 1980s

WILLIAM BOOTH
January, 1991

In a major reassessment of the health of U.S. coastal waters, federal scientists reported yesterday that overall the nation's marine environment may be less polluted now than a decade ago.

Contrary to the popular belief that the nation's waters grow more polluted each year, scientists monitoring toxic compounds and trace metals in fish livers and shellfish guts conclude that environmental efforts are paying off and chemical contamination on average appears to be either stable or decreasing.

"There are local problems. There are still big problems. But it appears the situation is improving or at least not getting worse," said Thomas O'Connor, manager of the program at the National Oceanic and Atmospheric Administration, which released its results yesterday.

"It's good news. If the data are accurate, this is a really hopeful sign," said Elliott Norse, a marine ecologist and chief scientist at the Center for Marine Conservation, an environmental advocacy group here. "I say three cheers."

Norse, however, said that despite some gains, the United States still has a large marine pollution problem. Moreover, the federal scientists caution that there are still high levels of chemical contaminants in the harbors and bays of Baltimore, Boston, New York, San Diego, Los Angeles and Seattle.

For example, while most of the Chesapeake Bay failed to show worrisome levels of contamination, Baltimore Harbor still shows high concentrations of lead and other trace metals, as well as the remnants of pesticides and fuel burning.

Yet the study suggests that the lawsuits, legislation, hard work and money spent in the 1970s began to show positive results in the marine environment during the 1980s.

"It is quite obvious that the decrease in chemicals in the environment is due to the banning of those chemicals," O'Connor said.

O'Connor and his colleagues saw less evidence of banned or restricted substances such as the pesticides DDT and chlordane. They also saw less polychlorinated biphenyls, or PCBs, which were used in electrical transformers and capacitors.

Lead levels also dropped, almost certainly due to the phasing out of leaded gasoline. In 50 "Mussel Watch" sites visited in the 1970s and 1980s, 39 showed lower concentrations of lead. Cadmium levels also dropped while copper levels increased. (Of the 11 contaminants examined, copper is the only one whose industrial use has increased.)

Federal scientists stress that their studies did not focus on levels of bacteria in the water or the effects of even low levels of pollutants on human health, nor did they examine the effects of urban and agricultural runoff.

"While these new findings suggest some improvement in the health of the marine environment, the prognosis isn't all good," said Charles Ehler, director of NOAA's Office of Oceanography and Marine Assessment. "Measurements of chemical contaminants alone aren't adequate to determine the overall health of our coastal areas."

Peter Montague, a senior research analyst in the toxics program at Greenpeace, said any optimism over coastal improvements should be tempered by the fact that the study did not examine the health effects of eating fish that harbor small amounts of toxic compounds or trace metals.

The federal study focused only on chemical contaminants found in sediments, the livers of bottom-feeding fish and the soft tissue of mussels and oysters at 287 coastal and estuarial sites around the country.

The samples were collected over the past six years and, in some cases, compared with mussels and oysters sampled at the same sites by the Environmental Protection Agency in the mid-1970s. Mussels and oysters are good sentinels, since they stay in one place and absorb what passes through their systems.

The program sampled sediment and oysters from "representative" sites, and it deliberately avoided obvious "hot spots" such as the highly polluted Houston Ship Channel, the Arthur Kill in New York or the Chelsea River mouth in Boston. The researchers said that these spots already are being monitored for compliance with federal regulations and, though highly polluted, do not offer much insight into the health of larger bodies of water. However, even though the Houston Ship Channel was avoided, seven other sites nearby in Galveston Bay were monitored.

The work reported yesterday follows a report by a group of international ocean experts assembled by the United Nations, who concluded in 1989 that the world's open oceans are relatively clean.

However, there is growing concern that the Third World is increasing its use of pesticides and PCBs, according to Ed Goldberg, an ocean chemist and an author of the U.N. report at the Scripps Institution of Oceanography. An international "Mussel Watch" program is in the works.

2 Ocean Contaminants Keep California Beaches Closed

LEEF SMITH
August, 1992

F ive miles of Southern California's popular coastline remained closed to swimmers seeking relief from sweltering temperatures today after discovery during the weekend of contaminants in the ocean.

Sanitation officials reported high levels in the water Saturday of coliform bacteria, an indication of untreated sewage, prompting Los Angeles County authorities to ban swimming at a series of beaches stretching from Venice to Playa del Rey.

"Generally, when people swim, they get water in their nose and mouth," said Shirley Fannin, director of the disease control office for the Los Angeles County Health Department. "Human waste can carry disease organism, and that's how you can get fecal-oral disorders."

Symptoms of exposure to coliform bacteria, she said, are diarrhea, nausea, headaches, fatigue and jaundice.

A sewage leak or backup is believed responsible for the contamination, but Health Department spokesman Richard Kebabjian said the source has not been found.

"Whatever it was, whatever happened, it occurred in Ballona Creek," which flows into the Pacific Ocean at Marina Del Rey about 15 miles southwest of downtown Los Angeles, Rebabjian said.

Sewage spills are more likely to occur in rainy weather when sewers overflow than in the dead of summer, he said. Los Angeles County averages about 10 to 12 sewage spills a year.

One of the most devastating sewage spills recorded in Southern California occurred last Feb. 2 when San Diego's main underwater-sewage pipe ruptured about two-thirds of a mile offshore. The pipe spewed about 180 million gallons of partially treated sewage into coastal waters each day until it was patched April 4.

The spill forced a 10-week quarantine of more than 20 miles of beaches from San Diego's Mission Bay area to the Mexican border.

Los Angeles beaches could be reopened as soon as Tuesday morning if water samples show improvement, authorities said.

221

Meanwhile, temperatures in the region have soared into the 90s and have occasionally topped 100, giving beachgoers in Los Angeles little escape from the heat.

Eighty miles to the north in Santa Barbara, beaches were packed today, with every hotel room in the city reported booked, authorities said.

3 Environmentalists Fear Drilling Plans in Chesapeake Watershed

D'VERA COHN
November, 1991

F aulkner, a rural crossroads on the Potomac River only 40 miles south of Washington, soon may be the closest place to the nation's capital with a producing oil well.

Texaco wants to sink a 10,000-foot exploratory well in a soybean field 1,500 feet from marshy Popes Creek, which feeds into the Potomac. The oil giant's proposal is part of the first concerted campaign by a major energy producer to hunt for oil or natural gas in a geological formation that stretches from southern Maryland across the Potomac River into Virginia.

For environmentalists and some local members of Congress, though, the Charles County community is altogether too close for comfort to the Chesapeake Bay and its tributaries.

"We are spending millions of dollars to save the bay," said Roy Hoagland, a lawyer with the Chesapeake Bay Foundation, the region's largest environmental group. "It's simply absurd to introduce the petrochemical industry into a region where you're trying so hard to preserve a resource."

In Charles County, Texaco has won local approval and is awaiting a drilling permit from the Maryland Department of Natural Resources. It recently obtained state and local permits in Virginia's King George and Westmoreland counties, and plans to begin drilling in Westmoreland next month. In Virginia's Essex County, Texaco won local permission and is seeking state approval. The three Virginia counties are east or south of Fredericksburg.

Texaco, which has leased nearly 400,000 acres in the two states for potential drilling, has promised state-of-the-art operations with meticulous environmental safeguards, even down to collecting and trucking out rainwater. The company argues that the nation needs to look for its own energy reserves to lessen dependence on imported oil.

"This project is good for the whole region," said Doug Weaver, a Texaco senior petroleum engineer. "I hate to get out the mom-and-apple-pie speech, but for a company like Texaco to try to open up a new region—that's the real big news."

Texaco officials say that the odds of a discovery are small—1 in 20—and that oil is a less likely find than natural gas, which demands a drilling rig no larger than a telephone booth.

The company promised not to transport oil by tanker, to use only non-toxic mud to lubricate its drills, to build barriers around the sites, to employ more accident prevention devices than state law requires and to truck out all waste except rock.

Critics say that the dangers of an accident to the area's large and most fragile natural resource remain too great and that if oil is discovered, today's tough standards may be relaxed.

In a letter last week, six members of Congress from Maryland, Virginia and the District urged Texaco to drop its plans because of those risks.

Rep. Tom McMillen (D-Md.), who organized the letter, said if persuasion does not work, the lawmakers are "looking at other possibilities, legislative and otherwise," although he did not give specifics. He said he is "not as concerned about natural gas" as about oil tankers on the bay.

The letter's signers included Rep. Wayne T. Gilchrest (R-Md.), whose district includes Charles County, but not Rep. Herbert H. Bateman (R-Va.), who represents the Virginia drill-site counties. A spokesman for Bateman said he believes the drilling permits are a state and local issue, and "shouldn't become a political battle."

This is Texaco's second stab at finding energy in the Taylorsville geological basin; it has leased 67,000 acres in Maryland and 324,000 in Virginia for potential drilling. In 1989, after several years of seismic tests, Texaco and Exxon jointly installed a 12,000-foot well in a cornfield in Virginia's Westmoreland County, yielding some natural gas but no oil.

Texaco's bids this time encountered little local opposition. In King George County, dozens of residents have signed leases—so many that one county supervisor said it amounted to a pro-Texaco referendum. In Essex County, Texaco spokesman Shawn Frederick said, the few residents who came to the public hearing were outnumbered by the Texaco delegation.

Each 24-hour-a-day well will cost $4 million, and Weaver estimated that 10 to 15 percent of the cost would be for safety steps. Texaco also is spending more than $50,000 for an archaeological excavation at the King George well, which may have been the home of a wealthy planter, Frederick said.

"I think it would be good for the whole state," said Alexander Dillard, chairman of the Essex County supervisors. "I can't see how it's going to hurt the bay. It's a long way from any body of water."

Not far enough, according to environmentalists, who say the drilling region is riddled with creeks and streams that lead to the bay, as well as lying over groundwater that flows to it. They raise other environmental hazards: air pollution from diesel-fueled drilling rigs, contamination of wetlands, disruption of bald eagle nests in Popes Creek and elsewhere.

Even more dangerous than the Texaco wells, they say, is the precedent they set.

"What happens in Charles County may happen all over the place," said Ron Huber, of Maryland's Earth First! "We don't think it's just a local issue."

"As much as we'd like to trust Texaco . . . that doesn't have any bearing on whether the ABC Company, a wildcatter from Louisiana, might have no qualms about shipping out on leaky barges," said William C. Baker, president of the Chesapeake Bay Foundation. "That's what opening the door does."

Baker and others say the Texaco proposals exposed weaknesses in Maryland's and Virginia's drilling laws.

Both states ban drilling in the bay itself and restrict it near the bay's shore, its rivers and streams. But environmentalists pointed out that several environmental safeguards promised by Texaco, such as trucking all waste off the site, are not required by state law and could be forgotten in the future.

The two state permits in Virginia included few of the extensive conditions recommended by the Council on the Environment, a state agency required by a 1989 law to give advice to the Department of Mines, Minerals and Energy. The mines department said it does not have the authority to require many of those conditions— among them a contingency plan for spills, and a reevaluation of the permit if Texaco decides to go into production.

"It's hard to believe that the lead environmental agency would absolutely be ignored," said the Chesapeake Bay Foundation's Baker.

The bay foundation says that Maryland law also apparently allows Texaco to convert an exploratory well to a production well without additional scrutiny.

Keith Buttleman, the Virginia council administrator, said the permit-writing process exposed weaknesses that should be remedied, either by the mining department toughening its procedures or the state legislature tightening the law.

"Something needs to be done to assure that the proper safeguards are built into any operation that is allowed to proceed," he said.

Virginia Gov. L. Douglas Wilder recently endorsed proposed legislation that would relax a ban on "slant" drilling into the bay from shore, as well as require future drilling to include the Texaco safeguards.

The proposal, drafted by a group that included oil industry representatives and environmentalists, would require all drilling to be accompanied by cleanup contingency plans and would ban drilling within 500 feet of the bay or its tributaries.

4 States Consider Tougher Restrictions to Ensure Success of Bay Cleanup

D'VERA COHN
January, 1992

T he campaign to clean up the Chesapeake Bay will fail without more restrictions on pollution, potentially affecting drivers, farmers, utility companies, developers and states that do not border the bay, regional lawmakers were told here today.

Maryland Environment Secretary Robert Perciasepe, who heads an interstate panel evaluating the progress of the cleanup, said research shows the bay states will meet their target of cutting phosphorus pollution 40 percent by the end of the decade. But he said the states will not meet their goal for cutting nitrogen pollution because population growth is offsetting other gains from current environmental restrictions.

Both pollutants come from chemicals such as fertilizers that run off from farming and lawn care. They encourage algae growth, which robs fish and other aquatic life of oxygen. Other sources are sewage plants and factories, runoff during rainstorms, and automobile tailpipes.

The evaluation convinced some bay state officials that they must get tougher on regulated polluters such as sewage plants and farms. The results also suggest that they must target pollution sources not regulated in the past because of politics or because they were not thought to be important enough.

"We have to do everything we are currently doing and yet do it better, and we may have to expand into new areas," said Jeffrey W. Coy, a Pennsylvania state legislator who was chairman of the meeting of the Chesapeake Bay Commission.

The wide variety of responses to Perciasepe's presentation indicated that agreement may not be easy to reach on the next step to restore the nation's largest estuary, where pollution from farms and cities has depleted a rich stock of fish, shellfish and plant life.

Some lawmakers said there is no money for new programs in tough economic times. Others said the report told them the cleanup is going well.

The final report will be presented for public comment in the spring, and the bay state governors will use it as a basis for deciding on the next stage of the bay cleanup effort at a meeting this summer.

Phosphorus pollution is down, but nitrogen has increased 7 percent since 1985 because of new sewer hookups, power plants, cars and other consequences of population growth, research shows.

One potential target is air pollution, which recently was discovered to be the source of at least 25 percent of the bay's nitrogen. The region's governors already have agreed to require cleaner-burning cars to be sold in their states to meet anti-smog goals. The panel also voted today to endorse that goal.

States also may target power plants, another source of nitrogen, and require them to install low-polluting burners, Perciasepe said.

New attention also is being paid to Delaware, New York and West Virginia, which dump 15 percent to 20 percent of the bay's nitrogen and phosphorus because their streams and underground aquifers ultimately drain into the bay.

The Chesapeake Bay Commission voted today to invite officials from Delaware, New York and Virginia to its May meeting to encourage them to get involved in the bay cleanup.

Perciasepe also endorsed requiring local governments to limit growth to conserve land and other resources. After an ambitious proposal failed to win support last year, Gov. William Donald Schaefer's administration will propose a scaled-back version this legislative session.

Ann Swanson, executive director of the commission, said bay states are leaning toward imposing mandates on farmers to use less fertilizer, fewer chemicals and more erosion control techniques, which now are largely voluntary. She said tougher rules are needed on sewage plants and factories, "to get our own house in order first" before asking concessions of others.

"Where are we going to get the money?" asked Maryland Del. Walter E. McClellan (D-Frederick), after hearing the report. "It's wonderful to have this dream of turning the bay back to where it was when the Indians were here, but we have different tribes now."

But William C. Baker, president of the Chesapeake Bay Foundation, cited Perciasepe's estimate that a 40 percent reduction in nitrogen and phosphorus would yield a 20 percent reduction in the bay's volume of oxygen-starved waters. Perciasepe said that may be enough, but Baker said a 1987 bay agreement set a goal of eliminating low-oxygen waters. "When the goal was 100 percent, is 20 enough? I say no," Baker said.

5 Bay Cleanup to Target Tributaries

Area Leaders Agree to Cut River Pollution

D'VERA COHN
August, 1992

The top elected leaders of the District, Maryland and Virginia, facing criticism about the pace of the Chesapeake Bay cleanup, signed an agreement today to extend their efforts against pollution to the Potomac River and other bay tributaries.

The agreement, signed here at the annual summit meeting of bay area governors, D.C. Mayor Sharon Pratt Kelly and Environmental Protection Agency Administrator William K. Reilly, was aimed primarily at reducing pollution runoff from farms, suburbs and cities that taints the rivers where much of the bay's marine life spawns.

The officials praised their progress on the cleanup of the bay itself, saying underwater grasses that are vital to fish and other marine life are coming back as the nitrogen and phosphorus that depletes oxygen is reduced.

At the same time, the officials acknowledged that correcting some problems, such as reducing runoff pollution, will be more difficult than once thought.

"We've made real progress," said Maryland Gov. William Donald Schaefer (D). "There are those who say we're not moving fast enough. . . . We have produced results."

The new bay pact comes as financially strapped state and local governments are trimming environmental programs to save money, or in some cases rolling back on previous environmental commitments. Fairfax County, for example, recently altered its stringent bay protection law at the request of local developers.

The bay cleanup drew criticism this week from the Chesapeake Bay Foundation, which said it relied too much on voluntary programs. The foundation said controls on real estate development near the bay, toxic pollution and fish protection were not strict enough.

In a letter to bay area leaders this week, the group said Maryland and Virginia had done nothing to "contain the commercial harvest of blue crabs at present levels" despite a 1989 promise to do so.

"Almost all activities seem to be to 'assess' instead of 'to do,'" foundation President William C. Baker said in the letter.

The campaign also came in for criticism today from the citizens advisory committee appointed by the governors and mayor, which said that there are "serious questions" about whether current policies will preserve wetlands and that "concrete programs have been slow to develop" to curb runoff pollution.

Edwina Coder, chairwoman of the committee, also urged the bay area's leaders to give more attention to installing controls on growth, a politically sensitive issue.

Maryland adopted a growth-control bill this year after a stronger measure failed last year. A Virginia commission will not even propose such legislation until 1993.

"You should be charging and directing and criticizing us," Maryland Sen. C. Bernard "Bernie" Fowler (D-St. Mary's-Calvert) said after Coder's report. "But don't forget there has been progress."

Schaefer's response was sharper. In an interview, he called Baker, head of the area's largest environmental group, "a nice young man," adding, "He's got to keep his membership up. He doesn't have to worry about politics. He doesn't have to worry about passing bills."

Schaefer also said he did not favor some mandatory programs, such as requiring farmers to reduce pollution or setting new limits on fish catches. He said that farmers will sign up for voluntary programs when they realize that using less fertilizer will save money and that fishing limits would be difficult to enact as well as potentially unnecessary.

In her speech to the conference, Kelly (D) said the District had been "somewhat disengaged" from the bay cleanup and other environmental issues, but that has changed. She said city officials plan to reduce nitrogen pollution of the Potomac River from the Blue Plains sewage treatment plant, the area's largest, and to step up efforts to restore the Anacostia River.

"We understand now in the District of Columbia . . . to talk about protecting the environment is in no way mutually exclusive of providing jobs and hope," Kelly said.

Schaefer and Virginia Gov. L. Douglas Wilder (D) also promised to revive legislation requiring new cars sold in Maryland and Northern Virginia to have enhanced anti-pollution devices.

Proposals to reduce automobile emissions died in both legislatures this year after opposition from industry. The primary reason for the devices is to combat smog, but advocates say they also will help reduce pollution to the bay, citing estimates that a third or more of nitrogen pollution in the estuary comes from the air.

The new focus on tributaries will begin with an evaluation of the sources and amount of pollution in each river, due in a year. Different plans to reduce pollution in each river will be written after the studies are finished. Some observers said they hope the emphasis on rivers will give new ammunition to calls for controls on runoff pollution from farms and suburban growth.

6   Fairfax Drawing a Line in the Soil

Officials Study Options for Easing Runoff Law for Chesapeake Bay

PETER BAKER
March, 1992

Carl Quitmeyer wants to clean up the Chesapeake Bay as much as anybody else. He just doesn't believe he should have to pay a lot of extra money to do it when he builds his dream house.

Under a landmark law pending in Fairfax County, owners of environmentally sensitive property such as Quitmeyer's could be told where and how they can build houses. Some would have to spend thousands of dollars to prevent soil disturbed during construction from running off into streams that feed into the pollution-choked bay.

To Quitmeyer, who bought a woodsy, sloping seven-acre tract near Sandy Creek Run in Fairfax Station in 1981 as the site of a future house, the new regulations are outrageous.

"That property, as far as I'm concerned, has done nothing to cause the problem in the bay," he said. "And yet, here I am being isolated to pay the cost."

To environmentalists such as Stella Koch, the rules are critical to saving the Chesapeake and its tributaries, and someone has to pay the cost.

"If you don't pay for it by keeping [pollutants] on your property, somebody else is going to have to pay for it downstream," said Koch, who works for the Audubon Naturalist Society.

This classic confrontation, with property owners and developers on one side and environmentalists and civic activists on the other, has consumed governments throughout the bay region in recent years.

But in few places has the issue been so sharply divisive as in Fairfax, where a new Republican-controlled Board of Supervisors recently decided to reconsider the stringent regulations approved last year when Democrats were in charge.

If the board scales back the ordinance, thousands of properties will be freed from the requirements, which worries environmentalists convinced that the bay will suffer as a result.

Like 88 other Virginia jurisdictions from Tidewater to the Washington suburbs, Fairfax was required by a 1988 state law to adopt land-use rules controlling building projects near streams that flow into the nation's largest estuary.

Last May, under then-Chairman Audrey Moore and her Democratic majority, the Fairfax board endorsed one of the toughest plans in Virginia.

Going far beyond the minimum state guidelines, the board designated about 15 percent of the county as critical areas where construction would be severely limited. In the rest of the county, builders would have to control erosion at their projects better than they do now.

For example, a homeowner living on a steep slope who wanted to add a wing larger than 1,000 square feet would have to plant new ground cover or provide special drainage for storm water runoff.

Supervisors said the expansive regulations were a logical next step in a county that has long had strong environmental controls. Builders and real estate agents complained that Moore's real motive was to slow growth rather than improve water quality in the bay.

The ordinance has not yet taken effect because it first had to be endorsed by the state. Debate about whether Fairfax had gone too far delayed approval until last month.

By then, Moore and two Democratic allies had been voted out of office, swinging control to a 6 to 4 Republican majority far more sympathetic to developers. Builders contributed thousands of dollars to their campaigns.

On a party-line vote last month, the board agreed to consider adopting the minimum restrictions set by the state. Such a move would cut in half the amount of land affected by the most severe rules and would mean that there would be no new rules for about 80 percent of the county.

Public hearings are scheduled before the Planning Commission on March 26 and 28, with the issue returning to the supervisors June 8.

How far the board will go remains unclear because the Republicans are divided. Moore's Republican successor, Thomas M. Davis III, has pledged not to push for the minimum guidelines.

"The county will do something in between the state minimums and what it did the first time," said Davis, who worked to loosen the original rules before voting for them last year. "Some of them make sense in terms of water-quality management. Some of them I never understood."

Developers and some homeowners complain that the Moore law is so restrictive that property values would plummet.

Michael S. Rolband, an Alexandria environmental consultant who often works for developers, produced a study concluding that the regulations would reduce the worth of county land by $750 million, costing the government $8.3 million in taxes each year.

Rolband also estimated that the average price of a new house could increase by $4,565. Another study produced for builders determined that in some extreme cases the ordinance could delay projects by nearly a year.

Rolband said there are more efficient ways of reducing pollution, such as controlling storm water runoff through an expanded system of holding ponds. "If we're serious about removing pollution from stream water, we have at our fingertips a way of doing it more effectively," he said.

But environmentalists scoffed at Rolband's study and its methodology.

"Most of the claims we've heard about the fiscal impact are just a crock," said Bruce G. Douglas, the county's chief environmental planner. "This stuff is ludicrous."

Douglas said homeowners would not be affected much, with requirements generally costing them hundreds of dollars, not thousands. Those targeted by the original ordinance are developers of larger projects, he said.

Environmentalists also said some large builders have insulated themselves with a new law passed by the General Assembly in the session that just ended.

Under the bay rules, any property with a detailed building plan already approved by the county is exempt. The new state law sponsored by Sen. Richard L. Saslaw (D-Springfield) extended the life of all such plans by five years, so that developers waiting out the recession don't have to worry about meeting the new regulations.

The law is retroactive to Jan. 1, instead of going into effect July 1 as most bills do. In Fairfax, that six-month difference affects seven plans, including the Centre Ridge project planned by developer John T. "Til" Hazel Jr., whose law partner lobbied for the Saslaw bill.

Saslaw said the bill was intended to help builders in trouble because of the wheezing economy and said he was not trying to thwart the bay rules.

"They aren't environmentalists, they're just no-growthers," he said of his critics. "If I thought that thing would have an iota of impact on the Chesapeake Bay, I wouldn't have put it in."

7   Setback Feared in Shift in Cleanup of the Bay

Individuals to Be Asked to Take the Burden

D'VERA COHN
September, 1993

A decade of progress in restoring the Chesapeake Bay could be endangered as antipollution efforts shift from industry to individuals, District, Maryland and Virginia officials acknowledged today.

At their annual summit, bay chief executives agreed that the cleanup program increasingly must address the contamination caused by suburban sprawl, cars and backyard chemical runoff.

But they conceded that many people living upstream from the bay will resist those changes.

"There's a tremendous untapped resource of people that we've been unable to get to," Maryland Gov. William Donald Schaefer said.

In fact, the officials said, much of the public still blames industry and sewage plants for the bay's problems. But that type of pollution is being addressed, they said.

District Mayor Sharon Pratt Kelly talked of the days when "we all rolled up our sleeves" to pick up litter or water trees in a community, and "no one thought it was the government's job" to clean the environment alone.

A similar theme was sounded Monday at a citizen conference on the Chesapeake Bay effort.

Support for bay programs "frequently becomes weak when personal interests are involved," Virginia State Sen. Joseph V. Gartlan Jr. (D-Mount-Vernon), a long-time Chesapeake activist, told that meeting in Baltimore. "Our political will has been sapped to some extent."

The need to build public support already has delayed plans to write separate proposals to reduce pollution in the Potomac, Patuxent and other Chesapeake Bay tributaries.

Those plans, originally due this month, will not be ready until next year because "people told us to slow down a bit" and involve the public, Schaefer said.

Despite concern over the future, bay program officials noted their progress: Phosphorus and nitrogen pollution is down. The rockfish is rebounding. The amount of vital underwater grasses is growing.

At today's meeting, the Chesapeake Executive Council, made up of bay state representatives, and Carol Browner, head of the U.S. Environmental Protection Agency, agreed to rewrite the plan to reduce pollution from toxic chemicals like mercury and copper.

A recent report commissioned by bay states said the bay has several toxic hotspots, including the Anacostia River.

However, officials say that the impact of low levels of toxic chemicals in the bay is unclear.

The conferees also agreed to increase efforts to restore bay grasses, remove barriers to fish migration and reduce farm pollution.

8   Plan to Fight Pollution at Blue Plains May Be Near after Two Years of Talks

D'VERA COHN
October, 1993

Every day, the Blue Plains regional plant in Southwest Washington treats 300 million gallons of sewage from the District, Maryland and Virginia. In a year's time, it discharges 14 million pounds of nitrogen as a byproduct of that treatment.

Those millions of toxic pounds ultimately reach the Chesapeake Bay, making the Blue Plains plant the single biggest source of nitrogen pollution in the bay.

For two years, federal and local officials have been negotiating how best to lower the facility's nitrogen discharges. Some say they're close to agreeing on a one-year experiment that would be the world's largest pilot program for nitrogen removal.

"It would be the single most cost-effective thing we could do to clean up the bay," said William Matuszeski, head of the federal Environmental Protection Agency's Chesapeake Bay office.

Although the Blue Plains plant is responsible for nearly one-third of the nitrogen in the Potomac River Basin, that's of little concern locally. Nitrogen becomes toxic only when it nears the saltier environment of the bay, 90 miles downstream from the District. There, it stimulates growth of algae, which block light and soak up oxygen, killing other marine species and stifling vital underwater grasses that offer food and a habitat.

"It's easy to point fingers and say it's somebody downstream that's causing that problem," said Alan Pollock, of the Virginia Department of Environmental Quality. But "the findings are that the Potomac River and the rivers north of there up to the Susquehanna all have very significant impacts on the water in the bay."

The effort at Blue Plains would be part of a regional undertaking. In both Maryland and Virginia, sewage treatment plants are considering spending millions of dollars to lower nitrogen discharges. All three jurisdictions have promised to reduce nitrogen and phosphorus discharges to the bay by 40 percent, compared with 1985 levels, by 2000.

Phosphorus already is a success story; levels have dropped 16 percent since 1985, mainly because of phosphate detergent bans and sewage plant improvements.

But nitrogen levels are up, mainly because the population and sewage levels are growing.

Nitrogen removal is a relatively low-technology process that relies on bacteria to convert ammonia nitrogen into nitrates and then into harmless nitrogen gas that vents into the atmosphere. Newer techniques use only bacteria, as opposed to such carbon-supplying chemicals as methanol.

By 2000, Maryland plans to install advanced nitrogen removal at 52 plants at a cost of $250 million. Washington Suburban Sanitary Commission plants in Upper Marlboro and Laurel already remove nitrogen, and design work is underway to convert the commission's third major plant in Accokeek. Bowie's sewage treatment plant also removes nitrogen.

In Northern Virginia, few plants have committed to removal programs because of the expense. Unlike Maryland, which is providing funds to help shoulder the cost, Virginia offers only loans. Prince William County officials are among the few who say they hope to install the necessary equipment within several years.

Virginia, however, is requiring that sewage treatment plants lower their ammonia discharges as a condition of renewing their operating permits. That will have the effect of removing some nitrogen as well. Pollock said state officials also are encouraging plants to install the second half of the process to finish converting the nitrates to nitrogen gas, which would further reduce nitrogen levels.

What consumers will pay for those programs remains uncertain. A consultant's report estimated that nitrogen removal could cost Northern Virginians $4 to $40 a year depending on where they live. In suburban Maryland, it accounts for about $1.50 of the average WSSC bill of $518 a year.

No District estimates are available, although the proposed Blue Plains experiment would cost about $2 million in construction and operating expenses, according to EPA officials. Permanent installation would cost an estimated $9 million a year in capital and operating expenses, city officials say.

The effort there could be a boon for smaller sewage plants. Because nitrogen removal costs more per pound for smaller plants, some regional officials have suggested that those facilities could underwrite additional nitrogen removal at Blue Plains instead of doing it themselves.

The Blue Plains talks have dragged on for more than two years because of various disagreements. They now are stalled over whether the city would be fined if the removal process backfired and instead worsened ammonia pollution in the Potomac.

"We have a treatment we think is going to work," Mayor Sharon Pratt Kelly said.

EPA officials say they have made several recent settlement offers to resolve issues of money and operating conditions. They note that City Administrator Robert L. Mallett got involved in the talks during the summer, a development they see as indicating new, high-level interest.

The Blue Plains method would use methanol to fuel the nitrogen-eating bacteria. Officials say that would not require major construction at the crowded facility. They estimate that a bacteria-only system would be eight times costlier.

Still, some question the plan. Virginia Tech professor Clifford Randall, a nationally known authority on nitrogen removal, said the methanol technique is costlier and generates more sludge for disposal.

The bacteria method, he said, "is much more environmentally sound than the other approaches. You're minimizing energy use. You're minimizing chemical use. You're minimizing sludge production. . . . It's something that virtually all the treatment plants in the Chesapeake Bay region should consider."

9 A Shell Game of Survival

Reef Project Is Latest Hope for Rescuing Oysters in the Bay

D'VERA COHN
May, 1993

A heap of shucked shells six feet high and 1,000 feet long rises from a quiet cove here, either a savior for the Chesapeake Bay's dying oysters or another failed experiment to keep them alive.

The reef is being built about three hours southeast of Washington, below the mouth of the Rappahannock River in Virginia's Middle Peninsula. Gulf of Mexico oysters are shucked in Virginia and the shells are taken down the Potomac River by barge and washed off the deck with a water cannon.

The shell pile is intended to provide a sanctuary from two diseases that are killing the bay's young oysters and a once-thriving shellfish industry.

Oysters flourished on such reefs when Europeans arrived in the bay, but years of dredging by watermen wore down the shell piles. Now, most oysters live on the silty bottom, where being in the muck saps their energy and makes them more susceptible to disease, according to one theory.

The Piankatank project will give the shellfish their start in life higher up on the new reef, where the water is clearer and food more plentiful.

For two decades, the state had been paying watermen to replenish shell beds on the bay bottom by dumping shells after the annual harvest. Even its sponsors say the reef is a chancy project that may not show results for five years. "We know everything we've been doing is not working," said James A. Wesson, project supervisor for the Virginia Marine Resources Commission. "The idea here is let's go back, set things at ground zero like we heard it was—pristine conditions—and see what happens."

Scientists increasingly view the oyster's decline as an ecological crisis, not just an economic one, because the mollusks perform the vital function of filtering out sediment and pollution. Scientists estimate that 100 years ago there were enough oysters to filter the whole bay in less than a week. Now, it would take nearly a year.

The oyster's decline has been sudden. Even six years ago, Chesapeake Bay watermen were pulling in more than 2 million bushels in a season, which runs from

October to March. But droughts in the late 1980s sent less fresh water to the bay, making it more salty. That created ideal conditions for a parasite called MSX and a fungus called Dermo. Many scientists also blame greedy harvesters and pollution.

This year's bay catch is estimated at 200,000 bushels tops—about the same number of shells being used to build the reef on Palace's Bar here.

As harvests drop, questions are being raised about traditional oyster policies.

Maryland is continuing to put new shells atop seedbeds on the bottom each spring. Baby oysters, called spat, settle on the shell beds during the summer. The following spring, the state moves the oysters to less salty waters, where disease is less prevalent.

One measure of the oyster's desperate state is that "the only harvest these days is coming from the propagation program," said Bill Outten, oyster program leader for Maryland's Department of Natural Resources.

Maryland will spend nearly $1 million this year to replenish seedbeds; this year's state harvest was worth about $2.5 million at dockside. The ratio is roughly the same in Virginia. "If you go on a strict cost-benefit ratio, it's going to raise eyebrows," said Erik Barth, Virginia's deputy fisheries director.

Maryland officials are trying some experiments, sinking tire reefs in the bay to encourage oysters and other species. They will hold an oyster summit next month to explore new ideas.

Virginia also is considering reviving a controversial proposal to drop sterilized Japanese oysters into the James River to see if they fight off disease. Maryland officials oppose the idea, saying a new species poses unpredictable risks.

Wesson says some drastic change is needed. Now 41, he grew up nearby and remembers a time when there were oyster harvests on the Piankatank. After a start as an academic, Wesson spent a decade as a crabber and served on save-the-bay committees before signing up with the state last fall to do something directly about the bay's fading fortunes.

He also is supervising construction of a 25,000-foot reef in the James River and the repair of oceanside reefs on the Eastern Shore. The state also is experimenting with removing all the shells from several beds and laying fresh shells. Total cost of the projects could reach $700,000.

Some of his watermen buddies do not like his reefs because the money to build them otherwise would have been paid to watermen to repair shell beds. Some also are unhappy because the reefs are being set aside as sanctuaries with presumably healthy oysters that will be off limits. "They're seeing this money spent on the reef as something they're not going to see tomorrow," said Tommy Leggett, president of the Virginia Working Watermen.

Wesson admits his project may not work, but he pointed out that the shells can be used for replenishment projects if the experiment fails.

John Register, Wesson's No. 2 man on the Piankatank, is more confident. "You all come back in five years," Register said, "and we'll have some for you."

10 Virginia to Consider Canceling Oyster Harvest

Yield from Chesapeake Has Fallen Drastically

D'VERA COHN and JOHN F. HARRIS

August, 1993

V irginia officials moved yesterday toward banning oyster harvests on the state's part of the Chesapeake Bay, where disease and overfishing have depleted the shellfish stock in the last three decades.

The state's Marine Resources Commission, responding to worsening Chesapeake Bay harvests that led to a record low last year, agreed to vote next month on whether to cancel this year's harvest on the bay's public shellfish beds. Such a ban also might include the seaside of Virginia's Eastern Shore. Shellfish beds leased by private farmers would be exempt.

"We have to protect the brood stock," said James A. Wesson, who is the commission's oyster management specialist and who recommended that the panel consider the ban. "If we get changes that help the disease ease off, we need some critical amount of oysters to . . . repopulate the bay."

The commission's decision yesterday was the latest sign of decline for the bay's once-bountiful fishery. Shad and sturgeon are nearly extinct. Rockfish catches are severely limited. Although blue crab numbers are not dangerously low, the bay states are considering new limits to protect the increasingly popular shellfish.

Chesapeake Bay watermen routinely brought in more than 2 million bushels of oysters a season less than a decade ago. Last year, the bay yielded less than 175,000 bushels.

State analysts have predicted that this year's oyster harvest, which runs from October through March, could be even worse because a huge influx of fresh water from heavy spring rains killed many of the mollusks.

The regional Potomac River Fisheries Commission recently imposed tight new time limits on the upcoming harvest in the Potomac, including a ban on harvesting in January.

This summer, Maryland officials organized a meeting of a range of groups, ranging from watermen to environmentalists, to begin trying to devise a new state

240

oyster policy in light of the dismal harvests. Maryland's harvest last year was about three times the size of Virginia's, but it also has dropped sharply in the last several years.

William Goldsborough, a fisheries scientist for the Chesapeake Bay Foundation who is a member of the roundtable, said it is "hard to imagine" that Maryland would impose a moratorium this year.

The Virginia commission will hold public hearings this month on Wesson's proposal, which is likely to be strongly opposed by watermen and packing companies. The head of a Virginia watermen's organization said he might favor incremental steps such as a shorter season, but not total closure.

"There are some people who can't, or won't, or don't know how to do anything else," said Tommy Leggett, of Virginia Working Watermen. "It's my feeling they are going to be a very minor contributor to the fishing pressure on the oyster."

Lake Cowart, who owns an oyster-processing plant near the mouth of the Potomac River in Luttsburg, Va., said the real culprits are the two diseases—MSX and Dermo—that have been ravaging the oyster stocks.

"Overfishing, in my mind, has not played a major role in the decline of the oyster," Cowart said.

The commission's action yesterday was praised by the Chesapeake Bay Foundation, which, along with scientists at the Virginia Institute of Marine Science, has for years called for a moratorium on oyster harvesting in the bay.

"We are at 1 percent of historic levels," said Ann Powers, vice president of the foundation. the region's largest environmental group. "We really feel there's a chance to do something here. By imposing restrictions, it will be possible potentially to see some rebound in the fishery."

The decline of the oyster is not just an economic crisis for watermen and the communities where they live, it's also a sign that the Chesapeake Bay is in poor health, analysts say. Oysters perform a vital ecological role in filtering sediment and pollution from the bay.

The proposed Virginia moratorium, which would extend for an undetermined period, would affect about 243,000 acres of public oyster beds. Nearly all of the productive public oyster beds are in the James River. The ban would not affect about 110,000 acres leased by private harvesters.

Wesson said he is undecided about whether a ban should include the Eastern Shore's seaside, which produces about a fifth of Virginia's harvest. Watermen there harvest by hand; in the rest of the state, they use tongs and dredges.

Some scientists believe that the bay's best hope for keeping oysters is to encourage the growth of a Japanese variety that has been successfully transplanted to France, California and other fishing grounds.

In June, Virginia officials began an experiment in which sterilized Japanese oysters were dropped into the York River to see how well they resist disease.

The study is not complete, and some scientists have urged caution in putting a nonnative species into the bay before the native oyster has died out.

Virginia also is trying another new tactic this year: building several high oyster reefs that may give the shellfish a sanctuary from disease. Wesson said the reefs are "not populating as fast as we'd hoped" but cannot be written off yet.

11 As Crab Yield Falls, Scientists Claw for Clues

Climate, Cannibalism, Man Seen as Culprits in Bay Decline

D'VERA COHN
August, 1993

The crack of wooden mallets punctuates hot summer nights at the Bethesda Crab House. Red shells, crusted with spice, pile up on newspaper-covered tables. For $14.95, you can eat all you want.

Even on weeknights, most tables are full, and owner Henry Vechery says he sells a hundred dozen Chesapeake Bay crabs on Saturdays. "The whole market's growing," Vechery says. "They want to eat them year-round."

But while the appetite for the bay's blue crab has never been stronger, there are signs that the crab may not be as abundant as it used to be. More watermen are seeking crabs for more months of the year using increasingly sophisticated equipment, yet the average catch is declining.

That has led scientists and environmentalists to try to determine whether the decline is chronic or merely a natural fluctuation in the crab population. And officials in Maryland and Virginia, alarmed by the idea that a symbol of the region could be threatened, are discussing broad limits on crab harvesting.

Scientists are conducting the first accurate count of blue crabs in the Chesapeake Bay, hoping to produce a forecasting tool that could be used to set harvest limits. Last winter, they estimated that about 400 million crabs of legal size lived in the bay.

Old beliefs about the crab's life cycle are toppling in the face of research that employs dredges, computers, Superglue and electronic tracking devices. Recent studies of the crab paint a picture of a violent life dominated by forces of climate and cannibalism. But they also conclude that man's actions, from the growing appetite for crabs to construction of shoreline homes that destroy habitats, also hurt the crab population.

Anxiety about the crab runs high because the bay's supply of other species also once thought to be boundless—shad, sturgeon, oyster and striped bass—has been gutted by disease, pollution and overfishing.

"As everything else fades out of the picture, there's nothing left but the blue crab," said scientist Chris D'Elia, of the University of Maryland. "Our resources are limited, whether it's timber in the Northwest or crabs in the Chesapeake Bay. We can only take so much before we destroy basic stocks."

No one believes the blue crab is about to be extinct: Catches vary wildly, ranging from 53 million to nearly 100 million pounds in recent years, with values up to about $40 million. It is a hardy shellfish that resists pollution and disease.

The effort to know more about the blue crab is driven by more than economics. For residents and visitors alike, it is a symbol of the region's uniqueness, and Maryland has honored the crab by naming it the official state crustacean. A staple of the local diet, its glory days date from the turn of the century, when ice and improved transportation expanded its market inland.

And the crab is a vital link in the ecological chain of the Chesapeake Bay: It lives in a wide variety of habitats, is the major consumer of bottom-dwelling fish and is itself consumed by predators.

Until recently, though, little was known about how many crabs are in the bay and whether the stock had fallen to dangerous levels.

So state and federal agencies have spent more than $2 million during the last four years to develop the first accurate Chesapeake Bay crab census and hope to use it to set 1995 harvest quotas.

The count takes place in the cold months—December, January and February—when crabs rest in the bottom mud throughout the 4,000 square miles of the Chesapeake Bay and its tributaries. Dredges drag the bottom at 1,500 locations, and the crab catch is sorted by number, size and sex.

Based on a complex formula, a computer spits out an "index of abundance" for tiny crabs and a count of 1- and 2-year-olds, which usually are large enough to be legally caught.

Scientists still are polishing the forecasting method. They predicted last year's harvest would be poor, and it was the worst in a decade, which is one factor driving the campaign for crabbing limits. This year's prediction calls for a somewhat better harvest.

Recent research also is rewriting the book on the crab's life cycle.

Crabs begin their lives when females spawn in the lower bay each summer. The microscopic larvae wash into the ocean, changing shape several times before the survivors make their way back into the bay and its rivers. Tiny crabs the size of holes in window-screen mesh settle in the bay shallows, shedding their shells more than a dozen times as they grow.

It takes 12 to 20 months for a crab to reach legal size—three inches for soft crabs, five inches for hard crabs. (They are soft-shell crabs during the interval it takes for a new shell to harden.) Females mate once, in the hours before growing their final shell.

For years, the crab seemed invulnerable because each female produces millions of eggs whose survival was thought to depend solely on climate forces such as currents. But recent research at the Virginia Institute of Marine Science found for the first time that the number of young hinges partly on the supply of adults.

That "means you can overfish them," said Bill Goldsborough, a fisheries scientist with the Chesapeake Bay Foundation.

Recent research, mainly at the marine science institute, the University of Maryland and the Smithsonian's Environmental Research Center near Annapolis, also is revising other assumptions about the crab's life cycle.

The dredge survey, for example, has found that crabs live in a wider variety of places around the bay than previously believed.

"People basically thought female crabs were in the lower part of the bay in the wintertime," said Brian Rothschild, a University of Maryland scientist and survey leader. "What we found were crabs distributed all over the bay."

The winter dredge also is turning up young crabs hunkered down in shallow-water sea grass beds, not the deep waters they had been presumed to occupy.

"Near-shore shallows—knee-deep water—is serving as critical habitat," said Smithsonian scientist Anson "Tuck" Hines. "That has implications for shoreline development."

Property owners who install bulkheads to protect their shoreline from erosion create instant deep water that can threaten crabs. Far better, Hines said, is to plant marsh grass or install riprap, a wall of broken stones.

Grassy creek beds near the Smithsonian's Annapolis center are a favored place for large male crabs to shed their shells. (Females molt in deeper waters.) The grass beds also offer a hiding place for small crabs—which is significant, because crab cannibalism is rampant.

At the Smithsonian, scientists glued small crabs to string and left them out overnight; they found that 90 percent of the small crab mortality in some areas was caused by larger crabs. At the Virginia Institute of Marine Science, marine ecologist Romuald Lipcius cut open large crabs and examined their stomach contents; 35 percent had crab remains, including claw tips. He also captured the act on videotape.

"It's a very quick pounce," he said.

Many animals eat their own, but the research confirmed that cannibalism helps determine how many small crabs reach full size. Thus, Hines said, a large number of small crabs may not mean a huge harvest later, because many may be eaten in the bay first.

There are other implications, Hines said: The soft clam is the crab's favored prey, but if its numbers drop, cannibalism among crabs could rise.

The Smithsonian also is the site of pioneering studies of crab behavior using electronic tracking devices. Strapped to a crab, a device tells scientists where the shellfish moves, how many bites it takes to chew its prey and when it splits its shell to molt.

Thomas G. Wolcott, a North Carolina State University marine biologist, has built a monitor at the Smithsonian lab that signals when a crab spreads its claws in a fighting display. Fighting, scientists found, is so common that a quarter of adult crabs have lost at least one limb.

Wolcott's latest invention is a hollowed-out fire extinguisher filled with electronic monitors that is intended to mimic the movement of a cloud of larvae. The "robot larva" may shed light on a question intriguing scientists: How do newborn crabs get pushed out to ocean, by winds or currents?

Other Smithsonian research, conducted in wire mesh pens in the bay or in children's wading pools, is turning a clinical eye on crab mating.

The ritual can last for days, during which the male cradles the female while she sheds, then protects her until her new shell hardens.

"You cannot possibly mistake these actions for anything other than lovemaking," William Warner wrote in his 1976 Pulitzer Prize–winning book about the crab, "Beautiful Swimmers."

But Hines said Smithsonian researchers noticed that some females, if released before new shells grew back, mated with a second male.

Perhaps the male's long and tender grasp is not only for protecting his female, Hines said, but also "protecting his investment" by ensuring that her babies are his.

Hines said one lesson of crab research is that protecting the species is a complex task because its life cycle is so intricate.

"You can't only deal with one part of it," he said. "Whatever happens in one part will have implications."

12   All around the Bay, Young Rock Strain the Seines

Amazing Recovery Appears Complete

ANGUS PHILLIPS
September, 1993

A fter eight years of strict conservation, rockfish have returned to Chesapeake Bay in numbers rivaling the best of times. Today, state officials suggested even better days are coming.

"This isn't good news," said Jim Peck, assistant secretary of the Department of Natural Resources, "it's great news."

Peck reported that state scientists surveying sites around the Bay this summer recorded the highest count of rockfish offspring in the 39-year history of their studies.

Biologists seining in the Choptank, Potomac and Nanticoke rivers and at the head of the Bay caught an average of 39.6 rockfish fry per haul, almost 25 percent more than the best previous year, 1970.

"This is a dominant-year class," said Peck of the abundance of juvenile rock, "where the population is so strong it can sustain the fishery for a number of years into the future. It's our first true dominant-year class since 1970," when scientists pulled just over 30 rockfish fry per haul of their nets at the same sites.

That 1970 spawning success led to nearly a decade of superb commercial and sportfishing for Maryland's state fish. But the bottom fell out in the 1980s, when year after year of poor spawning success, overfishing and habitat destruction nearly wiped out rockfish.

By 1985, so few remained in the Bay that Maryland shut down rockfishing altogether; a highly restricted season reopened in 1990. This year, the 45-day fall season opens for sport fishermen Oct. 1, with a limit of one fish per day per angler.

Peck said the strong spawning year could lead to relaxation of limits and expansion of seasons within a year or two, providing federal guidelines governing the states are eased.

State fisheries director Pete Jensen said no one is sure what precipitated the huge success in spawning, but he pointed out that this was one of the wettest springs on record, and the deluge may have diluted some pollutants. Also, he said improvements at Conowingo Dam at the head of the Bay helped spawning conditions there.

Whatever the reason, scientists roving the Bay to pull seines at selected sites said they were sometimes overwhelmed by the numbers of tiny rockfish they caught. Don Cosden, who heads the survey team, counted more than 1,100 rockfish fry on one haul at Castle Haven in the Choptank.

Cosden said spawning ranged from good to superb in every system checked, including backup sites in the Patuxent, Patapsco, South and other urban rivers that weren't included in the official tally.

The Patuxent, which runs through busy Prince George's, Anne Arundel, Calvert and Charles counties, had a seine count of over 100 fry per haul. Ten years ago rockfish fry were almost nonexistent there, Cosden said.

In the Potomac, the average this year was 36.2 fry per haul, up from 22.1 in 1992 and way up from an average of less than two fry per haul in 1988–91.

Happily, the spawning success for rockfish seems to have carried over to other troubled Bay species, as well. Peck said white perch and yellow perch fry also popped up in the seines in record numbers, blueback herring were at their third highest on record and hickory shad cropped up in record numbers at the head of the Bay.

The rockfish count bodes well for commercial and sportfishing over the next four or five years as the juveniles grow to legal keeper size of 18 inches, and for the long-term as well, as this year's fry reach spawning age and produce young of their own five or six years down the road, Peck said.

The effect of the historic spawn should be felt along the entire East Coast. Chesapeake Bay is the major spawning area for all Atlantic rockfish, which are known as striped bass elsewhere along the coast. As the fish grow to maturity, they leave the Bay and roam the coast from North Carolina to Maine, but return to the rivers of their origin in the spring to reproduce.

Peck guessed the sportfishing season could be expanded to 90 days within a year or two if rockfish stocks continue to prosper, but cautioned that the state will continue to follow a conservative path to ensure that the state fish won't fall again into a spiraling decline as in the 1980s.

Biological Diversity: Endangered Rain Forests 10

The preservation of plant and animal species is a topic that has received considerable attention in the past decade or so, and for many environmentalists, maintenance of biological diversity is the principal concern of our time. In addition to philosophical and aesthetic considerations, strong arguments can be made regarding the benefits of biological diversity in areas such as agriculture, industry, and medicine. Threats to biological diversity most often attract public attention when attempts to protect an animal species threaten economic interests, as illustrated by concern over the snail darter a decade or so ago and the spotted owl more recently. However, while intense interest is focused on a few highly celebrated cases, most people are oblivious to the fact that thousands of species of both plants and animals are being forever lost each year. A major cause of species loss is the destruction of natural habitats, as in the devastation of tropical forests, the damming of rivers, and the draining of wetlands. Other loss is the result of overharvesting of species, as in the case of the elephant and rhinoceros. The next three chapters present a number of recent *Post* articles concerned with maintaining biological diversity in the face of such threats.

In this first chapter on the topic, the focus is on preservation of the world's tropical rain forests. It is estimated that half of the world's plant and animal species reside in the Amazon rain forest alone. Yet, population and commercial pressures are resulting in the destruction forever of millions of acres of rain forest each year. This chapter presents seven *Post* articles describing the destruction of tropical rain forests and the problems encountered when attempts to preserve rain forests threaten economic interests.

Article 1 in this chapter presents the view of craftsmen that the exotic woods of their trade are being wasted by logging practices in the Brazilian rain forest. Many fine woodworkers now refuse to buy without documentation that the wood comes from well managed forests. Article 2 reinforces these fears with a description of the seemingly out-of-control logging practices in the Brazilian rain forest. Articles 3 and 4 present a more optimistic picture, with the first suggesting that the rate of deforestation is slowing, and the second describing evidence that soil in cleared areas of the Amazon rain forest continues to be of high quality a year later. This latter finding is contrary to the prediction that the soil would soon harden into concrete-like material and be unsuitable for agriculture. Article 5 describes the most recent problems with protecting the Brazilian rain forest. Although Brazil has numerous laws establishing reserves and limiting logging, enforcement is minimal. The final two articles in this chapter concern rain forests in other areas of the world. Article 6 describes an agreement between Costa Rica and a U.S. drug company that could provide a model of how tropical forests can be protected while limited commercial use is made of their resources. Article 7 describes how excessive logging is threatening British Columbia's rain forest.

1   Rain Forest Reprieve

Designers Are Switching to Ecologically Correct Woods

TERRI SHAW
November, 1991

There is nothing quite like the beauty of a lovingly finished piece of hardwood, whether it is a carved rosewood box, a polished aformosia coffee table or a sturdy mahogany desk.

Such woods have been used since the beginning of the 17th century, when European craftsmen began importing timbers from the tropical forests of Asia and South America. These woods, they found, were a pleasure to work with and offered a variety of colors and graining that added to the beauty of the products.

Brazilian rosewood, for instance, is prized for its striking grain. Satinwood has a golden color; purpleheart is bright purple; bubinga is a dark burgundy hue.

Mahogany has been a favorite of cabinetmakers for centuries. Teak, which is resistant to water, is used for boat making and outdoor furniture. Ebony and rosewood are essential for making musical instruments. Fine woodworkers love the textures of iroko, padauk and sapele.

Until recently these tropical hardwoods seemed in limitless supply, coming as they do from forests that normally regenerate themselves as part of a living ecosystem. But in the past few years, scientists and environmentalists have documented the rapid shrinking of tropical forests, and woodworkers, furniture makers and designers have been taking another look at those prized woods.

"When I started in this business I thought the rain forests would go on forever," said Andrew Poynter, president of A & M Wood Specialty, a Canadian company that sells 120 species of domestic and tropical woods to cabinetmakers, musical instrument makers and fine woodworkers. "I thought we would never run out. Now we realize that is not the case at all. I see what's going on and I'm appalled by the burning and waste."

A United Nations report using data from satellites estimates that tropical forests have been disappearing for a decade at the rate of about 40 million acres a year.

Roads built by logging companies in many tropical countries have been used by miners and farmers to move into the forests, cut down trees and burn underbrush, damaging the delicately balanced forest ecology and creating a phenomenon known as deforestation. Trees are cut down for fuel and the land is cleared for farming and ranching by people desperately seeking ways to support themselves.

The result can be measured by the disappearance of hundreds of plant and animal species that exist only in these forests. Many scientists also believe the destruction of tropical forests has a harmful effect on the earth's atmosphere and climate.

Faced with pressure from environmentalists and fear of dwindling supplies of tropical woods, many people in the design industry, from furniture giants Herman Miller, Knoll and Steelcase to individual cabinetmakers and interior designers, are reassessing the types of wood they use and how they use them.

Much of the wood used for mass-produced furniture, flooring and cabinets is oak, walnut, maple and cherry from North American forests that are not endangered. But for custom work such as lavish paneling and inlays for fine furniture, designers often have chosen exotic, or tropical, woods.

In response to concerns about tropical forests, Herman Miller, the second-largest office furniture manufacturer in the world, has adopted a policy of buying tropical hardwoods only from forests it is sure are "sustainably managed," said Bob Johnston, corporate relations manager. This term is used to mean logging that does not destroy the forest as an ecosystem.

The company has changed its teak supplier and stopped using rosewood altogether. The classic Eames chair is now being made with cherry and walnut instead of rosewood, Johnston said.

On a smaller scale, art furniture maker Silas Kopf, of Northampton, Mass., gives his customers a choice of woods. If they insist that he use a tropical hardwood, he charges a surtax, which he contributes to an environmental group.

"My customers are free to choose bubinga or walnut, but the surtax makes them think twice about the difference," he said. "It throws the ball into the court of the end user, the client."

New York furniture designer and manufacturer Dakota Jackson said he began working with exotic woods in the '60s as part of a "movement toward something very spiritual about personal identity." When "it turned out in the late '80s and early '90s to be something destroying the environment, it was very shocking," he said.

Now, he said, his company is using up its stock of mahogany, once its most popular wood, and shifting to ash and cherry.

Washington interior designer Lee Foster-Crowder became interested in the problem of the rain forests when her company, Foster-Crowder Design, worked on the offices of the environmental group Friends of the Earth. Now, she said, she recommends that clients avoid using endangered woods.

"The reason most designers were specifying tropical hardwoods in the first place is because they looked exotic," Foster-Crowder said. But, she added, "there are ways to use North American indigenous hardwood" that will look just as elegant. For example, she said, "if you want an exotic look, you use crotchwood or burlwood" of a species like maple or cherry. (Crotchwood is cut from a tree's branching part and burlwood is made from knots.)

At present, consumers who want to buy products made of wood from sustainably managed tropical forests may have to make a special effort to find suppliers, and pay a higher price for the products, furniture manufacturers say. But some predict that eventually the cost to the consumer will even out as more producers use the woods from plantations or sustainably managed forests.

Some users of tropical hardwoods, especially woodworkers, say they feel torn between their love of the wood and concern for the forests.

Ed Zucca, who makes art furniture in Connecticut, 2 1/2 years ago created a table 11 feet long by 30 inches wide called "Mystery Robots Rip Off the Rain Forest." He made the table top of a board of mahogany that "probably came from a virgin forest because it is so wide." The base of the table, he said, is formed by "four robots carrying the wood away."

Zucca's philosophy, he said, is: "There ought to be more trees and less people."

He said he is avoiding tropical hardwoods in his work for now, but has not made up his mind whether to buy more in the future.

"They're pretty," he said. "They have dramatic colors, flashy grain, reflective qualities about them. They have a depth to them."

Other woodworkers and suppliers of fine tropical hardwoods complain that they have been unfairly singled out for blame for the disappearance of tropical forests. Several said they use only the equivalent of the wood of one tree in a year—or even a lifetime.

"It seems everyone who uses a piece of wood is being attacked by environmental groups," said the owner of a San Francisco company that sells hardwoods and veneers. He asked that his name not be published.

But some environmentalists say that cutting down even a single tree can contribute to deforestation. Pamela Wellner, of the Rainforest Action Network, argues in her book "The Wood Users Guide" that "selective logging" can be just as damaging as clear-cutting. "Roads must be built to get into the forest, and heavy machinery is used to haul out the felled trees, which compacts the soil and kills seedlings. The removal of only a few trees per acre can destroy up to 40 percent of the remaining forest and kill nearly half of the young trees."

Importers of tropical timbers, including the largest companies, have formed a foundation to study the problem of forest preservation. Keister Evans, executive director of the Tropical Forests Foundation, said the United States imports about $3 billion in tropical hardwood products—$1 billion in raw materials (lumber, plywood, veneers and moldings) and the rest in furniture and parts for furniture to be assembled here. More than half of the raw material is plywood made from a tropical hardwood called lauan or meranti. The rest is sold to the furniture industry and lumberyards.

About 75 percent of the imported furniture parts, Evans said, are made from rubberwood, a byproduct of rubber manufacturing that would otherwise be thrown away. Only a small amount of finished furniture made of tropical hardwoods is imported by the United States, he said.

The international timber trade is very complex, with products going through a series of middlemen. This makes it almost impossible for consumers to know the origin of much of the wood in the market—whether plywood in a lumberyard or a rosewood tea tray in a gift shop.

When the problem of the tropical forests became apparent, some environmental groups recommended boycotting some or all tropical hardwoods. But as boycott efforts gathered steam it became apparent to people buying and working with hardwoods that reducing the market for timber would encourage people who live near the forests to cut down trees to clear land for other uses, such as cattle raising and farming.

Furniture manufacturers and consumers are "not going to solve anything by not using woods," said Evans. Instead, he said, the industry is looking for ways to make sure forests are well managed. "All major suppliers are now paying attention to trying to enforce good forestry programs," he added.

"It's very important to understand that the worst thing we can do is take away the economic advantage of the rain forest to people who live in the area," said Barbara Rapaport, manager of sales support service for Stow & Davis, the wood furniture division of Steelcase. "There has to be good reason for them to make a living."

Now representatives of the timber industry and some environmental groups encourage what is called "responsible," "sustainable" or "well-managed" logging so that tropical trees will retain their value. A U.N.-sponsored organization of producers and consumers, the International Tropical Timber Organization, has set a goal that all commercial timber be harvested from sustainable forests by the year 2000.

For now, Steelcase's Stow & Davis division, which uses mahogany veneer, has found "a source that can document and certify that . . . its veneer is from a supplier who is committed to sustained yield," Rapaport said.

The gardening supply company Smith & Hawken assigned its environmental director, Ted Tuescher, to spend almost a year researching the ecology of the teak it uses to make garden benches. As a result of his work, the company decided to use only teak from plantations on the Indonesian island of Java, where new trees are planted at the same rate old ones are cut down and other measures are taken to protect the ecosystem.

Other major furniture companies, such as Baker, Widdicomb and Century, say they are seeking, or have found, suppliers they believe can provide them with wood without damaging the forests.

But environmentalists say it is not easy to determine that wood comes from a healthy forest. Consumers "are being told by their suppliers who are being told by their suppliers that everything is being done properly," said Ivan Ussach, director of the tropical timber project for the Rainforest Alliance, an organization supported by its 18,000 members and foundation grants. This "usually means a country has a good set of laws on paper," he added, but "the actual doing of it is very different."

"It's a question of theory and practice. Most countries have good laws, but the practice leaves a lot to be desired. The [timber] trade has a pretty poor track record in terms of ecological impact."

A study by tropical botanist Duncan Poore for the International Tropical Timber Organization concluded that truly sustainable logging operations are found in less than one-eighth of 1 percent of rain forest lands used for logging, and perhaps one-half of 1 percent of the land has logging operations in which even an attempt is made at sustainable management.

One group that takes a hard line toward use of tropical hardwoods, advocating almost a complete boycott, is the 35,000-member Rainforest Action Network, based in San Francisco. Pamela Wellner, tropical timber campaign coordinator, said the group's policy is to "give exceptions for ecologically sustainable wood," but there is "such a minuscule amount" on the market that "the average person will never come in contact with it."

The network recommends reducing consumption of woods across the board and reusing wood products whenever possible. If new wood must be used, it recommends using woods from temperate forests.

The Woodworkers Alliance for Rainforest Protection (WARP) takes a more cautious approach. It was founded by Poynter, of A & M Wood Specialty, along with Kopf, the custom furniture maker, and other associates.

The organization does not advocate a ban, but stresses conservation and prudent use of exotic woods. "Don't stop using mahogany," Poynter said. "Think about how we are using it. If someone wanted to use 100,000 board feet of mahogany on an office building, I'd say, 'Take a hike.' "But it might be appropriate to use mahogany inlays or trim, he added.

Poynter and WARP are seeking funding to set up a telephone hot line for architects and designers "to ask specific questions about specific woods."

For consumers wondering what type of lumber or furniture to buy, two groups are trying to set up systems to certify those woods that come from well-managed forests.

The Rainforest Alliance has begun a project, called Smart Woods, to find and certify woods from sustainably managed logging operations Ussach has traveled to several tropical countries including Indonesia, Honduras and Belize to evaluate logging operations.

On these trips, he said, he tries to determine whether the logging companies fulfill his organization's criteria for well-managed forests: (1) The logging operations do not disrupt the lives of indigenous people; (2) the logging does not cause erosion and disrupt the watershed; and (3) it provides sustained yield production, that is, it allows the forest to continue to grow.

So far, the alliance, using information gathered by Ussach and a network of consultants, has certified certain logging operations in Java, Mexico, Brazil and

Honduras as sources of woods from well-managed forests. It has also certified seven companies that sell "tropical wood products made exclusively of Smart Wood." They include Smith & Hawken; Kingsley-Bate, and outdoor furniture wholesaler based in Arlington; and Mahogany Craft, a retailer of Chippendale-style furniture in Frederick.

A second certification effort has been initiated by the Green Cross Certification Co., a California-based organization that tests recyclability. Green Cross agreed to certify sources of woods for the Knoll Group, the world's third-largest designer and manufacturer of office furnishings.

A Green Cross representative has visited the Plan Piloto forestry project in the Mexican state of Quintana Roo to evaluate the logging of several types of woods, including mahogany, Spanish cedar and lesser known varieties, according to Debbie Hammel, of Green Cross.

Linda Brown, Green Cross's vice president for communications, said its program differs form the Smart Woods effort in that her organization plans to "look at the whole chain of custody" to make sure all parts of a product come from material obtained from sustainably managed forests.

David Bright, Knoll's vice president for communications, said the company plans to bring out a new line of desks and storage units made entirely of certified woods by 1992.

And for those who care enough about rain forests to want one in their own living room, custom furniture maker Paul McAnulty, of Valdosta, Ga., has created a six-foot-high terrarium containing 15 species of plants native to South America and Africa.

The $5,000 terrarium, complete with all the equipment necessary to maintain rain forest conditions inside, is made of solid oak, because, McAnulty says, "I stay away from using tropical hardwoods because of deforestation."

2 Brazil's Logging 'Free-for-All' Compounds Threat to Amazon Rain Forest

JULIA PRESTON
February, 1992

U ncontrolled logging is a growing threat to the Amazon rain forest, ecologists say.

Since the mid-1970s the Amazon region's lumber production has nearly quadrupled. Currently Indonesia and other Asian countries are the main suppliers of lumber for export, but their forests are being depleted and Brazil is expected to become the biggest exporter by the end of the decade. One-third of the world's rain forests are in Brazil.

Brazil's lumber exports currently are under 5 percent of the world total, but the potential in the Amazon has been valued at $600 billion. Today, Brazilian loggers bring down trees in ways that lead to widespread waste, researchers have found. Some types of trees are already in danger of running out. Management to ensure that logged forests regenerate is virtually unknown in the Amazon. And the financially strapped government has limited ability to monitor the industry.

According to Brazil's environment secretary, Jose Lutzenberger, in 1991 logging was one of the main and most "worrisome" causes of Amazon deforestation, which he estimated at 2 million acres. That is a decrease from 1990 because of diminished burning to clear agricultural land—the principal cause of deforestation.

Yet forestry experts also say that logging, if done carefully, could be a lucrative and long-term business for the Amazon. Logging began on a large scale in the Amazon's towering jungles only in the last 15 years. Still, just a fraction of the timber goes for export, principally mahogany and other hardwoods.

The growth of logging brought a potentially positive change in the way that Amazon settlers regard the rain forest. "In 1970, the forest had no value. It was just an obstacle to ranching and agriculture, to be cleared and burned away. Today the trees do have value. It changes the way people treat them," said Brazilian ecologist Adalberto Verissimo.

But so far Amazon logging has been dominated by unregulated lumbermen in "a complete free-for-all," according to Anthony Anderson, an ecologist working for the Ford Foundation.

President Fernando Collor de Mello has pledged to defend the environment, but in the struggle with foreign debts and budget deficits has had to cut back on monitoring in the Amazon. In 1991, the agency in charge of environmental enforcement, known by its initials as IBAMA, received only 10 percent of its programmed budget and the funds arrived 10 months late, agency officials said.

"We are terribly short of staff. We don't have basic infrastructure to organize information," said Randolf Zachow, head of IBAMA's forestry section. "There is a lot of talk about the environment but there is little in the way of funds for it."

Amazon loggers are required to pay a tax per tree for reforestation and leave half of their land as untouched reserves. But loggers in vast areas operate virtually free of government oversight. Often IBAMA inspectors can get out to look at a logging camp only when the logger pays for it. Collusion between inspectors and loggers in some areas is so blatant that Lutzenberger has denounced IBAMA, his own agency, as "just another branch of the lumber industry."

Paragominas, 110 miles south of the Amazon River in the state of Para, is the logging capital of Brazil, with 238 sawmills. A perpetual smoke cloud rises from ovens burning wood scraps for charcoal. Whining of saws is incessant.

Loggers use bulldozers to open swaths into the rain forest and pull out felled trunks. Entangled in giant vines, chainsawed trees that come crashing down bring many others with them.

"The forest is damaged much more than it needs to be for what is extracted," said Christopher Uhl, a biology professor from Pennsylvania State University. Uhl found that for every tree cut here, an average of 27 are damaged. Uhl's research also revealed that unlike virgin rain forest, which rarely burns, carelessly logged forests are much more vulnerable to fires. In Paragominas, fires set by ranchers to burn off pasture have begun to spread persistently into dense forests.

Ecologist Anderson looked at the logging of a tree called virola, the Amazon's second most important lumber wood, which grows in floodlands at the mouth of the Amazon River. Virola timber is already scarce for sawmills in the area, and Anderson concluded that the tree faces an "impending demise." In January, the government put virola on an endangered list.

In Paragominas, loggers generally do not own the property where they operate but buy cheap permits to log forests belonging to cattle ranchers. Prices for Amazon lumber remain low.

"The forest can't handle this level of production. It will have to diminish," acknowledged Norberto Antonio Hubner, a sawmill owner.

Sawmill owners complained that wood importers in the United States and Europe contribute to wasteful logging here. "Because of strict specifications, Brazilians cut five cubic yards of lumber for every one exported," Hubner said. "Half of the wood cut is burned."

Lumberman Joao Oliveira said he had conducted "a little survey" among foreign clients to find out if they would pay higher prices if they knew the lumber was coming from an environmentally sound company. "No one was taking," he said. "They're all big conservationists over there until you start talking about charging a dollar more."

3   Deforestation in Amazon Slowing

Last Year Saw 20 Percent Drop in Deforestation of Rain Forest

JULIA PRESTON
March, 1992

The rate of destruction of the Amazon rain forest dropped by 20 percent last year, according to satellite data released by the government today. It was the third year in a row that the level of deforestation had declined.

The figures were good news for President Fernando Collor de Mello, who has made protecting the Amazon a priority of his government. The condition of the Amazon's tropical forest is bound to be scrutinized in June when Rio de Janeiro hosts a U.N. conference on the environment, and the data should give him new leverage to press industrialized nations to improve their environmental records.

Based on photographs taken by the American satellite Landsat 5, the total area cleared last year was 4,286 square miles, or 0.3 percent of the Amazon region.

To date, deforestation has affected 8.7 percent of the vast region, which measures 1.5 million square miles. "At this rate, it would take us 330 years to finish off the whole Amazon rain forest," said Edson Machado de Sousa, Brazil's science and technology secretary.

However, the total area destroyed in 1991 is still more than twice the size of Delaware. "It's impossible to promote development in the Amazon without some deforestation," Machado said.

He attributed the decrease to government measures intensifying surveillance in the rain forest and canceling subsidies for cattle ranching. In addition, he said, the people of the Amazon are changing their attitudes and "learning to stay away from cutting trees."

Other data show that the number of fires set to clear land actually increased last year, but most were set where trees had already been cut down, Machado said.

Ecologist Willem de Foe Groeneveld, head of an Amazon research center, said Brazil's steep economic crisis is helping to slow tree destruction. "Nobody has any money to cut the forest down," he said. He also said patrols by the government's environmental monitoring agency, known by its acronym IBAMA, had been more visible in several western Amazon states.

But Eduardo Martins, who headed IBAMA for five months until he was removed from his post by Collor last week, said a study he had conducted showed that IBAMA inspectors succeeded in detecting and issuing fines in only 1 percent of the cases of illegal tree clearing in the Amazon.

Martins said impoverished subsistence farmers are responsible for a growing part of Amazon forest destruction. In the 1980s, in contrast, it was cattle ranchers who bulldozed and torched huge tracts. Martins blamed Brazil's fierce recession for the increase in deforestation caused by poor farmers, saying, "They have to clear to eat. You can't change that with fines."

Meanwhile, the June environmental summit generated new controversy here when Luiz Octavio Themudo, the chief Brazilian organizer of the event, resigned Thursday amid allegations of corruption.

4 Environment

Tropical Deforestation's Other Side

BOYCE RENSBERGER

September, 1993

T ropical deforestation can be blamed for many adverse environmental consequences. But according to new research, three of the most feared results don't
actually happen:

Most cleared soils do not lose their fertility for agriculture and harden into a
concrete-like material.

The land does not release large amounts of carbon to the atmosphere, encouraging global warming.

Deforested earth, though it initially releases nitrogen oxides to the atmosphere, eventually gives off less than forested soil does. Oxides of nitrogen
are chemical precursors of "bad" ozone in the lower atmosphere.

"It's a myth that most of these soils in Amazonia will turn to concrete and be
useless," said Chris Neill of the Ecosystems Center at the Marine Biological Laboratory in Woods Hole, Mass. Neill said it has been widely believed that most soils
in the Amazon region were of an aluminum- and iron-rich type called lateritic. When
deforested and exposed to weathering, such soils quickly lose fertility and harden.
Neill said that only about 30 percent of the region has such soil and most of that is
deep within the rain forest where clear-cutting has rarely reached.

It was also believed that as the organic compounds in deforested soil were
broken down by bacteria, they would release carbon dioxide, methane and other
greenhouse gases to the atmosphere.

Neill and colleagues examined soils deforested at various times in the past and
discovered that most had been sustained as pasture for generations. In one area
cleared 81 years ago, the land was still lush, requiring no synthetic fertilizer.

The carbon content of the soil had not been depleted. Instead, the longer the
land had been deforested, the more carbon it had taken up—absorbed from the
atmosphere by grasses, turned to carbohydrates in the process of photosynthesis,

and transported to plant roots. The amount of absorbed carbon, however, would not come near to compensating for the huge amount released by burning the vegetation originally on the land.

Finally, new research shows that when Costa Rican forests were cleared, the soil began releasing large amounts of nitrogen oxides. But after about 10 years, the rate of release dropped, eventually becoming lower than the amount that forested lands release.

In other words, Michael Keller of the International Institute of Tropical Forestry in Puerto Rico and colleagues report in the Sept. 16 *Nature,* deforestation eventually renders tropical soils better, at least in this limited respect, than when the trees were there.

5 Efforts to Save Rain Forests Raise Suspicions in Brazil

Outsiders' Campaigns Find Little Support

DON PODESTA
October, 1993

More than a year after scores of leaders met at the Earth Summit in Rio de Janeiro and declared their support for the protection of the world's rain forests, Brazilians remain defensive about the state of the Amazon and suspicious of any moves by foreigners to help preserve it.

Yet Brazil's own efforts to save the Amazon rain forest from destruction by miners, loggers and cattle ranchers clearing it for pasture continue to be anemic, hampered by a lack of financial resources and political will.

Interviews in several towns and cities across Brazil's Amazon region also make clear the difficulty of trying to preserve the way of life of those who make their homes in the forest. Rubber tappers and nut harvesters—whose work environmentalists promote as the sound use of the forest's resources—and nomadic Indians who have lived in the forest for centuries face a losing economic battle, according to officials, ecologists, rubber tappers and former gold miners.

The 2.7-million-square-mile Amazon basin, two-thirds of which is in Brazil, is home to half the world's plant and animal species, including 60,000 species of higher plants. An estimated one-third of the world's trees grow in the Amazon region and as much as 20 percent of all the fresh water flowing into the oceans comes from the Amazon river system, the world's longest. Its drainage area—a territory nearly as large as the continental United States without Alaska—forms part of eight countries.

From the air, Brazil's rain forest is a sea of deep green stretching to every horizon, an apparently uniform expanse of vegetation interrupted here and there by meandering tributaries of the Amazon. On the ground, the reality is something else.

The canopy shields an explosion of life: vines, flowers and birds of every shape and color, small monkeys, crazily scurrying lizards and tarantula-like spiders the size of saucers. At sundown the panorama of color fades to black and is replaced by a cacophony of insects buzzing, amphibians and fish splashing and small animals screeching as they are caught by crocodiles or other creatures of the night.

Some of the region is rich in gold, tin, diamonds and other minerals, drawing mining interests into lands traditionally inhabited by primitive Indians. Brazil's government has tried to protect Indians such as the Yanomami by establishing huge reserves in the forest, but it has been unable to halt mining in those areas. Encounters between gold miners and Indians have at times turned violent, most recently resulting in the killing of 16 Yanomami, several of them across the unmarked border in Venezuela.

The fact that Brazil's justice minister, on the scene to investigate the attack, did not know he actually was in Venezuela as he denounced the crime before television cameras speaks volumes about Brazil's inability to deal with the Amazon.

Rubens Ricupero, the newly appointed environment and Amazon minister, said in an interview in Brasilia that North Americans and Europeans often fail to understand that in many ways Brazil's Amazon, which makes up 58 percent of the nation's territory, is "a sector of our country where the state is only slightly present, and to a large extent this is part of the problem."

The economic pull of the Amazon is almost irresistible for a country with millions of its citizens living miserably in city slums or eking out a living in the parched countryside of the northeast. Thus, the huge areas reserved for protecting the forest and its Indians are politically unpopular among many Brazilians.

Setting aside more than 22 million acres for fewer than 10,000 Yanomami Indians in the northern state of Roraima "is crazy," said Ivan Frotas, an air force brigadier general who retired in August and plans to run for president. Foreigners, he said, "complain about the environment and massacres, but when it comes time to help us with things like trade concessions, they forget about us."

Gov. Gilberto Mestrinho of Amazonas, a state three times the size of France, accused foreign companies of pushing the environmental cause for economic reasons. "There's an interest that there be no development here," he said. For instance, the wood-exporting countries such as the United States, Canada and Sweden, do not want Brazil to become a competitive exporter, he said.

He accused environmentalists of making a living out of defending the rain forest. "There are 219 international groups concerned with saving the Amazon," he said. "Of those, I would say that 218 don't even know where the Amazon is."

In an interview at his home here, Mestrinho argued that the rain forest not only renews itself naturally—which ecologists dispute—but that it might even improve in the process. "Here, the danger is the forest invading the cities," he said.

"It's true that vegetation regenerates here much more quickly than people from areas with temperate forests are used to," said Philip Fearnside, an ecologist with the National Institute for Amazon Research in this state capital at the junction of the Amazon and Negro rivers. "But it doesn't cancel out deforestation because something other than rain forest is what grows." Environmentalists have long argued that clearing of the rain forest not only endangers uncounted biological species and native cultures but affects the planet's climate as well. The forest generates rain in Brazil's rich agricultural lands in the south. If it were burned entirely, 60 billion tons of carbon would be in the atmosphere instead of the forest, Fearnside said. As it is, the burnings are already contributing to the greenhouse effect and global warming. It is estimated that more than 8.5 percent of the forest has been cleared so far.

Last month, Discovery space shuttle astronauts reported clouds of smoke over the Amazon that indicated more forest fires than usual for September, traditionally the month of greatest burning to clear land for farming and ranching. President Itamar Franco's office issued a quick rebuttal, arguing that in 1992 the number of fires was unusually low, and that the 64,999 fires detected in the first half of September compared favorably to the 219,941 detected in September 1991.

The issue, much like the killing of the Yanomamis, embarrassed the government. Brazilian officials, particularly military officers, are sensitive about foreign criticism of the government's Amazon policy and often warn of plans to "internationalize" the Amazon.

In August, army generals told legislators that U.S. military maneuvers in neighboring Guyana were part of a plan to establish military bases on the fringes of the Brazilian Amazon. Last week, Brazil carried out exercises of its own in the northern Amazon, deploying 5,000 troops to demonstrate its control of the area near Guyana and Venezuela.

"The world covets the Amazon," Frotas said. "I don't understand the need for [U.S.] military exercises in a South American jungle. . . . It gives the impression that they are practicing to intervene in the internal affairs of our countries."

Brazil, particularly under the military governments of the 1960s and '70s, has had a "use it or lose it" view of the Amazon, a fear that if the forest was not occupied and developed by Brazilians it would be taken by foreign countries.

The Amazon remains at the center of Brazil's vision of itself as a country of the future. Brazilians have the idea that "when the giant awakens, we will have the resources to be a great power," said University of Sao Paulo sociologist Emir Sader. But until that day, Brazil struggles with an economic crisis and budget deficit that are making it difficult, if not impossible, for the government to protect the forest.

The branch of Brazil's National Indian Foundation, called Funai, charged with overseeing the Yanomami reserve in Roraima, has 60 employees for the 37,400 square miles, an area the size of Hungary. "We are overworked. We don't have enough people," said Funai official Manuel Reginaldo Tavares at the Boa Vista headquarters.

In Brazil, "everything is prohibited, but nobody complies," said Jose Guilherme Maia, director of a museum and Amazon studies center in Belem, a busy port near the mouth of the Amazon River.

There are strict laws against hunting, logging and mining in Indian reserves, but enforcement is spotty. "Nobody has been observing these laws," Stephan Schwartzman of the Environmental Defense Fund said by phone from Washington. "There's no enforcement whatsoever."

While officials plead poverty, environmentalists and others argue that agencies such as Funai are overstaffed. The real problem, they say, is that the agencies do not move people from office jobs in the cities to the more uncomfortable countryside where they are needed, and the government is constitutionally prohibited from firing public workers.

Meanwhile, rubber tappers and nut harvesters, whose livelihoods are supposed to be protected, are dealing in products that cannot compete economically with mining or logging.

6   A Biodiversity Pact with a Premium

U.S. Fears Rio Treaty Would Threaten Kindred Concessions in the Future

JULIA PRESTON
June, 1992

A Costa Rican deal with an international drug company illustrates the sort of hard-nosed commercial issue that lies at the heart of the Bush administration's worries about a biodiversity treaty to be signed later this week at the United Nations Earth Summit.

Costa Rica is a reserve of biological diversity. It has a population of only 3 million homo sapiens—about .05 percent of the world's total—but its small territory contains as much as 5 percent of all the other species of flora and fauna that exist on the planet.

In 1991 a private Costa Rican research center, the National Biodiversity Institute, signed a unique contract with Merck and Co. Inc., the world's largest pharmaceutical company, that is considered a model for the kinds of transactions the framers of the biodiversity I treaty hope to make common practice.

Under the contract, Merck paid $1.3 million to the institute, known as Inbio. In exchange, Inbio will collect and provide Merck with some 10,000 samples of insects, plants and microorganisms from all over Costa Rican territory. Merck has two years to screen and analyze the samples to see if they have hitherto undiscovered properties for healing cancer, diabetes, even AIDS, or other illnesses.

That's how biodiversity protection can work. But, Merck was able to achieve concessions from Inbio that the Bush administration feared American companies would lose if it signed the U.N. treaty.

One of Washington's principal complaints had to do with articles 15 and 16 of the text, which govern the control that nations will have over the results of their biochemical research. These clauses call on nations to "share in a fair and equitable way" these results. To the Bush administration, these terms diluted the American patent process.

Although President Bush has not got much support for this position in Rio, he has from many American businessmen. According to Abraham Katz, president of the U.S. Council for International Business, American companies feared the text of the treaty could be seen as a precedent for looser protections for other kinds of so-called intellectual property.

"We were afraid this treaty could give solace to countries that are engaging in nefarious practices" like pirating and copying of drugs and high-technology goods, Katz said. In his view, Bush's concerns "were not frivolous. They were serious."

Countries like Costa Rica, with large and little-studied rainforests and other tropical ecosystems, coupled with economies still struggling to develop, were the most interested in the treaty. The treaty is designed to ensure that the poorer countries' rights will be respected when industrialized nations use their plants or animals to make into commercial products. The rich countries want to make sure they will continue to have access to the little-studied abundance.

The Bush administration was nearly alone among major governments in deciding on two separate occasions not to sign the treaty. Germany, France, India and Australia have agreed to sign. Japan and Britain are leaning toward signing. The treaty has already been signed by more than the 30 countries needed to put it into effect.

The details of the Costa Rican agreement with Merck show the strange world of biodiversity research.

The samples to be provided to Merck under the agreement might include wasp glands, snake venom, spider webs, ant hill matter, a wide array of fragments of life. If Merck, which is headquartered in New Jersey, finds a product to develop and market as a drug, the company agreed to give Inbio a "very fair" share of royalties on the sales, Inbio director Rodrigo Gamez said in an interview today. The chances are that about one in every 10,000 samples will yield a marketable medicine, he said, and Inbio agreed to turn over any funds it obtains in royalties from Merck to Costa Rica's government for conservation of the country's national parks.

"It's the first time in history that a commercial enterprise paid for access to bio-technological resources," Gamez said. "Our philosophy is to use our biodiversity, to make it pay for its own development and help our country." Some critics have accused Inbio of giving away Costa Rica's resources for too little money, without keeping the possible patents. But Gamez said, "We are selling something that we don't yet know what it will be good for. You can't patent orange juice."

Merck senior scientist Lynn Caporale said the company is happy because Inbio can provide a regular flow of high-quality samples. "They didn't just say, give us a million and we'll give you the samples. It's a collaboration," she said. The contract gives Merck the right to patent any drug it develops out of Costa Rica's samples.

On another treaty issue, the United States found itself at loggerheads with European countries that are usually its allies. Article 19 calls for talks to establish a special protocol to govern the products of biotechnology—new forms of plant life created by changing the genetic structures of existing plants. The United States leads the world in this field.

"We don't think the biotechnology industry should be singled out for special treatment," said Richard Morgenstern, an administrator at the Environmental Protection Agency. "The Europeans view it as more of an unknown."

7   Canada, Conservationists Battle over Rain Forest

Logging Threatens British Columbia Area

CHARLES TRUEHEART
August, 1993

The ground-level view from the road and shore takes in some of the most spectacular forest in the world: centuries-old cedars and hemlocks a hundred feet tall on steep mountainsides traced by streams where salmon jump.

The aerial view across the mountainous top of Vancouver Island, off Canada's Pacific Coast, is not the same. It reveals vast slopes shaved of trees, littered with debris and scarred by now-useless logging roads the wounds left by the island's most important economic engine.

These two views are the ones at loggerheads in Clayoquot Sound, 800,000 acres of ancient rain forest whose name, pronounced *Clack-wot,* could become as familiar as the spotted owl and the ozone layer in the pantheon of late-20th-century environmental symbols. British Columbia, according to one parallel drawn by environmentalists, is "the Brazil of the North," its rain forest as biologically precious, and as threatened, as the tropical one being cut and burned in South America.

Emboldened by the support of U.S. and Canadian conservationists and greens as far away as Europe and Japan, young environmental activists have converged on the Clayoquot Valley this summer to build a "witness trail" through the still-uncut part of the forest and to stage symbolic confrontations against its depletion.

Every workday at dawn, a few more of the committed sit down in the middle of the road that carries the logging trucks and bulldozers into the forest, and submit to arrest. More than 140 protesters have been charged already, and increasingly the arrested are spending time in jail as provincial authorities crack down on what is viewed as an expensive and embarrassing nuisance.

But the battle over the future of the ancient rain forest is about to spread. British Columbia's government has dug in its heels after deciding last April to permit logging in two-thirds of Clayoquot Sound, barring it in the rest and pledging to reform logging methods.

Citing limitations on access roads and the size of clear-cuts, Premier Mike Harcourt said his compromise forest management plan contains the toughest logging regulations in North America.

Environmentalists, however, believe his government, which came to power with strong support from the province's logging industry union, sold out to British Columbia's powerful lumber interests, notably MacMillan Bloedel Ltd., which is licensed to harvest what remains of the last intact rain forest on the continent.

One prominent environmental advocate, Robert F. Kennedy Jr., believes he has found a key ally in forcing the Harcourt government to back down: local Indian nations who believe their rights to the disputed forest have been trampled by both private and governmental interests.

Seeking to yoke the defense of natural resources to what he terms the protection of human rights, Kennedy visited Clayoquot Sound last weekend to seal an alliance between the Natural Resources Defense Council (NRDC), the Washington-based environmental group for which he serves as a lawyer and high-profile voice, and the five Clayoquot tribes whose ancestral lands are at issue.

"MacMillan Bloedel has no interest in this land except to cut the lumber and run," Kennedy said in an interview, "but if the Indians lose their resources, they're through."

"The people who are injured most by environmental destruction are people who lack political power," he said after eight hours of private meetings with Indian leaders. The issues in Clayoquot Sound, Kennedy declared, "are the same ones our countries have been struggling with for 500 years. What's the difference between this and what happened when Custer went into the Black Hills [of South Dakota]?"

Kennedy's presence here provoked bitter resentment from many British Columbians. Gerry Stoney, president of the regional loggers union, said in a statement: "His support for the blockades is the ultimate in American-style bully tactics."

Native groups have not been easy allies of the more confrontational white environmentalists who reject any form of logging in the area. Indian leaders, who wish to reserve logging rights for their heavily unemployed people, have dissociated themselves from the daily arrests in the valley and have sought, with little success, to assert their claim over the forest through legal channels.

But after their meetings with Kennedy here, they were taking a markedly tougher line. "Our options are very limited," said Chief Francis Frank of the Tla-o-qui-aht First Nation, who spoke for the tribes. "We can go through your system, but we didn't create the justice system. Or we can take direct action. . . . The niceties of talking are almost over."

Frank would not rule out joining the blockades or seeking an injunction to block logging until the land claims are settled. But the direct action he and Kennedy have in mind, they said, is on the international stage. An NRDC-organized boycott of British Columbia timber products, half of whose markets are in the United States, is a distinct possibility, sources said, as are fresh legislative initiatives in the United States to require consumer labeling of wood products to indicate their origin.

To drive the issue home on Harcourt's doorstep, Frank said, the five bands also are prepared to call for a boycott of the 1994 Commonwealth Games in Victoria, the provincial capital on the southern end of Vancouver Island. Local Indian tribes are scheduled to participate in the ceremonies, and their withdrawal, Frank said, might spur other indigenous peoples of the Commonwealth countries to protest participation in the games.

For its part, the 170,000-member NRDC plans a direct-mail and advertising campaign in the United States this fall. Its Clayoquot Sound strategy is modeled on an earlier effort Kennedy led to pressure New York and New England states to cancel contracts to buy electricity from Quebec's public power company. The public utility's ambitious dam-building project in northern Quebec's James Bay subsequently was curtailed.

There too Kennedy linked environmental concerns with long-standing Indian claims to the land and its resources, and last weekend in British Columbia, a Cree leader instrumental in the James Bay struggle was in Kennedy's party. Deputy Grand Chief Diom Romeo Saganash pledged Cree solidarity to the Clayoquot cause and urged the Vancouver Island chiefs to overcome their reluctance about confrontation. "You have to kick them where it hurts—in the butt, and that's where the white man's wallet usually is," he said.

Kennedy was greeted by Indian leaders here with the kind of enthusiasm once accorded his father, the slain U.S. senator from New York and presidential candidate whose memory is still strong in native communities across North America.

The 39-year-old activist and law professor, accompanied by his 8-year-old son and namesake, was carried ashore in a dugout canoe for an outpouring of ceremonial gift-giving by Canadian Indian leaders. As he received robes, paintings, masks, bracelets and even honorific gifts of cash, Kennedy was told that one gift "gives you the right to speak to the world on behalf of the Clayoquot people."

The Fight for America's
Threatened Wetlands   11

O ne of the more frequent environmental topics in the news has centered on the effort by environmentalists to save America's shrinking wetlands. These areas are defined in terms of their flooded state, at least for certain portions of the year. Of course, everyone knows about the Everglades in Florida, perhaps the nation's most well known wetland. There are, however, thousands of such areas, and they serve the purpose of "purifying" natural water systems, and providing a habitat in which countless animals (especially birds) and plants thrive and reproduce. The reduction of wetland acreage for farming, urban sprawl, and "water management" has already resulted in significant reductions in habitat, with the consequent depredation of migratory waterfowl species. The wetland controversy provides an excellent example of the opposing forces of development and conservation that characterizes the dilemma of environmental preservation. It is also typical in that the connection between the problem and the pressure of overpopulation is clearly obvious.

    The *Washington Post* articles in this second chapter concerning biodiversity point out the difficulties associated with governmental attempts at environmental preservation and the compromises that ultimately follow. Articles 1 and 2 focus on the politics of how wetlands should be defined. Article 3 addresses the problem of well-intended laws to restore wetlands being subverted by the lack of subsequent legislative appropriations. Articles 4 and 5 look at the threat to survival confronting the Everglades and the recent proposals to save its ecosystem. Finally, Article 6 discusses Maryland's "mitigation banking system" as a partial answer to the destruction of the state's wetlands.

1   Wetlands Protection and the Struggle over Environmental Policy

MICHAEL WEISSKOPF

August, 1991

Arguing for strong wetlands protections at a recent White House meeting, Environmental Protection Agency chief William Reilly quoted a 1988 pledge by President Bush to protect the ecologically fragile areas—"no matter how small."

From across the table came a retort from Office of Management and Budget Director Richard G. Darman. Bush, he noted, "didn't say that. He read what was given to him in a speech."

Darman's demurrer, relayed by observers at the meeting, may have been wrapped in jest. But it gave a flavor of the manner in which the administration decided last week to relax the criteria for wetlands protection, a move that could open millions of acres to development, from Alaskan tundra to shrubby swamps in the Florida Everglades—as well as large tracts of land that rarely get wet.

The struggle over who should control environmental policy—the experts throughout government or the political and economic advisers to the president—is as old as this administration. But many federal wetlands experts complain that even for a White House whose top officials routinely get involved in the smallest domestic policy spats, the resolution of this issue reached new heights of political intervention.

What, from their standpoint, was supposed to be a scientific review of the swamps, marshes and bogs considered worthy of safeguarding ended up essentially rezoning thousands of acres for development. And what they planned to be a collaborative drafting effort by environmental specialists in four federal agencies was taken over by officials in the White House who have little direct knowledge of the issue. Indeed, they had to be given a special wetlands glossary at the decisive meeting.

A White House aide defended the process by saying that previous wetlands protection had gone too far in blocking development and denying landowners their rights to develop their land. He said its implications for private property and the environment were too important to be left to bureaucrats.

"Ultimately politicians make the decisions in Washington," the official said. "That's how the system works."

274

Wetlands is a catchall term applied to a wide variety of ecosystems ranging from prairie potholes that flood seasonally and become waterfowl breeding grounds to tidal salt marshes bordering estuaries such as the Chesapeake Bay. Wetlands are among the most diverse of wildlife habitats, but in the White House meeting, one characteristic was measured—how wet they were.

Vice President Quayle, wading into the complex debate over the extent to which soil must be soaked to qualify as a wetland, reportedly suggested a simple criterion: "When it's wet, it's wet."

"This was worse than the Reagan years in the amount of second-guessing and political involvement," one seasoned environmental official said. "Once the agencies achieve compromise, you assume you'll have the support of the principals. When the whole thing is reopened, the system goes awry."

Wetlands protection is the most recent flashpoint in an administration sharply divided over environmental policy. But unlike past disputes over broad policy questions, the wetlands issue centered on narrow, technical judgments such as the plant species that are characteristic of wetland habitats and the number of days soil must remain saturated at various depths to constitute a wetland that deserves protection against development.

At issue was a manual drafted by scientists in 1989 to set forth the factors that distinguish a wetland. The 100-page listing of criteria is used by the Army Corps of Engineers, which controls permits to fill in wetlands and decides whether projects threaten "unacceptable" environmental harm. Its decisions are subject to EPA veto.

The manual did little to curb development—95 percent of permit applications were approved last year. But industry complained nonetheless of unreasonable controls, which, for example, restricted development on cropland that had been tilled for generations.

Large sections of the Eastern Shore of Maryland and the state of Louisiana were technically off-limits to development under a strict reading of the manual.

The controversy, fueled by members of Congress who picked up the cudgels for angry landowners, sent the panel of government scientists who wrote the document back to work.

Reilly assumed leadership of the interagency effort that included the EPA, the Corps and the departments of Interior and Agriculture. He sought to establish what he called more defensible criteria and was willing to let go of marginal areas to concentrate on the most ecologically valuable wetlands.

It was not a popular cause. When Reilly forged a consensus to broaden soil saturation criteria, one scientist quit the panel in disgust and another asked to "disassociate" himself from its work.

The real fight began when Reilly took the consensus to the White House. Technically, the Office of Management and Budget is required to sign off on all regulations. But the wetlands review was so high on industry's list of concerns that the President's Council on Competitiveness entered the fray. The council, set up to ease regulatory burdens on industry, is chaired by Quayle and run by his staff.

Although the council is supposed to serve as an appeals board for agencies unhappy with OMB decisions, its staff participated at every stage of the wetlands debate.

On July 1, the interagency group reached agreement with OMB on annual revisions. But the next day, officials said, they were informed by a vice presidential staff member that the terms were unacceptable.

A White House official said that the agreement had been tentative and that objections by other interested parties, including the Council of Economic Advisers and the departments of Energy and Housing and Urban Development, kept the accord from becoming final.

A week later, Reilly attempted to deal directly with Quayle. Anxious to draft a proposal for public comment and unveil it at a Senate hearing on wetlands the next day, officials said, Reilly called Quayle the night before and offered a compromise.

The 1989 manual had conferred protections on wetlands saturated for at least seven consecutive days as deep as 18 inches below the surface. The interagency group raised the threshold, saying it wasn't a wetland unless it was saturated 14 straight days at the surface. Some administration officials wanted the criterion to be 30 days.

Reilly got Quayle's approval to propose 15 straight days of saturation and to ask for public comment on a range of 10 to 20 days, officials said. But Allan B. Hubbard, the competitiveness council's executive director, called back and told Reilly that Quayle had misspoken.

Another call by Reilly to Quayle just after midnight July 10 resulted in another compromise: a request for comment on the 10-20 day range and dropping the 15-day proposal. The EPA staff worked through that night to draft a proposal for the hearing the next morning.

But on his way to the Senate, Reilly received a call on his car phone from Hubbard, who directed him not to release the document, officials said.

That impasse set the stage for the competitiveness council meeting July 29. In attendance were the six council members or their representatives—Darman, the secretaries of commerce and treasury, the attorney general, the White House chief of staff and the chairman of the Council of Economic Advisers.

Also attending were officials from the interagency group. But although representatives of those agencies had earlier supported Reilly's compromise, they changed their minds in the more political atmosphere and none of them spoke in favor of Reilly's appeal for a 15-day saturation rule.

Interior Secretary Manuel Lujan Jr. told colleagues privately that he had come under pressure from the White House to break away. "I'm a politician, not a scientist," he said at the meeting, according to observers.

A knowledgeable official said that Quayle's staff had contacted council participants earlier in the search for a consensus, but that no one was pressured.

Lujan's spokesman said the secretary could not be reached for comment.

Darman, who is known as a critic of environmental policy, told the council that the dispute came down to deciding whether land that is dry for 344 or 350 days a year should be classified as wetlands.

"Boston was built on a wetlands," Darman reportedly said.

Quayle then interjected what he called a "supertest" for wetlands. If it is covered by water 80 percent of the time, it could be considered a wetland, he suggested.

"How about if we say when it's wet, it's wet?" Quayle suggested.

Darman then reportedly shot back: "Okay, Dan, and when it's dry, it's dry."

One observer said that Quayle was "thinking out loud," searching for a common sense approach to defining wetlands that would be easily understood and universally applicable.

Wetlands experts said Quayle's formula was more appropriate for classifying ponds or streams.

Although Reilly was outnumbered, the meeting ended without resolution.

Later in the day, Quayle offered him another compromise: 15 days of standing water and 21 days of saturation at the surface.

Hoping to bring public pressure to bear once the proposal gets out, Reilly accepted the formula. The new criteria are expected to be published in the Federal Register soon, starting a 60-day review period.

Reilly declined to comment on the deliberations.

2　Wetland Redefinition Shelved

EPA Abandons Controversial Rule Change

D'VERA COHN
January, 1993

With one week to go before leaving office, the head of the Environmental Protection Agency has abandoned a controversial proposal to narrow the definition of a wetland—a move that would have exempted millions of acres from protection.

EPA Administrator William K. Reilly told *Washington Post* reporters and editors yesterday that his agency has decided to use the same definition of a wetland as the one now used by the Army Corps of Engineers, "and I gather that will be accepted by the new administration," he said.

The definition is used in deciding whether a landowner needs a federal permit to fill or build on wetlands. The EPA's decision means it will use language employed in a 1987 Corps manual, abandoning a slightly broader definition in a 1989 Corps manual.

Reilly said that on Thursday he will release a memo signed last week by his agency and the Corps. Although the document does not mention the proposed redefinition, championed by Vice President Quayle, it "slams the door" on that issue for this administration, an official said.

"The Quayle manual is dead," the administration official said. "No one is going to adopt it while Reilly is here."

At the urging of farmers and conservative landowners, the White House announced in 1991 it would propose a relaxed definition to be used by the Corps, EPA and other agencies dealing with wetlands.

The proposal represented a victory for the President's Council on Competitiveness, but quickly drew fire from environmental groups that claimed it violated President Bush's campaign pledge to allow no net loss of wetlands.

Field tests by the government later showed that the change could exempt at least half the 106 million acres of wetlands currently protected, including portions of such well-known areas as Florida's Everglades, the New Jersey Pine Barrens, Virginia's Great Dismal Swamp and the salt marshes of Washington state.

The wetlands issue now apparently will be put on hold until a widely awaited National Academy of Sciences study, expected this year.

3 How Wetland's Fund Dried Up

Congress Traded off Popular Experiment in Its Infancy

TOM KENWORTHY
October, 1992

As the helicopter banks over a flooded field on his 6,800 acre rice farm, Ken Hofmann, one of almost 3,000 farmers who have applied to a pioneering federal program to reclaim U.S. wetlands, peers anxiously out the window to monitor his latest experiment.

Suddenly what had seemed to be an uninhabited shallow lake erupts into motion as thousands of ducks—mallards, pintails, widgeons and teals—explode from the vegetation where they have been hiding and take flight in a tableau straight out of a National Geographic special.

"Look at those birds," says a delighted Hofmann, 69, as he surveys what until last year had been just another 300-acre rice field but now is protected habitat teeming with the advance elements of the fall waterfowl migration along the Pacific flyway. "I can't believe it."

Under the terms of the 1990 farm act adopted by Congress, wetlands restoration projects like Hofmann's were supposed to begin sprouting by the thousands beginning this year. But in an abrupt policy reversal, Congress recently eliminated all funding for what is known as the wetlands reserve program for the 1993 fiscal year, jeopardizing an ambitious effort that had been enthusiastically embraced by both farmers and environmentalists.

In the annual game of winners and losers that marks the congressional appropriations process, the wetlands program lost big when the House and Senate passed the fiscal 1993 agriculture spending bill, halting the program in its infancy. In a direct trade-off during House-Senate negotiations on the bill, the Marketing Promotion Program, a controversial export-assistance program that has been criticized for paying the overseas advertising costs of such U.S. food giants as Burger King and Gallo Winery, hit the jackpot.

What happened to the wetlands reserve program is a classic example of how policy directives crafted one year by the authorizing committees of Congress can be undone completely by the appropriations panels the following year, particularly when such a program has an unorganized constituency and must compete for scarce funds against well-heeled and politically connected corporate interests.

Two years ago, the wetlands reserve program was being hailed as a pillar of the most environmentally conscious farm bill ever enacted by Congress. Under that legislation, the government embarked on a five-year effort to reclaim 1 million acres of wetlands, which are important for wildlife habitat, water purification and the prevention of soil erosion. The program would operate by purchasing perpetual conservation easements from growers if they agree to stop producing crops on former wetlands and restore them to their original condition.

Early last summer, as the Agriculture Department began the pilot phase of the program in nine states, officials were inundated with applications. More than 2,700 farmers offered to sell easements on 460,000 acres—nine times the amount that could be handled by the first-year appropriation of $46 million.

The response, said Agriculture Stabilization and Conservation Service official Jack Webb, reflects simple economics: Farmers who are growing subsidized crops on marginal land that is susceptible to periodic flooding will give up the use of that land if given an economic incentive such as the purchase of an easement. And in many cases, said Webb, that restored wetland can be rented out to hunters during waterfowl season.

Hofmann, a home builder, avid sportsman and director on the board of the National Fish and Wildlife Foundation, said such private-public partnerships are the key to slowing or reversing what has been an inexorable loss of wetlands to agriculture.

"If the public sector gets involved with the private sector, we can really do some good," said Hofmann. "Money's the big thing. You have to give the farmer direction and give him money. . . . You have to make sure they make a living. If you are going to cut their yield, you have to induce them to do it."

Though Hofmann has the personal financial resources and interest to restore wetlands without government help, federal financial assistance is an added incentive. His 300-acre wetlands restoration project here in the Butte Sink, an area north of Sacramento that is the heart of California's $180 million-a-year rice industry, cost about $59,000 and was done on a cost-sharing basis with the U.S. Fish and Wildlife Service. In order to double his wetland acreage, Hofmann has applied for enrollment in the Agriculture Department's wetlands reserve program.

By taking this land out of production, keeping it flooded most of the year and building levees and nesting islands, Hofmann has turned it into an enticing layover for ducks migrating along the Pacific flyway. Now this former rice field is the kind of land it would naturally be if the Sacramento River and other waterways hadn't been harnessed and diverted through the complex network of canals and reservoirs known as the Central Valley Project.

Such rest stops for migrating waterfowl are increasingly rare in California, where it is estimated that more than 90 percent of the state's wetlands have disappeared. Nationally, according to the Fish and Wildlife Service, about 290,000 acres of wetlands were lost annually between the mid-1970s and mid-1980s, the last period for which figures are available. Over the 30-year period ending in the mid-1980s, some 12 million acres of wetlands were lost, more than half of them attributable to farming. But "by creating the reserve, we gave these farmers an option they didn't have before," said Maureen Hinkle, the National Audubon Society's director of agricultural policy. "There's all this interest . . . and an obvious public benefit." By taking land growing federally subsidized crops out of production—acreage on which flooding often triggers federal crop insurance payments—the government actually could save money, said Ralph E. Grossi, president of the American Farmland Trust. "We're paying [the cost of the easement] two or three times now," he said.

Despite those arguments, and the Bush administration's request for $161 million to fund the wetlands program in the fiscal year starting Oct. 1, the conference committee on the agriculture appropriations bill zeroed out the program. As part of the deal, the conferees provided $150 million to the Marketing Promotion Program, which has been derided by members of both parties as "corporate welfare," but which enjoys broad support because of the political clout of the commodity groups and individual food companies that benefit.

"It looks like Congress is going back on the farm bill," said Ken Cook, vice president of the Center for Resource Economics, an environmental group active in agriculture issues. "They want to pass bills that authorize high-sounding environmental programs, then they want to duck the money issue."

4   Remedy for a Dying Wetland

More Fresh, Clean Water; Much-Altered Everglades Is Increasingly Hostile to Wildlife

WILLIAM BOOTH
July, 1993

From the air, the repair of the parched and polluted Everglades, with its interconnected chain of lakes, marshes, sloughs and bays, looks like a relatively simple proposition.

The solution: Simply add clean water.

But on the ground, restoring the Everglades has been anything but simple, and the tentative settlement reached today, after years of litigation and research, only emphasizes the fact that a final fix remains frustratingly elusive, if not completely uncertain.

The immediate problem is that the vast marsh known as the Everglades does not get enough clean water. "The wetland," as Jim Webb of the Wilderness Society has put it, "ain't so wet," because so much fresh water from the north has been diverted for agricultural and other uses.

Nor does Florida Bay, at the bottom of Everglades National Park, get its former share of fresh, clean water. Because less cool, fresh water is coming into Florida Bay, the onetime sports fishing paradise has become super-salty and warmer. Scientists suspect that the increased salinity kills the native sea grass, which decomposes and provides increased nourishment for algae. As a result, the bay now hosts a gigantic, miles-wide blob of blue-green algae that is clouding the once gin—clear waters—an effect that in turn kills more sea grass.

"It looks just like pea soup, doesn't it?" said Mark Robertson of the Nature Conservancy as he flew with a reporter last week over a bay so salty that it stings to swim in it.

The lack of clean water arriving at the right time of year appears to be responsible for the reduced vigor of both Florida Bay—home to tarpon, shrimp, turtles and redfish—and the Everglades wetlands, where populations of wading birds, among other species, have been drastically reduced.

"Think of South Florida as one big system, with all these different parts, each completely dependent on the other," said John Ogden of the Florida Institute of

Oceanography in St. Petersburg. "In other words, you mess with one part, you screw the whole system up. And that's what we've done. Screwed it up. Now all this effort, all these lawsuits and remedies, are nothing more than an attempt to make things something like they way they were."

The Everglades, once a vast natural drainage system, is now a vast artificial drainage system.

From south of Disney World in Orlando, the water slowly pours, from Lake Kissimmee, to the altered and degraded Kissimmee River, to the great inland Lake Okeechobee.

Lake Okeechobee used to spill over its southern banks. But the U.S. Army Corps of Engineers and the state of Florida dammed the lake, which now empties into Everglades Agricultural Area, to the giant sugar cane and vegetable farms, through a series of canals.

Lands that were once partially submerged for weeks and months are now subdivisions and farms. Everglades National Park, for instance, represents only about one-tenth of what was the Everglades.

Moreover, the little water that is released into Everglades from these farms is loaded with agricultural pollutants, such as phosphorus, which in turn encourages the growth of nonresident plants. Acres of once pristine wetland are now covered in cattails—a species that did not exist there in abundance prior to mass fertilization.

And so, the federal, state and local governments and the sugar cane and vegetable growers have pledged to release more water and to set aside some 40,000 acres to use as filtration marshes.

The idea, says Jim Webb, is basically to buffer the Everglades Agricultural Area with marshes to soak up the farms' pesticides and fertilizers and scrub the water clean.

"Water that once took months to get from Lake Okeechobee to Florida Bay now takes days," said Michael B. Robblee, research marine ecologist with Everglades National Park. "And so the nutrients and pollutants that would have been cleaned up and absorbed by the marsh grasses are not."

It is unclear, however, how much the newly created and set-aside marshes will clean the water. Environmentalists and some scientists have said they don't believe that 40,000 acres is enough.

The sugar and vegetable growers have pledged to reduce the amount of phosphorus in the water to 50 parts per billion. But again, some scientists and activists say it should be much cleaner—in the neighborhood of 5 to 15 ppb.

Yet, the farm industries can also abate their waste by using less fertilizer to begin with, and then employing other strategies, such as recycling water, to clean up the excess nutrients.

Finally, the tentative settlement calls for increasing the amount of water coming into the Everglades by 25 percent and providing that water in more "natural" quantities and more "natural" times. Before the ecosystem was changed, the Everglades used to get most of its water during the rainy season in late summer and fall.

Now its main flows occur when farms release water—for example, in the winter when fields are drained for the year's first crops. To achieve the 25 percent increase, levees would be opened, and some farm lands would be bought and allowed to flood.

The problem is, the scientists studying the Everglades are no longer sure what "natural" means, in a system altered in so many ways for so long.

5   Everglades Revival Plan Unveiled

$465 Million Government/Industry
Pact Arouses Controversy

TOM KENWORTHY
July, 1993

The Clinton administration yesterday announced a tentative agreement with the sugar industry and the state of Florida on a $465 million plan to begin restoring the Everglades, the once vast and pristine freshwater marsh now imperiled by agricultural runoff and development.

In unveiling the outline of an agreement whose details will be fleshed out over the next three months, Interior Secretary Bruce Babbitt called it "the largest, most ambitious ecosystem restoration ever undertaken" in the United States.

But the plan was roundly denounced by environmentalists, who charged that it does too much for the politically powerful sugar industry and not enough for the famed "River of Grass" whose natural processes have been severely disrupted by agriculture, development and one of the nation's most extensive flood control projects.

Babbitt's announcement ceremony—held in the department's ornate auditorium with a gaggle of officials and sugar industry representatives on stage—seemed to underscore the environmentalists' concerns.

"Today, the Clinton administration delivers," declared Alphonso Fanjul, whose prominent Palm Beach family controls several sugar companies and has been a major financial contributor to both the Democratic and Republican parties.

Under a "statement of principles" agreed to after furious negotiations that concluded near midnight Monday, the sugar industry would over 20 years pay a minimum of $232 million and as much as $232 million to help fund the restoration. In return, growers would receive guaranteed water supplies for their crops. Other payments would come from the state of Florida, water users in south Florida and the federal government.

The restoration fund would finance mechanisms to remove phosphorus from agricultural runoff and to increase by 25 percent the amount of water that flows into the Everglades. Phosphorus from fertilizer encourages the growth of cattails and non-native vegetation in the Everglades and degrades habitat needed by wildlife.

To absorb naturally much of the excess phosphorus from fertilized sugar cane land, a series of filtration marshes would be created on 40,000 acres of private and public land south of Lake Okeechobee. In addition, parts of the extensive network of canals and levees used to control flooding in south Florida would be altered to increase water flow.

Under incentive provisions in the plan, agricultural interests could keep their costs down as low as $232 million by reducing the amount of phosphorus they send into the Everglades.

Critics of the plan say it costs the industry too little, relies too heavily on engineering solutions rather than reclaiming sugar cane fields for marshland and lacks enforcement mechanisms to ensure the sugar industry lives up to its promises. They also charged that the plan would let the sugar industry off the financial hook while only meeting "interim" phosphorus water-pollution goals of 50 parts per billion, rather than "final" goals of 5 to 15 parts per billion prescribed in the settlement of a federal lawsuit brought against Florida over pollution of the Everglades.

"It has the potential to become the 'Munich' of the Everglades, in which the government buys 'peace in our time' with Big Sugar, leaving to others at a later day the difficult task of actually saving the Everglades," said Dexter Lehtinen, the former acting U.S. attorney in Florida who brought the original suit that led to yesterday's announcement.

But Interior officials said they had driven a hard bargain against an industry that only a few weeks ago was willing to pay far less. "We made it clear we were willing to litigate to the wall and made the terms pretty tough," said spokesman Jay Ziegler.

The plan announced by Babbitt seeks to end years of legal and regulatory wrangling over the Everglades, the world's largest freshwater marsh, which once encompassed 4 million acres but which is now less than half that size. Decades of intensive development and the draining of swampland for agricultural production have left one of the world's richest biological areas in critical shape, threatened by both a shortage of water and pollution by sugar cane and vegetable growers.

Five years ago, the federal government sued Florida for failing to enforce water-quality standards in the Everglades. In 1991, the state settled that suit, agreeing to a cleanup that was then challenged in about three dozen separate suits by agricultural interests and other parties. The plan announced by Babbitt seeks to put an end to that litigation, which has recently been the subject of mediation.

"We don't see this as the salvation for the Everglades," said Tom Weis, Florida program director for the environmental group Clean Water Action. "We see it as a contract to allow sugar growers to continue polluting the Everglades. . . . This is half of what we need. It says we'll just kill the Everglades a little slower."

Nelson Fairbanks, president of U.S. Sugar Corp., said the agreement forces the industry to contribute "much more than we wanted to pay." Nonetheless, said Fairbanks, "farmers can live with it—and it's the last bill."

6   Wetlands

As Ecological Value Is Documented,
State Is Banking on Their Future

ROBERT E. PIERRE

July, 1993

In the not-too-distant past, wetlands were viewed merely as sort of an inconvenience for developers, highway planners and lawmakers.

They didn't help get any votes, make any money or provide any recognizable benefits. But since the 1970s, there has been a growing awareness of their importance in purifying water before it reaches streams and rivers, soaking up floodwaters and providing a natural habitat for hundreds of species of plants and animals.

This recognition of the ecological value of wetlands is what led Maryland officials July 12 to join a national trend of designating wetland preserves, called mitigation banks. Mitigation banking is a system in which the creation, enhancement or restoration of wetlands is recognized by a regulatory agency as compensation for destruction of other wetlands.

Thirty years ago, Maryland law required only that state officials identify wetlands destroyed by highway construction. The policy of the late 1980s was to replace wetlands after destruction, usually at a site near a highway or other construction project.

But the new wetland banking pact signed last week by state and federal officials will permit Maryland to begin setting aside wetland banking areas from state highway administration projects. Currently, state law requires that wetlands be replaced after being diminished by construction, but banking allows these areas to be established in advance of destruction.

Regulatory approval is needed to destroy wetlands in the course of building a highway or other project. With a mitigation bank, a more central location is established where the enhancement occurs, and the developer in effect purchases that mitigation from the bank, said James McElfish, senior attorney of the Environmental Law Institute.

"Wetlands help with water purification, provide wildlife habitat and serve as a vegetative buffer for land activities," said Richard J. Dolesh, chief of the Maryland-

287

National Capital Park and Planning Commission's Interpretation and Conservation Division.

Most of the wetlands in Howard, Prince George's and Montgomery counties are located along the rivers and the streams that flow into them. Wetlands account for roughly 6 percent—more than 19,000 acres—of Prince George's County's 487 square miles of land surface. Most of the county's wetlands are non-tidal, also known as freshwater.

From 1981 to 1989, the county lost 229 acres of wetlands. Community development and construction of highways and gravel pits accounted for 67 percent of the loss.

In Montgomery County, there are 14,400 acres of wetlands.

Statewide, Maryland lost more than 1,000 acres annually of inland and coastal wetlands from 1955 to 1978 to erosion, development and agriculture projects. In recent years, however, state officials have enacted measures aimed at stopping any further loss.

The state legislature in 1991 passed a "no net loss" policy, which requires highway officials to replace wetlands lost to highway construction. For each acre destroyed, a developer would be asked to set aside one to five acres of wetlands.

Under the state's new banking agreement, a multi-agency task force would identify sites where highway projects are planned that might affect wetland areas. Once such a site is found, highway officials would enhance, build or restore the site as a wetland banking site in expectation of future effects. The banking site must be in the same river drainage system as the site that would be destroyed by highway construction.

Once the highway project is completed, highway officials would cash in acres as needed to make up for any wetlands loss.

Maryland Gov. William Donald Schaefer said that though it is imperative that the state continue to grow and create new jobs, the environment must not be ignored.

"Once a wetland is lost, it's gone forever," Schaefer said during a news conference last week at the Izaak Walton League's Patuxent River Park, near Routes 301 and 50 in Prince George's County.

Though state officials and environmental groups agreed that wetland banking is an improvement over building wetland areas piecemeal throughout the state, some were concerned it could lead to less protection for wetlands.

"I don't want this to become a wholesale excuse to just fill in wetlands just because there's a mitigation site somewhere," said Robert Boone, executive director of the Anacostia Watershed Society, an environmental group that cleans up the Anacostia River and its tributaries. "The concept is good, but there needs to be a provision for citizen comment and participation in individual projects. Human beings have yet to be able to construct a wetland with all the beneficial functions of a naturally occurring one."

A recent study of wetland mitigation sites nationwide seems to validate Boone's concerns. The District-based Environmental Law Institute released a report this month that said "banking is prone to misuse and ecological failure in the absence of clear, environmentally sound regulations and goals."

McElfish, one of the report's authors, said there are 46 active wetland mitigation sites throughout the country. McElfish said that though wetland banking is preferred to other methods of compensation, it is still best to avoid and minimize the loss.

"Wetland mitigation banking is a useful option for accomplishing compensation, but you have to be careful because these sites could fail," McElfish said. "Even if you compensate, it's not the same as having a wetland in place where nature put it."

Linda Kelbaugh, chief of the State Highway Administration's environmental programs division, said those concerns had been considered when the agreement was being drafted. The administration, she said, will continue to do studies in advance of large projects to avoid wetlands whenever possible.

The new agreement calls for the formation of a task force that would set site selection criteria, performance standards and criteria for exchange of credits and debits.

Schaefer said the agreement, which involved nine federal and state agencies, took too long to take shape. "This is a great day, but when we do something like this we've got to move faster. During those two years, we lost wetlands."

Still, a little late is better than not at all, said Barbara Taylor, executive director of Save Our Streams, a non-profit organization that promotes restoration and preservation of streams.

"This agreement is a recognition that the [Chesapeake] Bay can't survive without streams, and that streams can't survive without wetlands," Taylor said. "All of the rain that falls finds it way to a stream. Wetlands help to filter out the impurities and keep the stream clean. Ideally, you avoid wetlands . . . but realistically some are going to have to be destroyed. This way you can set aside larger areas and give the mitigated wetlands a better chance to thrive."

Biological Diversity: Endangered Animal Species 12

This chapter continues the theme of the previous two concerning the importance of preserving plant and animal species, here focusing on recent attempts to protect several animal species.

Article 1 in this chapter describes recent changes in U.S. policy concerning the designation of endangered plant and animal species designed to expedite federal protection of these organisms. The article points out that the U.S. Endangered Species Act has become a worldwide standard for the preservation of biodiversity. Article 2 concerns the designation of the Snake River sockeye salmon as endangered, although it appears to be too late to save this species. The article discusses conditions contributing to the decline of this species and actions necessary to avoid loss of additional species in the future. Article 3 presents the view that, at least in the case of the alligator, commercial trade is important for protection of both the species and its environment. The remaining articles concern worldwide attempts to protect various species, with Article 4 dealing with attempts to halt drift net fishing, particularly by Japan and South Korea. Articles 5, 6, and 7 address efforts to maintain the international ban on whaling and the threats of Iceland and Norway to defy this decree. Article 8 describes commercial seal killing in Namibia, and finally, Article 9 describes attempts to protect the few remaining rhinos and tigers in the face of demand by China and Taiwan for their body parts.

1 Endangered Species Rules Streamlined

U.S. Agrees to Hasten Process on Decisions

TOM KENWORTHY

December, 1992

I n a legal settlement hailed by conservationists, the Bush administration yesterday agreed to change its system of designating plant and animal species as endangered or threatened, a move that will expedite federal protection for hundreds of imperiled species over the next few years.

The administration's settlement, filed yesterday in federal district court here, ends six months of controversy over a suit brought against the Interior Department by the Fund for Animals and other groups and represents a major victory for environmental and conservation organizations. Those groups have long argued that the mechanism for officially designating (or "listing") individual species as endangered has become so gridlocked that the government has been acting in violation of the 1973 Endangered Species Act.

The agreement, in relatively short order, could lead to a doubling or tripling of the number of plant and animal species given government protection under the Endangered Species Act. The statute has become a worldwide standard for the protection of biodiversity but also has generated considerable political controversy because of cases such as the northern spotted owl, which has halted logging in vast tracts of forest land in the Pacific Northwest.

Since passage of the act in 1973, 750 domestic species have been declared threatened or endangered by the government, and the typical waiting time between the filing of a petition for listing and a government determination has extended to two or three years. Almost three dozen species, by the Fish and Wildlife Service's reckoning, have become extinct while awaiting designation under the act.

The government admitted no legal liability under terms of the agreement. But the Interior Department's Fish and Wildlife Service agreed by September 1996 to propose for listing some 400 species for which the agency has found substantial evidence to warrant protection but which have not been processed for listing.

In addition, the agency has consented to expedite final consideration of 900 species that it believes are worthy of protection but for which definitive scientific information has not been collected.

With some high profile exceptions such as the Florida black bear and the Montana arctic grayling (a trout), most of the 400 species likely to be listed by 1996 under the settlement are plant and animal species that largely are obscure to laymen. Among them are the greenest tiger beetle and the spring pygmy sunfish.

But in the long term, environmentalists said, perhaps the most important aspect of the settlement is the official recognition by the Fish and Wildlife Service that it should take a "multispecies, ecosystem approach" to protecting plants and animals rather than doing it species by species.

This could mean, for example, that rather than laboriously and separately going through the listing process for individual species such as the northern spotted owl, the marbled murrelet and salmon that inhabit the old growth forests of the Pacific Northwest, the government would evaluate that ecosystem as a whole and protect all of its components in one comprehensive plan.

The Fish and Wildlife Service has authority over most domestic plant and animal species that are endangered. Once a species is designated as in danger of extinction, the agency has broad authority to order measures to protect it, including the prohibition of actions that would further endanger the species, the designation of habitat critical to its survival, and the establishment of a plan to bring about its recovery.

"The importance of [yesterday's settlement] is that hundreds of species that were languishing in a bureaucratic box will now receive the special protection mandated by the Endangered Species Act," said Wayne Pacelle, national director of the Fund for Animals, the lead plaintiff in the suit against Interior Secretary Manuel Lujan Jr. and Fish and Wildlife Service Director John F. Turner.

"This finally makes the listing process what it was supposed to be 10 years ago," said John Fitzgerald, director of wildlife law for Defenders of Wildlife, another plaintiff. "Once this backlog is dealt with, you should be able to have a system that responds."

The agreement also was hailed by Assistant Interior Secretary Mike Hayden, whose office oversees the Fish and Wildlife Service. Hayden said the agreement would encourage the government to take a more comprehensive approach to species protection that could lead to more political support in controversial cases, as well as help persuade Congress to provide the agency enough resources to clear out its backlog.

"It's going to test us to get this done, but it is a reasonable settlement," Hayden said.

2 U.S. Designates Sockeye Salmon an Endangered Species

TOM KENWORTHY
November, 1991

The National Marine Fisheries Service yesterday formally designated the Snake River sockeye salmon an endangered species, a step that poses potentially enormous consequences for the agricultural and industrial economy of the Pacific Northwest. The region's huge appetite for cheap federal power and irrigation water might have to be curbed to save the once-mighty salmon runs of the Columbia River system.

The designation, which automatically triggers a federal campaign to restore the Snake River sockeye, probably comes too late to save the fish as a truly wild species. Only four of the fish this year completed the epic 900-mile journey from the Pacific to spawn in an alpine lake in Idaho's Sawtooth Mountains. The lone female in that group was taken for artificial spawning in a desperate attempt to produce hatchery-raised fish with the genetic traits of the wild species.

Although it may be too late for the Snake River species, the decision is expected to lend new urgency to longstanding efforts to restore threatened runs of other salmon species on the Columbia and its tributaries—magnificent, storied migrations that have symbolized the Pacific Northwest since aboriginal times.

Those attempts have made considerable progress in the past year but never quite succeeded, in part because of intense competition for the Columbia's water, which has been harnessed since the 1930s by a series of dams, including the famed Bonneville Dam. Those dams have turned millions of acres of arid land into some of the world's most productive farms and orchards and provided the cheap hydroelectric power that fuels the region's aluminum, aircraft and other industries.

The sockeye designation "is really a stalking horse for other salmon runs we still have a chance to save," said Ed Chaney, an Idaho natural resources consultant who has written a number of plans to restore the salmon runs, including a proposal by Idaho Gov. Cecil Andrus (D) that was largely endorsed by other governors in the region.

"The good news is that the region has been preparing itself for this listing for nearly a year and a half, and we are way ahead of the game," said Sen. Mark O.

Hatfield (R-Ore.) in response to the announcement. Last year, Hatfield convened a so-called salmon summit to develop a recovery plan for the salmon, an effort that fell short of success but which has been continued under the auspices of the Northwest Power Planning Council.

The National Marine Fisheries Service, a branch of the Commerce Department, has already proposed to list two other Snake River salmon populations, the spring/summer and fall chinook runs, as threatened—an interim step under the federal Endangered Species Act that is likely to lead to designations that they, too, are endangered and must be restored.

The designations would not affect most supplies of commercially harvested salmon because those fish spawn in other waters.

The decline of the salmon runs of the Columbia and its tributaries, including the Snake and Salmon rivers, involves a complex web of factors including overharvesting and habitat destruction. But a major reason, according to most experts, is the hydroelectric dams constructed beginning in the 1930s, a system that produces one-third of the hydroelectric power in the United States and provides people and industry in the Pacific Northwest with clean, abundant power at only 40 percent of the cost of electricity in most of the United States.

Despite the expenditure of about $1 billion in the last decade to build fish ladders, erect screens over turbine intakes, build hatcheries and truck salmon around the dams, the annual runs of all salmon species on the Columbia system have declined to about 2.5 million fish from historic levels of about 16 million per year.

Reversing the decline, say some experts, means undoing some of that massive engineering project by drawing down reservoirs behind the dams to let water pass faster downstream to assist juvenile fish in their journey to the ocean. That, in turn, means less water available to produce electricity, irrigate farmland and ship agricultural products from ports far inland.

However, utilities, industries that rely heavily on cheap power and the federal agencies that control the dams and the power they produce are likely to fight any solutions that rely too heavily on drawing down those reservoirs.

"Dams are not the only problem," said Jack Robertson, deputy administrator of the Bonneville Power Administration, arguing that some species of salmon have become extinct even though they spawn downriver from the dams. "It's a huge, complex biological cycle and you could blow up the dams and still drive the fish to extinction."

For the Snake River sockeye, the most perilous part of the journey is when the juvenile fish, or smelt, head downstream from their spawning ground in Redfish Lake in Idaho. Reservoirs created by the eight federal power dams on the lower Snake and lower Columbia slow water flow so much that many fish begin their transformation into their saltwater forms well before they reach the ocean. A trip that took about a week before the dams were built now takes up to six weeks, and the vast majority of fish die before reaching the Pacific.

Andrus said the endangered species designation will empower the fisheries service to overrule opposition to drawing down the reservoirs that is expected from the Army Corps of Engineers and the Bonneville Power Administration, which control the dams and the electricity they produce.

"They can look them in the eye and say 'do this and do that,' " said Andrus. "It's about time they did that to those yahoos."

3 Bag a 'Gator and Save the Species

Environmentalists Link Habitat Preservation to Sale of Skins

WILLIAM BOOTH
August, 1993

It is a long way from Ed Froehlich's gator farm to the floor of the Tokyo stock exchange. But in the brave new world of global economics and conservation, Froehlich's alligators and Japanese stocks are inexorably, if weirdly, linked.

The price of alligator skins is in free fall. The immediate reason is that the Japanese do not buy alligator handbags during a recession, and so alligator farms are going bankrupt. About one-third of them may go under in Florida and Louisiana.

But that is not all.

Environmentalists say the story of the rise and fall of the gator industry may illustrate a seemingly contradictory point: To save a wild species, such as the American alligator, society might have to decide that killing them is a good idea.

"It's a hard concept to get across, but if people in America want to protect the alligator, the best thing they can do is buy an alligator handbag," said Don Ashley, a consultant for the Florida Alligator Farmers Association and an expert in grading and selling classic crocodilian skins.

As Ashley sees it, by harvesting alligators from the wild and on farms, society gives them and the freshwater marshes where they live an economic value.

"Giving the gator a value gives their habitat a value," Ashley said. "It gives society another good reason not to dam and dike and drain the swamps. Look, Florida has lost half its wetlands. Half! And it's not going to save the rest unless there's a good reason."

The best reason to save something, Ashley maintains, is money.

Environmentalists agree. "We tell people: Buy alligator, if you can," said Ginete Hemley, director of a wildlife trade monitoring program at the World Wildlife Fund in Washington.

"There's little question in our minds that controlled hunting and ranching has helped provide incentives to protect both the species and habitat," Hemley said. "This is a great model . . . a success story."

The mere fact that an industry has been built around alligators is remarkable. In the early 1970s, the federal government listed them as endangered.

"The populations were severely depressed in some areas," said Nick Wiley of the alligator management section of the Florida Game and Freshwater Fish Commission. "But we questioned that they were truly endangered. There were still good numbers of alligators in remote areas. By the mid-1970s, we had alligators again coming out of our ears, so to speak."

Many Americans, however, mistakenly believe that the giant amphibious reptiles are still endangered. But alligators are doing so well in Florida that they have become a nuisance in many settings.

Not a month goes by without some new lurid report of a rogue alligator consuming someone's poodle, or worse. Trappers call the canals that crisscross Florida "alligator highways."

In June, a Little League canoe trip on the Loxahatchee River near West Palm Beach ended in tragedy, when an 11-foot alligator snatched Bradley Weidenhamer, 10, by the head, held him under water and killed him as his father struggled to free him.

Rogue alligators are shot and skinned, and all populations are being managed by the state, which allows limited hunting and egg collecting.

Gator farmers are a colorful bunch. In Florida, some are reformed poachers. Froehlich, a self-described "outlaw of the swamps," said he played hide-and-seek with game wardens for years, hunting alligators at night from his airboat and selling the illegal skins on the gray market. He was never caught.

Eventually, Froehlich said, he agreed to stop his nocturnal adventuring if the state would allow him to raise alligators on his farm, begun in the 1960s. Today, he is called "the father of alligator ranching" in Florida.

Froehlich's farm is located in this tiny town in central Florida, home of a roadside tourist attraction called Gator Jungle. The farm supports about 6,000 animals, and about 1,000 eggs should hatch within the next few weeks.

The eggs are collected from the wild, with the help and permission of the Florida wildlife agency, which charges Froehlich $5 for every egg he takes. He pays Ashley $6 for helping him to find eggs, and they use a spotter airplane and state alligator surveys.

Taking an egg from a mama alligator is not as insane as it might sound.

"I don't recommend it, but the danger is a little overstated," Wiley said. "They don't resist that much. They stay close to the nest, and they growl at you to demonstrate they don't understand what you're doing or why you're doing it. . . . I mean, they have a pretty small brain. Raccoons often clean them out."

The eggs go into hothouses. Under ideal conditions, all farm alligators would be raised in hothouses with a steamy, constantly warm, almost prehistoric condition. Hothouse gators eat year-round and reach a harvestable four or five feet in as little as 18 months.

An alligator raised outdoors takes as long as three years to reach the same length because the animals go into semi-hibernation when nights grow cool. In the wild, only 2 percent or 3 percent of alligator eggs mature into adults.

During the late 1980s, gator ranching was booming, and the industry was being compared to a living gold mine. Prices reached $60 a foot for wild alligator skins and $180 a foot for farm-raised. People rushed into the industry. Some farmers became temporarily rich.

By late 1990, however, the bottom had fallen out. Now, alligators sell almost for less than it costs to produce them. Prices have never been so low: Wild skins sell for $20 a foot and farm-raised for $75 a foot.

"It's killing us," said Kevin Foster, a gator farmer in Okeechobee, who not only raises alligators but also breeds them in ponds. "There are a lot of us just barely holding on."

In Florida and Louisiana, as many as one-third of gator ranchers may go out of business. The largest gator rancher in Florida recently filed for bankruptcy protection, and his farm is in receivership.

But the gators keep eating, hundreds of thousands of them, chomping on ground beef and chicken wings and gator chow, while a worldwide slump sends the new industry reeling.

The reason for the slump is well known: overproduction collides with lowered demand; too many skins for too few buyers.

A worldwide recession, particularly in Japan, reduced demand. About half of all alligator skins are bought by Japan, so a dip in the Japanese stock exchange or Tokyo real estate prices means fewer alligator purses sold.

There is another problem, gator farmers said. Many Americans think that buying alligator products is illegal or unethical. "Most people still think they're endangered," Ashley said.

But he and his colleagues would like to see a craze for alligator boots and belts sweep the land.

"This is the most regulated wildlife product in the world," Ashley said. "You make alligators worth $60 or $70 a foot. . . . I promise you people will look at swamps in a whole different way."

4   Japan to End Drift Net Fishing in Bow to Worldwide Pressure

U.S. Hails 'Victory for the Ocean Environment'

TOM KENWORTHY
November, 1991

The Japanese government announced yesterday it will shut down its drift net fishing industry by the end of 1992, ending its participation in a fishing practice that environmentalists and other governments said was wasteful and threatened the existence of many species of marine life.

The decision was hailed as a major victory by marine conservation groups and the U.S. government, which have fought for years to curtail use of the huge nets. They are used mainly to catch tuna and squid but stretch for 30 to 40 miles and ensnare and kill millions of pounds of other fish, birds and marine mammals, which are usually discarded.

Heart-rending images of dolphins caught up in the nets have inspired widespread popular concern about the practice and consumer boycotts in the United States of drift net tuna. In response, the major U.S. suppliers of canned tuna last year stopped buying tuna caught in drift nets. In a move seen as recognition of the power of environmental concerns in the marketplace, one firm labeled and advertised its tuna as "dolphin safe."

A scientific report issued this year at a meeting in Sydney, Australia, concluded that the Japanese drift net industry in 1990 swept up, along with 106 million squid, more than 39 million unwanted small fish, 700,000 sharks, 270,000 sea birds and 26,000 marine mammals. Japan has about 450 ships using drift nets, about half of the fleet operating in the North Pacific.

"This is a clear victory for the ocean environment," said State Department spokesman Margaret Tutwiler in announcing that the United States and Japan had agreed on a compromise U.N. resolution under which Japan will reduce its drift net effort by half by June 30, 1992, and eliminate it entirely by Dec. 31, 1992. This resolution, which could be debated in the United Nations as early as today, will supersede a pending resolution sponsored by the United States that would have called for the cessation of all drift net fishing six months earlier.

"We have the champagne on ice, but we won't uncork the bottle until the United Nations officially passes a drift net moratorium resolution," said Ben Deeble, who coordinates drift net opposition for the environmental group Greenpeace.

Citing the "unacceptable waste and adverse ecological impacts associated with drift net fishing," National Marine Fisheries Service Assistant Administrator William W. Fox Jr. said he hoped Japan's announcement would encourage other nations, particularly South Korea and France, also to comply with U.N. resolutions calling for a moratorium on drift net fishing. The international body two years ago adopted a far less restrictive, conditional moratorium to take effect by June 30, 1992.

"The government has no alternative but to suspend drift net fishing in view of the attitude of other countries toward Japan," said Foreign Ministry spokesman Taizo Watanabe, according to Reuter news service.

Japan is one of three Asian nations—the other two are South Korea and Taiwan—that have conducted large-scale drift net fishing operations in the Pacific Ocean. In August, after the United States threatened Taiwan and South Korea with trade sanctions if they did not abide by the 1989 U.N. resolution calling for an end to the practice, Taiwan announced that it would halt drift net operations by next July.

"South Korea remains the wild card, but we hope they will follow the Japanese lead," said Albert Manville, a wildlife biologist with Defenders of Wildlife who called the Japanese announcement a "sweet victory for the global environment."

The use of drift nets became widespread in the Pacific in the early 1980s, when Japan, Taiwan and South Korea dispatched hundreds of ships to catch squid and tuna. The apparatus, made of lightweight, almost invisible plastic netting, hangs from floats like a huge curtain about 30 feet below the ocean surface, entangling almost anything that swims into it. The nets are then hauled aboard ship, where the desired species are pulled free and processed.

Japan's announcement, following a vote of its cabinet, came as pressure was building both in the United Nations and in the United States to force a worldwide moratorium on drift net fishing. Although U.N. resolutions have no enforcement mechanism, legislation was moving in the Congress to impose trade sanctions on Japan if it did not adhere to the U.N. call for a moratorium.

Spokesmen for Japan's fishing industry bitterly criticized a decision they said would jeopardize the livelihoods of thousands of workers who depend on drift net operations.

"Our future is pitch black," said Kazuyasu Kando of the Japan Squid Drift Net Fishery Association, the Associated Press reported from Tokyo. "We really don't know what to do next."

5   Still Killing Whales

COLMAN McCARTHY
June, 1991

S ome modern Captain Ahabs, with Reykjavik, Iceland, as their home port and minke whales as their prey, are mad at the world. Claiming that their livelihoods are being threatened by international conservation meddlers, a group of Icelandic fishermen has announced it will defy the International Whaling Commission's six-year-old ban on hunting the endangered minkes.

A leader of the rebel whalers told a European newspaper: "We are not doing harm to anyone just trying to earn a living. We can't allow foreigners to tell us what to do anymore. If anyone tries to stop us, there will be a bloodbath."

It's past bathings in blood—whales'—that enabled the world's environmental and conservation groups to rally international support that either shamed or pressured the whale-hunting nations to put away their harpoons. Most have, except for Iceland, Norway and Japan.

The history of commercial whaling, with the fictional Ahab aside, is one of a scorched-earth policy applied to the high seas. That, combined with the overfishing of sea life, is leading to an oceanic desert.

The 19th-century image of brave New Englanders risking their lives in rowboats against leviathans has been replaced. Today's slaughter is done from factory ships using electronic explosive harpoons and guided by aerial tracking. Language is assaulted also: Whales are "harvested," not killed.

In the 1960s, when decimation peaked, Japan sent 10,000 workers to sea in more than 100 catcher boats and seven factory ships to kill as many as 15,000 whales annually. "humpback and blues, mammals slow to reproduce, were threatened with extinction. Japanese whalers then went after sei and fin. Those are now commercially extinct. The current prey is the smaller and less profitable minke.

The revolt of Iceland's whale hunters surfaced during last month's annual meeting in Reykjavik of the International Whaling Commission. The 36-nation group, which on notorious occasion has had as much spine as a jellyfish in making hard decisions, refused to lift the ban on commercial whaling. For another year, at least, it will be illegal.

Proposals are now before Iceland's legislature to pull out of the commission. This us-against-the-world stance might have a claim on public sympathy if Iceland's economy was even moderately dependent on whaling. It isn't.

The Icelandic whalers' self-description as oppressed working stiffs just hanging on economically deserves rejection. They are anything but subsistence fishermen, unlike some Eskimo communities.

"Iceland's whalers are earning incomes from other kinds of fishing," says Sally Shoup, a Greenpeace specialist on whaling who has attended the past three IWC meetings, including last month's in Reykjavik. "It's time they were a bit more candid about why they want to keep killing the minkes. It's for profit, which is how the problem was created in the first place. There's a small market in Iceland for whale meat, but the lucrative outlet is in Japan. It's a gourmet luxury food that can sell for over $100 a pound."

Iceland's whalers have sprung a major leak in their political boat. If they quit the IWC in a huff, they will lose the Japanese whale-meat market: Japan has domestic legislation forbidding the import of whale meat from non-IWC countries.

Instead of issuing blubbery threats to create "a bloodbath," Iceland's whalers ought to get in line with world opinion and stop the slaughter. They should be grateful that their coastal waters are not yet depleted of other stock.

If Iceland needs a model, the Soviet Union is available. Its whaling industry resisted joining the moratorium for years. In 1987, it did.

International pressure brought it around. Last year, some Soviet whalers came to the commission with a "research" proposal to kill 25–35 fin whales and 60–70 minkes, some from the protected waters in the Sea of Okhotsk. Scientists on the commission saw the proposal as having nothing to do with authentic research and rejected it. The Soviets came back last month with a slightly altered proposal, but already 26 international environmental groups have appealed to Mikhail Gorbachev to reverse the plan and stay with the moratorium.

That still leaves Japan prowling the seas, including Antarctica's, for "research whaling." Who's kidding whom? Last month in Tokyo, corpses of the scientific minke catch were served as deep-fried whale chunks, barbecued whale tail and slices of whale bacon at a banquet protesting the world's treatment of Japan's whaling industry.

The Japanese need to get with Icelanders and mutually try to wake each other up to the overwhelmingly strong arguments—environmental, ethical and economic—against prolonging the killing. A thought of Herman Melville, Ahab's creator, stands like a lighthouse that warns against the destruction: "The moot point is whether Leviathan can endure so wide a chase and so remorseless a havoc; whether the last whale, like the last man, smoke his last pipe, then disappear in the final puff."

6 Norway, Iceland Defy Ban, Will Resume Whale Hunts

GLENN FRANKEL
June, 1992

N orway and Iceland, two of the world's biggest fishing nations, announced plans today to defy a seven-year-old international ban and resume commercial whaling, setting off protests from environmentalists and officials from the United States and Britain.

Norwegian Prime Minister Gro Harlem Brundtland told a press conference in Oslo that her country would resume hunting next year for minke whales, one of the smallest and the most numerous of the species. Brundtland, a prominent environmental spokeswoman, said she was prepared for harsh international criticism of the decision, which her government made under pressure from its powerful fishing industry.

Iceland announced that it was quitting the International Whaling Commission as of midnight so that it too could resume hunting minke whales. Iceland's ambassador to Britain said the commission, which opened its annual meeting in Glasgow, Scotland, today, had become a captive of anti-whaling interests.

John Knauss, the U.S. representative to the commission, said he was "shocked and disappointed" by the Norwegian decision, which he said would "seriously undermine the structure of the only global body with authority to manage whaling."

"They didn't even give us the five days of this meeting to see if we could make progress in meeting their objections," said Knauss in a telephone interview.

British fisheries minister John Gummer, in his opening address to the meeting, made clear that the moves by Norway and Iceland would not compel the commission's 35 other member states to lift the ban. "The world will not allow us to risk a return to the barbarity of the past," Gummer told the delegates. "I firmly believe that the burden of proof for lifting the moratorium must rest with those who say they want to continue with whaling."

Whales are the largest and among the most intelligent of all mammals, and their preservation has become a key symbolic environmental issue. A cessation on hunting was adopted by the commission in 1982 and that took effect three years later, banning the killing of all 12 "great whale" species because of the threat of extinction. The ban permitted Norway, Iceland and Japan to continue killing several hundred whales each year for "scientific research" and allowed aboriginal subsistence whaling in four countries.

Environmentalists contend modern whaling, which often uses explosive harpoons and electric shock to snare and kill, is among the most brutal forms of mammal hunting. The conservationists, dozens of whom stood outside today's session holding anti-whaling placards, also allege that whaling countries have used scientific research as a smoke screen to conceal commercial hunting.

Ever since it agreed to the cessation, the commission has been engaged in a scientific assessment of just how many great whales remain in each of the 12 species. It has estimated a minke whale population of 860,000 in the areas it has assessed, but the size and accuracy of those estimates remain in dispute. Japan, Norway and Iceland were pressing to revise the commission's procedures to allow limited commercial minke whaling to resume. In opposition, France has offered a plan to create a new whale sanctuary in the Antarctic that would cut off that major feeding area from the hunters.

U.S. representative Knauss said he supports revising the commission's procedures for determining how many whales each country would be allowed to kill if and when the ban is lifted, while suspending judgment on whether to remove the ban until next year's session. That stand has placed him in conflict with environmentalists who contend there should be no easing of the current restrictive procedure.

7 World Whaling Body Riven by Dispute

Norway Threatens to End Moratorium

T. R. REID
May, 1993

The annual meeting of the International Whaling Commission ended in rancor today as Norway threatened to end a seven-year-old global moratorium and resume commercial whaling.

Throughout the week-long meeting of the world's whaling regulatory body, the United States and other countries joined to defeat all efforts to lift the whaling ban. But their "zero tolerance" position so angered the chief whaling nations—Norway, Iceland and Japan—that the organization was furiously split when the delegates adjourned today.

American observers at the meeting said the Clinton administration had adopted a considerably tougher anti-whaling position than the stance taken at past such gatherings by the Reagan and Bush administrations.

During the session here in Japan's ancient capital, the whaling countries repeatedly tried to gain the moral high ground in the ongoing argument about Earth's biggest animal. They argued that it is "cultural imperialism" for Americans, who shoot and eat wild animals such as ducks and deer to say it is wrong for others to eat whale.

Japanese fishermen and their wives demonstrated daily here, saying they had been deprived of their livelihood because of misguided environmentalism. "IWC—Humane to Whales, Inhumane to Humans," read the signs of the demonstrators.

The nations seeking to catch whales based their argument on a report from the commission's science panel that said certain whales are so abundant that they can be harvested without danger. Although some whale species—including the blue whale, at 100 tons the largest animal ever found on Earth—are in danger of extinction, there are whale species, with populations of hundreds of thousands or more, that are not endangered.

The commission's science committee reported last year that the minke (rhymes with "pinky") whale—relatively small by whale standards but still twice the size of an elephant—exists in the hundreds of thousands.

"In all reasonableness," concluded Ray Gambell, who heads the whaling commission, "we would have to say that a commercial catch could be taken without endangering [minke] stocks."

Nevertheless, delegates here rejected for the second straight year a Japanese request for permission to take 50 minke whales from its coastal waters. And the U.S.-led conservation faction easily defeated a proposal that would have permitted whaling nations to take a few thousand minkes each year.

These votes prompted Norwegian delegate Jan Arbesen to warn that his country may soon start commercial whaling on its own. "Our government decided last year . . . to resume traditional whaling," Arbesen said. "We wanted to wait until this meeting to see if we could reach an agreement with the IWC, but . . . no decision of any importance with regard to management of whales was made here."

Over the past dozen years, the United States regularly supported a ban on whaling but had been willing to discuss alternative approaches with whaling nations.

Under Clinton, however, "there's been a sea change in the U.S. stance," said Michael Sutton, of the World Wildlife Fund, a member of the U.S. delegation here and at several prior whaling conferences. "The new administration's policy is very clearly that the U.S. will just say no to commercial whaling under any circumstances."

Whaling nations sharply criticized this tough new U.S. stance. "I hope someone conveys to Washington that this is not an environmental position," said Iceland's representative, Gudmundur Eiriksson. "The administration's position is anti-environmental under the current environmental standard of sustainable use."

The doctrine of "sustainable utilization" of living resources was a central tenet of the U.N. environmental summit in Rio de Janeiro last summer.

Sutton argued that whaling should be banned everywhere. "There's no overriding human need for these whales. Whales are an internationally managed migratory species. They belong to the world, not to Japan or Norway," he said.

The IWC was created in 1947 by whaling nations as a control unit for commercial whaling. With the global spread of environmental concerns in the 1970s, however, the organization gradually turned into an anti-whaling body. Several countries that do not engage in whaling became voting members, leading to passage in 1985 of the complete ban on commercial whaling.

Since then, the whaling nations have mounted a counterattack, recruiting into the organization several small countries. A number of Caribbean island nations that receive financial aid from Japan have joined the body and generally support Japan and Norway on major votes.

8 Huge Seal Slaughter Defies Outcry

Namibia Defends Harvest; Activists Call It Cruel, Trivial

PAUL TAYLOR
August, 1993

For a man who makes his living clubbing baby seals to death with pick handles, shooting their fathers and selling their penises, Aldert Brink comes across as a disarmingly sensitive soul.

"If there's one thing I can't handle, it's a wounded animal," says Brink, a former nature conservation officer who runs a gigantic commercial seal harvest. "That's just not on. Especially if the animal flees into the ocean, where you can't put it out of its misery."

Brink prides himself on the humaneness of his slaughter. "The way we do it, there is no such thing as the animal suffering," he says.

Brink's critics are not impressed. Reviving a battle that raged in Canada for two decades, animal rights groups have launched a worldwide campaign to abolish the Namibian seal harvest. Their reasons: cruelty and triviality.

"Has mankind really sunk so low?" Brian Davies, founder of the International Fund for Animal Welfare (IFAW), asked in a recent fund-raising letter. "Is life so meaningless that we can allow people to kill babies and shoot their parents just to satisfy some perverse desire for a sex potion?"

Aphrodisiacs are at the center of the continuing save-the-seal movement. IFAW claims the main reason the Namibian government has doubled its seal-kill quotas over the past two years, to 48,000 pups and 2,800 bulls, is that the Cape Fur bull seal's penis, which can be ground up and sold as an aphrodisiac, fetches $1,250 a pound in Hong Kong.

Large-scale seal hunting around the world virtually ended in the 1980s after environmental groups focused attention on the Canadian hunt, causing the market for seal pelts in Europe and the United States to collapse. Both the United States and the European Community have banned the import of baby seal skins. Canada outlawed commercial hunting of seal pups in 1987, but subsistence seal hunting by native peoples is permitted.

David Barritt, IFAW's southern Africa director, said he has seen no evidence that the market for seal fur is reviving.

His organization, the largest animal rights group in the world, also objects to the way the seal harvest is conducted. Pups 6 months to 10 months old are clubbed to death; the bulls are shot.

"There is no humane way to kill any seal, but the worst situation is when you have highly mobile seals like the Cape Fur in Namibia, which are capable of trying to flee to safety," Barritt said. "You're bound to get a lot of injured seals."

During the four-month harvest that started earlier this month, Brink's day begins at sunrise, when the remote rock and sand beaches near his small, weather-beaten 100-year-old factory/slaughterhouse are still jam-packed with seals. By mid-morning, they will be in the ocean to feed and escape the heat.

The slaughter begins with some of Brink's 29 employees herding thousands of pups and cows away from the densely populated colony of several hundred thousand. The bulls are not herded, partly because their physiology requires a killing technique different from that used on the pups and partly because the bulls are hard to budge. They spend four or five months a year parked in the same spot—the place they mark out for themselves in the colony, where they maintain their harems and defend their territory from incursions by other bulls.

Once a group has been separated from the colony, Brink's men—seasonal migrant laborers who come from the impoverished Ovamboland region in northern Namibia—form a gantlet. Four to six men line up on each side, wielding pick handles or sticks up to six feet long.

The herders direct the prey through the gantlet, which lies in their path to the ocean. The seals move in tightly packed bunches, their heads cocked at an angle that gives them a beseeching look, batting their eyelashes, working their flippers in overdrive to produce an awkward movement that is part slither and part waddle.

Brink's clubbers aim for the pups' skulls.

"The cranial bone of a seal pup is paper thin, and it is very easy to smash," said Brink. "They go unconscious immediately."

Because the pups are a moving target, though, the first blow doesn't always strike the skull cleanly.

"I instruct my men to club each pup twice, just to make sure," he said.

It's not a pretty sight, but Brink says—and marine biologists confirm—it's the most efficient way to kill.

"The beauty of it—if I can use that word—is that you are so close to the animal, you have it under your control, so if the first blow misfires you are right there with a second," Brink said.

IFAW says seals are like cats or dogs—intelligent, social animals capable of feeling a range of emotions, including fear. Mothers nurse their pups for six to eight months, so when the harvest begins, most pups have not been weaned. But Brink said the killing does not seem to traumatize the cows.

"They don't seem to know what is going on," he said. "It doesn't set off a panic. To the contrary, it seems to have a calming effect; it's almost as if the seals think the pups have gone to sleep."

Within minutes after being clubbed, pups are stabbed in the heart, and their carcasses are lined up along the beach, to be taken by truck to the factory.

In the world of bull seals, which weigh up to 800 pounds, Brink himself is the predator. Bull seals' skulls are thicker, and they can be aggressive animals, capable of fighting back if not felled by a first blow. So instead of clubbing them, Brink shoots them in the brain with a .22-caliber bullet, using a silencer on his rifle so as not to cause a commotion in the colony.

A miss could wound another seal, but Brink claims he almost never misses. "If I go out with 100 bullets, I'll come back with 99 bull seals," he said.

His account could not be confirmed by this eyewitness. The morning Brink opened his operation to journalists for the first time, an unusually strong and warm east wind drove all the seals into the ocean. There was no harvest that day. Instead, Brink showed a videotape of pup and bull kills. This generally supported his description, although it was impossible to know what, if anything, had been edited out.

The kills here and at a second seal colony farther south are conducted under the eyes of inspectors from Namibia's Ministry of Fisheries and Marine Resources. IFAW is unimpressed.

"The inspectors are drawn from the local communities, and we think they are basically sympathetic to the kill," Barritt said.

No one at the ministry denies that the Namibian government supports the harvest—in contrast to the South African government, which suspended the kill along the same coastal waters in 1990 under pressure from animal rights groups.

"We are a poor Third World country," said B. W. Oelossen, a marine biologist with the ministry. "Why should we bend to the whims of the animal rights lobby when we have people who are starving?"

The Namibian sealing industry employs 100 people, most of them seasonally, and generates less than $1 million a year in revenue. But Brink hopes that a reviving market for furs will allow him to build a new factory, expand his catch and eventually employ up to 500 people.

The IFAW says the penis is the only part of the seal that is still profitable, especially since IFAW's earlier campaign against sealing in Canada virtually wiped out what had been a flourishing worldwide market for seal fur.

In the Far East, dried seal penises are either displayed whole or ground up and sold as pills, potions or food additives to enhance human sexual performance, IFAW says.

"For such a trivial use, should mankind really be allowed to kill a highly intelligent, social mammal who is capable of feeling terror?" Barritt asked.

But Brink says IFAW is exaggerating the importance of the penis issue. He said he sells all parts of the seal at a profit: the oil, the hide to make leather for shoes and bags, the carcass to be ground into meal for protein-rich animal fodder and fertilizer, and the fur—one of the densest in the animal kingdom—for clothing.

He refused to open his books, however.

Many here believe the real economic benefit of sealing to Namibia is that it removes from the waters a mammal with a voracious appetite.

"There's no question there are tough competitors for our fishing industry," said Oelossen, who notes that Namibia's seals consume an estimated 1.5 million tons of fish annually, while Namibia's commercial fisheries catch just 800,000 tons.

There is no scientific proof that seals diminish the catch of sardines and hake, Namibia's leading commercial species, but the fishing industry here considers seals a nuisance.

"They often get caught in the nets, and fisherman will tell you they often see seals swim into their net and feast on the catch," Oelossen said.

Top government officials acknowledge that allowing sealing is a sop to the commercially important fishing industry, although the official government position is that the seal kill is a harvest, not a cull.

"If we wanted to get rid of the seal population, our quotas would be much higher and we would allow the cows to be killed," Oelossen said. "But we don't. We consider seals as a resource to be harvested on a sustainable basis."

Oelossen said Namibia's seal population of an estimated 750,000 has never been larger and continues to grow at a rate of 3 percent a year.

To get IFAW off Namibia's back, Oelossen has proposed that animal rights groups buy out the sealing industry and turn the seal colonies into a tourist attraction—something IFAW has proposed that the government do.

"If they think it's feasible, why don't they try it?" Oelossen asked. "Why should we suffer financially?"

Tourism doesn't seem destined to be a big revenue producer, given the remoteness of the colonies from population centers. A small government-run seal-watching operation draws fewer than 25,000 tourists a year.

The battle over sealing leaves most Namibians a bit mystified and a bit cynical. They can't understand what all the fuss is about.

"It's the eyelashes," said Jimmy Rea, who runs a local sport fishing business. "Any creature with eyelashes will always get the Bambi treatment."

9   China and Taiwan Warned on Endangered Species

TOM KENWORTHY
September, 1993

A cting in tandem to protect two of the world's endangered species, the U.S. government and the international community yesterday took steps that could lead to sanctions against China and Taiwan if they don't halt their trade in rhinoceros and tiger parts sold for medicinal purposes.

Attending a meeting of the United Nations' Convention on International Trade in Endangered Species (CITES) in Brussels, Interior Secretary Bruce Babbitt announced that he has formally certified that the two countries are in violation under a U.S. law that could lead to broad trade sanctions against them.

The animals are killed to provide material for a brisk international market. Rhino horns and tiger bones are still frequently used in traditional Chinese medicine to treat fevers and joint and bone maladies such as rheumatism and arthritis. Recent investigations by the private, nonprofit Environmental Investigation Agency have shown that rhino horn is still available for sale in pharmacies in Taiwan and through government-run companies in China.

In a separate but related action yesterday, the CITES standing committee recommended that the 120 nations that are signatories of the international treaty protecting endangered species halt trading of plant and animal products with Taiwan and China. The recommendation could affect millions of dollars worth of trade in such products as flowers, timber and aquarium fish.

"The United States cannot stand by while the world's remaining wild tigers and rhinos slip into extinction as a result of illegal commercial trade in the world marketplace," said Babbitt in a statement released in Washington. "Our action today will send the message that continued unlawful trade in these rare species will not be tolerated."

But in letters sent yesterday to President Clinton and U.S. Trade Representative Mickey Kantor, Babbitt acknowledged that China and Taiwan have made some progress in stemming the trade in rhino and tiger parts and stopped short of recommending the imposition of sanctions.

"The Fish and Wildlife Service will continue to monitor the actions taken by China and Taiwan, and if they appear to be making expeditious progress toward compliance with CITES standards, I believe that the imposition of import prohibitions . . . would not be productive," Babbitt said in his letter to Kantor.

Under the so-called Pelly Amendment to the Fishermen's Protective Act of 1967, Clinton has broad discretion to impose trade sanctions against nations that undermine the effectiveness of international conservation agreements such as CITES. Following Babbitt's certification of China and Taiwan under the amendment, Clinton has 60 days to report to Congress with his response to the action.

Conservationists hailed the U.S. action yesterday as an important step in what they described as an increasingly desperate campaign to protect the world's 7,000 remaining tigers and fewer than 10,000 remaining rhinos.

"Implementing the Pelly Amendment sends a clear message to other nations at a time when the rhinoceros and tiger species are dangerously near extinction," said James P. Leape, senior vice president of the World Wildlife Fund.

Federal Land Use: Grazing Rights on Federal Range Lands 13

In a now classic article that appeared in *Science* in 1968 called "The Tragedy of the Commons," Garrett Hardin characterized man's assault on the environment in terms of the colonial New England tradition of allowing farmers to graze their animals on the village green or commons at no cost. Of course, the commons could support only so many grazing animals (its carrying capacity). Any given farmer, however, was tempted to put more animals on the green to increase his personal income even though it would mean that the entire group would eventually suffer. Thus, the farmer would pursue his own short-term welfare because the long-term negative consequences of his irresponsible behavior would be distributed over all of the farmers. Of course, the ultimate effect of his uncontrolled consumption was that everyone lost.

The tragedy described so vividly by Hardin seems to be occurring today on a vast scale. Millions of acres of federal lands are used by individuals at minimal cost for cattle grazing, logging and mining. Because these resources are limited, they will eventually be exhausted by uncontrolled consumption of individuals acting in their own self-interests. This chapter and the next present a number of *Post* articles concerning use by individuals of federal lands. The present chapter is concerned with cattle grazing rights and the next with logging rights.

Article 1 provides an overview of the issue and presents the differing perspectives of cattlemen and those concerned with environmental preservation. Articles 2 and 3 suggest that excessive grazing is harming the environment and that fees paid by cattlemen are too low. Article 4 describes how one cattleman has used environmentally sensitive range management practices with no loss of productivity. Articles 5 and 6 deal with the concerns over how management of federal lands will change as a result of a shift in national leadership from Republican to Democratic, but Articles 7, 8 and 9 show how difficult it is for government to implement policies that would limit immediate profits for the purpose of long-term preservation of resources.

1   Public Land, Private Profit

U.S. Ranchers Face off over Grazing Limits

JOHN LANCASTER
February, 1991

For generations, cattlemen have grazed their herds amid the parched and rugged mountains of the Gila National Forest, earning private profits from public land in a partnership steeped in the traditions of the Old West.

But now that partnership is at risk. Angered by new environmental restrictions on grazing in the 3.3 million-acre federal forest in southwestern New Mexico, ranchers and local governments have squared off with the U.S. Forest Service in a modern version of an old-fashioned range war.

"Here's Saddam Hussein, walked in and took Kuwait—and that's how it is with the Forest Service," said O. E. Grubb, 71, who recently was ordered to remove half his 200 Hereford cattle from the 15,000-acre grazing allotment he has occupied for nearly 30 years. "They run you down."

The conflict has echoes throughout the West, as ranchers fight for control of public lands that many long have treated essentially as their own.

Last summer, in a case closely watched by environmentalists and cattlemen's groups, one county government here went so far as to pass a law threatening federal land managers with jail if they impose new restrictions on grazing and logging, and the Forest Service promised to call in U.S. marshals if it were enforced.

"We're completely dependent on the management of these resources," said Dick Manning, president of the Catron County Cattle Growers Association and a prime mover behind the ordinance. "What we're looking at is protecting our stability."

Grazing is permitted on more than 250 million acres of federal forests and grasslands, roughly 12 percent of the lower 48 states. The land is managed by the Agriculture Department's Forest Service and the Bureau of Land Management, an arm of the Interior Department.

The system dates to the frontier era, when the federal government coaxed settlers westward with promises of ample public range on which to graze their livestock for nominal fees.

316

But critics cite evidence that the century-old grazing system has left lasting environmental scars: eroded streams, sinking water tables, trampled vegetation. Moreover, they say, the money-losing federal grazing program amounts to a generous subsidy to a handful of politically powerful "welfare cowboys" who produce less than 3 percent of the nation's beef.

Ranchers counter that their industry has been unfairly maligned by environmentalists bent on turning the nation's public lands into nature preserves. They note that grazing, properly managed, can benefit vegetation used by wildlife and suggest that ranching is a vital thread in the fabric of the West, its culture as well as its economy.

"It's not the money, it's the way of life," said Frances Biebelle, whose husband, Walter, 69, wears a neck brace from a "horse wreck" last October. ("My feet was in an oak tree and my head was in a rock pile," he explained.)

At first blush, the conflict over grazing may seem overblown in the Gila, an arid, Connecticut-sized expanse of sagebrush, juniper and pine forest. Cattle, after all, have been part of the landscape here since Spanish settlers drove them north from Mexico around 1600. The forests still are thick with elk, bear and other wildlife.

But there is little question that four centuries of ranching have taken their toll. Cattle are so pervasive here that Forest Service biologists complain they lack a natural "baseline" on which to judge range conditions.

"Other than mesa tops or a bench surrounded by rocky bluffs, everything has been grazed at one time or another," said Wayne Buckner, the ranger in charge of the Gila's Silver City district. But this is enough to give forest biologists a reasonable idea of how the range should look: a profusion of shrubs and grasses, lush stream banks shaded by willow and cottonwoods.

The reality often is quite different. Cattle are compulsive eaters, consuming an average of 900 pounds of vegetation each month. The result in many parts of the Gila is a landscape dominated by manure piles, juniper and "blue grama"—a grazing-resistant grass that has supplanted other native species.

John Baldwin, a Forest Service range specialist on the Gila, parked his truck in the midst of one heavily used area. "Just looking at it from the composition and density of the plants, it's not near where we want it to be," he said. "We may never get it back to where it once was."

Cattle also had left their mark on the banks of a nearby stream. "It's just like a bombshell went off," Baldwin said. "There's not a blade of grass."

The situation on the Gila is hardly unique. The BLM, which oversees the bulk of the nation's public range—about 174 million acres of it—reported last year that 52 percent of its land was in fair or poor condition, compared with 3 percent in excellent or "natural" condition.

Much of the worst damage occurs in streamside, or "riparian" areas, to which the cattle are drawn, and which are critical to biological diversity in the arid West.

More than half the streams on BLM lands in Colorado are in poor condition, according to a 1988 study by the General Accounting Office. The assessment for BLM lands in Idaho found that 80 percent of 12,000 miles of streams were "in some stage of a degraded condition."

"Cattle are alien creatures to this part of the world; it's too hot and dry for them," said Jim Fish, a New Mexico environmentalist and co-founder of the Public Lands Action Network. "It's like growing bananas in Alaska."

But grazing and environmental catastrophe do not necessarily go hand in hand. Range scientists say that grazing can actually improve vegetation, much as mowing a lawn stimulates the growth of grass. The trick, they say, is good management: rotating pastures, building fences to protect sensitive areas, placing salt blocks away from streams to prevent overuse by cattle.

"You can't just say, 'Take the cows off and everything will be fine,'" said Pat Morrison, a wildlife biologist for the Reserve ranger district. "So many changes have occurred that it's never going to go back to what it was in 1900."

Under pressure from environmental groups and some members of Congress, land management agencies have begun to enforce with more vigor rules protecting streams and other sensitive areas. But the changes have caused deep resentment among ranchers who see them as eroding their claim to the public lands.

Nowhere is the conflict sharper than in Catron County, where ranchers say an overabundance of elk is responsible for much of the overgrazing the Forest Service wants to eliminate. "We just finally stood up and said, 'We're not taking the cows off until you take the elk off,'" said Manning, of the cattle growers association.

He and other local ranchers contend that grazing permits are akin to property rights, and therefore should not be subject to "third-party" interference by environmentalists and others. They note that a ranch typically is priced on the basis of the grazing permit associated with the property, and that the permits are taxed as assets on inheritance. Under the county ordinance passed last August, any Forest Service official who tampers with a federal grazing permit theoretically is subject to criminal charges.

But the Forest Service takes a different view—namely, that a grazing permit is a privilege without monetary value, and that the government never intended to cede control of its public lands to a single industry.

"Somebody from New Jersey or New York, it's just as much their land as his," said Mike Gardner, the ranger in charge of the Reserve district.

Although the county ordinance has yet to be enforced, "it's made the job that we do a lot more difficult," said Toby Martinez, the Gila's chief range manager. "All of our employees are operating under threat."

Ranchers are equally resistant to another long standing charge by environmentalists and some federal land managers: that they don't pay enough for the privilege of running their herds on public lands.

Congressional studies have shown that federal grazing fees are only about one-fifth the rate for private lands, prompting criticism that the government is subsidizing the 27,000 ranchers who hold federal permits.

Last year, for example, the BLM spent $35.3 million on its grazing program while recouping fees of $18.5 million.

But repeated attempts to raise the fee have run into a wall of opposition from cattlemen and their allies in Congress. "Never has so much been given to so few so easily," said Rep. Mike Synar (D-Okla.), a leading proponent of higher grazing fees.

Don Cullum, an oilman turned rancher near the Catron County seat of Reserve, said he thinks the local ordinance is misguided. But he called Synar's grazing fee legislation a "crime" and insisted that the government already gets the better end of the deal.

Cullum, 54, who began running cattle here 13 years ago, lives with his wife in a spectacular log house so remote that he has to ford a stream to reach his front door. He is proud of the work he has done to improve range conditions on his allotment.

He recalled his success in blocking a logging company from clear-cutting near his property and the poachers he has run out of the forest.

And Cullum warned that if higher fees force him out of the cattle business, he might be forced to sell out to the vacation home developers who routinely scout the area. "And now they want to run me off the land," he said, voice rising. "The goddam government should just get out of our business."

2 Desert Grazing Poses Threat, GAO Finds

Study Says Sheep and Cows Harm Sensitive Environment in Three Areas

TOM KENWORTHY
January, 1992

Adding to an already vigorous debate over livestock grazing on public lands, a study by the General Accounting Office has concluded that cow and sheep grazing on three Bureau of Land Management desert areas of the Southwest damages the fragile desert environment, brings in little money to the U.S. Treasury and threatens endangered wildlife species.

The release of the study comes as both sides in the long-running dispute over public land grazing are gearing up for yet another fight in Congress over attempts to raise the fees ranchers pay for using federal lands. The House last year approved an increase in the fees, but the issue died in the Senate.

Rep. Mike Synar (D-Okla.), who has failed in several attempts to win congressional approval for higher grazing fees, last week called the GAO report "just more evidence of the obvious, that taxpayers are subsidizing fiscal and ecological disaster on public lands." But an official with the National Cattlemen's Association charged that the analysis by the GAO, Congress's investigative arm, is biased and reflects the views of the House member who requested it, Rep. Bruce F. Vento (D-Minn.), chairman of the House Interior subcommittee on national parks and public lands. "Western rangelands are in the best condition they've been in 100 years," said Pamela Neal, director of public lands for the cattlemen's association.

Ranchers are charged $1.97 for each unit of land capable of providing forage to sustain one cow, one horse or five sheep for a month, an amount known as an Animal Unit Month or AUM. The GAO report said the roughly 1,000 livestock operators holding grazing allotments on the 20 million acres of BLM land in the hot desert areas of Arizona, Nevada, California, New Mexico and Utah pay about $4 million per year in grazing fees to the government. That amount, the GAO said, is insufficient to cover the cost of administering the allotments because about 60 percent of it goes to state and county governments and to other BLM range-improvement programs.

"The economic benefits derived from livestock grazing on BLM lands in the hot desert areas [in the Mojave, Sonoran and Chihuahuan deserts] are minimal," the GAO report concluded.

But the study is particularly critical of the environmental impacts of grazing on desert rangelands that, because of inadequate rainfall and poor soil conditions, are quick to degrade and slow to recover.

Continued grazing on these fragile lands, said the GAO, has in some areas further damaged desert ecosystems that were severely harmed by overgrazing in the 19th century and early 1900s before the federal government began regulating grazing on the West's public lands.

"Domestic livestock grazing on BLM's hot desert allotments continues to impose the risk of long-term environmental damage to a highly fragile resource," the study said. "While recovery in some areas around water sources can occur quickly, in other areas recovery could take decades, and in some cases the damage may be irreversible."

Citing a number of other studies, the GAO also found that desert grazing can pose threats to endangered wildlife such as the Mojave Desert tortoise, bighorn sheep and pronghorn antelope.

The GAO also said grazing allotments in desert areas are not critical to local economies and provide little economic return to ranchers.

3 Federal Grazing Fees Found Too Low

U.S. Report Likely to Fuel Congressional Efforts to Increase Charges

TOM KENWORTHY

April, 1992

The federal government is losing up to $52 million a year by charging ranchers too little to graze their cattle on government land, according to a new report to be submitted to Congress today.

The report also found that the gap between what ranchers pay to graze their cattle, horses and sheep on private land and what they pay the U.S. government for grazing rights on land owned by the taxpayers is growing.

The 88-page report by the departments of Interior and Agriculture is almost certain to fuel long-standing efforts in Congress to raise the fees that about 27,000 ranchers and farmers pay for grazing their stock on more than 300 million acres of land managed by the U.S. Forest Service and Bureau of Land Management.

Last year, legislation to raise fees so they more closely approximate market rates passed the House but died in the Senate, and backers expect to renew the battle this year.

The study, a draft of which was obtained by *The Washington Post*, shows that, on average, ranchers paid $9.66 per animal unit month on private lands, but just $1.92 per animal unit month on public rangeland. Since 1987, the gap between what ranchers pay for using private and public lands has grown by almost 75 cents, according to the study.

An animal unit month, or AUM, is the amount of forage required to sustain a cow for a month.

Defenders of the federal grazing fee system argue that the disparity in costs between grazing fees on public and private land is justified because government land is often less desirable and more marginal than privately held land.

The study also found that the Forest Service and BLM lost the $52 million on their grazing programs because it cost almost $74 million to administer the program and manage the rangelands while the total fees they received from ranchers were just $27 million once the state and county shares of the fees were paid. While the government received $1.97 per animal unit month in 1990, it paid $3.21 per animal unit month to oversee the program.

A leading congressional critic of the current level of grazing fees, Rep. Mike Synar (D-Okla.), said the report provides more evidence that the grazing fee structure needs to be overhauled.

The report, said Synar, "underscores every one of our arguments supporting a fee increase; it demonstrates—convincingly—that fees are too low. . . . It's time to run federal rangelands more like a business."

4   The Lesson of the Black-Footed Ferret

Grazing and Conservation Compatible, Preaches Wyoming Cattleman

TOM KENWORTHY
August, 1992

I f Wyoming rancher Jack Turnell were rewriting the lyrics to that old standard "Home on the Range," it might begin something like this: "Oh give me a home, in a riparian zone."

At a time when ranchers and environmentalists throughout the West are at each others' throats over an assortment of issues involving cattle grazing on federal land, Turnell is something of an oddity, a cowboy who gets along with the greens and talks about biodiversity and streamside ecology as fluently as he talks about Herefords.

"I guess I've learned how to bridge the gap between the environmentalists, the bureaucracies and the industry," Turnell said as he took a visitor on a tour of the Pitchfork Ranch, a spectacularly beautiful spread south of Cody that extends into the Absaroka Mountains on the Shoshone National Forest. The ranch takes in 120,000 acres, including 40,000 acres of Forest Service land where Turnell has grazing rights.

This is a ranch rich in history: Butch Cassidy committed his first crime here— horse theft—and did his drinking at a saloon in town that is still in business.

Since he was converted to more environmentally sensitive range management techniques several years ago, Turnell has become something of a shuttle diplomat between cattlemen and the environmental movement. This year, for example, he spoke at the annual meeting of the Greater Yellowstone Coalition, a conservation group active in efforts to protect America's oldest national park and its larger ecosystem. He also makes the circuit of cattle groups, preaching to ranchers, some of whom "think I've lost my marbles."

For the first decade after he took over management of the Pitchfork Ranch, which has been in his wife's family for four generations, Turnell says he punched cows pretty much as his predecessors always had. He knew little about the plant physiology of native grasses or the sensitivity of riparian (streamside) areas in the mostly arid West.

"I'd never heard the word 'riparian,' even though I went to college," Turnell said.

Turnell's early indifference to range science is not atypical, according to numerous studies by the government in recent years showing the poor condition of much of the 250 million acres of federal forest and grassland used by about 26,000 public land ranchers in the United States.

Critics of livestock grazing on public acreage controlled by the Interior Department's Bureau of Land Management and the Agriculture Department's Forest Service charge that after decades of heavy use, America's fragile public range lands are in lousy shape from overgrazing, erosion of stream banks and depletion of water supplies.

The deterioration of this land has prompted some environmentalists to call for removing sheep and cattle from the public range and returning the land to the antelope and deer. "Cattle Free in '93" is their battle cry. At the same time, congressional efforts to raise the fees that public land ranchers pay the government are gaining strength every year.

Neither makes any sense, said Turnell, who believes that if cattlemen are kicked off the public range, ranches like his will quickly be sold off to developers and chopped up into vacation sites.

What does make sense, he said, is better stewardship of the land, a process that he began about a decade ago with the discovery of a small population of black-footed ferrets on the Pitchfork Ranch. The ferret was supposed to be extinct, and the discovery brought a flood of scientists and environmentalists to the ranch.

"The ferret forced me to cooperate with people who I'd traditionally been an adversary of," said Turnell, who had shared the prevailing western contempt for such agencies as the Fish and Wildlife Service. "I found out, by God, they were people and they were interested in something good."

One thing led to another, and Turnell gradually began changing how he operated the Pitchfork. He systematically began rotating pastures, keeping his cows away from the river and streams that course out of the mountains until the surrounding grasses had matured and spread their seed for the next season, gave up most use of fertilizers and pesticides, and crossed his Hereford and Angus with a French breed that does not like to congregate around water. Most decisions are now made in consultation with range and wildlife scientists, and progress is monitored religiously with photographic studies.

Over time, Turnell said, the results have been impressive. The Greybull River and other streams on the ranch are lined with willow and other plant life, providing lush habitat for an expanding population of wildlife. Antelope scamper almost everywhere, and the ranch is host to deer, moose, elk, bear and mountain lion.

And Turnell makes more money because better quality grass puts more meat on his cattle. "We're selling 300,000 more pounds of beef per year than we did in 1987," Turnell said. "It takes sense to do it right."

"Sure, we graze cattle on the top of that mountain," said Turnell, pointing up at the 13,000-foot peaks of the Absarokas and the Shoshone National Forest. "But we don't hassle the elk and the antelope and the deer when they come down here in the winter. To me, that's a fair trade."

5   Ranchers and Loggers Are Fearful Landlord Clinton Will Raise the Rent

Pressure Building to Overhaul 1872 Mining Law

TOM KENWORTHY
November, 1992

A s Democrats map out their plans for taking charge of the government in Washington, the people of Colorado's North Park region are casting an anxious eye eastward.

For more than a century, the economic foundation of this huge, grassy bowl surrounded by forested mountains has rested on ranching, logging, and the boom-and-bust cycles of coal mining and energy production, most of it on lands owned by the federal government.

Now, after 12 years of Republican administrations regarded as sympathetic to commodity interests in the West, residents of this part of north-central Colorado are openly fearful that the change promised by President-elect Clinton may extend to federal land management policies.

Here in Jackson County, where almost 70 percent of the land base is in the hands of federal agencies such as the U.S. Forest Service and Bureau of Land Management, a new Democratic administration with environmentalist leanings could dramatically alter the future of an area that is on precarious economic ground.

"I don't know what this new administration will do to us on public lands, but I'm afraid it will be bad," said Barbara Hughes, 62, the mayor of Walden, a town of about 1,000 people located 30 miles south of the Wyoming border.

During his campaign for the presidency, Clinton provided few if any clues to how he would approach issues such as the subsidy given ranchers who graze stock on federal land, the extensive, below-cost sales of timber from national forests, and the generous 120-year-old mining law that allows industry to profit from minerals found on U.S. property without paying royalties or reclamation costs.

But organized environmental groups and their allies on Capitol Hill see the election of Clinton, and his environmentally minded running mate, Sen. Albert Gore

Jr. (D-Tenn.), as an opening for fundamental change in how the government manages its hundreds of millions of acres.

A Clinton administration, environmentalists say, may provide the spark for reforming land use policies that grew out of the need to populate the West but have far less relevance more than a century later.

"The West is evolving, and land management policies must follow suit," Sen. Timothy E. Wirth (D-Colo.) wrote in a recent issue of the Colorado-based biweekly High Country News. Wirth, mentioned as a potential Interior or Energy Department secretary in the new administration, argues that Clinton can bring some much-needed balance to what has been a polarized debate over western resources.

Rep. Mike Synar (D-Okla.), one of Capitol Hill's loudest proponents of higher federal grazing fees and of eliminating unprofitable sales of U.S. timber, said Clinton can do the western environment and the U.S. Treasury a favor at the same time.

"Timber, grazing and mining are assets where we are literally losing billions of dollars because of poor management and below fair market sales," Synar said. "If Bill Clinton wants to have deficit reduction without cutting spending or raising taxes, I can give him a list of from $35 billion to $50 billion [in savings] over five years from better management of our natural resources."

Among the possible targets: Timber sales from the national forests. Critics say the forests are not only being overcut from an environmental standpoint, but also that the resources are being sold at a loss. Even the U.S. Forest Service concedes that timber sales on 69 of the nation's 120 national forests lose money, and opponents of the agency's policies contend the picture is far worse.

Mining on Federal Lands

Pressure is building on Capitol Hill to overhaul the 1872 law that governs mining of gold, silver and other "hard rock" minerals from federal lands. Under the law, miners can stake claims on federal land and for minimal yearly fees, eventually take title for as little as $2.50 an acre, and then pay no royalties on the minerals they extract. Over the years, miners have taken possession of 3.2 million acres of federal land in this fashion. According to a "conservative" estimate by the General Accounting Office this year, $65 billion in hard rock reserves remain on federal land.

Grazing on U.S. Lands

For the thousands of ranchers who have allotments to graze cattle and other stock on Forest Service and BLM land, the cost is now $1.92 a month per cow. By the BLM's own accounting, it costs more to administer the program than is gained in revenue. "There's a great deal of hope out there that we will be able to work with the Clinton administration to reverse a lot of the horrendous land management decisions made during the Reagan-Bush years," said Michael Matz, public lands director for the Sierra Club.

But people in Walden wonder if their community could survive the kind of changes envisioned by Matz, Synar and others.

Two years ago this area won fleeting national renown for two distinctions: providing the Christmas tree for the U.S. Capitol and being named by the National Association of Counties as one of the 10 American communities most endangered by potential changes in government land policy.

Walden and Jackson County face the same kind of problems that beset many other rural communities heavily dependent on federally owned natural resources. Isolated and with only a tenuous rail link to the outside world, Walden can offer few inducements for industry beyond the quality of life and a spectacular view of the Medicine Bow Mountains.

"I've lived here all my life and it's a nice community to live in, but it's a hell of a place to make a living," said Tony Martin, 47, a Jackson County commissioner and owner of the Elk Horn Cafe here. Martin has worked for two mining operations that fell on hard times, and now is on his fourth business.

A backbone of this community's economy is the Louisiana Pacific lumber mill on the outskirts of town, which provides paychecks for about 170 people who work in the mill or on contract, cutting in the woods and hauling 18 million board feet of logs each year from the Routt, Roosevelt and Arapaho national forests.

At the mill, manager Bill Fleming and Louisiana Pacific's northern division operations manager Dick Rydeen take a relatively sanguine view of the future, based on Gov. Clinton's history of good relations with the timber industry in Arkansas, his promise to emphasize economic growth and the prospect of a rebound in housing starts.

"If Bill Clinton leads the economy back and we get 1.7 million housing starts, either the cost of this lumber will go through the roof or they will loosen the resource [available from federal lands]," Rydeen said. "We are reasonably optimistic that logic and common sense will prevail."

But such optimism does not stretch very far in Walden, where residents recount the recent closing of another Louisiana Pacific mill 60 miles away and fear that environmental pressures will choke the timber supply from the surrounding national forests.

"With the current thrust of the new administration, the fear is there won't be a balance" between environmental and economic concerns, frets Harry W. Masinton, superintendent of the 325-student Jackson County School District. "We are very concerned whether the cattle and timber industries will be able to stay intact. That's our stability."

Local rancher Twist Meyering, who has been raising cattle for 67 of his 83 years and using federal land for grazing much of that time, is more succinct. "They'll cut our throats," he said.

Meyering's son, Dave, whose ranch abuts his father's, argues that urbanites and easterners fail to understand the importance of the federal resources to the region's economy. "These natural resources are where the real true wealth is developed. It's beef, it's timber. Services are important, but you have to start with the real wealth."

Officials in Walden and Jackson County have had little success in attracting employers, despite a campaign that has focused at various times on wooing a new state prison, setting up legalized gambling, establishing a ski resort and creating a wild horse sanctuary. With few new employment opportunities, most of the students who grow up here move, and the population continues to age.

One possible silver lining in a more environmentally sensitive administration is that the region's vast reserves of low-sulfur coal will become attractive enough to overcome what are prohibitive freight costs. But the skeleton crew that remains at a local coal mine is being let go in January.

So what does the future look like here as the Democrats sweep to power in Washington?

"Don't ask me that question," replied Hughes, Walden's mayor. "I don't know. I really don't know."

6   Natural Resource Users Facing Cuts in Subsidies

Mining, Timber, Grazing, Irrigation Affected

TOM KENWORTHY
February, 1993

The Clinton administration's economic plan calls for eliminating or reducing a wide range of subsidies long enjoyed by those who use federally owned natural resources—a proposal likely to prompt a multi-front battle with entrenched western economic interests and their allies on Capitol Hill.

Officials familiar with the plan said yesterday it would: impose for the first time a federal royalty on gold and other minerals taken from federal lands; phase out uneconomic timber sales at a majority of national forests; increase grazing fees paid by cattle raisers who use public lands; and impose a surcharge on large agricultural users of federal water. Recreational users of federal lands would also pay higher fees.

The administration projects the phased-in changes in policy on mining, timber cutting, grazing and irrigated water could save about $1 billion over five years, though congressional advocates claim far higher savings.

The comprehensive plan to begin charging market rates for resources that have historically been heavily subsidized constitutes a direct assault on the traditional economic foundation of the West, where miners, cattle interests, farmers and timber interests have used their political clout to fend off repeated attempts at change in Congress.

"It's a clear signal that [the Office of Management and Budget] is serious about advancing the principle that natural resources must move toward the market," said Interior Secretary Bruce Babbitt, who will face the politically arduous chore of pushing through legislation to effect many of the changes. The overall philosophy of the Clinton plan, he said yesterday, is "a deliberate attempt to take on every special interest in America all at once."

In a tacit acknowledgment of the political difficulty of such a broad-based initiative, Babbitt said he would have preferred his "honeymoon to last for a few more weeks." But, he said, the insistence by OMB officials to begin phasing out resource subsidies "reflects the feeling that you can't fight these battles piecemeal, one at a time."

The proposals constitute a virtual wish-list of the environmental movement, and if approved by Congress would have a dramatic impact on land-use policies in the West. They could reverse the trend of the past 12 years in which Washington has generally been receptive to arguments from industry that economic uses of national forests and other lands should be maximized.

But many of the changes could face heavy resistance in Congress, particularly in the Senate where western state senators have a long track record of blocking attempts to overhaul federal policies on mining, timber cutting and grazing.

Among the components of the package are:

Imposition of a 12.5 percent royalty on "hard rock" minerals such as gold and platinum taken from federal lands. Miners currently pay no federal royalties, and under the 1872 mining law can also take title to federal lands they mine for as little as $2.50 an acre. Some advocates of the royalty estimate that it could bring in as much as $400 million a year.

A phaseout of timber sales on national forests that consistently spend more money administering the sales than they receive in receipts. Congressional critics of such below-cost sales say that as many as 94 of the 155 national forests lost money last year on timber sales and that the Treasury could save hundreds of millions of dollars a year by eliminating them.

An increase in the grazing fee ranchers pay to graze stock on federal land. Babbitt is expected to be given discretion in devising a fee system that would reward good range management.

Environmentalists hailed the proposals yesterday as a sign of fundamental change in federal land-use policies. But industry spokesmen were generally more cautious in the absence of more details. Mark Rey, vice president for forest resources of the American Forest and Paper Association, said the proposals are "not a positive sign," but said his industry is ready to work with the administration to make timber sales more efficient through such actions as reducing environmental appeals.

7 Stepping Carefully into Public Land Grazing

Babbitt Using Hearings to Seek 'Reasonable Consensus' between Cattlemen, Environmentalists

TOM KENWORTHY
May, 1993

On a campus sometimes known as "Moo U.," in a room packed with hundreds of ranchers wearing their Stetson and Resistol hats, the Clinton administration on Friday came snout to snout with one of the West's most divisive resource conflicts, public land grazing.

Kicking off the first of what will be five public hearings in the West on overhauling the system under which western ranchers graze their stock at relatively little cost on U.S. land, Interior Secretary Bruce Babbitt said he is searching for a "reasonable consensus" between cattlemen and environmentalists. "We cannot turn the West into a battleground," he said.

But as Babbitt well knows, the West is already a battleground, fighting not just over grazing but mining and timber production and federal water policies as well. And if he needed any fresh evidence of just how hard it is to mediate those disagreements, Babbitt collected plenty here at a six-hour session at Montana State University practically in the shadow of the Gallatin Range.

As Max Robinson of McAllister, Mont., said in explaining why he was pinch-hitting for his uncle in speaking at the forum: His uncle "tends to use four-letter words when his lifestyle is threatened."

For years, ranchers and environmentalists have been at war over grazing fees and range management practices on the more than 250 million acres of U.S. Forest Service and Bureau of Land Management land that stockmen can use at a cost of $1.86 per head of cattle per month. The arguments on both sides are as honed and predictable as catechisms.

Cattlemen argue that in the 130 years since homesteading began, grazing has helped open up the West, improved the range, allowed wildlife to flourish and sustained a peculiarly American way of life. Raising the fees they pay for using the less-productive lands managed by the government will force many ranchers to sell their land for development and devastate the economies of countless western communities, they say.

Conservation groups and their allies counter that slipshod management by Federal agencies has allowed ranchers to degrade fragile, arid land throughout the West. Overgrazing encouraged by what they say are ridiculously low fees has compacted the soil, damaged fisheries, devastated native plant communities and created a "cowboy welfare" system that benefits only about 25,000 ranchers.

Babbitt, in a tough speech in Washington last week, lambasted the "giveaway" of publicly owned resources and promised that the Clinton administration will fundamentally overhaul federal land and water policies this year. A new grazing fee system, he said, would reward good stewardship practices such as stream protection, and environmentalists and others would have a say in how individual grazing allotments are managed.

Faced with a crowd of 800 people in which the cowboys appeared to outnumber the environmentalists 2 to 1, Babbitt softened his tone. President Clinton had reminded him, said Babbitt, that the Democratic ticket carried Montana last fall, and that any new grazing policy ought to be "sensitive to people who are living on the land."

The hearing here was another demonstration of the Clinton administration's fondness for government as talk show, with Babbitt even urging participants at one point to "mix it up a little here." Like the Little Rock, Ark., economic summit and the Portland, Ore., forest policy meeting, this grazing hearing was a blend of expert testimony by academics and personal testimonials by everyday Americans, in this case ranchers who were chosen by lot to say their piece from the floor of the student union.

John Duffield, a University of Montana economist, and Tim Gill, president of a firm that provides loans to ranchers, disagreed over what is a fair price to charge ranchers who use federal land. Duffield, author of a study of comparable state lands, said the market value of federal land is about $8 per head of cattle per month. Gill, noting the added costs ranchers pay on federal lands for fencing, water tanks and the like, said such a price would make one-third of Montana's ranches "immediately economically unviable."

But the fight over public land grazing in the West is less a dry argument over the proper price of an "animal unit month" or the complicated formula by which grazing fees are assessed than it is a fundamental dispute over how the land should be used in an increasingly developed region.

The ranchers' mantra is that the government can continue to foster a valued way of life or it can encourage the carving up of the West into 20-acre "ranchettes." In a play on the "Cattle Free in '93" slogan used by some militant environmentalists, Robert Van Deren, a Dillon, Montana, rancher, said: "We're not looking forward to condos galore in 2004."

Nonsense, say the environmentalists. "It's an issue of fairness," said Louisa Wilcox of the Greater Yellowstone Coalition, a regional conservation group. "This entire country is being asked to belly up to the bar and the ranching industry shouldn't be exempted from that."

Ultimately, said retired Forest Service employee John Mumma, the issue comes down to how the lands will be managed. "The time has come to start the management of our valuable rangeland resources in a sustainable way," wrote Mumma in an appeal to Clinton, Babbitt and Agriculture Secretary Mike Espy. Mumma's message ought to have a little resonance in Washington. He was once the regional forester for the Forest Service region that includes Montana, until political demands for higher timber harvests cost him his job during the Bush administration. Mumma resigned from the Forest Service rather than be forcibly transferred. Mumma served notice on the new administration: "The time has come to begin sharing the range with the other stockholders of the land," he wrote to Clinton.

8 Babbitt's Grazing Fee Increase Unsaddled by Westerners' Rider

Senate Bars Raising Ranchers' Cost of Using Federal Range for Year

TOM KENWORTHY
September, 1993

The Clinton administration's drive to overhaul the management of federal lands suffered a serious setback yesterday as the Senate voted to derail Interior Secretary Bruce Babbitt's plan to more than double grazing fees paid by western ranchers.

On a 59 to 40 vote, the Senate approved an amendment sponsored by Sens. Pete V. Domenici (R-N.M.) and Harry M. Reid (D-Nev.) that bars the Interior Department from spending money to implement the proposed policy for one year. The amendment was offered during Senate consideration of the fiscal 1994 Interior appropriations bill.

Domenici characterized the vote as "a major victory for small ranchers and townspeople who live in America's West. . . . The administration's plan would have fundamentally altered life in America's rural areas."

The defeat for the Clinton administration occurred despite a concerted lobbying effort by Babbitt and his top assistants at the Interior Department, who early in the day appeared guardedly confident they would prevail.

The issue must go to a conference with the House, which has supported raising the fees paid by western ranchers who use federal lands. The House, however, did not attach such an amendment to its version of the spending bill this year because Babbitt was proceeding to raise fees by administrative action.

Babbitt, responding to the Senate vote, said he is confident the administration can kill the one-year moratorium during the House-Senate conference committee and then move on to either negotiating a legislative plan with Congress or implementing one administratively.

"I'm going to go to work in the House tomorrow morning lining up the votes to kill this," Babbitt said. "Some of the western senators have said they want to sit down and talk this thing out and I, of course, am ready to do that, to find a reasonable solution that meets the administration's objectives."

The vote was an important one for the administration, which is under pressure from environmentalist allies to make good on promises to raise fees on those who use federal lands for mining, grazing and timber cutting, as well as those who receive cheap federal water for agriculture. Although the White House early last spring dropped those proposals from its budget plans, Babbitt and other administration officials have vowed the changes would be implemented through executive orders and separate legislation.

Last month, in the first installment on that pledge, Babbitt unveiled a comprehensive overhaul of federal grazing policies to be imposed by administrative edict after soliciting comment from the public.

The plan not only would have raised fees, but also eroded the long-standing power of ranchers to influence local grazing decisions, giving both the federal government and interested parties such as environmental groups more control over how federal lands are treated. The goal, Babbitt said at the time, was to improve the condition of federal range that, according to some studies, has been seriously degraded by overgrazing.

Under Babbitt's plan, which was not scheduled to go into effect before late 1994 at the earliest, ranchers who now pay $1.86 a month to graze one cow and calf or five sheep on federal land would have paid $4.28 a month after a three-year phase-in. About 26,000 ranchers hold permits to graze stock on land managed by the U.S. Forest Service and the Bureau of Land Management.

Western senators from both parties yesterday bitterly protested that the changes Babbitt proposed would have such a dire effect on the social and economic fabric of the rural West that they should be studied and negotiated with Congress over the next year.

9 Battle over Grazing Fee Plan Pits Visions of 'Old' vs. 'New' West

TOM KENWORTHY
October, 1993

T he argument between Interior Secretary Bruce Babbitt and a majority of the West's senators goes well beyond cows.

The escalating test of wills in the Senate over Babbitt's plan to rewrite the rules governing cattle grazing on federal lands is only the most visible part of a larger battle over the administration's entire agenda for overhauling public land policy—and over two very different visions of the West.

Western Republicans—plus a few Democrats—have three times in the past 10 days kept the Senate from ending debate on a compromise grazing plan. It would raise the fees paid by ranchers and give the federal government additional powers to regulate and protect lands managed by the Bureau of Land Management and the U.S. Forest Service.

"This is Secretary Babbitt's war on the West," thundered Sen. Pete V. Domenici (R-N.M.) in a refrain heard often during last week's debate.

In a sense, it is a war on the West. At least on that part of the West that still believes the first claim on the vast federal domain ought to be for traditional economic uses—ranching, mining, energy production and timber—at below-market rates, and not infrequently at some cost to the environment.

But even some western senators recognize that such a vision is increasingly at odds with new realities.

Despite the open spaces, uncluttered vistas and small resource-dependent communities that dot the landscape, the West has become a highly urbanized place. The percentage of the Rocky Mountain West's population that lives in urban areas is higher than that of the Northeast, the South and the Midwest.

About 60 million people live in the 16 western states where there is grazing on federal lands. But only about 2 percent of all the nation's livestock producers—or 27,000—hold grazing permits. A significant number of those with the largest grazing allotments are big corporations, foreign investors or wealthy individuals.

"Today's West is different," noted Sen. Harry M. Reid (D-Nev.), who opposed Babbitt's original grazing fee proposal but brokered a modified plan in the House. "This debate is about a new West."

Whether western senators are defending a myth or, as many argue, the economic underpinning of their region, they understand the stakes. If they can derail Babbitt on grazing, it will become much easier to fend off the administration's plans to change the way mining and logging are done and the way water is allocated.

"This is just the first step in an assault on the West," Sen. Conrad Burns (R-Mont.) said during Senate debate. "We do not stand here today discussing fees. We are discussing policy, and it has to do with timber, it has to do with recreation, it has to do with gas and oil and energy development, it has to do with hunting and fishing, it has to do with everybody that has a use on a public land."

Up to a point, Babbitt agrees. "If they can sink us in a dispute over the price of grass," he said, "I think it has ominous implications for our reform agenda, whether it is mining, whether it is the administration of wetlands or endangered species, whatever it might be."

But the western senators may have ridden into a box canyon.

With the stakes so high, Babbitt is engaging in some bare-knuckle politics. If the Senate impasse continues, he said on Thursday, he will use his administrative powers to impose his original grazing proposal—which would cost ranchers more than they would pay under the legislative compromise and put even more rigid federal controls on how they could use the land.

Ranchers currently pay $1.86 a month to graze a cow on federal land, far less than the rate for generally more productive private land and significantly below what almost every western state charges for state lands. Babbitt's original plan would, over three years, raise the fee to $4.28, higher than the $3.45 called for in the House-Senate compromise now bottled up by the filibuster.

But the struggle between Babbitt and the western senators is less about the cost of grazing than it is about how much control the federal government will exert over the public lands and the waters that run through them. Babbitt would reassert federal water rights on Bureau of Land Management relinquished by then-Interior Secretary James G. Watt during President Ronald Reagan's first term and reserve federal title to any permanent range improvements, such as stock ponds and water developments.

Babbitt's plan also contains numerous provisions to bolster federal authority to reward ranchers who practice good stewardship of the land and punish those who do not.

It is a "New West" regulatory structure. But it has run into an "Old West" mythology, which western senators have ably exploited to win the support of colleagues from other regions who have no public land grazing in their states.

"The mythology is a big barrier," Babbitt acknowledged. Although public lands ranchers are a tiny group, he said, they are able to exert significant influence "because of the culture and history and mythology of the West, in which the image of the cattle rancher has come to embody—through popular fiction, movies and the Marlboro man—all of the American virtues."

His home state of Arizona, Babbitt notes, is far more urbanized than Virginia and has fewer cows than West Virginia. "But that mythology kind of gets in the way of reality."

Federal Land Use: Timber Rights in Federal Forests 14

This chapter continues the discussion of use and management of federal lands, again focusing on the conflicting interests of individuals concerned with immediate profits versus others oriented toward long-term preservation of resources. The principal issue of this chapter is logging in federal forests. Articles 1 and 2 provide some historical background to this intense controversy as well as the positions of parties on both sides of the issue. Articles 3, 4, and 5 primarily concern attempts by the new Clinton administration to forge a plan that is satisfactory to both environmentalists and local citizens. Article 6 describes the administration's recently expressed determination to cut more timber than concerned environmental groups find acceptable in order to maintain the economy of the Pacific Northwest. Article 7 describes damage already done to old forests and speculations regarding what would be necessary for restoration.

1 Drawing the Line on West's Wilderness

Effort to Protect Federal Land Provokes Bitter Opposition in Utah

JOHN LANCASTER
April, 1991

A t the sawmill here, a secretary sells T-shirts emblazoned with a recipe for "Loggers' Stew." Among the ingredients: "4 large, well-plucked spotted owls," "3 finely chopped peregrine falcons'" and "2 well-beaten environmentalists."

Endangered species may play well in New York or Washington, but in southern Utah's canyon country, the traditions of the Old West die hard. Just ask a local what he thinks of Rep. Wayne Owens (D-Utah) and his plan to set aside 5.4 million acres of southern Utah—10 percent of the state—as protected wilderness, forever off-limits to roads, mining, logging and off-road vehicles.

"To sum it up right quick, we'd like to hang him," said Gene Griffin, pausing behind the counter of the dry-goods store that he runs when he's not tending cattle on his ranch. "It's government land, but we don't think they should take it away after we pioneered it. We don't go back [East] and tell them to take down all those tall buildings."

Rural westerners have always looked askance on federal efforts to restrict their use of public lands and resources. But the war over wilderness has reached a critical phase. Over the next decade, Congress will largely decide the fate of the nation's last big chunks of unprotected wild land—how much remains in its primeval state, how much is potentially open to industrial use.

"We fought over the easy stuff first," said Debbie Sease, public lands director for the Sierra Club. "What we're down to are the harder issues."

Since the Wilderness Act of 1964, Congress has designated about 100 million acres—roughly two Utahs, or 4 percent of the entire United States—as protected wilderness. More than half of it—57 million acres—is in Alaska. By the end of this year, the Interior Department is slated to complete its final recommendations on the unprotected wilderness that remains in the 11 contiguous western states. Congress then will consider the proposals along with its own wilderness bills, adding and deleting as it sees fit.

Polls indicate strong public support, especially in cities, for designated wilderness areas. It is no coincidence that Owens, a former mission president for the Mormon Church and former aide to Robert F. Kennedy, represents Salt Lake City and its fast-growing suburbs. But throughout the rural West, where economies rise and fall on the resources culled from public lands, no land-use topic is more divisive.

At a meeting in Denver last month, a coalition of 231 industry groups, off-road vehicle users and rural governments said in a statement that wilderness legislation "destroys job opportunities, removes land from "[the tax base] . . . and unduly restricts opportunities for motorized recreation."

The meeting was sponsored, in part, by the Wilderness Impact Research Foundation, producers of a recent videotape charging, among other things, that wilderness bills discriminate against wheelchair users by denying them access to the outdoors. "The preservationists' goals have become outrageous," said Grant Gerber, an Elko, Nev., attorney who founded the group.

Such complaints have found a sympathetic ear in conservative western politicians such as Sen. Jake Garn (R-Utah), who has called the Owens bill "so excessive it's not worth consideration," and in some quarters of the Bureau of Land Management (BLM), the Interior Department agency that oversees fully one-eighth of the nation's land area.

Conservationists were disappointed but not surprised earlier this year when the BLM recommended that 2 million acres of Utah wilderness receive permanent protection. Critics charge—and some Interior officials privately agree—that the BLM distorted its own standards for identifying wilderness in order to leave a door open for mining companies.

Environmentalists like to say that wilderness needs no defense, only more defenders. But they defend it just the same, citing evidence that designated wilderness can help lure tourists and nonpolluting industries, an alternative to resource-based economies subject to the whims of global markets. In any event, they say, society's priorities have changed and the rural West will have to accept the consequences, even if some of them are painful.

"Some of these towns are going to die, [but] they're not going to die gracefully," said Brant Calkin, director of the Southern Utah Wilderness Alliance (SUWA). "They're going to squeeze the last bit that they can from the federal lands." And it's the last stage that's the most dangerous because that's when the desperation is greatest and the little bit "of wilderness that remains is at greatest risk."

Since the 1930s, conservationists have agonized over the fate of southern Utah, a geologic wonderland of yawning "slickrock" canyons, ocher sandstone cliffs and seemingly limitless views. Harold Ickes, Interior secretary under Franklin D. Roosevelt, was so taken with the region that he once proposed making 4.4 million acres of it into a national park.

But in Escalante, residents take a different view.

"A lot of the environmentalists say [development] would ruin the sandstone," said DeLane Griffin, 67, a taciturn cowboy and brother of the dry-goods dealer. "Well, look at it." He pointed to a juniper-studded cliff through the window of his brother's store. "We've got a lot of it. We'll trade it off to them for green grass."

Small, conservative and overwhelmingly Mormon, Escalante is a dot in a sea of empty land, most of it federally owned. For generations, the town has lived and died by its public lands—chiefly the Ponderosa pine in the Dixie National Forest and the arid rangelands where the ranchers graze their cattle. Right now it is dying. Drought has forced cattlemen to reduce their herds, and recently the Escalante sawmill, the town's largest employer, laid off 35 of 120 workers.

Nevertheless, people here seem convinced that Escalante could prosper if only environmentalists, politicians and the federal bureaucracy would let it.

Louise Liston is a retired schoolteacher and the great-granddaughter of a scout on the first Mormon expedition to pass through the area in the 1880s. She is as good a spokesperson as any for the view that excessive environmental regulation, combined with the "lock up" of natural resources in national parks and other protected areas, is thwarting the region's economic growth.

"We could be the richest county in the state," said Liston, who serves on the Garfield County commission. "We have oil. We have titanium and zirconium. We have coal. We have tar sands."

Liston emphasized that "we love our national parks" and suggested that tourism is "a help." But she expressed deep resentment of environmentalists and their political allies, "suitcase saviors" who in her view have no business telling people in Escalante how to run their lives.

A favorite example is a congressional bill last year aimed in part at studying the expansion of Bryce Canyon National Park with an eye toward protecting the views. Such views cover "two-thirds of my county!" she said. "Can you say that the land is more important than the people? Our children are being endangered, our way of life is at stake and yet we don't get the same consideration as the spotted owl."

Officials in southern Utah describe the Owens bill as an economic catastrophe. A study commissioned by the Utah Association of Counties warned that the bill would eliminate livestock grazing in wilderness areas and estimated its annual cost at up to $13 billion, mostly in lost mining opportunities.

Environmentalists note that livestock grazing is permitted in wilderness areas as a matter of law, as is hunting, camping, horseback riding and, in some cases, mining. They also question how a bill that affects 10 percent of the state's land, all of it so far undeveloped, could cost Utah an annual amount that is nearly half its $27 billion gross yearly product.

In any event, there is considerable evidence that the fate of towns like Escalante may hinge less on the effectiveness of the environmental lobby than on broad economic tides over which it has little, if any, control.

The minerals industry is notoriously vulnerable to boom-bust cycles of the sort that eliminated hundreds of southern Utah uranium jobs in the 1980s. And the BLM acknowledges that the commercial potential of southern Utah's vast coal seams remains largely unproven. Indeed, a draft BLM study on the economic effects of setting aside 3.2 million acres of Utah wilderness concluded that "existing employment levels would not be affected."

"The people here are in a commodity economy on a global scale," said Calkin, the SUWA director. "[But] all of these economic supports are in trouble and there's nothing anyone can do. "So if you're a politician in Utah, if you don't have an answer, you've got to have scapegoats. And the convenient scapegoats here are the environmentalists."

Calkin, 60, is a wiry former Sierra Club president and former New Mexico cabinet secretary who flits about the state in a battered Cessna. The message he brings to county officials and others is that instead of destroying the economy, wilderness can actually enhance it.

A 1989 study by two University of Idaho geography professors, Gundars Rudzitis and Harley E. Johansen, found that counties with federally designated wilderness grew at two to three times the rate of other rural counties—capitalizing on natural amenities to attract tourists and industry alike. The newest business in Escalante is a store specializing in backpacks, trail maps and enviro-trendy Birkenstock sandals.

But Calkin acknowledges that while he is willing to "genuflect" to the cause of economic growth, it is not his main concern. "You look around, you see what's happened elsewhere, you see what's here to be lost, and you say, 'Not here.' "

Piloting his plane above the canyon country on a dazzling morning recently, Calkin dipped a wing toward the site of a proposed coal mine and 18-mile access road, and swung low over jeep trails from the uranium boom of the 1950s and 1960s. "The first use is gratuitous and short-lived—the guy out there with his Geiger counter," he said. "[But] there's never an end to it. It's a progression that doesn't have a plan and about the only plan you have to contain it is wilderness."

But to an agency committed to the doctrine of "multiple use," deciding which public lands to protect has proved troublesome.

Under the Wilderness Act, land agencies are supposed to make a complete list of potential wilderness areas based solely on natural or aesthetic qualities, such as uniqueness and "opportunities for solitude." Only after they have completed the task can they consider the potential for minerals or other forms of development in deciding whether to recommend them for permanent protection.

But in numerous instances cited by conservationists and congressional investigators, BLM officials who conducted Utah's initial wilderness "inventory" in the late 1970s excluded areas with minerals potential, often rejecting areas scores of miles from the nearest town on grounds they weren't lonely enough.

In a 1985 hearing, then-Rep. John F. Seiberling (D-Ohio), chairman of the house interior and insular affairs public lands subcommittee, cited the example of the Labyrinth Canyon area of the Green River. BLM included lands on one side of the river while rejecting mineralized lands on the opposite, virtually identical bank on grounds that they "obviously and clearly lacked any wilderness character." BLM also said the remnants of past mining operations made the area unsuitable.

Seiberling called the BLM's methodology "arbitrary and capricious," an assessment shared by some Interior officials. "They were much more willing to eliminate lands because of the perceived minerals potential," said an Interior official who asked not to be identified. "[But] if the land had wilderness characteristics it should have survived the inventory process."

BLM officials in Utah defended their approach. "I think it's really foolish to say these [mineral] resources are never going to be valuable," said Ron Montagna of the BLM office in Cedar City. "To have a really stable economy, just like a stable ecosystem, you need a myriad of factors."

Officials said some areas were excluded because they contained undeveloped mining claims, which would have to be bought out in order to preserve wilderness qualities. Furthermore, said Greg Thayn, BLM's Utah wilderness coordinator, wilderness is partly in the eye of the beholder: "I'm sure if you took different teams out and let them draw lines on a map, none would come up the same."

2 The Owl and the Lumberjack: Can Clinton Break the Logjam?

Oregon Conference Tests Ability to Reconcile Economic, Ecological Needs

TOM KENWORTHY
April, 1993

When President Clinton and Vice President Gore walk into the Oregon Convention Center today to negotiate an end to the prolonged stalemate over the northern spotted owl and management of the Pacific Northwest's forests, they will come face to face with a political and environmental tar baby.

Promised by Clinton during his presidential campaign, the forest conference—it was rhetorically downgraded from a "summit"—represents the sternest test to date of the president's belief that economic growth and environmental protection are not incompatible. "I will try to be fair to the people whose livelihoods depend on this and fair to the environment that we are all obligated to maintain," Clinton said at his news conference last week.

But the crisis confronting the majestic forests of Douglas fir, hemlock and cedar in the coastal forests of the Northwest is so profound and complex, and the animosities that surround it so intense and long-standing, that crafting a solution that all parties deem fair is enormously difficult. Washington is littered with the wreckage of previous attempts to satisfy loggers and environmentalists, Congress and the executive branch and the courts.

Even so, the one-day conference opens here riding a surge of optimism. Clinton, Gore, and several Cabinet officers—including Secretary of Agriculture Mike Espy, Interior Secretary Bruce Babbitt and Environmental Protection Agency administrator Carol M. Browner—are scheduled to meet with about 50 representatives of various regional groups affected by the forest crisis.

Although one conservation official predicted that the series of three roundtable discussions would turn into a gabfest "like the Geraldo show," many are more hopeful. "We have very, very high expectations," said Barry Cullen, senior vice president of the American Forest and Paper Association. Larry Tuttle, Oregon regional director for the Wilderness Society, agreed: "Something is going to happen out of this."

For the timber and forest products industries, almost any solution would be better than the status quo. Years of litigation over the threatened owl and its habitat, combined with Washington's policy impasse, have effectively left forest policy in the hands of federal judges who have repeatedly found the government's practices in violation of numerous environmental laws. In the past two years the courts have blocked new timber sales on millions of acres of federal land in the Northwest until the government comes up with better plans to manage the forests in ways that will protect the owl and other jeopardized species.

The owl injunctions have exacerbated structural problems of an already troubled industry where employment has been declining because of mechanization of mills and the annual export of more than 3 billion board feet of raw logs, primarily to Japan.

The forest products industry says that 132 sawmills have closed since 1990, throwing almost 13,000 people out of work. During the same period, according to the industry, federal timber sales declined by more than half, contributing to a supply crisis that it says is driving up lumber prices and slowing the nation's recovery from recession. Environmentalists argue that less than 10 percent of the nation's timber needs is supplied by federal lands in the Northwest, and that timber lost to owl protection can be made up by curbing exports and better management of private lands.

For all the angry rhetoric over the spotted owl, the reclusive bird that was listed as a threatened species three years ago is really a surrogate for the larger arguments over what is to become of the remaining areas of towering old-growth forests that once blanketed the Northwest.

Estimates and definitions of what constitute old-growth forest or ancient forest are imprecise. But it is generally accepted that only about 10 percent of the region's original 25 million acres of old-growth forest—characterized by stands of trees more than 150 to 250 years old—remains. There is a larger reservoir of habitat that is suitable for the spotted owl, not all of it old-growth, of about 7 million acres.

Owl or no owl, a mounting body of scientific evidence has concluded that the entire old-growth ecosystem of the Northwest is under severe strain from human activity, posing threats to the survival of many species including numerous runs of salmon and steelhead that have enormous symbolic and economic importance to the Northwest.

Forests in the region are "unraveling," Forest Service biologist Barry R. Noon testified before a government panel last year. "There is very strong and convincing empirical evidence that . . . the forest systems in Western Oregon are in decline."

"On numerous federal lands," a panel of scientists dubbed the "Gang of Four" concluded in a 1991 report, "many watersheds and riparian zones and much of the fish habitat have been degraded."

"I think we are approaching a critical point," said Jack Ward Thomas, a Forest Service biologist and Gang of Four member involved in numerous owl studies.

"When you are down to 10 percent, then you begin to worry about the integrity of an old-growth system."

Industries that rely on the forest for wood products disagree. "We should improve forestry practices, no doubt about it, but I don't see the forest as unraveling," said Denny Scott, an official with the carpenters' union.

The principal culprit in the decline, according to many scientists, is the fragmentation and degradation of wildlife habitat that comes with intensive logging. "Much of the late successional/old-growth forest is extremely fragmented," the Gang of Four concluded. The reserve areas set aside under current forest plans "will perpetuate this fragmentation," they said.

Very little old-growth timber remains on private lands in the Northwest, which were largely stripped of first-growth logs by the 1950s. Though replanted, much of that private land is still a decade or two away from being able to provide adequate second-growth volume for the industry.

What remains is largely on the 28 million acres of federal lands managed by the U.S. Forest Service, the Bureau of Land Management and the National Park Service. On Forest Service and BLM land, logging was accelerated in the 1980s, spurred on by the supply gap on private lands, pro-industry federal officials and a congressional delegation from the region that frequently dictated high levels of harvest. In the last three years of the decade, a record 20 billion board feet was harvested from federal lands in Oregon and Washington.

Land management practices by the federal government have come under increasingly sharp attack by federal judges, many of them Republican appointees, presiding over a spate of lawsuits. The judges, in often stinging terms, have found agencies like the Forest Service, the Bureau of Land Management and the Fish and Wildlife Service in violation of several federal laws governing environmental protection, forest management and endangered species.

U.S. District Judge William L. Dwyer, for instance, accused the Forest Service and Fish and Wildlife Service in one opinion of a "deliberate and systematic refusal . . . to comply with the laws protecting wildlife."

That view appears to be shared by the Clinton administration. "There hasn't been an administration policy in a decade," said Interior Secretary Bruce Babbitt, "other than passivity, neglect, stonewalling and abstinence."

With new timber sales on federal lands in the Northwest barred by the courts, the administration and the industry are anxious for a solution by this summer before some mills simply run out of supply. "We have to have a solution in place by near the end of the summer, or the economic dislocation that will occur here in the Pacific Northwest will be so severe that it will take years to rebuild," said Chris West, vice president of the Northwest Forestry Association. "People are going to be out of logs."

Two overriding questions must be decided at the meeting here: How many millions of acres should be put off limits to logging in conservation reserves to protect the owl and other imperiled species; and how should the remaining public forestland in the Northwest be managed?

"We want to go in and bargain hard and maximize [timber] volumes within the context of good environmental practices," said Scott, an economist with the carpenters' union, who along with industry officials believes the main issue is a timber supply crisis that is devastating local economies and driving up lumber prices. "We think you can do that if you don't hold out science for science's sake as some kind of religion."

Environmentalists who have made preservation of ancient forest a national crusade disagree, and say the lumber jobs dependent on old-growth forests are going to disappear soon in any case. Better to lose them now and preserve the remnants of the forest, they say, then lose both a few years down the road.

"Ultimately we believe the only possible way to bring a resolution of this issue is to stick to science and accurately assess the economic realities of the region and move ahead with forest management that is long term and scientifically based," countered Fran Hunt, a forest resource specialist with the National Wildlife Federation. "The reality is that anybody whose job depends on logging ancient forest has a dead-end job."

Much of the groundwork for making the difficult decisions awaiting the Clinton administration has already been done. What remain are the political decisions, not just on timber volume and owl reserves, but a host of subsidiary questions.

Said Rep. Peter A. DeFazio (D-Ore.), whose district will be the most heavily affected by the negotiations: "It's when you get to the details—how much old-growth to set aside, what kind of management changes, what do you do for rural communities—that's where we are going to have the knock down-drag outs."

3   Logging Is Top Goal in Policy Memo

Clinton Aides Outline Options for Northwest

TOM KENWORTHY
June, 1993

S enior administration officials have recommended that President Clinton adopt a potentially explosive solution to the long-standing conflict over use of Pacific Northwest forests and protection of the northern spotted owl. The plan would maximize timber cutting within legal limits, permit some logging in owl reserves and be at least partially immune to court challenge.

That proposal—known as "option 9"—is the preferred choice contained in a 47-page draft memo to Clinton from a special committee convened after the administration's forest policy conference in Portland, Ore., in early April. It is headed by Kathleen McGinty, White House director of environmental policy.

The memo says that the overriding goal is to cut as much timber as possible while still complying with the nation's environmental laws. It calls for "front-loading" a 10-year harvest program with higher yields in early years in order to meet political demands of Northwest lawmakers, but acknowledges that some scientists involved in the plan would oppose that policy.

If endorsed by the president, the plan would further threaten Clinton's relationship with the environmental community. That relationship already is strained following White House abandonment in March of a plan to revise the use of federal lands for mining, grazing and timber production. Labor and the timber industry would likely be more satisfied with the forest plan.

Clinton is scheduled to review the recommendations over the weekend and announce a decision early next week so that Congress can act on it quickly.

In his campaign and during the April forest conference, Clinton raised expectations that after years of deadlock he might be able to end the Northwest's feud over logging its national forests. Previous Republican administrations failed to find a way to satisfy the timber industry, its workers and environmentalists who have used lawsuits over the threatened owl and other jeopardized species to slow the pace of logging.

All nine of the options prepared for the committee by a team of scientists would result in timber cutting far below average levels during the past decade, when pro-industry government officials accelerated the region's cut to as much as 5 billion board feet a year. No option can both comply with environmental laws and produce more than 2 billion board feet every year, the committee memo states, and all the options would entail an estimated 6,000 to 9,000 job losses in the timber and wood products industries.

Option 9 was developed on a crash basis at the very end of the staff review, and only after the scientific team had finished the first eight. Environmentalists charge that it was ordered by the White House to satisfy Northwest politicians eager for higher timber harvests.

Marla Romash, a spokeswoman for McGinty and Vice President Gore, said no "specific instructions" were given to the scientific team. But Romash repeatedly emphasized the administration's concern for the region's economy.

"This is not just about forest management," she said. "It's about dealing with long-term economic issues."

Gore's office said last night he was not available to comment on the committee's recommendation of option 9.

Option 9, the memo suggests, would yield an average annual timber harvest of 1.2 billion board feet over 10 years, but would provide 2 billion in the first year and 1.7 billion the second. The high harvests in the early years, the memo says, would help it gain political support in Congress, particularly from Speaker Thomas S. Foley (D-Wash.) and other Northwest lawmakers.

Although they were not provided details of the plan, representatives of some of the nation's largest environmental groups emerged from a Wednesday evening meeting with McGinty profoundly discouraged. Many are convinced that Clinton will back a plan that would violate his pledge at the forest conference to construct a solution that would be "scientifically sound, ecologically credible and legally responsible."

"This is war," said Brock Evans, a vice president of the National Audubon Society. "It's political science, not biological science."

Among the elements in option 9 (also known as the "unified reserve") are: A new emphasis on protecting key watersheds, rather than just locking up owl habitat into reserves, in order to also protect threatened fish stocks. Some logging, through thinning and salvage of weakened trees, would be permitted in owl preserves in old-growth stands, a radical departure from earlier scientific studies that called for inviolate reserves. Creation of 10 "adaptive management areas" of 50,000 to 500,000 acres that would be the sites for "intensive ecological experimentation and social innovation." The experiments would include some local control over forest management decisions, a key goal of conservative western groups. At least some insulation of the plan from legal challenges in order to quickly get more timber moving through the pipeline in economically depressed communities.

The memo recommends that the fine points of this issue be worked out later, but strongly suggests provisions to prevent timber sale challenges under laws such as the National Environmental Policy Act and the National Forest Management Act.

Such provisions, known as "sufficiency language," would have to be enacted into law by Congress. They would declare that any timber sales approved under the administration plan are sufficient to meet the requirements of environmental laws governing forest management and cannot be challenged under those statutes. The environmental community is vehemently opposed to that kind of waiver.

4 Clinton to Slash Logging

Workers, Towns in West to Get Aid

TOM KENWORTHY

July, 1993

President Clinton, seeking a delicate balance among the demands of ecology, economics and politics, yesterday moved to reduce timber cutting on federal lands in the Pacific Northwest.

To protect the region's wildlife and old-growth forests, the administration plan will allow for average timber harvests over the next decade of 1.2 billion board feet per year. That is about half the level of the last two years, and only a third of the average rate between 1980 and 1992, when annual harvests swelled as high as 5.2 billion board feet.

To cushion the blow to the Northwest's timber economy—already battered by mechanization, exports and the loss of 20,000 jobs in the past two years—the administration will offer $1.2 billion in aid over five years for worker training, economic development and community assistance.

The plan, which grew out of a forest conference held in Portland, Ore., in April, is intended to end a long, bitter debate in the Northwest over management of federal forest lands and the fate of threatened wildlife such as the northern spotted owl, a bird called the marbled murrelet and stocks of salmon and other fish.

"This issue has been one which has beddeviled the people of the Pacific Northwest for some years now," said Clinton yesterday. "The time has come to end the logjam, to end the endless delay and bickering, and to restore some genuine security and rootedness to the lives of the people who have for too long been torn from pillar to post in this important area of the United States."

Clinton said the plan met his earlier test of being "scientifically sound, ecologically credible and legally defensible" and "provides an innovative approach to forest management, to protect the environment and to produce a predictable and sustainable level of timber sales."

But both the forest products industry and some environmentalists assailed the move yesterday.

"It's basically going to devastate the wood products industry," said Mike Draper, executive secretary of the Western Council of Industrial Workers, accusing the administration of a "betrayal" of its promise for a balanced solution at the forest conference.

"This is the best deal the timber industry could get without breaking the law," said Brock Evans, vice president of the National Audubon Society, one of many environmental groups that have softened their original criticism of the proposal.

Key members of Congress from the region also expressed disappointment. Senior members of the Northwest's delegation—who pointedly did not attend Clinton's announcement—say they will press for legislation mandating higher timbercutting levels than the administration wants. Among those who were not present for the announcement was House Speaker Thomas S. Foley (D-Wash.), who has suggested that legislation might be needed that is not "limited" by the administration goal of complying with existing environmental laws.

The administration seeks to protect old growth and wildlife by focusing on key watersheds, establishing a series of reserve areas around streams and rivers and in key habitat areas for the owl and other wildlife. Some thinning and salvage logging would be permitted in some reserves. In addition, 10 "adaptive management" areas would be established to allow for experimental efforts at joining ecological protection and economic uses.

Intensive cutting during the 1980s sparked a legal war by environmentalists, leading to a series of court decisions that halted logging on millions of acres in the region.

Under terms of a court order, the administration will present the plan as a draft environmental impact statement (EIS) to a federal judge on July 16. The court will then determine whether the forest-management prescriptions comply with federal environmental laws. If they do, the administration will ask the judge to lift his injunction at that time, circumventing some of normal EIS procedures.

Interior Secretary Bruce Babbitt said a key goal is to get logs quickly to Northwest mills. Babbitt said it should be possible to provide as much as 2 billion board feet this year, well above the 10-year average called for in the plan.

If approved by the court, the forest-management provisions of the proposal can be implemented by the administration. But some aspects of the economic aid, and any change in law to protect the plan against court challenge, would have to be approved by Congress.

Some key provisions of the administration's plan remain unclear. Among them are the details of forest management within the owl reserves and whether the administration will seek to protect timber sales under the plan from administrative and judicial review in order to speed up log deliveries.

A major goal of environmentalists in the long debate has been the legislative establishment of permanent, inviolate owl reserves where federal land managers would not be allowed to sell timber. In addition, many groups remain adamant that no plan should prevent them from using existing environmental laws to challenge timber-management decisions.

"With this proposal, the fate of the forests will stay in the hands of the very agencies that pushed them to the point of collapse," said Carl Pope, executive director of the Sierra Club. "It is a sincere attempt to protect the remaining ancient forests, but the way it is crafted won't accomplish that goal."

"This is a great step forward," said Karin Sheldon, acting president of the Wilderness Society, "but we think the plan has some very serious flaws. . . . They are talking about reserves, but they are not inviolate. There will be pressure on the Forest Service to use salvage and thinning as a cover for harvest."

And forest-products industry leaders, who say the plan will cost as many as 85,000 jobs—far more than the 6,000 predicted by the White House—complained yesterday that the administration has guaranteed a continuation of the policy gridlock that Clinton vowed to end.

"The Clinton administration has spent 90 days developing a solution to the crisis that will leave us exactly where we were when it began: court-ordered gridlock, with no timber being sold for the foreseeable future," said Mark Rey, vice president for forest resources for the American Forest and Paper Association.

5 Timber Plan Brings Little Peace to Oregonians

For Logging Industry and Conservationists, Worries over Old-Growth Forests Endure

TOM KENWORTHY
July, 1993

I n presenting his plan to overhaul the management of federal forests in the Pacific Northwest last week, President Clinton expressed the hope that it would end the region's drawn-out war over its old-growth forests and wildlife.

But here in the heart of one of the most timber-dependent counties in the United States, there is no immediate sign of peace.

Workers and executives in the forest products industry, which has sustained this area since the post–World War II housing boom began, predict that the administration's plan would only accelerate the economic tailspin that has closed five mills and cost Douglas County almost 1,000 of the 6,500 timber industry jobs that existed two years ago. The often-isolated members of local environmental groups worry that the "new forestry" techniques promised by the White House would amount to little more than, as one Oregon activist said, "clear cuts with a happy face."

Here, at least, Clinton seems to be the victim of raised expectations, of a bitter harvest from the seeds of hope he planted at his Portland forest summit in April. Then, the president spoke of "a balanced and comprehensive policy that recognizes the importance of the forests and timber to the economy and jobs of this region [and will] preserve our precious old-growth forests, which are part of our national heritage and that, once destroyed, can never be replaced."

But for those whose livelihoods depend on the massive Douglas fir trees cut from the nearby Umpqua National Forest and other federal lands, the president's plan represents a betrayal. The administration's proposal would allow an average annual wood harvest of 1.2 billion board feet over the next decade in forests that are home to the northern spotted owl and other threatened species. That figure is one-third of the average cut over the last 12 years.

"The impact is just crushing," said Roseburg Forest Products mill worker Darryl Middleton, a union activist who said he has watched the rate of family breakups and suicides climb in recent years as the legal battles over the spotted owl cut off new federal timber sales because of court injunctions. "It looks like it's just a plan to shut things down," he said.

Though no one can predict precisely the impact of Clinton's plan here, an accident of history and geography would likely mean the forests surrounding Roseburg would be particularly hard hit by the 3.7 million-acre system of owl habitats and stream preserves that would be established.

Because of Douglas County's isolation, timber harvesting on federal lands began later here than it did in many parts of the Northwest. As a result, this area has a far greater percentage of old-growth forests—those containing stands of trees older than 150 to 200 years old—than most of the region, where much old growth already has been felled. Clinton's plan aims to preserve about 80 percent of the remaining old growth.

"So here we are today with a wonderful old-growth resource base, and what was once a blessing is now a curse," said Allyn Ford, executive vice president of Roseburg Forest Products. The company, which employs 3,000 people in Oregon and whose plywood and specialty mills depend on old growth from federal lands, uses 500 million board feet of timber a year.

"They are talking about saving old growth," said Ford. "Boy, do we have old growth."

For all the gloomy talk, Roseburg appears bustling and full of vitality, with few outward signs of its 12.5 percent unemployment rate. Located between Medford and Eugene on Interstate 5, Roseburg is a regional commercial and medical center with new subdivisions sprouting on its outskirts. Planning for the inevitable decline of its timber economy began more than a decade ago.

Like many places in Oregon and Washington, Roseburg is a mecca for California refugees and retirees.

"We've had some success with diversification," Douglas County Commissioner Doug Robertson said, including the addition of a boat manufacturing facility and an aluminum cable plant in the last three years.

But because of the peculiar economics of timber country, even new manufacturers that offset the job loss in forest products end up providing far less tax revenue. More than half of Douglas County is owned by the federal government, primarily the U.S. Forest Service and Bureau of Land Management (BLM), and the county gets a generous share of all federal timber receipts in lieu of property taxes.

Of the county's budget of about $95 million, roughly $35 million comes from timber sale receipts paid by the federal government. Though the Clinton forest plan will guarantee initially that the county gets 80 percent of the average it received between 1986 and 1991, over 10 years the payments will decline to 50 percent.

The loss of federal funds will affect every county service, including education, roads and public safety, said Robertson. "Our ability to market Douglas County as a place with high livability will be diminished."

The sense of unease about Clinton's plan also extends to environmental activists who worked throughout the 1980s to preserve the magnificent old forests of the Cascade and coast ranges, now dwindled to 10 percent of the original old growth.

Diana Wales, a Roseburg attorney and National Audubon Society activist who participated in the April forest conference, said she is troubled that the plan, rather than establishing sacrosanct reserves, will allow some thinning and salvage in owl habitat. And, she said, the establishment of 10 large areas for experimental forestry techniques also worries her.

"The Forest Service and BLM have a long history of saying, 'We did it wrong, now we know how to do it right; trust us,' " Wales said. "It would be wonderful if we could have timber harvest and habitat protected in the same place, but we are not better than God."

"There have to be some areas set aside that we don't mess with just in case we are not as smart as we think we are . . . Science is wonderful and humans love to tinker, but we screw up a lot."

6   Interior, Allies at Loggerheads over Timber

TOM KENWORTHY
September, 1993

L ess than three months after the Clinton administration announced its plan to end the long conflict over the Pacific Northwest's old-growth forests, the White House and the environmental community are brawling over how much timber can be cut while the plan undergoes environmental review.

Eager to get more timber moving to northwest mills this fall and winter, the administration is threatening to support congressional efforts to insulate some timber sales from judicial challenge unless environmental groups agree to higher interim timber harvest levels.

Since President Clinton announced the forest plan on July 1, the administration has been negotiating with the 12 environmental groups that are plaintiffs in a lawsuit over the threatened northern spotted owl and northwest forests. Court rulings in that case have enjoined the government from cutting timber on millions of acres of federal forest land in the Northwest. The goal of the talks, which continued yesterday in Portland, Ore., has been to identify specific timber sales that could be released from the injunction while the administration's plan goes through the Environmental Impact Statement process.

The environmental groups have proposed for release sales that would provide about 83 million board feet of timber. The administration has proposed sales totaling 137 million board feet and has threatened to seek the judicial review protections from Congress if it does not get at least 100 million board feet, according to environmentalists close to the talks.

Any attempt to insulate the forest plan, and the timber sales that would be permitted under it, from judicial review would provoke a confrontation between the White House and its usual conservation allies.

But a spokesman for Interior Secretary Bruce Babbitt said yesterday that the goal of replenishing the supply of timber to northwest mills is so important to the regional economy that the administration would press for congressional approval of sufficiency language if the talks with environmental groups hit an impasse. The vehicle would be the Interior Department appropriation bill awaiting action by a House-Senate conference committee.

"We have said . . . we wanted to find some way to pursue fast-track implementation and that our preference was to deal with the plaintiffs," said Kevin Sweeney, Babbitt's spokesman. "But we have always said if we couldn't get an agreement to move significant amounts of timber, or reasonable amounts of timber, that we would look for other places to get that kind of authority, and that one place is Congress."

"Our view is this is staff running amok," said Richard Hoppe, a spokesman for the Wilderness Society. "We thought we had an amicable agreement to review these sales in return for them holding off on sufficiency. Now we have to question their sincerity."

7 'Unraveling' of Ecosystem Looms in Oregon Forests

Scientists Say Recovery Could Take Century

TOM KENWORTHY

May, 1992

W hen settlers pushed up the Oregon Trail into the Blue Mountains of eastern Oregon in the mid-1800s, they encountered a strikingly beautiful forest unlike any they had seen on the way west. Widely spaced ponderosa pines formed a towering canopy over an understory so free of brush and smaller trees that the settlers could sometimes drive their wagons through the forest as if it were a park designed by a landscape architect.

"Our road has been nearly the whole day through the woods—that is, if beautiful groves of pine trees can be called woods," wrote Rebecca Ketcham in her journal in 1853 as her party left the Grande Ronde Valley. "The country all through is burnt over, so often there is not the least underbrush, but the grass grows thick and beautiful."

If those settlers could come back today, they would find these forests, managed for most of this century by the U.S. Forest Service, nearly unrecognizable.

Gone are most of the ponderosa pine, cut up by the timber industry into lumber for moldings and doors. With the ponderosas cleared out, and the Forest Service so successful at fighting fires, other species have taken over the forest in tightly packed stands of grand fir, Douglas fir and lodgepole pine.

But those usurping species are far more susceptible to insects and diseases, and now millions of acres of trees are dead and dying from repeated outbreaks of such insects as western spruce budworm and tussock moth. Combined with six years of drought, this has created conditions ripe for monstrous wildfires.

Forest scientists describe this ecosystem as "unraveling," and say it could take as long as a century to restore it by encouraging the return of ponderosa pine and larch. With thick bark and few branches close to the ground, ponderosa pine is resistant to the kind of low-intensity fires that used to creep through the forest understory and eliminate competing species.

But Congress, now writing legislation to protect the old-growth forests west of the Cascade Range in Oregon, Washington and northern California that are home to the endangered northern spotted owl, may ignore pleas of conservationists to use that legislative opportunity to preserve the remaining old-growth ponderosa pine on the east-side forests as a genetic base for restoring the ecosystem.

Whether protection for old-growth stands on the east side is included in the legislation now being written by the House Agriculture and Interior and Insular Affairs committees will depend to a great extent on House Speaker Thomas S. Foley (D-Wash.), whose position gives him a key role in the debate. Foley's district in eastern Washington includes one huge national forest and parts of two others that are now beginning to experience some of the same problems affecting the Blue Mountain forests to the south.

But Foley remains skeptical of the need to deal with the east-side forest issues in the legislation now moving through the House. "We probably need to do an inventory of old-growth timber on the east side before we make assumptions about it," said Foley last week.

So the national debate over forest policy may continue to bypass this region, drowned out by the cacophonous arguments over the owl and jobs in the timber industry.

"If we weren't blathering about old growth and owls, this would be the hottest story in forestry," said Jack Ward Thomas, a Forest Service biologist who heads his agency's research station in the Blue Mountains.

Here in what is called the Inland Empire, it is a hot story.

Conservationists, arguing that the only way to restore the east-side forests to health is to allow them to return naturally to the way they were, call for a moratorium on further cutting of old-growth ponderosas, an intensive scientific study of how to manage the forests and a new policy of using fire as a tool. This week, arguing that the Forest Service has turned these forests into a "virtual salad" for insects and diseases, a coalition of environmentalists filed suit in Spokane, Wash., to prevent further timber sales that would "degrade forest health."

Timber interests argue there is plenty of old growth reserved in wilderness and roadless areas and push for an aggressive program to salvage dying and dead trees before they become useless.

Forest Service employees, while acknowledging past mismanagement, say these ecosystems are so complex that letting nature run its course is foolhardy and that intensive manipulation by man will be needed for decades if the forests are to become healthy again.

How much a ban on logging the remaining old growth would cost is anybody's guess. While there are numerous estimates of the cost in jobs of protecting old-growth forests on the west side of the Cascades, there are no reliable projections for the east side.

Adding urgency is a final decision two weeks ago by the National Marine Fisheries Service to list Snake River chinook salmon as threatened species. East-side forests provide spawning grounds for some chinook, and logging could be halted to prevent further degradation of salmon habitat hit hard by clear-cutting and cattle grazing that raise water temperatures and cloud streams with sediment.

"Salmon and steelhead are now at record low numbers," said Tim Lillebo, east-side forest coordinator for the Oregon Natural Resources Council, a 6,000-member conservation group. "There will be endless appeals and lawsuits over the same thing, so why not do it now?"

Environmentalists fear that decisions putting millions of acres of coastal forests off limits to logging because of the owl will only shift timber pressure eastward, onto national forests that have suffered from heavy logging and where thin soils and a shortage of rainfall make reforestation difficult.

"If you have a shirt with one hole, it's still a shirt," said Andy Kerr, conservation director for the Oregon Natural Resources Council. "If you have two holes, it's still a shirt. But pretty soon you don't have a shirt. We don't need to make any more holes."

Flying over the crest of the Cascades, which trap precipitation moving to the east, the fabric of the landscape changes abruptly. Left behind are the moist climate, rich soils and relatively fast-growing forests of the west side with their impossibly tall Douglas firs. Ahead is a far more arid terrain, with spindly lodgepole pine and firs competing fiercely for the scarce rain and soil nutrients.

In spots, the forest looks almost lunar: Millions of dead trees have turned it into a mottled gray-and-green kaleidoscope threaded with logging roads connecting thousands of 40-acre Forest Service clear-cuts and even larger gaps cut on private timber industry land.

These Oregon forests—among them the Winema, the Deschutes, the Ochoco, the Umatilla, the Wallowa Whitman and the Malheur—are so stressed that the regional Forest Service forester last year said their ecosystems are "unraveling."

"The Blue Mountains are suffering declining forest health on a landscape scale," Forest Service entomologist Boyd E. Wickman wrote in March.

At the Blue Mountains Natural Resources Institute, a state/federal/private re-search consortium in La Grande, Wickman and others have watched with growing alarm the results of man's management of these forests. In a report last year on conditions in three of the forests, they reported that "past management practices such as fire exclusion and selective timber harvesting, though carried out with the best intentions and using the best information of the time, have led to potentially catastrophic buildups of [dead wood], insect infestations and disease-caused dam-age."

Insect infestations are nothing new in these forests, but they began worsening after World War II, by which time much of the ponderosa pine had been logged, allowing dense stands of firs and other fire- and insect-prone species to take over. A variety of diseases have also attacked the forests.

A spruce budworm epidemic since 1980, for example, has affected 2.7 million acres in the Blue Mountains. In the Wallowa Whitman National Forest, according to forest health coordinator Steven L. Fletcher, 1.1 million of the forest's 1.4 million wooded acres are affected by bud worms that eat the foliage and needle buds, stripping the limbs.

The insect epidemics, combined with the prolonged drought, have produced a forest floor covered with enormous quantities of dead wood. Fires have been increasing in number and size the past few years, and the Forest Service is bracing for catastrophic wildfires that could equal those that burned 700,000 acres in Yellowstone National Park four years ago.

Although the Forest Service has accelerated its salvage sales of dead and dying timber under pressure from Rep. Bob Smith (R-Ore.), the pace is not quick enough for the timber industry. "Each day that we wait, the quality of usable "dead" timber declines," said Chris West, vice president of the Northwest Forestry Association.

Conservationists like Lillebo of the Oregon Natural Resources Council say that nature is taking care of the forest's problems on its own, through insects and disease, and that the key to restoring its health is to stop cutting old-growth ponderosa pine so it can reclaim the forest. Fire, natural and prescribed, must also be part of the rebuilding, they say.

"The Forest Service has screwed it up and we have to do something different," said Lillebo, who argues that "We have to have fire on the ground . . . and we have to stop cutting old growth right now. That's what it comes down to."

But the solutions seem far less straightforward to the people who manage the forests. Both salvage sales and allowing fires to burn, for example, have potential implications for wildlife, including elk that need substantial cover, and salmon that need cool, clear water.

Re-creating forests dominated by ponderosa pine and larch over a vast area with such varied conditions, the institute's Wickman wrote, "is going to be difficult biologically, operationally, economically and socially. It will require drastic steps on a landscape level over a very long period—perhaps 100 years."

Meanwhile, the timber industry scoffs at the notion of returning to the old ponderosa pine forests. "We can get into just as much trouble going to all ponderosa pine," Boise Cascade's regional chief forester Bob Weinberger said. "The answer is to keep a good, healthy mix of species," he said, adding that there are sufficient reserves of old growth.

But Judy Johnson, who has led 200 volunteers in an east-side forest mapping project for the National Audubon Society, said the Forest Service has no real "idea of what's on the ground." One-fifth of what the Forest Service has marked as old growth, she said, is either not old growth or has been logged.

"If you've never inventoried and you don't know what's out there, it's hard to decide what the forest can sustain," said John Osborn, a Spokane physician and board member of the Inland Empire Public Lands Council who has pushed to slow timber cutting on the Colville National Forest in northeast Washington in Foley's district. In the Colville, Osborn and other forest activists said, swamps are misidentified as "old growth," whereas actual old growth is scheduled to be cut down in drainages that are already 35 percent clear-cut.

"This is the speaker's forest and whatever happens to it will be his doing," Osborn said.

Government's
Limitations in
Environmental
Preservation 15

Idealistically, one of the primary functions of government would be to protect and preserve environmental quality. Realistically, however, performing this role is hindered by significant limitations—limitations of inefficiency, politics, economics, and resolve. Since the early 1970s, the issue of environmental quality has been part of every presidential campaign in the United States, as well as part of the campaigns of most other politicians at the state and federal levels. As history has shown us, the promise to be "the environmental president" is easier to make than it is to keep. Attempts to foster environmental preservation through the political process invariably result in a balancing act, with pressures from other economic forces tempering legislative and executive resolve to act in the environment's behalf.

Critics of the Reagan-Bush administration's pedestrian record in the environmental arena abound. A few of the articles in this section provide accounts of some of these two presidents' efforts at "compromise." But the same pressures faced by Reagan and Bush continue to plague the Clinton administration, as other articles in this section attest, and they raise a question regarding the extent to which the political process can be counted on to protect environmental quality.

The 17 recent *Washington Post* articles in this chapter highlight some of the problems associated with the government's role in environmental protection as it struggles with the reality that immediate economic and political considerations often are of far greater concern than are environmental issues. The position of government leaders is made even more difficult by well-organized and well-funded special interest groups, both in and out of government.

The first six articles are presented to show how serious and pervasive this problem of political expediency is. Articles 1 and 2 discuss efforts of the Bush/Quayle government to circumvent the Clean Air Act, in the first case by allowing increases in pollution emissions without formal notification and hearing, and in the second, by weakening requirements for emission controls in new plants. Article 3 deals with relaxing the Endangered Species Act to allow cutting of more timber, and Article 4 concerns a policy change allowing drilling for oil and gas on federal land during appeal procedures. The next two articles reflect the international nature of political expediency, with Article 5 detailing the struggle of the Bush government to identify a position on the issue of global warming that would be acceptable to both the world community meeting at the environmental summit in Rio, as well as to political constituents in the United States. Article 6 describes efforts of the Clinton administration to gain approval of the North American Free Trade Agreement despite serious concerns over environmental standards in Mexico.

The next three articles focus more specifically on the role of special interest groups in both the enactment and implementation of environmental policy. Article 7 describes how the powerful oil lobby and legislative allies were able to exempt refinery wastes from inclusion under the Superfund program established by Congress in 1980. Article 8 describes how a powerful Congressional lobby has been able to block changes in grazing policies on federal land proposed by the Clinton administration. Article 9 continues this story, but also suggests that a determined leader has approaches available that do not depend on Congressional authorization.

Another issue that receives frequent media attention is waste and inefficiency in government programs, and the area of environmental preservation contains some striking examples. Article 10 describes how different government programs work at cross purposes, with some designed to protect the environment while others are harmful to the environment. Article 11 focuses on waste in the administration of the Superfund program and on efforts of the EPA to increase efficiency of the program and greatly increase the rate of actual toxic waste clean-ups. Article 12 describes objections to efforts of the EPA to increase efficiency of its research labs. Article 13 in this chapter concerns the general question of the overall value of government regulations in the battle to protect the environment.

The final four articles address some of the difficulties government encounters when attempting to protect the environment. Article 14 describes problems with protecting wilderness areas in New York State. Article 15 describes President Clinton's plan to deal with global warming, based almost entirely on voluntary participation by industry; and Article 16 points out that often the main costs of implementing programs falls on cities and communities. The last article reports on how the Clinton administration's attempt to make environmental policy changes through executive orders, rather than through legislative action, led to criticism by elements of the business community.

1   Bush between Push and Pull on Clean Air

President Being Compelled to Choose Strict Enforcement of Law or Eased Rules for Industry

ANN DEVROY
April, 1992

C aught between competing political imperatives, President Bush is being forced to choose sides in a bitter debate over a proposal championed by Vice President Quayle that opponents say could cripple enforcement of the Clean Air Act of 1990.

The clash over how to enforce the law, the major environmental legislation enacted during Bush's presidency, pits the advocates of easing regulations on industry, spearheaded by Quayle and the President's Council on Competitiveness he chairs, against those promoting strict regulation of air pollution, led by William K. Reilly, administrator of the Environmental Protection Agency.

With Bush having embarked Friday on what aides called "Deregulatory Week," highlighting the need to end burdensome regulations as part of his effort to spur the economy, White House officials predict Quayle and his allies will prevail.

The issue underscores a broader debate over the need for tougher environmental controls that has existed since Bush took office. While Bush proclaimed that he would be "the environmental president," the danger posed to his reelection campaign by the faltering economy has pushed him "toward the economic argument more than he might have," as one aide put it.

"At the heart of this debate is really a different world view inside this administration," one senior official said. "One view is extremely suspicious of business and industry and feels that government must watch it at all costs and that goals like clean air must be pursued to the final inch. Another view is that watching has to be balanced and that goals to be achieved have to be balanced by the cost to business and ultimately the consumer."

The 1990 reauthorization of the Clean Air Act left it up to the EPA to write the rules used to enforce it, a process that has been going on for more than a year. But administration officials, principally through the Competitiveness Council, have become involved in the rule-making process, and, according to critics, are using the process to achieve exceptions rejected by Congress.

The issue that has brought this struggle to a head is a proposed rule that would allow large industries to forgo public notice, hearings or EPA review and simply notify federal and state pollution control authorities when changes in their operations will increase emissions beyond the levels specified in their permits.

A key provision of the Clean Air Act requires industry to obtain the permits. During debate over the legislation, industry representatives fought unsuccessfully for more flexibility on the limits specified by the permits and the ability to exceed the limits without going through the process of obtaining new permits.

But the Competitiveness Council has said the public notice requirements are burdensome and expensive for what it says would be only minor changes in emission levels. It has vehemently pushed the limited notice, insisting that the Clean Air Act does not require such potentially broad and expensive review of minor emission changes.

Reilly says the Clean Air Act in fact stipulates that any revisions in emission levels require a public review process, and he has two legal opinions, environmental groups and the congressional authors of the act on his side.

From 30,000 to 40,000 large businesses, including utilities, oil companies and manufacturing plants, would be affected by the decision, with the EPA estimating the cost to each of the public hearing requirement to be $500,000, but with industry officials arguing that billions would be spent over small amounts of increased pollution.

Quayle, Reilly and other senior officials met Wednesday on the issue, one of a series of contentious sessions in recent months, and were unable to reach a resolution. The conclusion was the sides were so far apart that Bush would have to make the choice, a distasteful outcome for a president who prefers governing by consensus.

Asked if there is a middle ground in the debate, one official said, "If there is, George Bush will find it."

Most of those involved in the debate say there is no middle ground. Rep. Henry A. Waxman (D-Calif.), one of the authors of the legislation, said in an interview that the law requires such notification and that if Bush sides with Quayle, the president is violating the law and opening a huge loophole in it.

"The decision on this permit goes to the very heart of the Clean Air Act," Waxman said. "It is the key, the linchpin to the whole thing working that industries have to get a permit on these emissions and that they not go beyond that without a full public examination. What they want to do is allow industries to increase pollutants through the back door."

Beyond that, Waxman accused Bush of a "cynical manipulation" in hailing the Clean Air Act as a major achievement and using it as his premier environmental credential while administration officials are gutting it through the rule-making process. "He has a responsibility to enforce this law and his own expert lawyers" say the Quayle position has no legal standing, Waxman said.

Waxman's reference is to an August memo by Donald Elliott, then the EPA's general counsel, which stated, "It is highly unlikely that the courts would uphold as 'reasonable' an interpretation of the statute that would authorize environmentally significant changes to be made in emissions without appropriate opportunities for public notice and opportunities to participate."

In addition, the comptroller general, asked for a legal opinion, found in December that "revisions to permit requirements must be subject to public oversight."

According to administration officials, the Justice Department communicated to the Competitiveness Council that either the EPA approach or the Quayle approach was legally defensible. Challenged to produce a written, signed legal opinion, department lawyers did so last week, administration officials said. "We did not think it would go this far, but obviously it has and Bush will now have legal opinions on both sides," one official said.

The issue has reached critical mass at a time Bush is emphasizing his efforts to ease the burden of regulations on business, not his environmental credentials. He has scheduled a series of events to highlight that theme this week, including extending the 90-day moratorium on new regulations that was announced in his State of the Union address, a new effort to ease regulatory burdens on the securities and transportation industries, and several others.

To buttress their case that Americans believe government regulation is too onerous and is hurting them, officials last week were circulating a Penn-Schoen poll done March 23–25 for an industry group that shows strong anti-regulation sentiment.

The poll findings are that a "significant majority" in the 605-person nationwide sample feels government regulators have "gotten out of control," that the country has too many unnecessary and costly regulations, and that regulators do not take into account the cost to consumers.

But the questions are couched in language that seems to play directly into the current anti-Washington mood: "Do you think right now that the country has a lot of unnecessary and costly regulations or not?" asks one question, to which 83 percent replied yes. The poll does not ask if government should make strong efforts to strictly limit industrial pollution.

2   Administration Considers Weaker Protection for Unpolluted Air

MICHAEL WEISSKOPF
October, 1992

A mid a barrage of environmental announcements during the last week before the election, the administration is quietly planning to weaken a key provision of the nation's clean air laws after the presidential contest, according to officials.

The plan, which would relax a regulation designed to preserve air quality in unpolluted areas, was finalized two weeks ago by high-ranking officials of the Environmental Protection Agency and Office of Management and Budget who decided to delay announcement of the proposed change until after the election to shield Bush from probable criticism by environmentalists, officials said.

As the regulation stands today, industry must install state-of-the-art controls on new plants whose emissions pose a threat to the air quality of unpolluted areas. The changes that the administration is planning to propose would permit companies to install cheaper and less effective devices.

Assistant EPA Administrator William G. Rosenberg, a political appointee and close friend of Bush campaign chairman Robert M. Teeter, agreed to the plan despite warnings by his staff that it would endanger air quality, complicate regulation and anger environmentalists, according to officials.

Rosenberg did not consult EPA Administrator William K. Reilly before reaching agreement with the White House, officials said. Reilly must sign the proposal before it becomes public. Normally he approves recommendations of his assistants. But informed of the plan that Rosenberg agreed to, Reilly issued a brief statement yesterday, saying that he intends "to look myself at the options."

Rosenberg, the EPA's air pollution chief, has helped orchestrate a White House strategy this week to strengthen Bush's environmental credentials by issuing long-delayed regulations mandated by the revised Clean Air Act.

Rosenberg denied that politics was the reason for delaying plans for the new technology standards. He said he wanted to issue more important regulations first.

But according to another administration official involved in the matter, "This is one that's been controversial. Obviously we're in an election period, and one thinks of those things."

At stake is a provision of a 15-year-old law designed to protect clean air in unpolluted areas of the country, such as national parks. The law requires industry to install "best available" technology on new sources of emissions in those areas, except when the costs of those controls are excessive.

In 1987, the EPA stiffened that requirement by imposing a "top-down" standard to determine the best control devices, whereby the best available technology is supposed to be taken as a starting point for any new pollution sources. If companies can demonstrate that they cannot install the best for technical or economic reasons, they are then permitted to go to the next lower level of stringency.

But under the planned amendments, companies would not have to consider state-of-the-art technology as a starting point. Rather, they could consider devices "representative of the range" of technologies, subject to interpretation of permitting authorities.

And instead of having to justify why the best was not selected, they would only have to show that their choice of older or less effective devices is "consistent" with legal requirements.

Although EPA officials sought initially to retain essential elements of the "top-down" approach, they gave in to changes drafted by the White House counsel's office and the Council of Economic Advisers, documents show.

The proposed changes are similar to those advocated by some pulp and paper companies and electric utilities. They argue that the current rule is unreasonably strict for emissions in unpolluted areas and that it complicates planning for equipment purchases because state-of-the-art technology is constantly evolving.

Millions of dollars per plant are at stake. In the case of utilities, for example, the "top-down" approach has led to requirements that new power plants in Virginia install devices capable of removing up to 90 percent of the nitrogen oxides emitted from smokestacks. The removal rate of most technology currently in use is 40 percent.

The cost of the current system is about $400 for every ton of pollution removed, compared with $2,700 per ton removed by the new, more effective devices, industry statistics show.

In an interview, Rosenberg defended the changes as "making for a more rational decision," instead of automatically requiring that the toughest technology be considered first.

But most of the EPA's regional officials who commented on the plan have complained in writing that the changes unduly relax an important environmental rule.

A memo to Rosenberg's office from the Pacific Northwest region said the revisions "weaken, not improve, the effectiveness" of efforts to preserve unpolluted areas. "Whether EPA chooses to acknowledge it in writing, we all recognize that the effect of this rule-making is to force [state] permitting authorities to make less stringent [technology] determinations," wrote Jim McCormick, director of the Pacific Northwest's air and toxics division.

3   Endangered Species Act Must Change, Bush Says

People and Jobs 'Deserve Protection Too'

RUTH MARCUS
September, 1992

President Bush vowed today that he would not sign an extension of the Endangered Species Act unless it is changed to take more account of the economic cost of protecting threatened wildlife because "people and their jobs deserve protection too."

Bush came to this remote logging town to make the case that he would strike the proper balance between jobs and the environment while Democratic rival Bill Clinton and his running mate, Sen. Albert Gore Jr. (D-Tenn.), would sacrifice the well-being of workers to environmental extremists who are "twisting" the law.

The 1973 law designed to protect endangered species from extinction has become a major issue in the Pacific Northwest, where threats to the northern spotted owl have halted logging in millions of acres of national forests in Oregon and Washington and been blamed for the loss of thousands of jobs for loggers and other forest products industry workers.

The spotted owl, which Bush once described as "that little furry, feathery guy," inhabits western Washington, but the president told a rally here in the northeastern part of the state that "it is time to make people more important than owls."

Campaigning in Oregon and Washington four years ago, Bush promoted himself as the environmental president. Today, revisiting both states after a campaign stop in Southern California, he presented himself as the environmental president with a healthy dose of economic realism, in contrast to the Democratic ticket.

"My opponent talks about putting people first," Bush said, referring to the title of Clinton's economic plan. "Well, we can start right here in the Pacific Northwest."

Bush quoted a passage from Gore's recent book, "Earth in the Balance: Ecology and the Human Spirit" calling for protection of the spotted owl because "the jobs will be lost anyway."

"I challenge Governor Clinton: Do you agree with your running mate? Do you endorse the book that you once called 'magnificent'?"

Clinton was also in Oregon today to talk about the dispute between environmental groups and the timber industry and told a small group in Eugene that there should be "no net loss" of jobs because of restrictions on logging to protect the spotted owl or because of other environmental concerns.

Clinton met in a back yard in Eugene with a group of people whose economic well-being is tied to timber, who told him of hardships that had occurred because of environmental lawsuits that have tied up the sale of timber from federal lands.

He said that part of a $100 million tax subsidy program now used to encourage the export of raw logs should be diverted to retrain timber industry workers, upgrade logging mills and otherwise bolster the Pacific Northwest's economy.

"I can't promise to make things the way they were," Clinton said. "We can't go back to that."

Environmentalists have challenged Bush's diagnosis of the Northwest's timber industry woes, saying the loss of jobs that occurred there stems from a combination of automation, increasing exports of raw, unprocessed logs and a series of court decisions that have halted logging because the Bush administration was in violation of environmental laws including the National Environmental Policy Act and the National Forest Management Act.

"The Endangered Species Act is not what has led to injunctions [against logging] in the Northwest," said Kevin P. Kirchner, an attorney with the Sierra Club Legal Defense Fund. "The administration's failure to comply with the National Environmental Policy Act and the National Forest Management Act have led to the injunctions."

Appearing in Rancho Penasquitos, near San Diego, before coming here, Bush simultaneously attacked Clinton's environmental record in Arkansas and suggested that Clinton would be an environmental extremist if elected president.

"Under Governor Clinton, Arkansas ranks 50th, worst in the country, for utility of state environmental initiatives, according to an independent analysis," Bush said. "But in his zeal to capture his party's nomination, Governor Clinton has made every promise to every environmental group who sent him a survey."

Later at Burril Lumber Co. in Medford, Ore., Bush derided Clinton as "Governor Doublespeak."

Describing the Endangered Species Act here today, Bush said, "The law is broken and it must be fixed."

Clinton told the back yard gathering: "If I win this race in 50-odd days, I am determined to break this logjam. You're entitled at least to have all these federal government agencies on the same side and to have a coherent policy and to have a commitment to the region and to the people that resolves this in a fair and balanced way."

The Endangered Species Act, which restricts development or other activities once a species is declared to be in danger of extinction, is up for reauthorization this year. With the issue of jobs versus the environment a politically volatile one, it will not be considered by Congress this year. However, the law will remain in effect with passage of the Interior Department appropriations bill, now before a congressional conference committee. Under a 1978 amendment, the law allows for exemptions if protection of a threatened species jeopardizes a national or regional economic interest.

After the U.S. Fish and Wildlife Service declared the owl a threatened species in June 1990 and said excessive logging was a threat to its survival, Interior Secretary Manuel Lujan Jr. convened a Cabinet-level committee, nicknamed the God Squad, which in May granted limited authority to permit logging on about 1,700 acres of federal land in Oregon.

The administration has also submitted a plan to Congress that would reduce the number of acres set aside to save the owl from 5.4 million to 2.8 million. The administration acknowledges that change would "highly likely" result in the extinction or near extinction of the owl after more than a century.

Staff writers Edward Walsh in Eugene and Tom Kenworthy in Washington, D.C., contributed to this report.

4   Some Environmental Rules Loosened, Some Tightened

Oil Drilling on Federal Land May Proceed during Appeals Process, Interior Department Says

TOM KENWORTHY
September, 1992

Moving to stem what it maintained was a flood of "frivolous" environmental challenges to energy exploration on federal land, the Interior Department yesterday announced that beginning next month oil and gas drilling would be allowed to proceed while appeals of the agency's decisions are under review.

The new rules, which will affect oil and gas activities on the 270 million acres managed by the Bureau of Land Management, represent a significant departure from current practice. Now, no exploration or drilling is permitted to proceed until the appeal is decided by Interior's Board of Land Appeals.

At the same time it announced the final rules covering oil and gas exploration, the department proposed similar rules for appeals of activities conducted by other agencies in the department such as the Bureau of Indian Affairs and the Office of Surface Mining. For example, efforts to control predators by the Animal Damage Control office in the U.S. Fish and Wildlife Service, would go forward while under appeal.

The changes are part of a broad effort by federal land management agencies to insulate natural resource industries from citizen appeals and administrative challenges to activities on government-owned land. The changes come in response to a directive from President Bush to eliminate excessively burdensome economic regulation. Earlier this year, the U.S. Forest Service proposed to eliminate procedures allowing citizen appeals of timber sales on its land.

But that Forest Service proposal to do away with an appeals process in place since early this century, would be blocked under legislation approved yesterday by a House-Senate conference committee. In completing negotiations over the fiscal 1993 Interior appropriations bill, the conferees accepted provisions providing for a 45-day Forest Service timber sale appeals process.

House Speaker Thomas S. Foley (D-Wash.), who earlier this year asked Agriculture Secretary Edward R. Madigan not to jettison the appeals process, said he was "pleased by the action of the conferees . . . in continuing the opportunity for administrative appeals."

Also yesterday, the Interior appropriations conference committee defeated a House proposal to raise grazing fees on ranchers who use federal lands. The panel also jettisoned a provision that would have put a moratorium on the "patenting" of federal land by miners, who under an 1872 law can take title to federal land for as little as $2.50 an acre.

In announcing the appeals rules for oil and gas drilling, David C. O'Neal, the assistant secretary of Interior for land and mineral management, said they would protect the rights of citizens to be involved in the drilling planning process while insulating industry from the expense and inconvenience caused by an increasing number of "frivolous" appeals filed by environmental groups.

The new rules also allow for decisions approving drilling to be stayed by the Board of Land Appeals pending consideration of appeals if it determines there is a significant threat to the environment or public safety.

O'Neal said the change came in response to a "growing public demand for more efficient and effective government." It is "ludicrous and unfair," said O'Neal, to permit environmental groups to stymie energy production with boilerplate appeals that often take up to two years to decide.

Though O'Neal and other Interior Department officials repeatedly said frivolous appeals that manage to stall drilling had risen, they could not document the trend. Figures provided by Interior show that the number of appeals filed with the Board of Land Appeals has been relatively constant for three years. There were 597 oil and gas decision appeals in fiscal 1990, 541 in fiscal 1991 and 545 for the first 11 months of this fiscal year.

Representatives of some conservation groups sharply criticized the new rules, saying they will restrict the public's right to prevent environmental degradation before it occurs. "Even if you think this is an environmentally sensitive area where there shouldn't be oil and gas drilling, they can go in and begin drilling and by the time of the ruling on an appeal, the environmental damage will probably be done," said Cindy Shogan, Washington representative for the Southern Utah Wilderness Alliance.

5   Bush Was Aloof in Warming Debate

Climate Treaty Offers View of President's Role in Complex Policy

MICHAEL WEISSKOPF
October, 1992

He had promised in the 1988 campaign to use "the White House effect" to fight the "greenhouse effect," but as President Bush sat down with a dozen advisers at the White House last April he confronted an issue to which he had given little personal attention during his presidency.

While environmentalists had warned of a potentially devastating peril to the world climate from the buildup of heat-trapping gases, and scientists—joined by Bush's former chief of staff John H. Sununu—had engaged in a sharp public debate over the accuracy of such predictions, the president had remained aloof. But in April, with an environmental summit meeting due to convene in Rio de Janeiro six weeks later, Bush was faced with a difficult diplomatic problem: The U.S. position on the first international treaty to deal with global warming was sharply at odds with the rest of the industrialized world.

As his advisers reeled off the economic, environmental and diplomatic implications of the treaty, Bush sat silently, showing little interest in the issue, participants at the meeting recall, until the discussion turned political: Congressional Democrats were threatening to embarrass him by legislating the very terms his negotiators were opposing.

"Since when does Henry Waxman run the government?" he asked, referring to the liberal California congressman who was sponsoring the legislation.

In June, when the Earth Summit took place, the public disagreement between the United States and its allies resulted in a public relations disaster for the Bush administration at a critical time in the presidential campaign. A reconstruction of the global warming policy debate at the administration's highest levels offers an insight into the way Bush addressed complex domestic concerns.

In background interviews with two dozen officials involved in setting policy on global warming, Bush was described as being detached, uninterested, and as his brief remarks in the April meeting showed, responsive only to the politics of a complex issue. He never sat for a full-dress scientific briefing on it or exercised

379

control over administration policy even after infighting among administration officials became public or leaders of other industrialized nations pledged action.

Instead, he delegated policy decisions on global warming, as he did on other key economic and social issues, to Sununu, a conservative former governor of New Hampshire.

In the absence of any presidential involvement, Sununu followed his personal belief that global warming projections were alarmist and overruled the recommendations of the administration's own environmental officials. Stressing his engineering credentials, Sununu commissioned government-supported scientists to develop a simplified climate model that he ran on his office computer. His strong arguments—even in the face of contrary scientific evidence—that excess heat from the burning of carbon fuels would be absorbed by oceans earned him the nickname "plankton man" from the president.

Scientists generally agree there is a warming trend, but their estimates of how fast and how far the planet will heat up vary widely. Rather than recognize an emerging consensus, Sununu seized on the differences in opinion as a reason to avoid action and turned global warming into an issue to be politically finessed. When criticism of the president would intensify, the White House responded by taking public relations measures, such as issuing an "action agenda" that repackaged existing policies and plans to plant trees that absorb the primary greenhouse gas.

"We debated tactics," one former White House official said, "but there just was no examination of the core elements of policy."

Sununu squelched a full-scale debate on the issue, engineering the firing of a deputy assistant secretary of state who argued for a more aggressive policy, and got so deeply involved in the politics of the issue that he planned a White House workshop on global warming right down to the hiring of a Republican conventions expert for $24,000 to handle the logistics, choosing speakers, editing press releases and demanding hourly reports.

No one else in the administration had the power or access to challenge him. Secretary of State James A. Baker III, an early proponent of action on global warming whose department was intimately involved in international negotiations on the issue, recused himself in early 1990 from any policy decisions because of his investments in oil companies.

After Sununu resigned last December and U.S. negotiators were more intent on reaching accord, politics still was a driving factor, this time out of the need to avoid alienating the Republican right just as conservative Patrick J. Buchanan was challenging Bush in the presidential primaries.

Bush eventually approved a global warming treaty tailored to meet U.S. demands for a narrower, less specific pact than most other nations wanted. It set approximate deadlines and limits on emissions of greenhouse gases, but failed to explicitly link the two.

The accord is nonetheless considered a decent start, and perhaps a prudent one—given the usual fickleness of science.

But Bush's involvement in developing the accord was minimal. When European Community President Jacques Delors at a White House visit in April tried to break a deadlock with a last-minute compromise, Bush responded with only a few words and moved to another topic. When top aides asked his approval of treaty language, he threw up his hands in frustration at the technical details as if he could not be expected to understand them. And lunching with advisers a few days before the treaty signing in Rio de Janeiro, he asked, "Tell me again, why is it we couldn't do what the rest of the world wants to do."

Issue Divided Administration

To some extent, Bush acted like any president in relying on his advisers to direct key issues. If he differed in his approach to such domestic concerns as global warming, critics say, it was his failure to ride herd on the staff and take charge of major developments.

The issue drove his advisers into factions, dominated for the first three years by Sununu, who declined to be interviewed for this article. Sununu had powerful allies in Richard G. Darman, director of the Office of Management and Budget, and Michael J. Boskin, chairman of the Council of Economic Advisers. They argued that limits on greenhouse gases, produced by burning oil and coal, would be economically ruinous because of U.S. dependence on those fuels. As Boskin warned before the 1990 economic summit in Houston, "Remember, Mr. President, this is a bet-your-economy issue."

Heading the environmental camp was Environmental Protection Agency Administrator William K. Reilly, a career conservationist who sought a more detached analysis of the scientific forecasts and called for energy conservation measures that would carry their own economic benefits while reducing warming gases.

An occasional ally of Reilly's was Robert E. Grady, then head of environmental programs for the OMB, who wrote Bush's environmental speeches in the 1988 campaign, including the now-famous promise in Michigan to use the "White House effect" to combat the "greenhouse effect."

In the center was a faction of pragmatists, led by Clayton Yeutter, the short-lived domestic policy coordinator under former White House chief of staff Samuel K. Skinner. Yeutter took charge of the issue after Sununu left. By bringing together warring parties last spring, he managed to find enough common ground for a pair of results-oriented diplomats to negotiate a treaty in time for the Rio summit.

After Baker recused himself in 1990, he handed the issue to Robert B. Zoellick, the State Department counselor. A Darman protégé and Bush campaign aide in 1988, Zoellick had good standing in both the White House and the diplomatic community.

Zoellick's chief negotiator was Robert A. Reinstein. Blessed by background and politics, his career in energy and trade included work for Yeutter, who recommended him as deputy assistant secretary of state for the environment, after Sununu forced the firing of his predecessor, William A. Nitze.

Campaign Call for Action

Ironically, Bush was one of the first world leaders to warn of global warming when he pledged Aug. 31, 1988, to "do something about it" and called for an international agreement.

But like other promises that later haunted him, the global warming pledge was born out of political considerations. He picked the issue out of a briefing book that aides had brought to the vice president's mansion to gear up for the environmental vote. Turning the pages, Bush said, "Let's try this one."

His timing was right: 1988 was the warmest year on record, joining five earlier record-breaking years, and it focused interest on environmental issues. Scientists said it signaled a long-term trend in which world temperatures would rise at least 3 degrees by about 2050, causing floods in some places, droughts in others.

But when the new administration had its first chance to act, it balked. In May 1989, a diplomatic panel formed by the United Nations was set to meet in Geneva. Reilly suggested support for a framework treaty to define the problem and its remedies.

Sununu blocked the idea, arguing that the threat was too tenuous and the cure too costly to start down the path of international agreements.

It was a Pyrrhic victory for Sununu. Newspapers reported the Reilly rebuke, plus stories that OMB diluted global warming warnings in the congressional testimony of a respected federal scientist. Members of Congress asked, was this the "White House effect" Bush had promised?

A chastened Sununu called Reilly to the White House late one evening. The president was embarrassed, he said, "What do we do?" The EPA chief suggested committing to a framework convention and offering to hold the first negotiating session here.

Only a week earlier, Sununu had rejected a similar proposal. But now he ran the idea by Bush, a former aide recalled. "Whatever you both think is necessary," the president said, and the announcement was made. The United States thus had been committed, in reaction to political criticism, to participating in an international event that top presidential advisers still opposed. Politics paved the way to Rio, but the failure to resolve the substantive differences resulted in more political infighting.

Although Sununu retreated to quiet critics, he was determined to hold the line in any treaty to simply identifying the problem and listing possible remedies without committing the parties to any concrete action. He put White House science adviser

D. Allan Bromley, rather than Reilly, in charge of coordinating global warming policy.

Sununu consolidated his control after Baker withdrew from involvement in the issue. The secretary of state recused himself after Sununu tore up and rewrote a Bush speech that Baker, Reilly and Energy Secretary James D. Watkins had approved for delivery to a global warming meeting here Feb. 5, 1990.

The president delivered Sununu's draft, stressing the "scientific uncertainty" of global warming and the U.S. commitment to spending more on research.

But as diplomatic criticism mounted and a U.N. panel of 300 climate experts projected unprecedented temperature rises if nothing is done, Bush continued to defer to Sununu and did not personally engage the issue.

He invited environmental officials to the White House but when global warming came up, he changed the subject. At one point Bush encountered aides in an informal gathering and broached the issue, but he exited quickly as the discussion got technical, saying, "Let me know when you get it figured out."

By the opening of treaty talks in February 1991, European nations raised the ante. Instead of a hollow framework convention, they wanted a treaty with "targets and timetables" to stabilize emissions of the main greenhouse gas—carbon dioxide—at 1990 levels by the year 2000.

The administration called for nonbinding "national action plans" to level off all greenhouse gases, not just carbon dioxide, the industrial byproduct of burning coal and oil. The negotiations remained at a stalemate until Sununu resigned in December 1991.

Clamor for a Treaty

When Yeutter took over domestic policy last February, he saw a crisis brewing. The Rio summit was four months away, and every other industrialized nation was clamoring for a treaty to sign there. He found the decision-making process frozen, with the president uninformed and his advisers badly split. Reilly and Grady favored some form of stabilization, and Darman and Boskin argued against a treaty and summit. To complicate matters, Buchanan was running well in early primaries and was bashing environmental issues.

Yeutter knew how much Bush enjoyed the pageantry of state visits, but if there was no treaty, the president would be held accountable at Rio. If he accepted "targets and timetables," he faced conservative criticism at home.

A treaty acceptable to both sides had to be worked out.

Reinstein enlisted help from British officials at an April meeting of industrialized nations in Paris. On April 29, two days after Bush's briefing, British Environment Minister Michael Howard came to Washington to go over final details of a compromise with Zoellick and Reinstein. When they emerged, they had a deal: "Targets and timetables" were replaced by nonbinding, unspecific goals that left much room for interpretation.

Before the language could be formally presented at the last round of talks prior to Rio, Yeutter had to get the president's approval.

In the Oval Office, he explained how the compromise was carefully devised to permit the president to go to Rio without committing the nation to drastic economic measures. According to an observer, Bush threw up his hands at the technical details, asking "How is anyone supposed to understand this stuff?"

But 15 minutes later, he ruled: "Let's try it."

Reinstein took the next shuttle to New York in time to have the new language unveiled in the last round of talks before Rio.

On May 8, agreement was reached. The language worked out by Zoellick and Howard was refined into what Jean Ripert, who chaired the U.N.-sponsored talks, called "constructive ambiguities." Industrialized nations agreed to submit reports "with the aim of returning" to 1990 levels of greenhouse emissions. But no deadline was given for reaching the goal.

Still, other governments, as eager as Washington to make the Earth Summit succeed, saw it as their best chance for the first global warming treaty. Only after agreement was reached in New York did the White House announce that Bush would attend the Rio conference.

While the treaty was being wrapped up and the White House was making arrangements for Bush to go to Rio, the administration continued to manage the issue politically. To assuage conservative concerns, Yeutter wrote a letter May 8 to the powerful chairman of the House Energy and Commerce Committee, Rep. John D. Dingell (D-Mich.), explaining that the key language in the pact was contained in two sections.

"Neither binds the United States to specific commitments of any kind," he said.

6   Cloud over Trade Pact—Texas Too

Mexican Pollution Fuels U.S. Criticism

TOD ROBBERSON
June, 1993

A smoky gray cloud has formed on the horizon of this Rio Grande border community, and depending on which way the wind blows, it could cast a shadow over U.S.-Mexican relations at a crucial point in negotiations linked to the proposed North American Free Trade Agreement.

The sulfury cloud comes from the smokestacks of two coal-fired electrical plants on the outskirts of Piedras Negras, and prevailing winds are carrying it straight across the border into Big Bend National Park, a wilderness area 100 miles to the northwest that is one of the most popular outdoor recreational sites in Texas.

The cloud and the smokestacks, which have virtually no anti-pollution devices and eventually could pump up to 230,000 tons of sulfur dioxide into Big Bend each year, are at the center of a controversy between Mexico and the United States over territorial rights to clean air. Sources at the U.S. Environmental Protection Agency said the problem threatens to bog down talks on an environmental side accord to the proposed free trade agreement, known as NAFTA.

President Clinton has said that without the environmental accord, as well as two other side agreements on labor issues and sudden cross-border trade surges, he will not submit NAFTA to a vote on Capitol Hill.

Critics of NAFTA have argued that Mexico-based companies already have a competitive advantage over their U.S. counterparts because of lax Mexican environmental standards, low wages and other factors that permit them to produce products much more cheaply. They have said NAFTA, which would eliminate tariffs and other trade barriers among the United States, Mexico and Canada, will encourage U.S. companies to relocate to Mexico, taking American jobs and capital with them.

Promoters of NAFTA say it will create the world's largest free-trade zone uniting more than 350 million consumers and eventually presenting dramatic opportunities for increased employment in all three countries. NAFTA promoters also point to the political capital that could accrue to the United States in Latin America with approval of the free-trade accord. In an interview earlier this year, Mexican President Carlos Salinas de Gortari called NAFTA a "historic window of opportunity" for the United States to improve the often uneven relations it has had with its neighbors to the south.

In many ways, the smokestacks at Piedras Negras are the NAFTA debate in miniature, pitting the economic goals of employment, free enterprise and increased cross-border commerce against concerns about unfair trade practices and the environment.

Environmental experts say air pollution at Big Bend would not pose a serious threat to the health of wildlife, vegetation or visitors. However, it would destroy the ambiance that national parks are designed for: as a nature reserve where beautiful scenery and clean air can be enjoyed without the irritants normally associated with urban life—in this case sulfurous smoke.

If advisers to EPA Administrator Carol Browner get their way, at least one of the two border electrical stations will be closed or radically modified—at a cost of hundreds of millions of dollars—to meet U.S. environmental standards.

If Salinas gets his way, the power plants, known as Carbon I and Carbon II, will remain operative and unmodified. With much international fanfare, the Salinas administration announced in May that it would privatize Carbon II, half of which is still under construction, in an unprecedented move to open Mexico's government-owned power generators to free enterprise. Carbon I, a 1,200-megawatt station built in the mid-1980s, will remain under control of Mexico's national power utility, the Federal Electricity Commission.

If international financing can be arranged, the 1,400-megawatt Carbon II station will be sold to a private joint venture 49 percent owned by Mission Energy, a subsidiary of Southern California Edison, and 51 percent by Grupo Acerero del Norte, a big Mexican steel and mining corporation. Talks reportedly are underway to hook up Mexican border power plants to the U.S. power grid, enabling stations such as Carbon II to compete with U.S. utilities.

Nearly 10 percent of the electricity produced by Carbon II will go directly to steel mills owned by Grupo Acerero. The U.S. Department of Commerce placed sanctions against those same steel mills in January for dumping cheap steel products on the U.S. market.

The two power plants sit atop their own fuel source—a large vein of medium-sulfur, high-ash coal—that crosses under the Rio Grande and abuts the neighboring border community of Eagle Pass, Tex. If both power plants stay open, coal-mining operations here and in Eagle Pass could provide an important source of employment for decades to come. If the plants close, this already depressed region probably will sink further into poverty.

Despite the plant's potential economic infusion, specialists at EPA are warning of serious hazards posed by Carbon I and II, neither of which were built with stack scrubbers or other anti-pollution devices to control emissions of sulfur dioxide, nitrous oxide or ash, according to EPA documents obtained under the Freedom of Information Act.

Thomas Reed, Mission Energy's project director for Carbon II, said in a telephone interview that his company is not willing to spend the estimated $200 million to $300 million necessary to retrofit the plant with scrubbers and other anti-pollution devices. "Those plants were built to meet Mexican standards, and they meet those standards," he said.

Social Development Secretary Luis Donaldo Colosio, whose ministry oversees environmental protection, said in an interview last March that his country imposes standards that meet or exceed those of the United States. EPA officials, however, described Mexico's standards for coal-burning power plants as equivalent to what the United States imposed in 1970. U.S. standards have since been dramatically tightened.

Carbon II "does not meet EPA new source standards, and it will not do it without installing scrubbers," Reed acknowledged. A typical scrubber injects a watery spray containing a basic substance, such as lime, that combines with the acids of sulfur dioxide to form a heavy compound. This compound, which is solid as opposed to the sulfur dioxide gas, is more easily collected before it leaves the smokestack.

Reed added that Carbon II's prospective new owners are under no obligation to meet U.S. standards—or even to supply EPA with data about the plant's design and emissions rates—because the plant is not located in U.S. territory. Aside from the standards set by the Mexican government, Reed said, the plant also must meet specifications set by the World Bank, which is considering financing the plant's privatization.

Nevertheless, Reed said his company's analysis indicates that "there will be no impact" on the environment.

But in a June 4 memorandum to EPA Administrator Browner, two assistant administrators and a regional administrator strongly disagreed with Reed's assessment.

"Despite Mission's assurances, EPA and National Park Service staff remain concerned that existing and planned units may significantly impact U.S. national park areas" administrators Alan Hecht, Michael Shapiro and Joe D. Winkle said in the memo. "Neither the existing facility nor the new units could be permitted anywhere in the U.S. because of their failure to meet EPA new source performance standards, let alone the best available control requirements mandated by the Clean Air Act."

The memo added, "Moreover, at this point we have no information indicating the facility would be barred by the Mexican government from burning even dirtier, higher sulfur coal" than what is being extracted from the Piedras Negras area.

Browner, a supporter of NAFTA who has praised Mexico's environmental cleanup efforts, has taken no position regarding Carbon II, EPA staff members said.

In other EPA internal memos, advisers to Browner appeared divided on whether to make a high-profile issue about Carbon II's problems or to be low—key for fear of impeding the progress of talks on the NAFTA environmental side accord. Asked whether the Clinton administration is concerned about repercussions that the Carbon II controversy could pose for NAFTA, an EPA staff member replied, "Absolutely, there's no question about it."

In hopes of making a more precise evaluation of Carbon II's environmental impact, EPA regional officer A. Stanley Meiburg sent a letter April 21 to Rene Altamirano, Secretary Colosio's environmental director, requesting various technical details about the power plant's design and test results on its emissions rates.

EPA staff members said that so far Altamirano and other Mexican officials have not acted on the request for reasons they could not explain. Altamirano was unavailable for comment in Mexico City.

An EPA source said it appeared that the Mexican government was withholding environmental impact data for fear it could negatively influence Mission's and Grupo Acerero's pending applications for international financing. Potential financiers include the International Finance Corp., the private arm of the World Bank; Barclays Bank; Citibank, and two Mexican banks.

Susana Romero, spokeswoman for the International Finance Corp., declined to comment specifically on the Carbon II loan application but said environmental concerns always weigh heavily in World Bank loan considerations. Another World Bank source confirmed that the lack of scrubbers on Carbon II's smokestacks poses a serious impediment to financing. "No scrubber at all does not meet World Bank guidelines," the source said.

The source said the World Bank also is concerned that Carbon I and II could be closed as a result of the NAFTA environmental negotiations, which would mean that the plant's financiers could lose everything.

Reed said his company is prepared to pull out of the project altogether if the financiers or the Mexican government requires the plant to be retrofitted with scrubbers. "The economics of retrofitting are just not there," he said. Even if Mission withdraws from the privatization effort, he added, "the plant is going to run—regardless of who owns it. This is just a question of ownership."

One option, Reed explained, was a provision in the sales contract permitting the private owners to pass on the cost of retrofitting to the plant's customers. Under Mexican law, however, Carbon II would have only one customer—the government-owned electricity utility. Carbon II's owners plan to give nearly 10 percent of the electricity they produce to Grupo Acerero's steel mills under a "private service" contract unregulated by the government. Under current arrangements, Grupo Acerero would retain its source of cheap energy for steel production while the Mexican public would bear the cost of retrofitting the plant.

Meanwhile, pollution from Carbon I and II is having a negative ripple effect across the border in Texas. An EPA staff member said the federal and state governments impose "incremental" air-quality standards that must be met by all U.S. companies in Texas. Those standards are set by region, and when a region exceeds its pollution limit—regardless of whether the pollution comes from Mexico or

Texas—Texas-based companies are required to reduce their own emissions to bring pollution levels down.

In the June 4 memo to EPA Administrator Browner, her senior advisers warned that Carbon I and II are already using up Texas's pollution increments. As a result, the state may have to cut back on new permits for industries and utilities hoping to open in southern Texas, while existing factories may have to reduce production to compensate for pollution produced by Mexico. "Thus, this source as presently configured can preclude industrial growth in the U.S.," the memo stated.

"This is unfair competition," said an executive with a major Texas utility. "What happens if they decide to export this electricity? There's no way we could compete."

The executive added, "We had hoped that with privatization, these environmental problems would be taken care of. But I guess now it will just be private companies invading our airspace."

Special correspondent Ted Bardacke contributed to this report from Mexico City.

7   Oil's Superfund Loophole

Law No Help to Victims of Oklahoma Spills

MICHAEL WEISSKOPF
November, 1988

The fumes from Mae Morgan's basement grew so pungent last year that she awakened every night with raging headaches and nausea. Bubbling up from cracks in the cellar floor was an orange, gooey liquid so caustic that it burned Morgan's feet right through a pair of shoes. The frothy substance, which she believes is the result of wastes from a nearby refinery, saturated the rug and wood paneling, and she could do nothing to seal off the odor.

Morgan may seem like the classic victim of toxic waste the federal Superfund program was devised to help. Under the program, the government has the power to evacuate residents from dangerously contaminated areas and order industrial spoilers to thoroughly clean up their pollution.

But Morgan traces her problems to petroleum, and in the oil patch, all pollution is not equal. When Congress set up the Superfund in 1980, it exempted refinery wastes under pressure from the powerful oil lobby and its legislative allies, including Sen. Lloyd Bentsen (D-Tex.), the Democratic nominee for vice president. They argued that refinery wastes occur in low concentration and that they quickly break down in the environment, unlike the man-made chemicals, such as PCBs, that are targeted by the Superfund.

But the refinery wastes that are exempt from Superfund protections include natural constituents of oil ranked among the most toxic industrial debris, namely the neurotoxins xylene and toluene and the known human carcinogen benzene.

Because of oil spills and leaks from storage tanks, unlined pits or underground pipelines, those toxic substances can seep into the earth around refineries, penetrate underground streams and spread into the ground water of surrounding communities, threatening sources of drinking water and polluting the air.

Although other laws can be used against oil wastes, critics say the petroleum exclusion clause of the Superfund denies the most comprehensive, protective statute to hundreds of places such as Ponca City, population 30,000, where Conoco Inc. has operated a refinery for 75 years.

Years of complaints about oil wastes prompted the Oklahoma health department to monitor the air and standing water of the basements of houses near the refinery in the southern part of town last March. The tests turned up benzene, toluene and xylene.

Dr. Frederic E. Gerr of Mount Sinai Medical Center in New York, who reviewed the data for a citizens group here, noted the "potential for serious health effects" from benzene in the basement water alone and called for a reduction of excessive exposures to a substance considered dangerous at any level.

Two households were evacuated and bought out by the city in 1986 after the local fire marshal found explosive or volatile levels of gas vapors in the cellars. One of the evacuees recalled how vapors ignited by the gas flame of his hot water heater produced flashes of fire in his basement.

A Conoco analysis of ground water turned up benzene concentrations thousands of times higher than the federal drinking-water standard. Fortunately, the town gets its drinking water upstream of the refinery. But puddles smelling of oil soak back yards and playing fields even during dry spells, and streams of a viscous, sheeny substance course down streets and ooze from sidewalks here.

For similarly dislocating toxic waste cases, the Superfund's managers at the Environmental Protection Agency send a team of specialists to determine if evacuation or Superfund cleanup is necessary.

If the site qualifies for the Superfund, the EPA commissions a comprehensive health survey, looks for the source of contamination, develops a cleanup strategy, requires the polluter to pick up the costs and pays the community for outside experts to review the plan. Cleanups are supposed to restore the environment, leaving the ground water, for example, pure enough to drink.

In Ponca City, the EPA helped the state conduct its health survey and hopes to use a less stringent law to achieve some cleanup. Otherwise, citing the oil exclusion in the law, it has deferred to the state.

The state rules out the oil wastes as a serious health problem. Dr. Mark Roberts, state environmental epidemiologist, said benzene detected in home air does not exceed state guidelines. He cited statistics showing similarly high levels in other industrialized parts of the country, such as Bayonne, N.J., and Houston.

Such analysis is branded as typical of industry favoritism in Oklahoma, where oil and government have always mixed. Gov. Henry Bellmon owns oil wells and Lieutenant Gov. Robert S. Kerr III is the scion of the Kerr-McGee oil empire.

Despite high levels of benzene found in the city's ground water, the state has not officially identified the polluter, allowing Conoco to clean up the pollution essentially in a manner and time of its choosing, subject to state supervision.

"We don't have a pollution problem," refinery manager Dennis R. Parker said in an interview. The oily odors probably result from "swamp gas," not petroleum wastes, he said, and the ground water pollutants are from "unknown sources." Another Conoco official said the oily sheen of water in basements and streets is due to bacteria in iron from the ground water that turns rusty in the air.

Nevertheless, Conoco, acting as a "good neighbor," according to Parker, has agreed to lower the water table to reduce the threat of flooding. Ground water will be pumped out and treated and biochemical measures used to neutralize remaining pollutants.

The plan falls far short of demands by hundreds of families wedged between the Conoco refinery and the Arkansas River in south Ponca City. With health complaints ranging from sinusitis to abnormally high cancer rates, the families want to be evacuated from houses where insulation, walls and floors are saturated with benzene. They want the two-square-mile area fenced off and tons of polluted soil removed.

And they want the southside's ground water—so contaminated that a jar of it exposed to a lighted match has been known to flare up—restored to drinking-water quality.

For Morgan, 63, the demands were so far from realization and the problem so unbearable that she was forced to choose another course of action last November. Noxious sludge oozed onto her basement floor as quickly as she mopped it up. Samples sent to a private lab showed traces of kerosene and heating oil. Viewing the benzene readings of a neighbor, she decided she had no choice but to leave.

Over the front door of her abandoned, frame house that she insures at a value of $70,000, Morgan hoisted a sign: "For Sale: Own Your Own Toxic Waste Dump."

Not everyone has the resources to move out. Mostly low-income families and retirees on fixed incomes, they seethe with the frustration of living amid disabling odors, watching children play in a polluted ditch nicknamed "Acid Creek" and fighting a company that is the town's principal employer with 4,000 jobs.

"You go to your local officials, and they refuse to help you because they're afraid to get into a fight with Conoco," said Anna Sue Rafferty. "Your state officials won't help you because Conoco pays their campaign funds. The EPA says we don't qualify."

"It leaves you no where to go," she said.

When Congress exempted refinery wastes from the Superfund in 1980, lawmakers focused on what appeared to be the more pervasive, dangerous threat of toxic chemicals. The oil lobby, with friends on congressional environmental and finance committees, was poised for a fight to exclude oil, which no one then deemed a serious enough risk to jeopardize the entire program, legislative aides recalled.

Congress also suspended regulation of oil and gas drilling wastes in 1980, requiring the EPA to determine if they should be regulated in the same manner as hazardous chemicals. Eight years later, after lobbying again by Bentsen and other oil-state lawmakers, the agency decided last June to extend the exemption to production wastes.

A spokesman for Bentsen said the exclusion was intended to "recognize the special category of high-volume, low-toxicity waste where state regulatory regimes have performed fairly adequately" and where new federal rules would be financially "crippling" to the industry and offer "no significant environmental benefits."

But, he emphasized, the exemption was not intended as a "broad brush" to ignore communities polluted by high levels of hazardous oil refinery wastes. The

EPA "can't just hide behind the cloak of exemption," the spokesman said. "There ought to be a presumption to help people in situations like this."

In Ponca City, the EPA's presumption is to "act as a partner in pollution by not using the strictest of available remedies to get these people out of danger and to prevent the contamination of other communities further downstream," said Adrienne Anderson, western director of the National Toxics Campaign.

According to Allyn Davis, of the EPA's office in Dallas, the agency is limited to the "tools Congress provides us." Although the EPA is "hamstrung" by the oil exclusion in Ponca City, he said, the state seems to have the problem "under control."

The state directed Conoco to survey the ground water here in 1986, but it has not taken the administrative or legal steps necessary to order cleanup of the contamination by a specific date and to a specific extent, said Dave Dillon of the state water resources board. Instead, the company volunteered a remedial program that the state has accepted.

"We never got into the mode of telling them, 'You must do this,' " he said. "States have limited resources. It's counterproductive to get into an adversarial role. As long as I see progress, I'm going to continue down the path of least resistance."

8   Babbitt's New American Land Ethic Faces Crucial Test on Hill This Week

Senate Defeat on Grazing Policy Portends Further Difficulties

TOM KENWORTHY
September, 1993

I nterior Secretary Bruce Babbitt's oft-stated goal of creating a "new American land ethic" faces a critical test in Congress this week as the administration tries to rebound from an embarrassing Senate defeat of Babbitt's plan to overhaul grazing policies on federal land.

A House-Senate conference committee is about to take up the issue on the Interior Department appropriations bill. But if Babbitt and his deputies are to prevail, they will have to be more adroit, and work harder, than they did before the Senate's 59 to 40 vote on Sept. 14 placing a one-year moratorium on the grazing plan.

More may be at stake than just Babbitt's proposal to more than double grazing fees and pressure western ranchers to take better care of federal range lands, congressional sources said. The ease with which the Senate routed the White House plan demonstrates the hazards that await other parts of the administration's efforts to "reinvent government," and leaves the administration even more vulnerable to questions about its commitment to a strong environmental agenda.

The vote also demonstrated anew the tenacity of small but politically muscular interest groups in holding onto federal programs. It served as a warning to the White House that Congress can use the appropriations process to thwart administration initiatives—even those designed to be implemented by executive order and admin- istrative actions.

Babbitt and the administration, said one senior congressional aide, made a fundamental tactical error by announcing the comprehensive grazing overhaul last month, before Congress had completed action on the Interior appropriations bill. "This was a sitting duck" for an amendment blocking it, said the aide, adding that he would not be surprised to see other elements of the Clinton-Gore plan to restructure government get the same treatment in other spending bills.

The administration's allies in the environmental community say the setback is another disturbing example of the administration's habit of promising a more ambitious agenda than it is willing, or able, to deliver. The White House promised a broad assault on natural resource subsidies in the budget early this year, then backed off in the face of opposition from western Democrats. The administration later promised a broad-based energy tax and then buckled. Clinton pledged to make the government a leader in buying recycled paper, chlorine-free paper and low-pollution autos, yet there are signs of retrenchment under industry pressures.

The grazing-fee vote has worried Babbitt's allies in Congress who share his view that the whole array of federal resource subsidies—including mining, lumber and water—needs to be overhauled. They say the Senate vote puts the administration in a weakened position as it heads toward efforts later this fall to rewrite federal mining law to charge royalties for mineral production on government land and provide greater environmental protection.

"If we can't cut [the grazing subsidy], where are we going to cut?" asked Rep. Mike Synar (D-Okla.). "This is so clearly an unjustified subsidy. . . . This is an important beginning for the Department of Interior and we can't afford to lose it."

To many observers in Congress, administration response to the Senate threat to undo Babbitt's grazing proposal was lackluster at best. "They could have had the votes if they'd worked it," said one House aide. "They didn't communicate that it was a priority."

Western senators opposed to Babbitt's grazing overhaul, by contrast, were well-organized. They took Babbitt's argument that the issue was less about grazing fees than about the overall management of public lands and turned it against him. In the process, they won over a number of senators, including John H. Chafee (R-R.I.) and Daniel Patrick Moynihan (D-N.Y.), who have voted for higher fees in the past.

Babbitt's plan, designed to be installed administratively by late next year, would have done far more than raise the grazing fees over three years from the current $1.86 per cow per month to $4.28.

It also would have abolished local grazing advisory boards and given the larger public, including environmentalists, a say in range management decisions; established national rangeland environmental standards; shortened grazing leases if ranchers did not abide by those standards, and given the government sole title to range improvements such as fencing, as well as water rights associated with range improvements.

In a coordinated drumbeat that was never effectively answered on the Senate floor, westerners said the proposals' net effect would be a wholesale change in the longstanding relationship between ranchers and the federal government. That kind of thorough overhaul, they argued, should not be done by executive fiat, but through consultation with Congress.

That has left Babbitt pursuing a delicate, two-track strategy—beginning negotiations with western senators who want less burdensome changes while at the same time lobbying the House for a strong vote instructing its conferees to reject the Senate position.

The House is likely to vote on those instructions Monday. Although it is a non-binding vote and the conferees on the appropriations bill can do as they please on the grazing question, a strong margin of victory for Babbitt may well say a great deal about his chances of building a new land ethic.

9   Showdown on Grazing Fees

Babbitt Acts after Filibuster Vote Fails

TOM KENWORTHY and ERIC PIANIN
October, 1993

W ith western senators blocking legislative enactment of new policies governing cattle grazing on federal lands, Interior Secretary Bruce Babbitt yesterday said he will move to implement even higher fees and tougher management restrictions through administrative action.

Babbitt said at a Capitol Hill news conference that he has instructed his staff to prepare for publication rules to implement his grazing plan and for western hearings on the new rules that could take effect as early as next spring.

"So long as the gridlock persists, the Department of the Interior can't stand idly by waiting interminably for reform, which just never seems to happen," Babbitt said.

Babbitt's announcement came shortly after the Senate failed for the third time to shut off a filibuster by western senators angered by the administration's drive to charge western ranchers higher grazing fees and to impose more stringent federal management of some 260 million acres of public rangelands. The Senate vote was 54 to 44 to end debate, six votes short of the three-fifths majority required.

Although the western senators led by Sen. Pete V. Domenici (R-N.M.) have prevailed so far, Babbitt and the administration appear to hold the high card. The proposal before the Senate is a milder version of what Babbitt proposed in August; he has the authority to impose the tougher measures through the federal rule-making process without congressional authorization.

In addition, the House has voted by a 3 to 1 margin for the changes and appears resistant to giving any more ground.

If the impasse continues, warned Sen. Harry M. Reid (D-Nev.), the compromise likely will be stripped from the bill and "Secretary Babbitt gets everything he wants."

House Natural Resources Committee Chairman George Miller (D-Calif.), appearing at the news conference with Reid and Babbitt, said the House "cannot yield to a small minority in the Senate that is committed to engaging in the rules of obstructionism and gridlock."

Under Babbitt's original plan, grazing fees for western ranchers who use Forest Service or Bureau of Land Management rangeland would rise over three years from the current $1.86 per "animal unit month" to $4.28.

An animal unit month is the forage to sustain one cow/calf combination, five sheep or one horse for a month.

The plan now before the Senate, contained in a $13.4 billion Interior Department appropriations bill, would increase the fee to $3.45. About 27,000 ranchers hold permits to graze stock on federal land in 16 western states.

Beyond the costs, however, Babbitt's original proposal would go further than the Senate plan in imposing tougher environmental standards on ranchers, including allowing environmentalists a role in rangeland planning and tying the length of grazing permits to how ranchers treat the land.

Both measures would ensure federal title to water rights and permanent range improvements such as water wells, eliminate rancher-dominated grazing councils and establish national standards and guidelines for good rangeland management.

Domenici and his colleagues have argued that the changes constitute a wholesale rearrangement of the ranching community's traditional relationship with the federal government without benefit of public hearings.

Flushed, angry and pounding a lectern, Domenici yesterday accused the administration of trying to "turn over the destiny of our people to the secretary of the Interior."

But Reid, who brokered the compromise with the House, said many of the policies had been in effect for years on land managed by the Forest Service. The legislation, he said, would merely bring the Bureau of Land Management into conformance with its sister agency.

The protracted Senate battle over grazing fees has prevented Congress from completing work on all 13 spending bills for the fiscal year that began Oct. 1. Yesterday, the House and Senate for the third time in a month approved a continuing resolution to keep the government running while lawmakers finish work on the Interior and the Defense Department spending bills.

10 'Earth Budget': Waste Not, Want Not

Group Urges Redirecting $14 Billion in Spending

THOMAS W. LIPPMAN
February, 1993

S ince the first days of the administration, think tanks and interest groups hoping to shape the Clinton team's agenda have flooded members of Congress, their aides and reporters with policy papers, "alternative budgets" and issue analyses.

One example is the "Earth Budget" issued last month before Bill Clinton took office by Friends of the Earth, an environmental group.

According to this 208-page study, the federal government spends $34 billion a year for programs designed to protect the environment at the same time it spends or subsidizes $14 billion a year on programs that damage it.

Expenditures protecting the environment involve pollution control projects, mass transportation subsidies, agricultural conservation programs and international assistance, such as Energy Department funding to clean up coal-fired power plants in Poland.

Not surprisingly, the Friends of the Earth study concludes that this $34 billion—"slightly more than two cents of each federal dollar spent"—is not enough. Stop spending the $14 billion a year on programs that actually damage the environment, the authors say, and more federal funds would be available. That $14 billion can be found in low-cost access to federal grazing, mining, water and timber resources, unnecessary nuclear weapons activities, tax breaks for oil drilling and subsidies for heavy trucks, and civilian nuclear power, the study says.

Many groups, of course, will argue strongly to keep the expenditures Friends of the Earth proposes to cut. "Tax breaks for oil drilling," for instance, could be defended as aid to a troubled domestic industry and insurance against disruption of imported supplies.

Authors Ralph De Gennaro and Gawain Kripke maintain that "most of the subsidies in the anti-environmental budget" were well intended. Timber sales and irrigation projects, for example, were supposed to provide jobs and pay for themselves but may have lost more than $100 billion since they began. "Nuclear power was to be cheap. Rural electrification and irrigation were intended to help family farmers and rural folks of modest means. Many of these obsolete programs began during the nation's youth to encourage development of the West, and are no longer justifiable, they argue.

The list of "anti-environmental" federal expenditures and subsidies includes:

$300 million annually spent by the U.S. Army Corps of Engineers and the Interior Department's Bureau of Reclamation for unnecessary dams and irrigation projects.

A $173 million broadcasting tower that the Voice of America proposes to build in Israel "along one of the most important migratory bird flyways on Earth."

The Forest Service's timber sales. Not only does the program lose about $400 million a year, but "thousands of miles of new roads" are being constructed through national forests each year, the report says.

Pleasure boat exemption from the 20.1 cents a gallon federal diesel fuel tax. "Removing this tax break would encourage efficiency and could raise about $144 million a year," the study says, citing research by the Congressional Budget Office.

Free parking provided by employers, "a massive subsidy of $17 billion annually" that should be a taxable fringe benefit. Congress began dismantling this subsidy in the 1992 energy bill, which set a monthly limit of $155 on tax-exempt parking benefits.

About $200 million a year in loan guarantees provided by the Rural Electrification Administration. This agency originally had "a noble mission of bringing light to rural areas which for-profit utilities refused to serve," but many of its below-market loans now go to profitable enterprises, according to the report.

The 1872 federal mining law, "the granddaddy of the anti-environmental budget." This law has been denounced as "a license to steal" by Sen. Dale Bumpers (D-Ark.) but is fiercely defended by mining companies and western-state legislators. The law encourages mining companies to buy federal land at rock-bottom prices, and exempts them from royalties on much of the mineral wealth they find.

"Some companies," the report says, "have used the law to buy federal land and make large profits by converting the property to ski resorts, golf resorts and condominiums."

Similar conclusions about federal energy and environment spending were reached by a coalition of conservation and industry groups and published in December as a "A Sustainable Energy Budget." That report recommended that funds be cut from long-term programs such as fusion energy development for short-range benefits such as insulation of low-income housing. At her confirmation hearing last month, Energy Secretary Hazel R. O'Leary promised to "closely examine the department's energy investment portfolio," but she said it would be premature to make specific commitments. The first test of the new administration's policy will be the fiscal 1994 budget, which is to be sent to Congress in late March.

11   EPA Plan to Cut Payments to Superfund Contractors

Agency Hopes to Triple Toxic Waste Cleanups by 1993

MICHAEL WEISSKOPF

October, 1991

E nvironmental Protection Agency Administrator William K. Reilly said yesterday that EPA's payments to private contractors for the management of toxic
waste cleanups are excessive and sometimes improper, and he announced reforms
intended to cut them substantially.

Reilly also announced steps to triple by 1993 the number of cleanups of
contaminated sites under the Superfund program, which Congress created in 1980
to rescue communities from the toxic debris dumped by industry for decades.

The new policies closely follow recommendations of an EPA task force that
criticized the management payments and turned up new evidence of questionable
charges by private contractors. Among the charges for which EPA reimbursed one
midwestern firm, according to officials, were $650 for a Christmas party, $2,730 for
rental and maintenance of office plants and an 80 percent markup in the charge for
data processing services, which brought the company an extra $35,000.

"Potted plants and Christmas parties and expenses of that sort don't belong in
this program, and we'll do our best to get them out," Reilly said at a news conference, adding that none of the charges appears to be illegal.

Reilly appointed the task force in June after *The Washington Post* reported that
nearly one-third of the $200 million paid to 45 contractors since 1988 to plan and
oversee cleanups had gone not to clean up anything but to compensate the contractors for the costs of paperwork and coordination of their projects nationwide.

That money—about $62 million—was spent on what the EPA terms "program
management," a loosely defined category of overhead that included "start-up" funds
for contractors that had no projects to manage; bonuses for work criticized by the
EPA as wasteful and sloppy; purchase of pollution detection devices that sat unused
in rented warehouses, and travel expenses and time spent at professional conferences, including $210,000 paid by the agency to host one meeting of contractors in
Dallas.

Meanwhile, the Superfund has cleaned up only 63 of the 1,200 sites listed by the EPA as the most threatening to communities or their underground water supplies.

Although the government customarily reimburses contractors for the cost of administering their projects, the percentage of Superfund money that has gone to "program management" dwarfs that of most federal contracts as well as the 9 percent targeted by Superfund planners when the 45 management firms were signed up.

Unlike most government contracts that pay only for actual time and expenses devoted to administration, the EPA agreed in advance to set up semipermanent offices for Superfund contractors to manage their cleanup projects. Rent and salaries are paid, business costs such as recruitment and training are covered, and profit and bonuses are awarded, regardless of how many cleanup jobs they have to manage, or whether they have any.

Reilly said yesterday that the EPA overestimated the need for contractors to plan and conduct cleanups. More polluters have come forth to pay for the work, hoping to avoid court suits by the agency. But the EPA is still locked in to 10-year contracts with the 45 firms that include many fixed costs of program management.

Yesterday's plan seeks to cut program management costs to no more than 20 percent by cutting administrative staffs of contractors, intensifying EPA oversight, pooling cleanup equipment and withholding jobs from inefficient and profligate contractors.

Congress's conference committee on appropriations has recommended an even lower 15 percent target for program management.

The task force also called for termination of contracts if firms fail to straighten up. As a result, Reilly said he is "actively reviewing" such a strategy. The EPA office in Atlanta is seeking to end contracts with two of the six companies hired to handle Superfund jobs in the South. Officials estimate EPA will save more than $500,000 a year by canceling the two firms, which have scored lowest in the agency's regular performance evaluations.

"It is vitally important that we ensure better value for our contract dollar," Reilly said.

The drive to triple the number of cleanups within two years includes steps to speed up selection of cleanup plans and standardize the remedies for getting rid of toxic waste.

12   EPA Researchers Say New Directives Mean Too Much Paperwork

GARY LEE
October, 1993

Until a year ago, David Lewis, a veteran microbiologist with the Environmental Protection Agency, devoted 30 hours a week to investigations on global warming and five to contract management. Now his work week requires more than 30 hours of paper shuffling, leaving the remainder for scientific research.

The shift results from an avalanche of new directives on how EPA's federal employees should manage the agency's contract workers. Reacting to congressional complaints about contracting abuses, EPA has issued 120 rules in the past two years explaining in intricate detail how contract workers should be handled.

The directives range from requirements that every contact between regular federal employees and contract workers must be recorded to extensive instructions on how federal employees should direct contract employees to perform tasks and how the workers should respond. Many of the rules, which require elaborate written reports, are designed to minimize contact between agency staff and contract workers.

"Because of these rules I can no longer work in my lab, since it would give the appearance that I'm [personally] supervising the contract scientists there, which is against the rules," Lewis said. "The situation is ludicrous."

EPA researchers in labs at various locations across the country concur.

At the EPA's research facility in Duluth, Minn., scientists responsible for research in dioxin, wetland contamination and other water problems now must devote up to half their work time filling out paperwork required by contract-worker regulations, compared to 10 percent previously, said Allan Batterman, a research scientist there.

At EPA labs from Gulf Breeze, Fla., to Ada, Okla., the contract regulations have had similar effects, managers say. At Narragansett Bay, R.I., the new paperwork requirements have resulted in a two-thirds drop in the output of scientific papers, researchers there said.

"I have never seen morale so damaged," said Philip Cook, a Duluth-based EPA researcher. "It will take at least five years for us to get our footing back as scientists."

Gary Foley, EPA's acting chief of research, said the complaints stem from a minority of research staff.

"For the majority of scientists working at EPA, that is not the case," he said. "It may be for some, and we are working to do what we can for additional training for them in management to make sure that this doesn't go on for long."

In any case, the directives on contract employees do not constitute new regulations but an attempt to better enforce existing ones, Foley added.

EPA's Office of Research and Development has 12 field research offices with 1,800 employees and several hundred contract workers.

The directives on contract workers were issued in reaction to a 1992 report by EPA's inspector general that charged agency employees with exercising favoritism among contract workers, permitting gross overcharges and allowing government funds to be spent for sporting events and alcoholic beverages.

The report apparently was prompted by an earlier study by the House Government Affairs Oversight Subcommittee, under the direction of Rep. John D. Dingell (D.-Mich.), which criticized EPA's inspector general's office for failing to adequately prosecute contract worker abuses.

The two reports set off a chain reaction, starting with a crackdown at the EPA labs and peaking with the interrogation of managers in the labs in Duluth, Athens, Ga., and Narragansett. In the end, dozens of contract workers were fired.

Gilman Veith, director of the Duluth lab, originally was charged with mismanagement of contract workers and fired from the EPA. But a federal judge cleared Veith of all charges last August and ordered him reinstated. The EPA is appealing the decision.

EPA researchers interviewed for this article said they feel that the Draconian tone of the investigations and the subsequent directives show that EPA's inspector general went to the extreme in addressing congressional criticism of contract work.

One policy particularly irksome to Lewis, who works in Athens, requires labs to close out cooperative arrangements with outside institutions after three years in order to encourage competition for contracts. As a result, he is being obliged to curtail a cooperative agreement on the effects of global warming on soil with the Woods Hole Marine Biology Laboratory just when it was beginning to yield results.

"You can't just treat all research projects like you're setting up specialty hot dog stands," Lewis said, "shutting them down every three years just to see if anyone else wants to sell that kind of weenie."

13   At Issue in '92: Environment

Oil Recycling Success Provides
Support for Differing Messages

MICHAEL WEISSKOPF
October, 1992

With know-how and moxie, Jake Voogd built Evergreen Oil Inc. into a $15 million-a-year recycling business that could be a campaign advertisement for President Bush's market-based environmentalism—except for one thing.

Were it not for a California regulation of the sort championed by Arkansas Gov. Bill Clinton, Evergreen may never have gotten off the ground.

Evergreen's story is telling in a presidential campaign in which the environmental issue is framed chiefly in economic terms: Does regulation make or break jobs? The usual debate over pollution has been recast by the country's all-consuming financial difficulties. Instead of the cleanup of Boston Harbor in 1988, for example, the focus this year would be on the long-term economic impact of such a cleanup.

It was no coincidence that both camps visited Evergreen this summer to deliver very different messages. Bush, apparently unaware of the importance of the state regulation to Evergreen, praised the company as a symbol of free enterprise in service of the environment. He criticized government intervention as a drag on business initiative.

Clinton's running mate, Sen. Albert Gore Jr. (D-Tenn.), gave just the opposite pitch: Evergreen's success shows how regulation can benefit the economy by encouraging new technology and corporate efficiency.

The debate over regulation is important because the next president will have to deal with an environmental problem more deeply rooted in the economy and potentially more disruptive than any other in 20 years of pollution controls. The threat of global warming comes from the buildup of gases emitted by every car and factory in America.

Presidential hopefuls usually compete over ways to curb such pollutants. But Bush and Clinton are waging a more basic, philosophical duel over the costs of those controls. They often sound more like candidates for union boss fighting for the jobs of their local. Whether the issue is auto fuel-efficiency standards or protection of the northern spotted owl, they pepper their arguments with job statistics and economic projections.

To get perspective, however, it is possible to put their general approaches to the test in California, a longtime leader in environmental law whose 1986 regulation on the disposal of used oil is a handy reference point for the presidential debate.

In many ways the California legislative debate of six years ago mirrored the differences of today's candidates. Clinton supports regulations like this one to trigger technological change that helps the environment and, at the same time, creates jobs.

Bush's anti-regulatory position echoes the arguments of those who opposed California's regulation as a damper on profits and competitive advantage.

After five years of the state law, California has piled up enough practical experience to shed light on the larger clash of candidates. If their regulatory approaches are scored on the basis of what happened to jobs in a single industry of a single state, the Democrats win in a tight match.

The California experience bears out some of Bush's forebodings. Generators of used oil, such as service stations and factories, pay more today to dispose of their oil wastes. Companies that used to collect and resell it as fuel for industrial boilers have gone out of business or are squeezed by the high costs of pollution control, insurance and state fees.

Even Voogd gripes that the new red tape and permit rules have stymied his plans to build a Southern California plant with triple his current capacity.

But there were overall economic benefits of the regulation. Evergreen, for example, was able to refine its technology in a more conducive business climate and grow from a small tank farm to a company large enough to keep 70 percent of the cars and trucks in San Francisco running on recycled motor oil.

Layoffs from companies unable to meet the new standards were more than offset by the 100 jobs created at Evergreen and 98 by Gibson Environmental Inc., which converted a failing refinery into a $22 million-a-year business removing oil from contaminated soil and water. For each new job in the oil industry, economists estimate that another six are created in associated work.

The new businesses boosted tax revenue for the state, and Evergreen's marketing of its know-how overseas at $1.5 million a deal helps the nation's balance of payments.

Moreover, the environmental payoff for which the regulation was devised is bigger than expected. Nearly twice as much used oil was collected and removed as was predicted in the first three years of the law.

"I haven't seen any significant damage to the job market, and it definitely has had a good effect environmentally," said Leif Peterson, the state's hazardous materials specialist. "Less used oil is being burned and dumped into the environment."

For Voogd, a longtime Republican resident of conservative Orange County, where the term "regs" is considered a four-letter word, the 1986 regulation was "very important."

"It allowed our small plant, which was on the learning curve, to survive," he said.

A National Problem

Used oil may be a serious environmental hazard, but it is by no means one of the burning national issues of the day. For purposes of critiquing the philosophical leanings of Bush and Clinton, it is simply a symbol.

Nevertheless, waste oil is a national problem that needs remedying, and one on which the candidates have spoken. Gore, a "green" leader of the Senate, wants more stringent controls nationally. Bush doesn't—he or his appointees have twice rejected plans to extend California-like standards nationally.

About 1.4 billion gallons of used oil are drained every year from auto crankcases and industrial motors nationwide. As a lubricant, the oil gets contaminated by toxic metals from engine wear and fuel. It has to be changed regularly to remain effective.

Most dirty oil, generated by car dealers, repair shops and truck depots, is collected by "reprocessors." They remove large particles and resell it as fuel for ships and industrial boilers, which emit more lead than any other industrial process—600,000 pounds last year, according to the Hazardous Waste Treatment Council.

Low exposure to lead can impair the mental and physical growth of children and cause hypertension in adults.

More than a third of the nation's waste oil is dumped into sewers, storm drains or fields where it threatens to seep into groundwater. Only 5 percent is stripped of contaminants and recycled into motor oil by Evergreen and one other U.S. plant.

At Evergreen Aug. 2, Gore called for national limits on the lead byproducts of waste oil and charged that Bush was propagating a "false message that there has to be a choice between jobs and the environment."

Noting earlier that day that foreign rivals realize the huge market in "products and processes that make it possible to have economic progress and a higher standard of living without destroying the environment," he asked: "Why are Bush and [Vice President] Quayle saying that Japan and Germany are wrong?"

Bush's involvement with used oil dates back to 1981 when as vice president he headed a deregulatory task force that stopped a plan by the Environmental Protection Agency to regulate used oil as a hazardous waste, similar to California law.

Under court order to reconsider the regulation, the EPA ruled again in August—this time on Bush's watch. The decision declined to regulate used oil, but issued "management standards" widely regarded as too weak to prevent pollution.

The decision came amid a larger White House regulations moratorium that Bush imposed last year in the hope of stimulating the economy.

Speaking at Evergreen June 18, Bush gave his rationale: "I believe less regulation means more jobs. I have an obligation to guarantee health as best one can. But we can overdo it by frivolous regulations. And sometimes . . . in the environmental area we can get too regulatory."

Public Health Argument

The California fight to regulate oil was led by environmental and Evergreen lobbyists who argued for strict limits on the lead content of reprocessed industrial fuels. They argued on public health grounds.

But only Evergreen, then being developed, would have had the technology to remove lead from waste oil.

Reprocessors countered that a tough lead standard would kill their industry and that Evergreen was too small to recycle the state's huge flow of used oil, 10 percent of the nation's total. Generators of waste oil would have no choice but to dump their waste.

Lawmakers passed a compromise: Used oil resold as industrial fuel could not exceed 100 parts per million (ppm) of lead, to be halved after two years. Average lead levels then were 1,000 ppm, Peterson said.

The law designated used oil as a hazardous waste and required a permit for anyone seeking to burn or dispose of it on land or in state waters.

By the time the law went into effect, Voogd was trying to get the bugs out of Evergreen, the nation's first state-of-the-art "re-refiner" able to remove pollutants from used oil and produce a premium grade lubricant.

Luckily for Voogd, the new regulation changed the economics of used oil. Previously, reprocessors paid gas stations and other generators up to 10 cents a gallon to haul their waste. They could resell it as industrial fuel for four times as much.

But once used oil was designated as "hazardous," the tables turned.

Generators, held liable by federal law for environmental damage caused by such hazardous waste, became more interested in getting rid of the oil than selling it.

So Voogd started to charge for the pickup of used oil, starting at a nickel a gallon. As the only California facility fully licensed to handle the waste, the plant was especially attractive to large industrial generators eager to avoid long-term liability.

The fees allowed Voogd to meet his costs while Evergreen was ironing out technical problems. "If we had to pay for the oil, we would've gone bankrupt," he said in an interview. But it raised the costs of doing business for those who used to sell used oil but now had to pay to have it hauled away.

Now Evergreen collects 15 million gallons a year from 6,000 customers and charges 20 cents a gallon. More than 7 million gallons are re-refined into base oil, the primary ingredient of hydraulic and motor oils that sells for $1 per gallon. Pacific Gas and Electric Co. (PG&E) buys Voogd's oil for much of its fleet.

Evergreen workers average salaries of $37,000 a year. The firm's economic impact extends beyond the plant gate to equipment vendors, cleanup and repair crews and distributors like the San Jose man who blends additives into base oil for the PG&E account.

Although the regulation was indifferently enforced at first, it imposed such high standards and costs that "gypsy" collectors who owned a truck or two to collect waste oil had no choice but to get out of business or sell out. Voogd bought eight small companies, steadying the supply of oil, or "feedstock," for Evergreen.

For larger reprocessors, the price of survival includes lab fees to certify that their product meets standards; $2 million in insurance coverage for losses from accidental spills; a hazardous waste facility tax of $64,000 a year; worker training costs, and engineering and legal fees.

The lead limit poses technical problems for reprocessors. They have to blend used oil with enough low-lead diesel to dilute the metal content. But that further raises costs.

California's oldest reprocessor, Leach Oil, was driven into bankruptcy. John Shubin, owner of Industrial Service Oil Co., lost his bank credit line and is planning to broker crude oil to overcome what he calls "too much regulatory overkill."

"I knew when this law passed, it was going to drive companies out of business," said Rick McAuley, president of Petroleum Recycling Corp. (PRC).

But it also eliminated competition for the fitter firms, like PRC, the state's largest oil reprocessor. Gobbling up smaller companies and expanding his service territory, McAuley increased his work force from 30 in the early 1980s to 150 today.

The 17 cents he now charges for each gallon of used oil helps to increase his gross profit margin by a dime for each gallon that PRC resells as fuel for industrial boilers and marine vessels.

"We didn't know we were going to be as successful as we were," he said at his office south of Los Angeles.

Cost of Controls

Few question the overall value of the California law. But whether it is representative of the huge body of regulations is subject to debate. Industry spends $130 billion a year to implement government controls for everything from cars to hunting.

The consensus in one industry of California is that regardless of its merit, regulation is a force for change.

"There's a concentration of businesses, one or two lead companies and a bunch of also-rans," said McAuley of PRC. "The price to society is in the higher costs of services."

Evergreen has turned Voogd into at least a limited believer in regulation.

"The government should work with business to promote good opportunities while cleaning up the environment," he said. "There are those things costly to a taxpayer and those things that can be done at a profit."

14　Adirondack Park at 100 Years Old

Public, Private Pressures Converge; Battle Rages over Potential Development, N.Y. State's Control of Land

TOM KENWORTHY

May, 1992

One-hundred thirty-four years after James Russell Lowell and Ralph Waldo Emerson established their first "philosophers' camp" there, Follensby Pond serves as an apt symbol of the battle raging over New York's Adirondack Park as it celebrates its centennial this week.

The pond and the 14,000-acre tract that surrounds it, located adjacent to one of the park's premier canoe routes, have been offered for sale to the state.

Environmentalists say it would be a stellar addition to the 2.6 million acres of wilderness within the 6 million-acre expanse of Adirondack Park. But many of the park's 130,000 residents, chafing for two decades under state control over private land-use decisions within park boundaries, say the state already owns enough land in the park. And the state itself, after the defeat two years ago of an environmental bond referendum, has no money available to purchase the property.

Like Follensby Pond, the whole of Adirondack Park, a magnificent refuge of mountains, lakes, rivers and woodlands, today stands at a crossroads, a case study in the collision between environmental and aesthetic values, property rights and lean state budgets.

At nearly three times the size of Yellowstone, Adirondack is the largest park in the continental United States. But it sits within a day's drive of 70 million people, and development pressures are building every year. Some of the same qualities that give the park its unique character—the patchwork of state wilderness, vast tracts of land owned by timber companies and wealthy families, and small private lakefront lots—have combined to produce a roiling debate over the park's future.

At issue are some broad and difficult questions for a park that was a model of ecosystem protection long before that term was coined. How much wilderness is enough when some 2.6 million acres are forever off limits to the developer's bulldozer and the logger's chain saw? How much control should the state exercise over development of privately owned land within park boundaries? At what point does the construction of vacation homes and condo developments on the park's thousands of lakes begin to degrade the aesthetics that draw visitors in the first place?

Two years ago, a special commission appointed by Gov. Mario M. Cuomo (D) came up with what it thought were daring but workable answers to those and other nettlesome questions.

"The state today has a great opportunity—probably its last clear chance—to establish and implement a bold vision for the Park," chairman Peter A. A. Berle wrote in a letter accompanying the commission's report. "The state must not let the Park be overwhelmed by the shortsighted interests that would destroy the forest industry and treat the Park as a mere piece of saleable real estate."

The commission made 245 recommendations to protect the park from a surge in vacation-home development and the breakup of large parcels owned by timber companies and wealthy individuals who face increasing financial and tax pressures to sell.

According to the commission and the Adirondack Park Agency, about 21,000 new homes and 6,500 building lots, 4,000 of them waterfront lots, were added in the park between 1967 and 1987. Subdivided property sales tripled between 1982 and 1985 and doubled again by 1988. Under existing land-use rules, the commission said, the population of the park could grow fivefold, with several hundred thousand new houses constructed.

To combat those trends, the commission sought a new state land-acquisition fund to add another 654,850 acres to the roughly 2.6 million acres it already owns, land that the state constitution directs shall be "forever kept as wild." It sought to protect open, private lands through strict new development and subdivision controls, the purchase of conservation easements and the transfer of development rights. And it sought new ways to manage the park and create economic opportunities and affordable housing for the 130,000 year-round residents whose poverty and unemployment rates almost always exceed the state average.

The commission had an answer to everything, it seemed, except the storm of opposition that greeted its report. Its proposals, which included a one-year moratorium on development in the most sensitive areas, generated a powerful backlash from Adirondacks residents and their political leaders who have formed a flock of new property-rights organizations to fight for more local control over park decisions.

Only a few months after the report was released, New York voters narrowly defeated a $2 billion environmental bond issue that would have provided $800 million in state funds for land acquisition. And Cuomo, who had earlier spoken of "unbridled land speculation and unwarranted development that may threaten the unique open space and wilderness character of the region," unveiled an Adirondacks plan that was something of a retreat from the ambitious goals of his own commission and that relied heavily on tax incentives to preserve open space.

In this atmosphere, Adirondacks residents and their chief political ally, the local state senator who holds the third-ranking leadership position in the state Senate, say that any legislation tightening the state's grip over land-use decisions is doomed.

"The depth of feeling is unbelievable," said Robert F. Flacke, a Lake George businessman and former official in local and state government who served as head of the Adirondack Park Agency and the state Department of Environment and Conservation. Adirondacks residents, said Flacke, "feel that outsiders are dictating to them, that they own the land and they pay taxes on it and they have to compete in a market economy."

The anger of Adirondacks residents has been building for more than 20 years, since an earlier commission appointed by Gov. Nelson A. Rockefeller (R) led to legislation creating the Adirondack Park Agency and giving it control over building densities in the park's four different land-use classification areas.

Though regarded as a model at the time, environmentalists say the laws establishing the park agency and its powers are in need of an overhaul, particularly to protect against strip development along roads and to preserve shoreline along the park's more than 2,700 lakes.

"The Adirondacks are dying the death of a thousand cuts," said Harold A. Jerry Jr., who served on both Cuomo's commission and its predecessor. "The long-term future is really bleak unless we can bring a halt to the development. . . . I don't care if you only build 10 houses a year, slowly but surely you are going to lose the open space in the park."

Canoeing near Follensby Pond last week, National Audubon Society representative Dick Beamish said the future of the park depends on state acquisition of such pristine private holdings.

"As these large parcels go on the market, we're going to have this whole park go to pieces," said Beamish. "We have something that is very rare in this country, a whole ecosystem. We want to protect the integrity of the whole park, not just pieces of it."

15   Clinton Offers Package to 'Halt Global Warming'

GARY LEE
October, 1993

P resident Clinton yesterday unveiled a broad package of initiatives to curb the threat of global warming, including projects for planting more trees, increasing use of hydroelectric power and raising efficiency standards for home appliances.

In a White House ceremony, Clinton appealed to U.S. industrial leaders, many of whom were in the audience, to help reduce greenhouse gases by voluntarily taking part in the initiatives—only a few of which make industry participation mandatory.

"In concert with other nations, we simply must halt global warming," Clinton told the crowd. "It is a threat to our health, to our ecology, and to our economy."

The "Climate Change Action Plan" is designed to reduce the emission of carbon dioxide and other greenhouse gases to their 1990 levels. In all, the measures would reduce emissions by 100 million metric tons a year. Total emissions in 1990 were 1,367 million metric tons, according to the plan.

The plan calls for $60 billion in private investment in energy-saving programs—encouraged by federal programs to increase energy efficiency—and $1.9 billion in federal spending, most of which would be redirected from existing programs. No new taxes would be required.

Set in the Rose Garden, yesterday's ceremony was designed to enhance the Clinton administration's image as environmentally progressive. The event also featured a speech by Vice President Gore and remarks by John H. Adams, executive director of the Natural Resources Defense Council, a leading environmental group.

Gore, who has made the fight for environmental protection a mainstay of his political career, favorably compared the administration's environmental record to that of the Bush White House. President George Bush, many of whose advisers warned that the costs of combating global warming could hurt the economy, never offered a comprehensive plan for reducing greenhouse emissions.

But Bush did sign the United Nations Framework Convention on Climate Change at the Rio "Earth Summit" in 1992, committing the United States to eventually cut back emissions to 1990 levels. Yesterday's plan is designed to comply with that document.

"The action plan reestablishes the United States as a world leader in protecting the global climate," Clinton told yesterday's gathering.

However, many environmentalists said they doubt that industry participation will be high enough to reach the goal of returning to 1990 levels. After administration officials briefed it last week, a coalition of environmental groups held a news conference to criticize the heavy reliance on voluntary action.

"What we need is tougher measures to achieve real reductions," said Dan Becker, a spokesman for the Sierra Club.

"This tells the international community that they don't have to use tough measures to fight global warming," said Steve Kretzman of Greenpeace. "It tells them that voluntary measures are enough and that's the wrong signal."

Corporate leaders, who had feared that the administration would introduce stricter measures to cut emission levels, such as increased fuel efficiency standards, praised the plan widely.

"The plan is a good first step," said Thomas Kuhn, president of Edison Electric Institute, an umbrella organization for utility companies. The utilities, he added, are "committing to work with administrative representatives to see what kind of programs companies can undertake to limit overall emissions."

The plan outlines 50 measures, many of which would require joint participation between federal agencies and the private sector.

One section of the plan calls for the Agriculture Department to provide assistance for tree-planting programs in privately owned forests. Because forests are regarded as gas-absorbing "greenhouse sinks," the measure would reduce greenhouse levels by 4.5 million metric tons over the next six years, according to the plan.

The plan also includes a proposal for Congress to change tax laws so that employers could give employees the cash equivalent of the cost of subsidized parking in order to encourage increased use of public transportation. In all, U.S. corporations provide more than $50 billion a year in free or discounted parking, according to Transportation Secretary Federico Pena.

An estimated 4.5 million drivers are expected to take advantage of the provision by the year 2000, an administration official said. The reduced automobile use, in turn, would cut the release of carbons by more than 6 million metric tons a year, the plan says.

The White House rejected a proposal to impose higher fuel efficiency standards for automobiles as a means of decreasing emissions, but the plan calls for a task force to study the issue for a year. Increasing the standards at a later date was not ruled out, Environmental Protection Agency Administrator Carol M. Browner said in an interview.

Following the ceremony, members of the Clinton Cabinet held a news conference to discuss criticisms of the plan. Energy Secretary Hazel R. O'Leary, defending the non-mandatory nature of the programs, said that "*voluntary* is not a dirty word." EPA's Browner, dismissing naysayers as "disingenuous," said that in fact many of the programs proposed in it had already shown signs of success. Pena defended the plan as a sound way to cut back on driving.

16   Costly Federal Mandates Spur Protest

States, Counties Seek Relief from Programs Imposed without Funding

GARY LEE
October, 1993

A coalition of state and local officials, led by the United States Conference of Mayors, yesterday launched a protest against programs introduced by federal agencies or Congress that require enforcement—and funding—by city and county governments.

The "unfunded federal mandates," which give local governments responsibility for measures such as improving air quality and protecting endangered species, are too costly and take resources cities need to fight crime and fulfill other urgent duties, said Louisville Mayor Jerry Abramson, president of the mayors group, at a news conference.

The coalition, which includes the Council of State Governments and the National Governors' Association, among other groups, does not oppose the substance of the federal programs defined by the mandates, Abramson explained. But it is opposed to the federal government's imposing new programs without giving local authorities additional money to operate them.

"We are objecting to a bankrupt federal government that continues to pass laws without the wherewithal to fund them," he said.

This year, 314 U.S. cities reviewed as a sample will spend $6.5 billion enforcing 10 such programs, according to a survey released at the conference. Enforcing the Clean Water Act alone in 1993 cost those cities $3.6 billion, the survey said, and will cost them $29.3 billion over the next five years. On average, U.S. cities spend about 11.7 percent of their revenue enforcing the federal mandates, the survey found.

In an apparent bid to preempt the campaign against federally mandated programs, President Clinton used a morning meeting with mayors to sign a new executive order directing federal officials to consult with local officials before issuing unfunded mandates.

The order also established new terms whereby cities and other local bodies can be granted an exemption from the mandates if the required activity is not widely applicable in their jurisdictions. For example, municipalities that have only minimal drug-abuse problems could be exempted from certain drug law enforcement requirements.

In a countervailing attempt to defuse criticism of federally unfunded mandates, a group of environmental and consumer groups yesterday called a news conference of their own.

Bob Adler, an attorney for the Natural Resources Defense Council, an environmental group leading the defense of mandates, told the gathering that the federal requirements are essential to maintaining environmental quality.

"We agree that the federal government should share more of the burden for funding these programs," he said, "but we caution against those who will use the criticism as an excuse to abolish some of the programs."

The news conference, which included representatives of the Sierra Club, Friends of the Earth and other groups, was held an hour before the mayors' gathering and in the same downtown Washington hotel.

In their dueling media shows, the two groups differed over a wide array of unfunded federal mandates, from the Immigration Act of 1990 to the Americans with Disabilities Act.

Critics pointed to the 1974 Safe Drinking Water Act as particularly burdensome. The law, which requires local governments to guarantee that tap water meets federal standards, will cost the 314 cities $8.6 billion to enforce over the next five years, according to the mayors' survey. Besides the cost, the program is too rigid and will become increasingly difficult to enforce, according to a position paper released by the mayors.

In a paper issued to counter those charges, proponents of the federal requirements pointed out that violations of the law are common, that the list of contaminants found in drinking water systems is long and that strong local enforcement is badly needed.

Abramson praised Clinton's new executive order. "It shows the president is on our side . . . and goes part way in addressing our concerns" about federal mandates.

NRDC's Adler criticized the directive. "Our fear is that it will put a chilling effect on federal officials who have a hard enough time doing their jobs with limited resources." However, he said, the order is ambiguous enough to create "a big question of interpretation."

A separate report issued yesterday by the National Association of Counties said that county governments across the U.S. are spending $4.8 billion a year complying with 12 specific mandates involving issues from disposing of solid waste to improving air quality. The costs of these programs to counties will total $33.7 billion from 1994 to 1998, the study said.

17   Environmental Orders
Irk Business Groups

White House Accused of Bypassing Congress

TOM KENWORTHY
September, 1993

For a business community that often applauded the behind-the-scenes work of the Bush administration's anti-regulation Council on Competitiveness, the shoe has been on the other foot since the Clinton administration came to power. Yesterday business leaders began to complain about it pinching a little.

At a news conference and in letters to congressional leaders, representatives of more than 20 business and industry groups objected to what they say is a tendency by the White House to make broad environmental policy changes through executive orders rather than legislation.

The process, the business representatives said, locks Congress, the public and affected industries out of the debate and produces policies that can hurt the economy.

At issue are two recent executive orders. The first, signed by President Clinton last month, directs federal agencies to develop plans for reducing or eliminating "unnecessary" purchases of products containing "extremely hazardous substances or toxic chemicals." The second, still under development at the White House, is aimed at increasing federal purchases of recycled paper and reducing federal use of paper manufactured using chlorine.

Chemical Manufacturers Association president Fred Webber, acting as a spokesman for the business groups, charged that the executive orders were overly broad, were developed without assessing risks from various chemicals, would hurt business and cost jobs, and should be subject to congressional review.

"Every president issues executive orders, but here they've crossed the line and are dealing with major public policy," said Webber, accusing the White House of conducting an "end run around Congress."

In fact, 54 members of the Senate and 42 members of the House wrote Clinton in March asking him to issue the executive order on materials containing hazardous substances. That order also brings the federal government into compliance with "right to know" legislation by directing agencies to inform the public of the release of hazardous substances into the environment and seeks to encourage pollution prevention by the federal government.

"The thrust of the order was to have the federal government behave in a way that Congress has mandated for years [about] how the private sector should behave," said Kathleen McGinty, director of the White House Office on Environmental Policy. Noting that the two orders apply only to government purchases, McGinty said "we are not making new rules or regulations that will impact all the private operators in the private sector."

Jim Edward, the Environmental Protection Agency's director of pollution prevention who wrote the order issued by Clinton, said that outdated federal specifications often force manufacturers to use materials they either no longer use or recycle when making the same products for private purchasers.

"This is not an anti-chemical industry-bashing kind of thing," said Edward. "It's just trying to eliminate things where it makes sense."

Among the groups supporting the Chemical Manufacturers Association are: the U.S. Chamber of Commerce, the National Association of Manufacturers, the American Forest and Paper Association, the American Petroleum Institute and the National Agricultural Chemicals Association, among others.